ON
VALUE JUDGMENTS
IN THE ARTS
and Other Essays

Elder Olson

On
Value Judgments
in the Arts
and Other Essays

The University of Chicago Press

Chicago and London

For My Wife, Jerri Hays

ELDER OLSON, a native of Chicago,
received his Ph.D. from the University of
Chicago, where he has taught since 1942.
In 1971 he was named Distinguished Service
Professor. Among his many literary awards
are the Emily Clark Balch award, the
Tietjens award, and awards from the Poetry
Society of America and the Academy of American Poets. He is the author of numerous works
of literary criticism including *The Poetry
of Dylan Thomas, Tragedy and the Theory of
Drama*, and *The Theory of Comedy*, and is the
editor of *Aristotle's Poetics and English
Literature*. Professor Olson has published
several volumes of verse including *Collected
Poems* and *Olson's Penny Arcade* (1975). His critical
writings and poetry are the subject of a study
by Thomas E. Lucas. He is married to the
artist Jerri Hays.

The University of Chicago Press, Chicago 60637
The University of Chicago Press, Ltd., London

© 1976 by Elder Olson
All rights reserved. Published 1976
Printed in the United States of America

Library of Congress Cataloging in Publication Data

Olson, Elder, 1909–
    On value judgments in the arts and other essays

    Includes index.
    1. Criticism—Collected works.
PN85.054   801'.95   75-9057
ISBN 0-226-62895-7

CONTENTS

PREFACE

The pieces gathered in this volume represent nearly four decades of concern with the theory and practice of criticism. A good number of them have been repeatedly anthologized (indeed, sometimes pirated) and translated into various languages, and so might be deemed sufficiently accessible; but I have collected them here chiefly for the convenience of students and fellow-workers who wanted them to be available in a single volume. They include essays, lectures, reviews, review-articles, and—in one instance—a letter to a friend. Save for the correction of misprints and such, they are presented here in their original form. The reason for this is not that I deem them beyond all improvement, but that this seems to me the only fair procedure; I am as responsible for what I said nearly forty years ago as I am for what I say now. If these pieces reveal inconsistencies—I am not aware that they do—so be it; I must bear the responsibility for these also.

I have divided the book into five sections. The first deals with practical criticism—the criticism, as it happens, only of poets and poems. For this limitation I ask your indulgence. I am, after all, a poet first and everything else afterward. The second involves the theory and practice of hermeneutics, limited here to drama, and indeed, a particular drama. The third section contains examinations of critics and critical positions. The fourth includes theorizings, both "Aristotelian" and Platonic. I may say at this point that if the two dialogues can be shown not to have used the actual Platonic dialectic, I shall consider that they have failed in their intention. They are part of a projected series of twelve dialogues in which I hope to present a complete Platonic theory of art. The final section deals with "metacriticism"— that is, theorizing about theories in general. The last essay, begun somewhere around 1936 and finished about 1941, was originally the first chapter of a book on general poetics which, except for a few other chapters, remains unwritten. I have left it, too, in its original form.

Many of these pieces contain passages of destructive criticism, sometimes polemical and harsh. I am sorry about that—up to a point. Destruction is often necessary if one wishes to build; I destroyed only because I thought, rightly or wrongly, that I could build better.

I have dedicated this book to my wife, but I do not wish that dedication to constitute a denial of my multitudinous debts to friends and colleagues living and dead, or to seem to diminish my gratefulness to them.

ACKNOWLEDGMENTS

The author wishes to thank the editors of the following journals in which many of these pieces first appeared: *Chicago Review, College English, Critical Inquiry, Modern Philology, Poetry, Texas Quarterly,* and *University Review* (Kansas City University).

1

PRACTICAL CRITICISM

"SAILING TO BYZANTIUM": PROLEGOMENA TO A POETICS OF THE LYRIC

Though the critic who seeks to discuss and the poet who seeks to construct a lyric poem are apt to discover all too quickly that in this particular province of literature, extensive and important as it is, little has been said which affords them any real guidance. At first sight, critical discussion of the lyric appears abundant, even though scarcely commensurate with the importance of the lyric itself; but closer examination readily reveals this abundance to be one of bons mots on the character of the lyric poet, of startling analogies to the psychological or physiological effects of lyric poetry, of "dull receipts how poems may be made," of oracular statement in which the tradition of ambiguous if portentous declamation is usually preserved by the oracle, and finally, in very considerable part, of mere *loci* within a general discussion of literature which is concerned with the lyric only because the lyric possesses some characteristic in common with other forms. In the last quarter of a century, to be sure, literary magazines have often been clamorous with disputations concerning the nature of the lyric; but perhaps without exception these have been declarations of purely individual predilections, or, as in the case of Ezra Pound's famous ten precepts for Imagists, definitions of a doctrine or of a convention rather than of a lyric poem. One might be tempted to conclude that a subject so persistently slighted is perhaps not worth discussion, were it not for the fact that, more than frequently, the critical statements suggest abortive attempts at precisely that.

What has been so often attempted unsuccessfully must be approached with caution. To rectify all errors, to supply all deficiencies, to strike out a poetics for the lyric at a single blow would be a noble and ambitious project, but the causes that make it so also operate to make it improbable of achievement. It is only prudent to propose something at once less striking and more feasible; to propose an

Reprinted from the (University of Kansas City) *University Review* 8 (1942): 209-19.

attempt to discover—through the analysis of a particular poem—some index as to how, eventually, a poetics of the lyric might be framed.

It should go without saying that any attempt to furnish indices toward a poetics of the lyric can be significant only in a philosophy in which the arts and sciences are held distinct from each other; for, unless that is the case, the inquiry into principles peculiar to poetics would turn on a nonsense question: if, in any sense whatever, all knowledge is one, then it must follow that the objects of knowledge must also be one in that same sense, and the question of peculiarities appears as a meaningless one. Further, it should be clear that poetics in such a system cannot deal with every question which may possibly be raised about a work of art, but only with those raised concerning it *qua* work of art; it is not merely conceivably but actually the case that questions about works of art may fall under many sciences, according to the manner of consideration. For instance, a question relevant to a poem as an existent thing falls under metaphysics, a question relevant to it as productive of, say, social consciousness, falls under politics; lacking the proper peculiarity to poetry neither of these questions would be poetic questions in the sense in which I propose to employ the term *poetic*, for *being* and *political instrumentality* are predicable of things other than poems, and whatever answers could be found to such questions would turn, not on the nature of poetry, but on a community between poetry and something else. Further, poetics in the present conception would be analytical and inductive, since the work is the object of consideration, and therefore, like any object of knowledge, must exist prior to any knowledge of it.

The scrutiny of particular poems would thus be the beginning of the critical enterprise; but the principles eventually reached, as disclosed by analysis, would not be rules governing the operations involved in the construction of any further poem, nor would the enumeration of poetic parts and poetic devices suffer extension beyond those objects to which analysis had been turned. In other words, poetics as conceived here would not afford a series of recipes for making poems, nor a set of rules according to which they must be made, for the very character of poetics is such that it must be subsequent to the inventive utilizations of the medium by the artist. Obviously, anything which should constrain invention would be detrimental to rather than productive of art. Properly taken, poetic questions would be concerning the poetic structure of a particular work, in the sense of inquiring what form has been imposed upon the medium of words. Such an inquiry, properly prosecuted, would terminate in a discovery of the parts of a work and of the interrelations through which the parts are parts of a whole.

The philosophic criticism of literature has provided us richly with instruments for almost every other mode of consideration; but with respect to this one mode, only one treatise—the *Poetics* of Aristotle—is relevant; and while that treatise serves both to differentiate and to illustrate the manner of working of that mode, generally, its specific concern is only with such species of poetry as have for their principle a tissue of incidents, a plot. To attempt to find a plot in the lyric, however, would be a profitless if not impossible task; to attempt on the other hand to find in the lyric some analogue of plot in the drama and in epic, for the mere sake of imitating Aristotle, would be to run counter to the broader indications of his very method—a method involving the distinction of diverse departments of inquiry diversely prosecuted. In the absence of any specific formal treatment of the lyric, then, its analyst must not only fulfill his proper function, but find his own warrant for his operations as well. Complex as his task is, however, it is by no means hopeless; the procedure reduces to an attempt to discover some principle in the work which is the principle of its unity and order—a principle which, it goes without saying, will have to be a purely poetic principle, i.e., a formal principle of the poem, and not something extrinsic to it such as the differentiation either of authors, audiences, subject-matters, or orders of diction would afford. Since in a formal consideration the form is the end, and since the end renders everything else intelligible, a mark of the discovery of the formal principle would be that everything else in the poem would be found to be explicable in terms of it.

We may take as the subject of our analysis the lyric "Sailing to Byzantium" by Yeats.

> That is no country for old men. The young
> In one another's arms, birds in the trees,
> —Those dying generations—at their song,
> The salmon-falls, the mackerel-crowded seas,
> Fish, flesh, or fowl, commend all summer long
> Whatever is begotten, born, and dies.
> Caught in that sensual music all neglect
> Monuments of unageing intellect.
>
> An aged man is but a paltry thing,
> A tattered coat upon a stick, unless
> Soul clap its hands and sing, and louder sing
> For every tatter in its mortal dress,
> Nor is there singing school but studying
> Monuments of its own magnificence;
> And therefore I have sailed the seas and come
> To the holy city of Byzantium.

O sages standing in God's holy fire
As in the gold mosaic of a wall,
Come from the holy fire, perne in a gyre,
And be the singing-masters of my soul.
Consume my heart away; sick with desire
And fastened to a dying animal
It knows not what it is; and gather me
Into the artifice of eternity.

Once out of nature I shall never take
My bodily form from any natural thing,
But such a form as Grecian goldsmiths make
Of hammered gold and gold enamelling
To keep a drowsy Emperor awake;
Or set upon a golden bough to sing
To lords and ladies of Byzantium
Of what is past, or passing, or to come.

In "Sailing to Byzantium" an old man faces the problem of old age, of death, and of regeneration, and gives his decision. Old age, he tells us, excludes a man from the sensual joys of youth; the world appears to belong completely to the young, it is no place for the old; indeed, an old man is scarcely a man at all—he is an empty artifice, an effigy merely, of a man; he is a tattered coat upon a stick. This would be very bad, except that the young also are excluded from something; rapt in their sensuality, they are ignorant utterly of the world of the spirit. Hence if old age frees a man from sensual passion, he may rejoice in the liberation of the soul; he is admitted into the realm of the spirit; and his rejoicing will increase according as he realizes the magnificence of the soul. But the soul can best learn its own greatness from the great works of art; hence he turns to those great works, but in turning to them, he finds that these are by no means mere effigies, or monuments, but things which have souls also; they live in the noblest element of God's fire, free from all corruption; hence he prays for death, for release from his mortal body; and since the insouled monuments exhibit the possibility of the soul's existence in some other matter than flesh, he wishes reincarnation, not now in a mortal body, but in the immortal and changeless embodiment of art.

There are thus the following terms, one might say, from which the poem suspends: the condition of the young, who are spiritually passive although sensually active; the condition of the merely old, who are spiritually and physically impotent; the condition of the old, who, although physically impotent, are capable of spiritual activity; the condition of art considered as inanimate—i.e., the condition of things which are merely monuments; and finally the condition of art considered as animate—as of such things as artificial birds which have a human soul. The second term, impotent and unspiritual old age, is a privative, a repugnant state which causes the progression through the other various alternative terms, until its contrary is encountered. The first and third terms are clearly contraries of each other; taken together as animate nature they are further contrary to the fourth term, inanimate art. None of these terms represents a wholly desirable mode of existence; but the fifth term, which represents such a mode, amalgamates the positive elements and eliminates the negative elements of both nature and art, and effects thus a resolution of the whole, for now the soul is present, as it would not be in art, nor is it passive, as it would be in the young and sensual mortal body, nor is it lodged in a "dying animal," as it would be in the body of the aged man; the soul is now free to act in its own supremacy and in full cognizance of its own excellence, and its embodiment is now incorruptible and secure from all the ills of flesh.

About these several oppositions the poem forms. The whole turns on the old man's realization, now that he is in the presence of the images of Byzantium, that these images have souls; there are consequently two major divisions which divide the poem precisely in half, the first two stanzas presenting art as inanimate, the second two, as animate; and that this is the case can be seen from such signs as that in the first half of the poem the images are stated as passive objects—they are twice called "monuments," they are merely objects of contemplation, they may be neglected or studied, visited or not visited, whereas in stanzas 3 and 4 they are treated as gods which can be prayed to for life or death, as beings capable of motion from sphere to sphere, as instructors of the soul, as sages possessed of wisdom; and the curious shift in the manner of consideration is signalized by the subtle phrasing of the first two lines of stanza 3: "O sages standing in God's holy fire/ As in the gold mosaic of a wall." According to the first part, the images at Byzantium were images, and one should have expected at most some figurative apostrophe to them: "O images set in the gold mosaic of a wall, much as the sages stand in God's holy fire": but here the similitude is reversed, and lest there should be any error, the sages are besought to come from the holy fire and begin the tuition of the soul, the destruction of the flesh.

Within these two halves of the poem, further divisions may be found, coincident with the stanzaic divisions. Stanza 1 presents a rejection of passion, stanza 2 an acceptance of intellection; then, turning on the realization that art is insouled, stanza 3 presents a rejection of the corruptible embodiment, and stanza 4, an acceptance of the incorruptible. There is an alternation, thus, of negative and affirmative: out of passion into intellection, out of corruption into permanence, in clear balance, the proportion being 1: 2:: 3: 4; and what orders these sections is their dialectical sequence. That is, passion must be condemned before the intellect can be esteemed; the intellect must operate before the images can be known to be insouled; the realization that the images are insouled precedes the realization that the body may be dispensed with; and the reincarnation of the soul in some changeless medium can be recognized as a possibility only through the prior recognition that the flesh is not the necessary matter of the soul. The parallel opposition of contraries constitutes a sharp demarcation: in stanza 1 a mortal bird of nature amid natural trees sings a brief song of sensual joy in praise of mortal things, of "whatever is begotten, born, and dies"; in stanza 4 an immortal and artificial bird set in an artificial tree sings an eternal song of spiritual joy in praise of eternal things, of "what is past, or passing, or to come"; and similarly, in stanza 2 a living thing is found to be an inanimate artifice, "a tattered coat upon a stick," incapable of motion, speech, sense or knowledge, whereas in stanza 3 what had appeared to be inanimate artifice is found to possess a soul, and hence to be capable of all these. A certain artificial symmetry in the argument serves to distinguish these parts even further: stanzas 1 and 4 begin with the conclusions of their respective arguments, whereas 2 and 3 end with their proper conclusions, and 1 is dependent upon 2 for the substantiation of its premises, as 4 is dependent upon 3.

This much indication of the principal organization of the work permits the explication, in terms of this, of the more elementary proportions. The first line of stanza 1 presents immediately, in its most simple statement, the condition which is the genesis of the whole structure: "That is no country for old men"; old men are shut out from something, and the remainder of the first six lines indicates precisely what it is from which they are excluded. The young are given over to sensual delight, in which old men can no longer participate. But a wall, if it shuts out, also shuts in; if the old are excluded from something, so are the young; lines 7 and 8, consequently, exhibit a second sense in which "That is no country for old men," for the young neglect all intellectual things. Further, the use of "that" implies a possible "this"; that is, there is a country for the old as for the young; and, again, the use of "that" implies that the separation from the country of the young is already complete. The occupation of the young is shrewdly stated: at first sight the human lovers "in one another's arms" have, like the birds at their song, apparently a romantic and sentimental aura; but the curious interpolation of "Those dying generations" in the description of the birds foreshadows the significance they are soon to have; and the phrases immediately following remove all sentimentality: "the salmon-falls, the mackerel-crowded seas" intend the ascent of salmon to the headwaters, the descent of mackerel to the deep seas in the spawning season, and the ironic intention is clear: all—the human lovers, the birds, the fish, do but spawn, but copulate, and this is their whole being; and if the parallel statement does not make this sufficiently evident, the summation of all in terms merely of animal genera—"fish, flesh, or fowl"—is unmistakable. The country of the young, then, is in its air, in its waters, and on its earth, from headwaters to ocean, wholly given over to sensuality; its inhabitants "commend all summer long" anything whatsoever, so long as it be mortal and animal—they commend "whatever is begotten, born, and dies"; and while they "commend" because they have great joy, that which they praise, they who praise, and their praise itself are ephemeral, for these mortals praise the things of mortality, and their commendation, like their joy, lasts but a summer, a mating season. The concluding lines of the stanza remove all ambiguity, and cancel all possibility of a return to such a country; even if the old man could, he would not return to a land where "Caught in that sensual music, all neglect / Monuments of unageing intellect." The young are "caught," they are really passive and incapable of free action; and they neglect those things which are unageing.

Merely to end here, however, with a condemnation of youthful sensuality would be unsatisfactory; as the second stanza expounds, old age itself is no solution; the old man cannot justly say, like Sophocles when he was asked whether he regretted the loss of youth and love, "Peace; most gladly have I escaped the thing of which you speak; I feel as if I had escaped from a mad and furious master"; for merely to be old is merely to be in a state of privation, it is to be "a paltry thing / A tattered coat upon a stick," it is to be the merest scarecrow, the merest fiction and semblance of a man, an inanimate rag upon a dead stick. A man merely old, then, is worse off than youth; if the souls of the young are captive, the old have, in this sense at least, no souls at all. Something positive must be added; and if the soul can wax and grow strong as the body wanes, then every step in the dissolution of the body—"every tatter in its mortal dress"—is cause for a further augmentation of joy. But this can occur only if the soul can rejoice in its own power and magnificence; this rejoicing is possible only if the soul knows of its own magnificence, and this knowledge is possible only through the contemplation of monuments which recall that magnificence. The soul of the aged must be strong to seek that which youth neglects. Hence the old must seek Byzantium; that is the country of the old; it is reached by sailing the seas, by breaking utterly with the country of the young; all passion must be left behind, the soul must be free to study the emblems of unchanging things.

Here the soul should be filled with joy; it should, by merely "studying," commend changeless things with song, as youth commends the changing with song; it would seem that the problem has been resolved, and the poem hence must end; but the contemplation of the monuments teaches first of all that these are no mere monuments but living things, and that the soul cannot grow into likeness with these beings of immortal embodiment unless it cast off its mortal body utterly. Nor is joy possible until the body be dissolved; the heart is still sick with the impossible desires of the flesh, it is still ignorant of its circumstances, and no song is possible to the soul while even a remnant of passion remains. Hence the old man prays to the sages who really stand in God's holy fire and have merely the semblance of images in gold mosaic; let them descend, "perning in a gyre," that is, moving in the circular motion which alone is possible to eternal things, let them consume with holy fire the heart which is the last seat of passion and ignorance, let them instruct the soul, let them gather it into the artifice of eternity and make the old man like themselves; even Byzantium, so long as the flesh be present, is no country for old men.

What it is to be like these, the soul, as yet uninstructed, can only conjecture; at any rate, with the destruction of the flesh it will be free of its ills; and if, as in Plato's myth of Er, the soul after death is free to choose some new embodiment, it will never again elect the flesh which is so quickly corruptible and which enslaves it to passion; it will choose some such form of art as that of the artificial birds in Theophilus' garden[1]; it will be of incorruptible and passionless gold; and it will dwell among leaves and boughs which are also of incorruptible and passionless metal. And now all sources of conflict are resolved in this last: the old has become the ageless; impotency has been exchanged for a higher power; the soul is free of passion and free for its joy, and it sings as youth once sang, but now of "What is past, and passing, and to come"—of the divisions of Eternity—rather than of "Whatever is begotten, born, and dies"—of the divisions of mortal time. And it has here its country, its proper and permanent habitation.

Although the argument as we have stated it clearly underlies the poem, it would be erroneous to suppose that this in itself constitutes the poem, for in that case there would be no difference between our paraphrase and the poem itself. The poem itself comprehends the argument and collocates with it many terms which, although they

1. In his note to the poem (*Collected Poems* [New York, 1933], p. 450) Yeats remarks: "I have read somewhere that in the Emperor's palace at Byzantium was a tree made of gold and silver, and artificial birds that sang." Undoubtedly the Emperor was Theophilus (829–842), and the birds conform to the descriptions of certain automata constructed for him by Leo Mathematicus and John Hylilas. Cf. *Hist. Byzan. Script. post Theoph.*, Anon. Cont. Theoph., 107; Constantini Manassis, *Brev. Hist.*, 107; and Michaeli Glycae, *Annales*, 292. See also Gibbon, *Decline and Fall*, chapter LIII, and George Finlay, *History of the Byzantine Empire* (London, 1906), pp. 140, 148, where further references are given.

could scarcely be formulated into some order approximating the pattern of the argument, nevertheless qualify the argument and determine its course. The basic analogies of the poem—of the natural world to a country, of the aged man to a scarecrow, of the world of art to Byzantium, and of artificial to natural generation—all these function as do the definitions of terms in actual argument; they serve to delimit the sphere of discourse and to make the argument intelligible.

This point is worth some discussion. The criticism of poetry has often turned chiefly on the so-called psychological connotations of readers with single words or phrases; but one may doubt whether the reader is at liberty to intrude such irrelevances as the accidents of personal experience or the inevitable ambiguities of language would necessarily afford. Surely the ultimate consequence of such assumptions must be either that the poem becomes a mere stimulus to independent poetic activities on the part of the reader—that is, the reader becomes the true poet, his reading the true poem—or, on the other hand, that the reader becomes the matter or medium of art, in which case all the arts would have a common medium, the soul of the spectator. Neither of these consequences, it need scarcely be said, complies with the stipulations which initiated this discussion.

If the basic terms of a lyric poem do not receive their meanings from the chance associations of the reader, neither do they have their dictionary meanings; like terms in most discourse, they take their significance from their context, through juxtaposition to other terms with which they are equated, contrasted, correlated, or combined. In the present poem, for instance, the term "singing" is explicitly extended beyond its usual meaning to cover two kinds of jubilation, the rejoicing of the natural creature and that of the artificial; as a consequence, all the terms which relate to jubilation and song are affected; for example, "commend," "music," "singing-school," and "singing-masters" suffer an extension commensurate with that of singing. Similarly, the term "intellect" and all the terms associated with it suffer extension; and the monuments here are not ordinary monuments, but changeless embodi- ments of the changeless soul—by no means effigies, but truly living creatures, capable of will, of desire, of jubilation, of local motion, of intellection and instruction. Nor is Byzantium the historical city; the tourist is not invited to recall that here once he was overcharged, nor is the historian invited to contribute such information as that this was a city visited by Hugh of Vermandois; Byzantium is not a place upon a map, but a term in the poem; a term signifying a stage of contempla- tion wherein the soul studies itself and so learns both what it is and in what consists true and eternal joy.

Furthermore, if the words of a poem have meanings which the poet may arbitrarily determine, the "objects" in poetry are also given whatever "properties" the poet sees fit to assign to them. That is, whereas the physical thing has its determinate nature and is subject to physical laws such as Newton's laws, the "things" of a poem—the artificial and natural creatures here, for instance—have only such properties as statement within the poem affords them. Poetic statements must not be confused, however, with propositions; since they are not statements about things which exist outside the poem, it would be meaningless to evaluate them as true or false; they have rather the status of definitions or resolutions; and while in certain poems the coordination is dialectical, as in this poem, no criteria of dialectic could be significantly applied to them, for a dialectic is necessarily regulated by the natures of things external to the dialectic and must ultimately be evaluated by references to these externals, whereas the coordination of elements in a poem cannot involve reference to anything outside the poem. Even when poetic statements are incidently true propositions, even when their coordination is also cogent argument, these coincidences would not affect their poetic status. Thus, "To His Coy Mistress" is an excellent poem, whether the lover's argument is valid or not. In a sense, every poem is a microcosmos, a discrete and independent universe with its laws provided by the poet; his decision is absolute; he can make things good or bad, great or small, powerful or weak, just as he wills; he may make men taller than mountains or smaller than atoms, he may suspend whole cities in the air, he may destroy creation or re-form it; within his universe the impossible becomes the possible, the necessary the contingent—if he but says they do.

I have said that the bare argument of "Sailing to Byzantium" is not the poem; but I should argue that the argument (considered not as a real argument, but, according to what I have said, as a certain collocation of terms) is the *principle* of this poem, in a sense analogous to that in which, for Aristotle, plot is the principle of tragedy. For if the principle is that for the sake of which all other things in the poem exist, and that, consequently, in terms of which all are intelligible, what could be the principle, other than the thing we have supposed? There is here no plot, no ordered tissue of incidents, for, first of all, the whole poem is of a moment—the moment in which the old man confronts the monuments and addresses them—whereas a tissue of incidents, a plot, must extend over a span of time. And second, there can be no plot because there are no incidents; the "events" in a lyric poem are never incidents as such, connected by necessity or probability, but devices for making poetic statements. Again, since there is no action, there is no agent, that is, *character*, in the sense in which there are differentiated agents in drama or epic, each duly discriminated for his distinct part in the action; rather, the character in the sense in which character may be said to exist here is almost completely universalized. Hence, if plot does not constitute the principle of the poem, neither does character; for not all the parts of the poem would be explicable in terms of character, nor are we presented with any precise depiction of character here, as we should be if it were the end. On the merely verbal level, again, we can account for nothing; the words must be explained in terms of something else, not the poem in terms of the words; and further, a principle must be a principle of something other than itself; hence the words cannot be a principle of their own arrangements.

Rather, it is clear as we look at the poem, that a certain problem orders the whole—the problem of finding a suitable compensation for the losses suffered in old age; the poem begins with exclusion from the pleasures of youth, develops among ordered dialectical alternatives, and ends when the problem is permanently solved. As the problem determines the limits of the poem, so it determines all else; the character is determined by it, for example, because—according to the very nature of the problem—a young man could not have conceived of the problem as it is stated, nor could a raging and sensual old man, nor could an old man who was contented with age, like Sophocles; since an ideal and permanent solution was to be given to the problem, a character conscious of loss, and capable of conceiving an ideal solution, was necessitated. Nothing beside this is indicated with respect to the speaker. Again, the words themselves are determined by the problem; while the choice of metaphors of a "country," or "song," and of modes of embodiment was initially arbitrary, once the metaphors have been stated they must be carried out according to the dictates of the problem; indeed, it is possible to trace variations in diction precisely proportional to the stages of the dialectic. For example, the stages are verbally signalized by the succession "flesh," "stick," "dying animal," "gold," in terms of expressions of embodiment, or "no country," "Byzantium," "the artifice of eternity," which is amid "holy fire," in terms of habitation; and the metaphor of the artificial bird in the fourth stanza bears such relation—in terms of setting, song, character of joy, object of joy, and "bodily form"—to the real birds—"those dying generations"—in stanza 1 as the solution of the problem bears to the element the negation of which generated the dialectic. In a similar manner the presence of nearly every word in the poem might be justified if space permitted.

On the basis of our examination, then, we may say that there exists a kind of poem (since we have here one instance of it) which has argument, in the sense we have stipulated, as its principle; not, let us remember, a dialectic referable to externals, but a certain formal collocation of terms which is referable to nothing outside itself and

which may be called the soul of the poem in the sense in which
Aristotle calls plot the soul of tragedy. This kind of poetry has the same
means as tragedy, epic, and comedy, but whereas the latter are
imitations of human action, so that their principle is a certain
collocation of incidents organized by necessity and probability—
whereas, that is, these are dynamic, for they imitate change—
the kind which we have been scrutinizing is static; it abstracts
from motion and change, and though it sometimes appears to recount
events, these are not events as parts of a plot connected by probability
or necessity, but events in the sense in which we speak of events in a
philosophical dialogue—they are only dialectically separable stages in
the treatment of a problem, and are reducible to statements within the
problem. Whereas in the Aristotelian treatment of poems which have a
plot as their principle, certain qualitative parts of the various species
resulted from an analysis of the object of imitation, that is, the action,
a different procedure is necessary here; the principle is a tissue not of
events but of ideas, and the ordering of the poem will not be by
necessity and probability, by the antecedents and consequents of
action, but by dialectical priority and posteriority. Lastly, while
character will be necessitated here as where a plot is the principle, it
will be determined, not by its share in an action, but by its role in a
drama, not of action, but of thought. That is, it is determined, as the
characters in a Platonic dialogue are determined, by the nature of the
discourse which they are to utter.

It would be a mistake, however, to assume that all lyrics are of the
order considered here. The term lyric itself has been given an
extraordinary variety of applications, and the scrupulous analyst and
critic will attempt to keep the variety of critical approaches almost
commensurate with these, on the assumption that great art—however
familiar the pattern in which it is apparently laid—is always in the last
analysis *sui generis*.

commensurate is overused
in terms of is used

RHETORIC AND THE
APPRECIATION OF POPE

A certain danger attends the attempt to revaluate the work of a writer whose literary fortunes have included his repudiation by the taste and doctrine of a whole century of criticism; the danger that, even if a certain restoration be effected, it may be for reasons utterly foreign to those underlying his original eminence. In the case of Pope, whose elevation and degradation were alike complete, the danger of such equivocal restoration is all but unavoidable, for the literary reversal which discredited him made both his theory and his practice unintelligible; it seems hardly grateful, therefore, to meet the labors of his advocates with the objection that these labors involved a danger which they have not avoided. Yet, to the modern defense of Pope, at least, the objection might well be made; and in the instances of Mr. Tillotson and Mr. Root, who are perhaps the most recent defenders,[1] it can be made for almost identical reasons. Both men evince an essentially similar reading of Pope; both operate upon his works with assumptions and distinctions of a similar order; and both attempt his restoration in terms which, however different superficially, are fundamentally equivalent.

Some restatement of their arguments may make my meaning clearer. Mr. Tillotson is engaged largely with the demonstration that Pope is "a true poet"; as he says,[2] the early nineteenth-century controversy centered mainly about the nature of the true poet, with Pope figuring merely as the stated subject; and it is that controversy, through which Pope has fallen into modern disfavor, which the critic sets out to resolve. For Mr. Tillotson it is the doctrine of classicism which stands in the way of our appreciation, as an external condition which might have deformed wholly the genius of the poet; hence he

Reprinted from *Modern Philology*, vol. 37, no.1 (August 1939).

1. Geoffrey Tillotson, *On the Poetry of Pope* (Oxford, 1938); Robert Kilburn Root, *The Poetical Career of Alexander Pope* (Princeton, 1938).

2. Tillotson, p. 18, n. 1.

seeks to show that there was no such deformation; that "Pope took over nothing that he thought unreasonable"; [3] that Pope escaped the servility which the doctrine of imitating the ancients might have imposed by being "himself"; [4] that, in short, he was actuated by precisely the motives, and possessed of precisely the emotional qualities, of the "true poet"; [5] and that his supposed limitations are evidence merely of his absorption with man rather than with nature (*Nature* in the Romantic sense), [6] or, on the other hand, of the manifestation, in poetic technique, of stern moral control. [7] Thus, for Mr. Tillotson, Pope is clearly akin to Wordsworth, Keats, and even to Mozart; [8] and with that kinship established, we may proceed to read and appreciate him without further difficulty.

Happy as this reconciliation of literary contrarieties may be, it is hardly acceptable. "The problem for the critic of Pope's poetry is that of relating the mechanics of the verse to its quality for the emotions"; [9] and Mr. Tillotson's approach to that problem has proceeded by the importation of certain terms central in Pope's literary doctrines—e.g., "correctness"—into a psychological context. For Pope these terms had had a strictly literary meaning: they were predicates of a good poem in the neo-classical conception; [10] for Mr. Tillotson, however, they have an ethical or a psychological significance: they are predicates of Pope. [11] Between the "true poet" and the works and doctrines of Pope, then, a discussion of Pope's character and psychology is a necessary mediation; poem and critical proposition alike become but indices of

3. P. 2.
4. Pp. 5, 11.
5. See particularly pp. 18–32; also pp. 160–69.
6. Pp. 18–32.
7. Pp. 41, 169, *et passim*. The idea is stated with particular clarity on p. 16: "In his [Pope's] own poetry of this kind, the mood is preserved from sentimentality by the technical control, which is the evidence of a moral control."
8. For example, pp. 166, 169, 171.
9. P. 160.
10. Compare, for example, the use of such terms in the *Essay on Criticism* as "whole" (l. 235), "part" (ll. 243–52), etc.
11. E.g., as "technical control" was "evidence" of "moral control" (p. 16), so such terms as "correctness," "design," "propriety," etc., suffer extension into moral or psychological meanings. Perhaps the quotation of a passage will give, better than the enumeration of shifted terms, the direction of Mr. Tillotson's dialectic: "Shelley is all for light and wind, Keats for colour and luxurious substance. But they seldom see how the materials provided by the earth can attain a perfection of form, and even of symbol, in the work of man's hands" (p. 29). Note that here the literary fact is taken as evidence of the poet's perception or lack of perception; i.e., qualities of the work are taken as qualities also of the man. Whether the argument is intended to turn on potentiality and actuality, or on image and idea, the reasoning of Mr. Tillotson is fallacious: the absence of a potentiality may not be argued from the absence of the actuality, nor is the characteristic absent in the image necessarily missing in the idea.

character; and the character is easily equated to the ideal. In such analysis, clearly, the poet and the work are not separable; historical guarantee of Pope's moral excellences affords a guarantee also of excellences in the poem, and conversely the sensitive critic can ascertain in the excellent poem the moral excellences of the poet. Thus Mr. Tillotson can quote historical evidence, [12] for example, to certify the presence of Romantic qualities in Pope's writings, and he can exhibit the *Second Dialogue* as infallible testimony of Pope's virtue. [13] Apparently the man is the exemplar or paradigm of which the poem is a kind of image or copy; if we wish to understand the image, we must first know its model; but the way to that understanding is, in the main at least, through an examination of the literary genius of Pope. Here the criticism is plainly Platonic, and quite irrefutable in its Platonism; the objections are not upon that score, but on grounds more relative than this: the Platonism, unlike that of Plato, is a somewhat unfruitful Platonism, and the truth to which it leads us is quite unplatonically implausible. If we submit to the unification of doctrine and poem, and both with Pope, and Pope with all other good poets—and I think this is indubitably the course of Mr. Tillotson's dialectic—we deserve to discover the nature of the True Poet, and hence the nature of the True Poem; but the True Poet turns out to be merely the good man, and the True Poem merely the literary evidence of the good man's goodness. Denied the proper revelation, the literal-minded are apt to be captious; they are apt to point out, for instance, that the whole body of neo-classical doctrine becomes so distorted by the analogy as to have only a verbal connection with its former meaning; that such interpretation of the doctrine would perhaps be as little acceptable to Pope as the portrait of Pope the True Poet would be to the Romantics; and that, besides, the paradigm of the True Poet is a purely Romantic creation which Mr. Tillotson assumes without question, and which Pope —and many another—would have questioned very much. One thing, at all odds, is clear: whereas a critic of the eighteenth century —Johnson, for example—could on occasion debate the status of a work in purely literary terms—terms which could apply only to a literary work considered in isolation from the man or the society that produced it [14]—Mr. Tillotson's argument, originating in the erasure of that distinction, can do no such thing; one may question, therefore, whether critical methods so different could reach an agreement concerning Pope which would not be equivocal.

For Mr. Root likewise the restoration of Pope involves the recog-

12. E.g., pp. 15, 23–25.

13. Pp. 39–40.

14. See, for example, Johnson's commentary on the *Essay on Criticism* in his *Life of Pope*.

nition of Romanticism and Classicism as opposites. Although his book
is a series of discrete essays tracing the development of Pope as a poet, a
certain unity of method is discoverable; and the method is again one in
which man and work are inseparable: the argument progresses,
consequently, through a genetic analysis of the work, identifying
models, reconstructing doctrines, and expounding in general the
character and career of Pope, since these are the character and career
also of his poetry. For Mr. Root, the modern reader's difficulties with
the poetry arise from difficulties with the man, and the latter are
twofold: Pope was a man of a society, a century, considerably different
from ours, and Pope was so successfully the satirist that bitter
animosity has continued to plague his memory.[15] The first difficulty
Mr. Root removes by establishing an analogy between the time of Pope
and the present century:[16] once the history of Pope's life is before us,
the analogy is clear. That clarification immediately results in another,
a literary one: we can now observe the analogy, on the one hand,
between the canons of Pope's art, and modern common-sense poetic
doctrines,[17] and, on the other hand, between the "Rape of the Lock"
and similar modern poems.[18] The second difficulty Mr. Root destroys
somewhat more startlingly. Pointing out that the portrait of Pope
which forms the frontispiece of the 1717 volume is that of "a
completely Romantic figure, every inch a poet,"[19] Mr. Root solves the
problem nicely: "There can be no doubt that to many readers of poetry
throughout the nineteenth century, Pope the man was an entirely
unsympathetic figure; and for nearly every one in that century, at any
rate, it was difficult to dissociate a work of art from the personal
character of the artist. All that personal prejudice would have been
averted if Pope had died in 1718; instead we should have had another
sentimentalized figure of the young poet cut off in the first flower of his
genius—and a genius which was apparently to develop into the great
precursor of the Romantic movement."[20] Pope unfortunately lived
twenty-six years longer, as Mr. Root admits; but his diversion into
moral essay and satire is now pardonable as a metamorphosis of the
true poet, and in that light the later works are intelligible. Even if we

15. Root, *Poetical Career*, p. 103.
16. Pp. 1–11. Perhaps the term "analogy" is misleading; the point is that the genetic,
i.e., historical, analysis clarifies the work by revealing the process of its generation.
Seeing the work develop under the conditions which determined its character, we
understand how the work came to be what it is, much as we can understand Pope the
man better, according to Mr. Root, by knowing his origin as a precursor of
Romanticism and his end as a poet of moralized song (pp. 159–60).
17. Pp. 11–31.
18. Pp. 81–82.
19. P. 103.
20. P. 104.

grant all this, however, it is difficult to see how we may apply our discovery to the explication of the texts; comprehension of the analogy between Pope and any other whom we know to be a true poet ought to spring rather from an examination of the writings than from an examination of the man, or of his portrait; and it is precisely upon the writings that Mr. Root is least satisfying. We reach thus a dilemma: either Mr. Root's essay is, or it is not, to be taken literally; if we take it literally the question is begged, because the similarity of Pope to good poets is precisely the point the anti-Papists would not grant; if, on the other hand, we do not take the essay literally, then the whole essay is beside the question.

Both of these works illustrate, I think, the danger that attends a method when familiarity with its use makes the recollection of its principles a tautology. Both works are in the analogical method; when predicates strictly literary are attributed to a human subject, or when human attributes are applied to a work of art, as in these essays, the literal interpretation of the statements so formed could result only in their falsification. For Mr. Tillotson and Mr. Root the method has become so familiar that to them it is, quite simply, the way in which literature must be approached; an alternative method seems not to have occurred to them. Both, consequently, discuss the works of Pope as a whole; while they admit that each poem is unique, the admission is conventional rather than functional, for the poems are never considered as unique structures; rather, the individual poems enter the discussion, not as solitary objects of consideration, but as illustrations of some quality of Pope's work as a totality, some quality of Pope the poet or Pope the man, some quality of a doctrine, a convention, or an era. This illustration of qualities proceeds necessarily by the revelation, rather than by any causal explanation, of their presence. The unity of the work exists for these critics in the authorship, i.e., in the author; since the reason for the presence of elements in each poem cannot, then, be found in terms of the poem, it must be adduced from the conditionings, doctrinal or biographical, of the poet; and the statements so derived take the form of analogues in which one term signifies the character of the poet, the other the characteristics of the poem. There is nothing in the least wrong with this method of literary criticism, although literary criticism perhaps affords a surfeit of it; but unless the critic operating in any method is perfectly aware of its manner of operation and of the nature of its solutions, he is likely to take his own statements unqualifiedly, i.e., without respect to the context which developed them; and in both Mr. Tillotson and Mr. Root that qualfication is sufficiently lacking to justify us in believing that they are not perfectly aware of their method. The nineteenth-century controversy which both critics here attempt to resolve had terminated in the general conviction that Pope was not a poet; that conviction is not to be corrected by pointing out, as Mr. Root and Mr. Tillotson do, that there is another sense in which Pope may correctly be said to be a poet; if any contradiction is intended here, it is an equivocal contradiction; yet both writers are obviously directing their efforts toward the removal of that conviction. [21] Both, furthermore, attempt to argue literally from the analogues which they provide: Mr. Root, for instance, seems to me to attempt a literal explication of the *Essay on Man* from the (by now almost commonplace) analogy between the philosophical professions of Pope and the Deism of his time; [22] Mr. Tillotson similarly essays a justification of the diction of *Windsor Forest* by a history of the terms present in that diction. [23] Moreover, both writers frequently include statements which are irrelevant or meaningless in their discussion; for example, both imply the unique character of the individual poem; [24] but the proposition is not used in either of these studies.

The appreciation of Pope is not a question of interpreting his works so that they fall, however equivocally, under what we know, under what we are accustomed to appreciate; rather it is a matter of the discipline of reading: we must discover what these works are, we must learn to appreciate them as they are. This is a point that, I think, most modern critics of the neo-classical have neglected; the feeling for classicism of Mr. T. S. Eliot or Miss Sitwell, for instance, seems to me rather an ability to find Romantic qualities in the neo-classical than any real ability for the appraisal of the neo-classical itself. Primarily, of course, the problem is not necessarily one of the opposition of Classicism and Romanticism at all, although the hypostatization of these contraries has made their distinction seem one which literary criticism cannot avoid. The problem of the appreciation of Pope is quite the same as that which arises in the appreciation of any writer: one appreciates a work either for extrinsic or for intrinsic reasons, that is, one appreciates it for general "values" or "qualities" which it reflects, or for the unique literary structure in which it is constituted. Generally, there are as many reasons for the lack of appreciation as there are variables in the problem, whichever of the alternatives we choose, and we can obtain an analysis of these by an analysis of the propositions we make about appreciation: a lack of appreciation is due either to (1) a lack of excellence in the work itself, or (2) a lack of intelligibility in the work, or (3) a lack of sensitivity in the reader, or (4) a lack of education

21. See Tillotson, pp. 18 ff., 32–42; and Root, pp. 103–4.
22. Root, pp. 179–82.
23. P. 88. The section on "Correctness in Language" (iii) argues in general in this fashion.
24. Tillotson, p. 55; Root, p. 64.

in the reader, or (5) some prejudice in the reader. The appreciation of a work for extrinsic reasons has perhaps been sufficiently illustrated, not merely by Mr. Tillotson and Mr. Root, whose fundamental criteria are of an ethical nature, since these critics are primarily concerned with the works as a manifestation of the character of the man, but by the host of critics who have appraised literature in the light of criteria that were ethical, logical, political, or psychological. Appreciation of an intrinsic order—appreciation that might be formulated in terms of exclusively rhetorical or poetic criteria—has not, on the other hand, been sufficiently illustrated. The criticism which results as reasoned statement from such appreciation is in kind with the work; and if one reads the works of Pope as unique structures, one reads with a growing suspicion that the criticism has not been in kind with the work. The scholar, the casual literary essayist, the literary historian, and the writer of textbooks and outlines, all present a treatment essentially similar: whatever the variations of method, purpose, or point of view, whatever the differences in the final evaluation, the characteristics of Pope's work apparently turn out much the same. And when these have been enumerated, whether for stricture or defense, they remain on the whole the characteristics of the rhetorician rather than of the poet— characteristics which, in poetry, are somewhat difficult to explain away. It is curious, then, that, in the face of this general admission, the position that Pope *is* a rhetorician, that his works are best explicable in the light of rhetorical rather than poetical principles, has not been assumed. The absence of this assumption seems especially curious when we observe that the greater portion of Pope's work, if we set aside the translations, is either satire or didactic, and that satire and didactic, as invariably involving a consideration of the audience, would fall, not under poetics, but under rhetoric. If we suppose, too, as the criticism of Pope has done invariably, that the doctrines of a writer have some influence upon his work, it is not irrelevant that the doctrines which Pope held were derived from men who either were rhetoricians or who sought, in their writing, what was primarily a rhetorical end.

If we are thinking of rhetoric in its truncated modern sense, as mere stylistic, the supposition that Pope is a rhetorician rather than a poet has little meaning other than of derogation; the truncation effects the substitution of a merely immediate end for the popular rhetorical one, effects, that is, the substitution of verbal ornamentation for persuasion; the result is that—since the end which alone makes intelligible the means is not regarded—the rhetorical work, which is the actualization of the means, cannot be intelligible.[25] If, however, we take rhetoric in its

25. What weakens the work of Mr. Tillotson and Mr. Root is that, however much of a poet Pope may seem to them, their main concern with him, insofar as it is a literary

more ancient and more useful sense, as that faculty by which we are able in any field of discourse to induce belief or conviction in our audience, [26] the supposition enlarges the possibilities of accounting for what is present in Pope, not merely by permitting the consideration of the various devices as ordered to a more general and, it may be, a more proper end, but by enlarging the scope of the means whereby that end might be attained. [27]

Perhaps the only way in which these statements may be substantiated is by indicating roughly, through actual analysis, what a rhetorical approach to Pope would be like. Suppose we take, quite arbitrarily, the *Epistle to Dr. Arbuthnot.* If we assume Pope to be a rhetorician, the *Epistle* (like its counterpart, the *First Satire of the Second Book of Horace: To Mr. Fortescue*) is of extraordinary rhetorical importance: these works attempt to re-establish Pope, after such attacks as the *Lines to an Imitator of Horace* and the *Epistle to a Doctor of Divinity*, as a man of good moral character. To a rhetorician the appearance of having a good moral character is a first concern; as Aristotle says, [28] goodness of character is almost the most effective

---

one at all, takes the form of rhetorical explication; but the rhetoric underlying the explication is mere stylistic. It is for this reason that much which is fresh and excellent in these two books does not, after all, reach very far. Mr. Tillotson, for example, can illuminate some aspects of Pope's diction commendably, as can Mr. Root (see, e.g., Tillotson, pp. 71–84; Root, pp. 37–46); neither can get much beyond the grammatical level, however, since the diction is not systematically considered as ordered to a rhetorical end. While both authors can talk rather prettily of "transitional devices" and "propriety," it is never made clear, precisely, what the transitional device effects, or what it conjoins, or why the elements of the conjunction should be so conjoined; and it is never made clear what is appropriate, or to what it is appropriate, or in what sense it is appropriate. The whole uncertainty in the consideration of the context sometimes betrays these critics into patent absurdities: Mr. Tillotson, for instance, contrasts the full treatment of Nova Zembla in the *Temple of Fame* with the bare mention of the name in *Dunciad*, I, 74, as an example of Pope's steadily developing thrift in description (pp. 60–61); Mr. Root *summarizes* poems to indicate the appropriateness of a passage, as if poetic unity were a question of material conjunction (pp. 64 ff.). Both critics leave one with the impression that what Pope does cannot be accounted for—an impression which, since the poet should have some justification for the use of his devices, is most disturbing. The justification can be only in terms of the end; here the end is not considered.

26. Aristotle *Rhetoric* i. 2. 1. 1355b26.

27. The preference for the second mode of consideration is best argued, I think, from the greater fruitfulness of the mode; but it might be argued as well upon historical grounds. If we hold that neo-classicism embodied much of ancient rhetorical theory, and that the doctrines of neo-classicism constituted the main direction of Pope (and these are in fact the traditional assumptions), there is some ground for supposing that Pope's own conception of rhetoric would not have been limited to stylistic. In other words, Pope was aware of the many devices suggested by Aristotle, Cicero, Quintilian, and others, and would have been likely to employ them.

28. *Rhet.* i. 2. 4. 1356a4–13.

means of persuasion the orator possesses, since good men are more completely and more readily given credence than others, and since the possibility of persuasion is dependent upon credibility. Thus didactic and satire would have been vitiated alike, had such charges against Pope remained unanswered. The *Epistle to Dr. Arbuthnot* is, there-fore, a piece of forensic in which Pope answers the accusations of his enemies; his audience consists of judges, not spectators, and they are judges of what has been done, rather than of what may be done, and because the end of the discourse is the "proof" of the justice of Pope's actions, i.e., the rehabilitation of his character. [29] One thing must be remarked at once: such questions as whether Pope's indignation is sincere, or whether Pope was actually a man of good character— questions about which his critics have troubled so much—are entirely irrelevant here. The rhetorician need not actually be sincere, need not actually be a good man; he must, however, *seem* to be these things, that is, he must through his art effect the impression that he is these things; it is far more important, from the standpoint of rhetoric, to seem to have good character when one actually does not, than to have it when one does not seem to.

Two rhetorical devices of extreme importance may be noted at the outset. First, the casting of the defense into the form of a dialogue was a stroke of rhetorical genius. By the portrayal of himself as closeted with a very close friend, Pope permits himself the most congenial and most disarming setting: the circumstance is one in which sincerity and frankness can be expected. Arbuthnot, moreover, is a great and good man, and as such serves a triple function: he can raise, as interlocutor, questions that might have been awkward for Pope himself to initiate, he serves as a warrant for the truth of the dialogue, and, most important of all, he offers a model, by his concurrence after reasonable objection, which an audience would be extremely likely to imitate; he validates, one might say, both the argument and the report of it which constitutes the *Epistle*. Again, the device of dialogue avoids the difficulties that a direct address to the audience might have entailed; it is very cunning that here the audience should seem to be not an audience, that Pope should seem to be unaware of any other hearer than Arbuthnot; the strategy obtains for Pope the opportunity of using every device of rhetoric while appearing to use none. The dramatiza-tion, moreover, sets the matter before the eyes of the audience; the audience is, in a manner, admitted as witness, and what we witness we are most assured of; and, what is more, the presentation as a kind of play insures a much sharper attention than a bare answering of charges could possibly provoke. Secondly, there is much rhetorical force in that

29. Ibid. i. 3. 1358a36–1259a29.

the answer to Pope's enemies should have been drawn up, not as the response of a defendant, but as Pope himself says, as a "sort of bill of complaint." To have answered as defendant would have been to indicate the charges as worthy of serious consideration, and the defense would have been much more difficult; to file a bill of complaint, on the other hand, is to propose one's self as the wronged person and to lay the burden of disproof upon the opposition.

According to Aristotle, there are three modes of persuasion furnished by the spoken word: the first is dependent upon the personal character of the speaker, the second upon the frame of mind of the audience, the third upon the speech itself. [30] Hence the rhetorician must be able to argue well, to comprehend human character and goodness in their various forms, and to understand the emotions. [31] We may test Pope as a rhetorician, then, according to his abilities in these directions; that is, we may take for criterion the consideration of whether he has employed all the available means to his particular rhetorical purpose. Aristotle mentions three things as productive of confidence in the character of the speaker—the three, namely, that induce an audience to believe a thing apart from any proof of it: good sense, good moral character, and good will; these are all requisite because false or mistaken counsel is due to the absence of these. [32] Pope effects the characterization of himself as a man of good sense by a dozen devices: by his attitude toward flatterers (e.g., ll. 109–24), toward fools (*passim*), toward sober criticism (e.g., ll. 156–57), toward bad art (e.g., ll. 33–46), and in general by his sharp insight into character and motive, and his ready and certain evaluation of human action and production. Furthermore, he brings authority to testify to his good sense: the great have approved his studies (l. 143), and the ancients and the approved moderns (Horace, Persius, Boileau, etc.) furnish him with maxims (e.g., ll. 40, 105–6, etc.). [33] His opponents, on the other hand, are men of folly, susceptible to flattery (e.g., ll. 231–48), congenial with other fools (e.g., ll. 209–12), impatient of just criticism (e.g., l. 40), and in general the contraries of Pope. The characterization of himself as morally good is even more full: Pope has all the virtues in the calendar. He is courageous (e.g., l. 343), temperate (if we can so construe l. 263), liberal (e.g., ll. 371–72), properly ambitious (e.g., ll. 334 ff.), gentle (e.g., ll.368–87), amiable (e.g., ll. 35, 37), sincere in self-profession (e.g., ll. 261 ff.), witty (this scarcely requires illustration), and just (e.g., ll. 283 ff.). Again his opponents are his

30. Ibid., i. 2. 1356a1–21.
31. Ibid. i. 2. 1356a21 ff.
32. Ibid. ii. 1. 1378a6–19.
33. L. 3, Pers. *Sat.* iii. 5; l. 20, Boileau, *Art poétique*, Chant I, l. 22, from Mart. *Ep.* xii. 62; l. 40, Hor. *De arte poet.* 388; l. 128; Ov. *Trist.* iv. 10. 25–26; etc.

contraries; some are vicious through deficiency, as Atticus; some through excess, as Sporus. The characterization of himself as well disposed toward the audience, i.e., as having good will, Pope effects easily; his audience is those who are or who think themselves virtuous; and this generalization of the audience escapes, of course, the sharp antagonisms which might have arisen through a more specific pleading. As the matter stands, virtue is the solitary characteristic of the audience; hence Pope needs only to reassure his audience that he is a man of virtue, and that "A lash like mine no honest man need dread." The enemies of Pope, on the other hand, are haters of virtue, hence enemies also of the virtuous, hence enemies of the audience.

So far, however, we have considered only what Pope professes himself and his enemies to be; about that profession in itself there is nothing remarkable, since most people characterize themselves as having every virtue, their enemies as having every vice. The preceding discussion has served but one purpose: it has shown us that Pope has omitted nothing requisite to the character of the speaker. If, now, we can find out in what ways he is able to establish himself as possessed of these characteristics, we shall be dealing with the more properly artistic aspects of his rhetoric. And the chief device is certainly the dialogue itself; for through the dramatization Pope avoids the necessity of stating that he is morally good or sensible or well-disposed, and needs only to show himself as actually acting in such character. This is excellent for several reasons: in the first place, statement analyzes out the various attributions, making refutation or doubt much easier, whereas dramatization presents, like reality itself, complexes of characteristics in such a fashion as often to baffle analysis; secondly, statement gives the impression of hearing a report or testimony, whereas dramatization gives the impression of actually witnessing; hence the latter is clearly more credible. Notice how the attribution proceeds by dramatization; in lines 333 ff., for example, Pope breaks into a heroic declamation which has the effect of attributing extremest moral excellence to him; he does not, however, *state* that he is virtuous; he merely shows himself acting as if he were. There is not a single declarative idea in the whole speech; the whole is one subjunctive sentence. The moral indignation which he assumes in the angry interruptions (e.g., ll. 78 ff.), the ironic amusement at flattery (e.g., ll. 115 ff.), the disgust with "the whole Castalian state" (e.g., ll. 215-54), the regret at the fate of Gay (ll. 256 ff.), the apparent justice of the portrait of Atticus, the earnestness of such passages as lines 135 ff., as lines 261 ff., as lines 334 ff.—all these are speeches appropriate only to a man of distinguished virtue and prudence; the audience assumes therefore that Pope, who is saying these things, *is* virtuous and prudent, much as spectators at a play imagine an actor to be actually like the character he is impersonating. Nor can the audience take this as fiction; Arbuthnot is there, as it were, to certify that it happened. The result is something very difficult to doubt, something practically impossible to refute. Once Pope's character, moreover, is established, it tends to establish certain other things which, reciprocally, assist in the further establishment of the character; for instance, it is because we believe Pope virtuous that we believe his account of his parentage, and it is because we believe his account of his parentage that we tend to be more assured of his virtue, not merely because Pope exhibits filial piety and a wish to emulate his father's virtue, but because it is generally thought that what springs from good parentage tends itself to be good. The good will toward the audience is similarly, as I have suggested, established.

The audience here needs hardly any other characterization than that it is composed of all those, of whatever age, birth, state, or similar determination, who are virtuous or who think themselves virtuous. Their state of mind may be any state from fear and hatred of Pope[34] to mere anger with him; the rhetoric seems devised for the removal of any prejudice against him as a kind of "mad dog" satirist. It is the state of mind of the audience that orders the work: the ordering, that is, is not logical or poetical, but one determined by the stages in which such prejudice can be removed, and in which the proper conception of Pope as a man can be constructed. The most important thing is to allay the fear of the reader that he may be the next to be attacked, since such fear would make it impossible for Pope to appear as one of good will, and hence to persuade at all; consequently Pope shows himself as besieged by the rabble of bad poets; because one who is himself hard pressed is unlikely to attack new enemies, the fear is temporarily, at least, allayed. But Pope immediately proceeds to characterize his opponents as the mad; they, then, and not he, are the proper objects of fear. Even so, Pope is civil to them in their madness and folly; the audience is likely to judge, therefore, that he will be more than civil to the sane and wise. Indeed, Pope must be even hospitable to the mad; else the poetaster sallying forth from the Mint would not be happy to catch him "just at dinner-time." Also, Pope is apparently kind to his servant—witness "good John"; therefore it is likely that he will be kind to those who are not his servants. What is more, Pope has been wrongly accused: Arthur and Cornus impute to him what it is absurd to think he could have caused. All of these details would operate upon the minds of the audience to an obvious end; so that by line 68 it is established that Pope, far from being a mad dog satirist, far from being a perpetrator of unprovoked literary outrages, is a man of civility and

34. *First Sat. Bk. II. Horace: To Mr. Fortescue*, l. 41: "Ev'n those you touch not, hate you."

humanity, as well as of acumen, who has borne the extremest provocation that a character so constituted can bear. His enemies, on the other hand, are men of the opposite stamp; they fit the description of those whom Persius, Martial, and Boileau had satirized,[35] and they will not in their literary folly profit by the advice even of Horace;[36] thus the authority of the ancients and moderns is invoked against them. It is to be noted that as the speech progresses, as Pope obtains increasing control over his audience, the satire sharpens with more and more serious allegations: thus, for example, the portrait of Atticus is sharper than the ridicule of the fools at the beginning, and the portrait of Sporus is sharper than that of Atticus.[37] The jesting tone of the opening lines, moreover, permits exaggerations which a more serious statement might have made to appear falsity; in addition, the pleasantry is most disarming.[38]

The fear of the audience is perhaps, for the moment at least, sufficiently allayed; but certain possible prejudices against Pope's character must be removed. For example, the audience may feel that while Pope's satire is certainly not unprovoked, the punishment may be excessive, and Pope, consequently, may be cruel. This charge is answered in lines 83–101, and it is notable that Pope himself raises the question rather than Arbuthnot: as one who punishes justly, Pope must himself have weighed the punishment; for Arbuthnot to have raised the point would have been to suggest that it was an issue overlooked by Pope. The charge is, of course, answered casuistically; but while the argument itself is fraudulent, it is posed in such a fashion as to provoke laughter; and laughter, as Pope himself once said,[39] is a kind of assent. The anger of those who might object to Pope's attacks upon royalty, as arising from the most serious prejudice, has been removed previously: in lines 70–72 Pope's reference to "queens, ministers, and kings" had been innocent and accidental; and the fear of Arbuthnot that such a reference might be turned against Pope suggests in the most cunning fashion that all such charges had had similar origin.[40] Lines 101–24 remove any prejudice which the audience may have against Pope on the score of imprudence; lines 115–24, any which the audience may hold on the score of vanity. Following this, Pope attempts to move the audience into a positive conception of him; the appeals to the authority of nature (ll. 125–28) and of the great who had approved his labors (ll.

35. See n. 33, above.
36. L. 40.
37. Cf. the increasing sharpness in the speech of Mark Antony in Shakespeare's *Julius Caesar*, III, ii, 74–260.
38. Arist. *Rhet.* iii. 18. 1419b3–5.
39. *First Sat. Bk. II. Hor: To Mr. Fortescue*, ll. 155–56.
40. Note other attempts to remove the same charge in this epistle; e.g., the canceled verses after l. 282 in the MS; ll. 356–59, etc.

135-46), together with the brief appeal to the pity of the audience (ll. 131-33), signalize the beginning of this attempt. Certain of the minor enemies can be discredited now that the audience has been fairly caught; but the attack must begin mildly, or the old prejudices will revive. Accordingly Pope, while apparently illustrating his restraint, discounts Gildon and Dennis (ll. 146-56) by adumbrating the causes of their attack upon him. Similarly, the momentary fury of the attack upon his "more sober" critics is made pardonable by the apparent aptness of the metaphor in lines 169-72, although the punitive force of the passage is thereby increased and not lessened; and similarly, too, the treatment of the "others angry" moves assent by the inclusion of aphorisms on the difficulty of pleasing the proud (ll. 175-78). Immediately thereafter we have Atticus. A good deal has been said on the apparently nice justice of these lines,[41] so that any extended treatment here is unnecessary; however, it may be noted that in the character Pope is professing himself to be, any purely scurrilous treatment of Addison would have been inappropriate, and that, at the same time, some treatment of Addison was requisite: Addison was too distinguished an adversary to be ignored. He must, moreover, be removed as early in the argument as would be consistent with safety, since to reserve him for later answer would have been to effect in the audience only a tentative acceptance of the greater part of Pope's argument. Hence Pope, using what Aristotle calls a "method of thoroughly skillful and unscrupulous prosecutors,"[42] mixes the virtues and vices of Atticus in such fashion as to disguise perfectly that this is special pleading. The statement is not even plain and flat; as Mr. Tillotson admirably suggests, the whole "hangs on a condition."[43] Even so, the attack may have been too daring; hence, lest the audience feel that it has proceeded from literary envy, Pope hastens, in lines 215-70, to indicate himself as one quite without ambition of the worldly kind, whether literary or otherwise; the portrait of Bufo the patron is introduced to show the kind of character to whom "the Castalian state" would be desirable, to provide an object for the contempt of Pope, and so to disclaim any similar ambition. This is followed by several self-characterizing speeches in which the audience is further impressed with Pope's good will: if certain works attributed to Pope have given offense, the attribution is questionable;[44] Pope is a friend of the virtuous, hence of the audience. Thus the shocking portraiture of

41. Mr. Root has some excellent suggestions; see *Poetical Career*, pp. 201-5.
42. *Rhet.* iii. 15. 1416b5-7.
43. *On the poetry of Pope*, p. 38.
44. Cf. ll. 279-82 and 351.

Sporus—in this instance the main enemy, since he and Lady Mary[45] had brought the charges—is prepared for: at the precise moment when the identification of Pope with the audience is most complete, Pope turns on Sporus; and the assent of the audience is a foregone conclusion. The contemptuous interruption of Arbuthnot reinforces the ferocity of the attack; and the coincidence of the audience is counted upon to such an extent, now, that Sporus's very best parts—his "eternal smiles," his personal beauty, his evident charm, his wit, his possession of royal favor—all suffer a horrid inversion. That removes all charges against Pope; and Pope proceeds to stamp home, once and for all, the impression of himself which he wishes to create: all his acts have virtue as their source (ll. 334–59); his very enemies can give evidence of that (ll. 368 ff.); he is good in origin (ll. 382–403) and he will so continue (ll. 404–17). Arbuthnot acquiesces completely, closing the dialogue. What is left last of all with the audience is, therefore, a proper picture of Pope, duly approved by Arbuthnot, to bear in mind against any further attacks.

The argument itself is relatively simple: it must first be shown that Pope's action in the present instance is just retaliation; next, that he did not initiate the literary war; and finally, to provide against further charges of a similar nature, that Pope's intentions are virtuous and that it is improbable that he will depart from those intentions. Accordingly the argument falls into three parts: the first (ll. 1–124) arguing the present charges (i.e., of the *Verses to an Imitator of Horace* and the *Epistle to a Doctor of Divinity*), the second (ll. 125–248) arguing that Pope was not the original aggressor, the third (ll. 249–end) arguing the guarantee of Pope's future conduct.

In the first part Pope spends lines 1–68 in establishing, by rhetorical induction, his minor premise, namely, that his case is worse than that of Midas' minister, since every coxcomb perks asses' ears in his face; the major, that all who have secrets similar to that of Midas' minister cannot retain them, is suggested in lines 69–74 and the conclusion appears in lines 79–80 through the false *a fortiori*: Pope is "forced to speak or burst," hence "Out with it, Dunciad! Let the secret pass." Two objections are posed, one with respect to the possible cruelty, the other with respect to the possible imprudence of retaliation; each of these meets a threefold argument of counter-objection. The first objection is answered first by enthymeme; the major is "Fools do not suffer pain" ("No creature smarts so little as a fool"); the minor, that

45. Lady Mary is mentioned by name only in l. 101 and, still with considerable reticence, in l. 369—probably because a too furious attack might have been out of character here.

these are fools, is taken as *ex concesso* and is suppressed; the conclusion, that these do not suffer pain sufficiently to constitute the
infliction of it a cruelty, then follows. [46] Next, the objection is refuted
by analogy (ll. 89–94): if a scribbler is like a spider and it is no cruelty
to destroy the fabrication of the spider, then by analogy it is no cruelty
to destroy the fibs or sophistries of the scribbler. The analogy is so
skilfully drawn as to command the assent of the audience; but with the
assent to the analogy the conclusion apparently follows. Thirdly, Pope
refutes, by seemingly perfect induction ("Whom have I hurt?") for the
last time the objection of cruelty (ll. 95–101). In turn the objection of
imprudence is answered by enthymeme or maxim (l. 104), analogy (ll.
105–6) fortified by an appeal to authority ("if the learned are right"),
and finally by induction (ll.109–24).

The second part of the argument establishes the innocence of Pope's
conduct previous to the present warfare. The cause of his writing is
nature ("the numbers came"), not vanity, since he wrote as a child,
when he was not yet "a fool to fame"; and the natural capacity was
realized in accordance with duty, piety, and friendship; hence his
writing is in origin and in actualization good. The cause of his
publication is authority; and the *ad verecundiam* argument serves the
double purpose of supporting the contention and of characterizing
Pope as amiable, sensible, modest, and talented, as indeed does most of
the argument. The writing so generated, so developed, and so
published could have given no offense; yet he was attacked by Gildon
and Dennis, who wrote not through nature but through want, and
who published not by authority but through madness; Pope is not,
then, the first aggressor. Indeed, he did not act even then; though he
may have angered some (l. 173), it was only an attempt upon his part
to evaluate them justly; and since the evaluation was truthful, it could
have given anger only to the proud (ll. 173–78). It is notable that
nowhere in this part does Arbuthnot pose an objection; these are
matters that Arbuthnot could not have called in question without
ruining the rhetorical effect. For the most part the argument has
proceeded by enthymeme and induction; but the analogy in lines
169–72, like that of the spider, is of telling force.

In the third part the argument is of extremest simplicity; here Pope
for the most part falls back, quite properly, [47] upon moral discourse his
future conduct is suggested from his wishes (e.g., ll. 249–62) and his
present virtue (ll. 283 ff.), the latter being in fact the reason why his

46. Depending upon grammatical interpretation, the argument is either maxim or
enthymeme. For the distinction see Aristotle *Rhet.* ii. 21–22.
47. Cf. ibid. iii. 17. 1418a37 ff.

genius, by nature literary, should have been given a satiric determination. [48] The piece closes with the purely rhetorical exhibition of Pope as it were, in the bosom of his family.

Space has not allowed more than the adumbration of an analysis but even from this it would be easily possible to show how the style, the prosody, and even the grammatical constructions are appropriate to the rhetorical work we have outlined. The style, for example, is excellent if for no other reason than that it is in the great rhetorical tradition of Horace, Juvenal, and Persius; to write in that fashion is in a manner to invoke the authority of these writers; and to write so, furthermore, would be rhetorically justifiable if only upon the ground that such a style was demanded by the audience. More specifically, however, the appropriateness of the diction can be seen from the manner of its exhibition of character and emotion and from its suitability to the subject matter. For example, in the passage describing the simplicity of Pope's life (ll. 261 ff.) the diction itself is simple; the words are among the commonest in the language and they are used in their literal sense; mostly, indeed, the speech is monosyllabic; there are almost no epithets, and there are no ambiguous or unusual grammatical constructions. That simplicity of diction of course makes for clarity; but to appreciate how it exhibits character and emotion we have only to consider what a more fanciful or elaborate diction would have effected; any such departure from the simple would have belied the simplicity of taste that Pope was attempting to establish as characteristic of him, and furthermore, would have given a flavor of artificiality to his professions, snice people tend to believe that sincerity is attended by simplicity of speech. I think the very grammatical structure here is defensible; the subjunctive sentence, particularly when exclamatory, as here, is much more effective than a declarative sentence could have been, since it has an emotional tone; we have only to substitute "I wish to live my own and die so too" for "Oh, let me live my own and die so too!" to observe how the emotion disappears. The exhibition of emotion is particularly important here; the good man ought not merely to wish a good life but to feel strongly about it, so that all his emotions are ordered to it; and the best argument that one has such and such desires is the exhibition of one's self as actually moved by the contemplation of them. The use of the verbs "maintain," "see," "read" without the auxiliary construction (i.e., without "let me") is also defensible; it gives the passage a rational tone through grammatical co-ordination, where a series of short exclamatory sentences would have made but hysterical declamation. It is proper, too, that the

48. Ll. 334–59.

analysis of what it is to "live my own" should be brief; a long series of statements about the simple life would have made the life seem not simple but complex. The entire absence of grammatical inversion in this passage was almost necessitated by the need for an air of plainness and simplicity; hence, once the kind of sentence has been determined, the organization of the words is according to normal order; and although ellipsis is employed, it is normal ellipsis only: the omission of a subject before predicates in series, or of verbal auxiliaries. Wit could have no place in this passage; it could but make suspect Pope's sincerity. Simple though the verses are, the diction is saved from meanness through its employment in moral discourse, through the absence of any low referents, and through the verse.

Viewed generally, even in this crude sketch of an analysis, the *Epistle* presents certain striking peculiarities of form. Not the least striking of these is the circularity of the rhetoric; the work is intended to establish the character of Pope through argument, but the warrant for the credibility of the argument is the character of Pope, and, strangely enough, the particular arguments establishing each trait of character depend upon the previous assumption that Pope *has* the very trait in question; for instance, we can grant the argument establishing truthfulness as a characteristic only if we already believe in the truthfulness of the speaker advancing the argument, and we can grant the thesis of his prudence only if we have previously ceded that characteristic as present in him. There is a reciprocal relation, consequently, between the principles and the conclusion of the rhetoric; a circularity not even broken by the presence of Arbuthnot as witness, since in the end we have only Pope's word for that. But the peculiarities do not cease here; the internal rhetoric is one in which speaker, audience, and speech are one: Pope is the speaker, Pope is the thesis in question and the argument supporting it, and finally, since Arbuthnot, the apparent audience, is nothing more than the creature of Pope, Pope is the audience as well. The effect on the actual audience, i.e., the readers for whom the rhetoric is designed, is most curious; it is as if they were overhearing one more *Débat de cuer et de corps*, one more *A son esprit*. [49] What is more, there is here, in a sense, rhetoric within rhetoric; there is the rhetoric by which Arbuthnot becomes convinced of the propriety of Pope's satire, and there is the rhetoric effecting conviction in the reader through the example of Arbuthnot's conviction. Here again a circle is evident; the first can be effective only if the second is effective, and the second can be effective only if the first is.

49. It was apparently Warton who first mentioned this latter, the ninth Satire of Boileau, as strongly influencing the *Epistle to Arbuthnot* (*Essay on the Genius and Writings of Pope*, [London, 1782], 2:264). Certainly there are important similarities.

The rhetoric is not thereby vitiated, strangely enough; it is saved by Pope's lively simulation of virtue, which is sufficiently impressive to establish part, and hence all, of the circle. As Aristotle remarks, an audience generally tends to commit the fallacy of the consequent, to suppose, in other words, that because the speaker acts just as virtuous men do under the circumstances, he is himself virtuous. [50] In appraising the *Epistle* as forensic, then, it should be sufficient for us that the semblance of virtue is good, that the part is well acted; to judge the work as demonstration there would be requisite a certitude, which no historical information could provide, that Pope was in fact virtuous. If we assume that Pope is dissembling here, the rhetoric is much like that of the first speech of Socrates in the *Phaedrus;* [51] unlike the speech of Lysias, [52] it has an ordering principle, and unlike the second speech of Socrates, [53] which is the true rhetoric, i.e., dialectic, it does not possess truth. The conception of rhetoric which is exemplified in the first speech of Socrates approximates Aristotle's conception of rhetoric; it is an art of uttering semblances of truth rather than the truth itself; and it bears that relation to the true rhetoric, dialectic, which in Aristotelian statement rhetoric would bear to demonstration; it seeks, that is, its warrant in the opinions and emotions of the audience rather than in principles of scientific demonstration.

I have suggested, thus roughly, a possible approach [54] to the *Epistle to Dr. Arbuthnot;* I think that a similar treatment of the *Moral Essays,* the *Essay on Man,* the *Essay on Criticism,* the *Dunciad,* and in general the rhetorical works of Pope, might prove not unprofitable. Such

50. *Poetics* xxiv. 1460a19–25.

51. 237 C ff.

52. Ibid. 231 A ff.

53. Ibid. 244 A ff.

54. Since literary analysis, like any analysis, involves variables (e.g., the sensibility or erudition of the reader, the certainty of the text, etc.), its status is that of hypothesis. There can, consequently, be no proof positive of the present analysis, if by proof positive we mean something of the order of demonstration; but there may be derived from the definition of the term *hypothesis* eleven topics which can be taken as criteria for the evaluation of hypotheses. If we define *hypothesis* as a supposition explaining data, it is clear that (1) the hypothesis must be more intelligible than the data (since explanation is always of the less well known in terms of the better known); (2) the hypothesis must be clearly formulated; (3) it must have a single principle governing the admission of data as evidence; (4) it must take into account all the evidence resulting from the application of that principle; (5) it must imply all the admitted evidence; (6) it must in that implication have systematic unity; (7) it must be self-consistent; (8) it must rest upon no hypotheses less probable than itself; (9) it must be economical; (10) it must constitute an explanation of the data, i.e., the data must be intelligible through it; and (11) it must be consistent with known truths.

The present analysis is intended, thus, not as a final and absolute explanation of the poem, but as an illustration of a critical method.

works as the *Pastorals*, the *Temple of Fame*, the "Rape of the Lock,"
and the translations of Homer, Statius, and Donne are not, on the
other hand, likely to yield much in such analysis; these seem to me
rather to be translations in the sense in which any attempt to construct
a literary analogue of a given work is a translation, and must be
approached accordingly. Whatever approach be adopted, however, it
will tend to be more fruitful if it examines systematically the nature of
the equivalences which may exist between literary analogues. The
problem of Pope's Homer, for instance, is not touched, much less
solved, when we point out that Pope is or is not Homer, or when we
underscore similarities or dissimilarities of diction; we cannot operate
properly apart from a clearly formulated theory of translation if we are
to make any literal statements concerning a work *qua* translation. In
the case of Pope we have been provided with a statement of what he
considered translation to be;[55] the danger has been that we have
interpreted that statement too easily, too naïvely; the larger critical
doctrines in which it was included, and without reference to which it is
unintelligible, have in a similar fashion been construed too readily, or
ignored. In the main the concern of Popian critics has been with the
conventions that are considered to have limited, fortunately or unfortunately, the genius of Pope; it might be profitable to remember that if

55. Although the term "translation" is usually defined as the rendering of a literary
structure in different diction, certain loosenesses of its application have extended its
meaning to include both imitation and adaptation. In its broadest literary sense,
translation is the construction of a literary work similar in some respect to a given work
or a given kind of work; hence there are as many modes of translation as we distinguish
qualitative parts of the work to be translated, or, to put it differently, as there are
respects in which we take works to be similar. Thus if we distinguish plot, character,
diction, and thought as qualitative parts of the epic, the equivalences between original
and translation may be stated in terms of these; and the criteria of translation *qua*
translation would be derived, in any case, from the fact that a translation is dependent
for its character upon those aspects which the translator held either to be chiefly
characteristic of a work, an author, a *genre*, or a mode of composition, or, on the other
hand, to be relevant to some circumstance affecting the translator. In the *Preface to the
Iliad* Pope sets up two ways in which his translation may be tested; one may test
intuitively (i.e., by sensibility) by referring the work to Fénelon's *Télémaque*, a poem
which according to Pope has caught the proper spirit or quality of Homer, or one may
test intellectually by referring to Bossu on the epic for the "justest notion of
his [Homer's] design and conduct." In the first, the intuitive test, the "chief character" of Homer is revealed as "fire"; but if the reference to Bossu is anything
more than a fashionable gesture, there is no need to consider "fire" a property of diction
only, or to suppose that Pope's doctrine of translation was exclusively concerned with
diction, in spite of Pope's somewhat lengthy analysis of possible stylistic equivalences,
viz., equivalences either in variations of style, modulations of numbers, diction, or
grammatical or rhetorical figuration. In other words, the *Iliad* of Pope might be
examined without reference to the Popian stylistic to which so much objection has been
raised.

convention, as a postulate, constitutes a limitation, it is also the source of a structure the realization of which is possible only through it. If we are to study Pope, that study might include what the works of Pope are, as well as what they are not. In such fashion alone are we likely to comprehend how, in the judgment of a whole century, and by no means without reason, Pope must be reckoned among the few first figures of English literature.

LOUISE BOGAN
AND LÉONIE ADAMS

It would be generally conceded, I think, that Louise Bogan and Léonie Adams are among the four or five American women thus far in this century who have produced poetry of high distinction. Their reputations, solidly established in the twenties, have survived a number of spectacular revolutions in literary taste, theory, and practice; certain of their poems seem to have become permanently embedded in anthologies of contemporary poetry; in short, their situation is excellent, except for the danger that the greater part of their work may be ignored precisely because a piece or two remains in high favor. [1] I, for one, should be sorry to see all their craft and skill come to be represented merely by so much as is manifest in a few poems; and I should like to do what I can to prevent this, by considering the larger aspects of their art.

The greater part of Miss Bogan's poems deal with the experiences of love; love, that is, as suffered by a certain individual. Like many other lyric poets, Bogan tends to portray a single character who appears constantly, or nearly so, in her work; whether this character is the poet or a dramatic figment, whether her experiences are real or imagined, it would be impertinent, and indeed pointless, to inquire. What is to the point is that this character is of a certain order, and that her experiences, as suggested by the individual poems, tend to follow a certain pattern. The character is a woman, sensitive, passionate, sensuous, and, I should say, strong-willed; intelligent, but emotional rather than intellectual; led against her reason, almost against her will, into love; loving violently and prodigal in her love, but quick to resent any betrayal or any attempt at domination by her lover. For her, love is neither a merging of two into one such as we see in Donne's "The Ecstasy," nor the ensouling of woman by man, nor of man by woman; it is a conjunction of two distinct persons, the essential condition of

Reprinted from *Chicago Review*, vol. 8, no. 4 (Fall 1954).
1. Louise Bogan, *Collected Poems: 1923–53* (New York: Noonday Press, 1954); Léonie Adams, *Poems: A Selection*, (New York: Funk and Wagnalls Co., 1954).

which is that, as conjoined, they should remain distinct. It is neither love wholly spiritualized, nor merely physical attraction. It is likely to be transitory, not because romantic conventions demand that it should be so, but because the difficult conditions of its existence cannot be long maintained. Like romantic love, it has its pleasures and pains, but these are not always alternations of rapture with anguish; they remain pretty much life-size.

For such a woman, the history of love is almost bound to follow a certain course; there are, thus, poems which express intense desire, or bitter resistance to it; delight, not merely with love itself, but with life as transformed by love; resignation, pain, bitterness, or regret as love ends. This course seems to grow out of the conflict between selfhood and love, and special emotions are generated as now one triumphs, now the other; significantly, love is often seen in the poems in terms of war, with its wounds, surrenders, victories, and scars, or of some natural force raging beyond control, or else of some thralldom or bitterly resented enchantment, some "bitter spell" that must be suffered.

This may remind some instantly of Millay; but in fact there is very little, if any, resemblance. In Millay, when the woman is not simply "feminine" in the sense of whimsical, fickle, impulsive, and so on, she is supposedly of divine or heroic mold; and the whole history of love is similarly magnified and exaggerated. The fates are involved, the fortunes of nations hang in the balance, the gods watch or even intervene, the lover is not a man but a god, love makes the woman godlike, too, or at any rate comparable to Danae, Europa, Leda, and others who "had a god for guest." All pain is insupportable agony; all pleasure is transcendent ecstasy. (Lest it be supposed that I exaggerate this, look at sonnets I, IV, V, VII, XII, XIV, XV, XVI, XXVI, XLII, LII of *Fatal Interview.*) Millay sought to give the love she described something of tragic stature by equating it with the great loves of myth and legend; she failed, I think, because in her poems we are told rather than shown that the love is of so exalted an order. It is one thing to claim that you are suffering as much as Othello or Lear; quite another to be what they are, and suffer such anguish as they do.

Miss Bogan never attempts this tragic or epic strain. She shows us a human being suffering perfectly human, if violent, passions; lovers are brought together or separated, not by the Fates or Cupid or Aphrodite, but by the course of nature; the love depicted is not that of Iseult or Dido, but love as most of us know it; we see the events, not against any romantic background, but in perfectly ordinary, if vivid, settings— chiefly New England countryside; and what happens is important because of the individuals concerned, not because of any greater consequences.

We must beware of reading independent lyric poems as if they made up a novel. Miss Bogan's poems, for instance, are independent lyrics, and they nearly always depict a single moment of passion or thought. But poems which deal with a moment may or may not deal with it as involved in a context of other events. In the case of Herrick's "Whenas in silks my Julia goes," for example, we never dream of asking in what particular circumstances the lover spoke, or of asking what happened before or after; the moment is separated from all circumstance and from any other event. Miss Bogan's poems sometimes deal, similarly, with the isolated moment; more characteristically, however, they imply a context of events; and it is that context which I am attempting to suggest here. Moreover, I should say that she scores special triumphs by selecting, not the moment when affairs themselves are at a crisis, but the moment which makes its context most significant and intelligible. I have a distinction in mind which a single example may make clear. Think of "Porphyria's Lover." Browning had the choice of depicting a moment of crisis, say the strangulation of Porphyria, or the moment when the whole course of events could best be manifested and contemplated; quite different effects must follow, of course, as one or the other is shown, though in any case the tale must be one of violent emotions. Hardly anyone would doubt, I think, that Browning gets a particular effect by showing the lover, serene and mad, holding his strangled mistress in his arms as if she were still alive, and musing calmly on what has happened. Passions do not rage to the point of murder in Miss Bogan's poems, but she does similarly select the comprehensive rather than the climactic.

I have been speaking of *what* she depicts; the manner in which she depicts it serves to heighten and reinforce the characteristics of her subject. She tends to be reticent as to what is happening or what has happened, while at the same time she sets forth the attendant circumstances in vivid detail. That reticence she manages in various ways; her character speaks with all the assumptions consequent upon shared experience, as in "Old Countryside," or makes guarded references to what has happened, as in "For a Marriage," or interprets something as only a person who has suffered devastating passion would interpret it, as in "Feuer-Nacht," or uses a narrative technique which simply does not tell all it might, as in "The Changed Woman."

The consequence is that the personages of these poems appear to us as they might by a lightning-flash, or as they might be glimpsed from a swift train; they are caught in attitudes obviously significant, which we cannot interpret; they make gestures passionate but mysterious. In "Porphyria's Lover," Browning tells us what happened; Bogan hints. But the setting, the whole circumstantial periphery of action, is shown with great vividness; the sharp images compel our imagination and our belief; the reticent and yet pregnant method of representation forces us to wonder and conjecture; and a part of the inexhaustible fascination of these poems surely resides in the fact that no conjecture fully satisfies us. Her poems are like pictures of scenes from some passionate and bitter play which we have not seen: the decor is brilliantly clear; the characters are fixed in poses which betray much, if only we could interpret.

"Old Countryside" is a perfect example of this method:

> Beyond the hour we counted rain that fell
> On the slant shutter, all has come to proof.
> The summer thunder, like a wooden bell,
> Rang in the storm above the mansard roof.
>
> And mirrors cast the cloudy day along
> The attic floor; wind made the clapboards creak.
> You braced against the wall to make it strong,
> A shell against your cheek.
>
> Long since, we pulled brown oak-leaves to the ground
> In a winter of dry trees; we heard the cock
> Shout its unplaceable cry, the axe's sound
> Delay a moment after the axe's stroke.
>
> Far back, we saw, in the stillest of the year,
> The scrawled vine shudder, and the rose-branch show
> Red to the thorns, and, sharp as sight can bear,
> The thin hound's body arched against the snow.

Here the physical circumstances are as clear as possible; but what is the further history which is hinted at in "all has come to proof"? Perhaps only the growth of love; perhaps more.

"A Packet of Letters" is less concerned with circumstance, but is charged with bitter mystery:

> In the shut drawer, even now, they rave and grieve—
> To be approached at times with the frightened tear;
> Their cold to be drawn away from, as one, at nightfall,
> Draws the cloak closer against the cold of the marsh.
>
> There, there, the thugs of the heart did murder.
> There, still in murderers' guise, two stand embraced, embalmed.

Again, in one of her best and longest poems, the extraordinary "Summer Wish":

> . . . the betraying bed
> Is gashed clear, cold on the mind, together with
> Every embrace that agony dreads but sees
> Open as the love of dogs.

Indeed, she can imply a whole history of terror and pain in a line or so:

> Never, for them, the dark turreted house reflects itself
> In the depthless stream.

Her images range over all kinds of feelings. Here are a few samples of her visual imagery. First, from "Statue and Birds":

> The birds walk by slowly, circling the marble girl,
> The golden quails,
> The pheasants, closed up in their arrowy wings,
> Dragging their sharp tails.

From "Winter Swan":

> Here, to the ripple cut by the cold, drifts this
> Bird, the long throat bent back, and the eyes in hiding.

From "Summer Wish":

> The cloud shadow flies up the bank, but does not
> Blow off like smoke. It stops at the bank's edge.
> In the field by trees two shadows come together.
> The trees and the cloud throw down their shadow upon
> The man who walks there. Dark flows up from his feet
> To his shoulders and throat, then has his face in its mask,
> Then lifts.

And from "The Flume," a remarkable narrative poem which she does not include in her *Collected Poems:* [2]

> At night his calm, closed body lay beside her...
> Her hair sweeps over his shoulder, claiming him hers...

She is as brilliant in depicting other sensations:

> ... she gave her kisses
> Beside rough field-stones piled into a wall
> Cold as the wind in every particle.

2. Both Miss Bogan and Miss Adams have omitted excellent and characteristic poems from their volumes, to my very great regret.

Miss Adams's collection contains many drastic revisions, particularly of the poems in her second published volume, *High Falcon.* In every instance they seem to me very much for the worse, even where a point of grammar was involved (e.g., in "Winter Solstice" she had originally written "gamester's shop," on the mistaken notion that a gamester dispensed game; I should rather have that than "steamy shop," where the idea of steam contradicts the feeling of intense cold given by the rest of the passage). I have, however, followed her latest text in every quotation; perhaps my reactions to her revisions are merely the consequence of having carried around *High Falcon* until I wore it out.

Here is a tremendous auditory image, from "A Letter," which I believe she has not reprinted since her first book:

> the scene where that girl
> Lets fall her hair, and the loud chords descend
> As though her hair were metal, clashing along
> Over the tower, and a dumb chord receives it?

These images are striking even in isolation, because of the perceptions which they record. In one way, as I have just said, they are quite various; in another, they are all of a single kind. Images can be classified according as they give us the unmodified perception or the perception as modified by the state and circumstance of the perceiver. [3] Miss Bogan limits herself, I think almost entirely, to the first kind; she

3. Perhaps these points should be developed, in case anyone is interested in them. The terms *image, symbol, description,* and *metaphor* are often used interchangeably. I think this usage blurs important distinctions; at any rate, for the purposes of this essay I should like to distinguish them as follows:

An *image* is any verbal expression immediately activating the imagination, whether a phantasm of some sensory impression is formed (as when a sight, sound, taste, and so on are imagined) or some other "feeling" (such as of pressure, motion, weight, heat, cold, vertigo, lassitude, energy, or the bodily conditions attending particular emotions). A *description* is an account which addresses the intellect rather than the imagination, dealing with ideas rather than with imaginative syntheses; if the imagination is thus activated, it is through the mediation of an idea. When I say the ice was one hundred twenty feet high, I describe it; the reader who wishes to imagine it does so of his own accord, and he must do so by first visualizing an object which he knows to be of similar height, say a water-tower. When I say the ice was mast-high, the reader immediately forms a picture of a berg in relation to a ship.

A *metaphor* is a transposition of names or terms, on the ground of similarity. Mr. Charles Feidelson, Jr., argues to the contrary (*Symbolism and American Literature* [Chicago: University of Chicago Press, 1953], pp. 58 ff.). I can only say here that I can accept none of his arguments. Metaphor may be present without image, image without metaphor: Marvell's "My love is of a birth as rare," etc., in "The Definition of Love," involves metaphor without image, even though the metaphor of birth is insisted upon; conversely, there is no metaphor in "Ice mast-high came floating by / As green as emerald"; but there is certainly an image.

A *symbol*, as I have argued elsewhere (*Critics and Criticism, Ancient and Modern,* ed. R. S. Crane [The University of Chicago Press: 1952], pp. 567–94) results from an identification of one concept with another; when an image is linked to a symbolic concept, the image is itself symbolic; but it is neither the case that all images are symbols, nor that all symbols are images.

Taking the term *image* as thus distinguished, we may, for literary purposes, differentiate three kinds: (1) images which present an unmodified perception, so that we feel we have received an "objective" account; (2) those which seem modified by the character or condition of the perceiver, and in this group we may distinguish between images in which (a) we primarily conceive the object to be possessed of certain qualities, or (b) we primarily interpret the perception as significant of the condition of the perceiver. Thus Miss Bogan's images give the effect of accurate perceptions; Miss Adams's, as I shall try to show later, give the effect of imaginative interpretations of perceptions and feelings; while the speaker in Tennyson's "Maud," saying of the gives the object simply, "as it is"—that is, as any good perceiver, unaffected by emotion or a particular point of view, would see it; and as a consequence she builds up a very real and solid world to serve as the theater of her brief and poignant dramas. Any reader of Defoe knows how circumstantiality produces belief; conviction is even greater when the circumstance is rendered in a vivid image.

Imagery of this order has to be an "accurate" depiction of the object; Miss Bogan is accurate to the point where her images seem to deal with permanent and inalienable aspects of the objects, and to do so definitively; one has the feeling that, whatever else might be said about the objects, these things *must* be said, and that it would be difficult if not impossible to say anything further about them, in this objective fashion. For example, she speaks of

> the pillared harp, sealed to its rest by hands—
> (On the bright strings the hands are almost reflected,
> The strings a mirror and light.)

After that, I submit, it is a little hard to say anything more about harps.

She does not merely choose the salient and "essential" characteristics, however; she chooses those which in addition imply other characteristics, and thus she effects wonders with a few strokes. Look at that winter swan again; it is not merely a swan, but a whole season seen in terms of a swan. Or see how, in two lines of "Hypocrite Swift," she conveys the silence, the immobility, the spaciousness, the chill and formal elegance, even the eerie loneliness of a scene:

"dreadful hollow" that "Its lips in the field above are dabbled with blood-red heath, / The red-ribbed ledges drip with a silent horror of blood," is actually telling us less about the hollow than about his own condition. I intend this not as a distinction of images as good or bad but as differing in kind and as having different effects. Nor do I mean to imply that images of the first class involve no poetic imagination; on the contrary, I assume that the poetic imagination is at work, though diversely, in all of them.

All these images permit various modes of construction, which cause the imagination of the reader to operate in different ways. It may be worthwhile to note a few of these: (1) images based on comparison, in which we are forced to imagine one thing as a standard for another, as in "ice mast-high"; (2) those based on mental transit from cause to effect, whenever the cause is in some way remarkably potent for good or evil, or simply remarkable, as in Bogan's "Like fire in a dry thicket / Rising within women's eyes"; (3) those based on transit from effect to cause, under the same conditions, as in Keats' "And the long carpets rose along the gusty floor"; (4) those based on startling contrast, as in Wallace Stevens's "rouged fruits in snow"; (5) those based on dynamic interrelation, as in "And the owls have awakened the crowing cock." There are many more which cannot be discussed here.

All of these have varying effectiveness in varying contexts; hence we can, in these terms, reach judgments as to a poet's art in handling them. To offer a single example here: nothing is more trite than the comparison of passion to a flame, and the imagination will not respond to it; Bogan's "Like fire in a dry thicket" is another matter entirely.

On walls at court, long gilded mirrors gaze.
The parquet shines; outside, the snow falls deep.

Since she deals with experiences which we all have, seen clearly and
without exaggeration and distortion, she usually avoids figurative
language, and remains perfectly literal; when she does use metaphor,
it is with telling force. In the lines just quoted, "gaze" is the only
metaphor; but it gives us immediately an impression of fixity, of still
brightness untroubled by reflected motion, over a long period of time.
"The parquet shines"; and "shines" echoes that notion; we get the
impression that the mirrors reflect the parquet, the parquet reflects the
mirrors; there is nothing else, except that, dumbly, "outside, the snow
falls deep." No presence, no sound, no motion—not so much as a can-
dle's flickering—in the chambers, though our view has ranged from ceil-
ings to floors with the word "long" and along the floors with the word
"shines." When we see a place once noisy and crowded, now vacant
and silent, an eeriness comes over us; the more spacious it is, the more
crowded with tokens of its former busyness, the sharper the feeling;
that is why, I think, we feel it so keenly here. In short, late winter
night in the eighteenth century, in a palace, complete in all essentials;
expressed in sixteen words.

Her style is generally plain, terse, bare to the point of austerity,
seldom involving uncommon words or constructions; we are not likely
to notice this because of the absorbing thing she does with it. When we
do notice it, we are likely to conclude hastily that hers is simply the
style of common speech. This is not quite the case; indeed, she achieves
some startling feats by using a common word, literally and apparently
in its usual sense, and yet with extraordinary force. A single example
must serve here. "Mix" is surely a common enough word; few would
suppose, offhand, that it could be used to much poetic effect, let alone
for a whole variety of effects. But look what she can do with it:

A mirror hangs on the wall of the draughty cupola,
Within the depths of the glass mix the oak and the beech leaf....

The crafty knight in the game, with its mixed move...

Dream the mixed, fearsome dream.

In brief: Bogan is a poet of the violent emotions; she depicts with
severe economy, with reticence and by implication; her images are "objective," and her language is plain and natural. In each of these respects,
Léonie Adams is her opposite. Miss Adams is a poet of the calm and
gentle emotions; life and love and death are here, to be sure, but not as
arousing any fierce passion; grief is changed to melancholy; even joy,
perhaps, to quiet delight. Bogan deals largely with thoughts and

emotions aroused by external events; Adams's poetry is private, in the
sense that she is moved not so much by what happens as by what her
subtle and exquisite mind makes of it. She depicts, not with economy
and implication, but by aggregation and suggestion. Since the starting
point of her emotions and reflections is generally a particular imaginative perception, her imagery is seldom objective; and since her poems
record the experiences of a mind of extraordinary quality, literal
language and the forms of common speech are inadequate for her; she
is forced to use many metaphors and other figures, and her diction is
elaborate, rich, and artificial.

A mind and a style really unique are impossible to describe; and Miss
Adams's art is so delicate that to say it produces an effect of
enchantment, that it places one in landscapes of vision or dream, is at
once to vulgarize it. It does produce enchantment, and does deal in
visions and dreams, however. Her imagination translates her sensations into something rare and strange. Common objects appear as they
would under special conditions of light and atmosphere, strangely
brightened and enhanced, and somehow made portents and tokens of
something still more strange. I have said that Louise Bogan's imagery is
solid and substantial because it ranges over all forms of feeling, and
gives us objects as they naturally and familiarly appear. Adams'
imagery is chiefly visual and auditory; objects seem weightless as they
do in dreams, shapes are etherealized, colors are made purer and more
luminous, sounds clearer and more delicate. All things appear, whatever sense they appeal to, as they might to one in a drowsy fever, or
between sleeping or waking, or fast in a spell.

Chiefly she seems to "outstare substantial stuff," as she herself says:

> The day comes wildly up the east,
> Because the cup of vision broke,
> And those clear silver floods released
> Go ravaging the calm sky of night;
> And all who to that seeing woke
> Look coldly on a common sight,
> As to outstare substantial stuff.
> The substance never is enough
> When lids are drenched apart by light. . . .

Her marvelous imagination, or, if you will, her vision, thus gives her
extraordinary things: waters, for instance, so clear

> They will stain drowning a star,
> With the moon they will brim over.

or sky

> . . . in which the boughs were dipped
> More thick with stars than fields with dew

or leaves

> . . . deepening the green ground
> With their green shadows, there as still
> And perfect as leaves stand in air . . .

When she does offer us what I have called "objective" imagery, however, she does so with great effect. Here, for instance, is the very essence of a winter nightfall, more economical and precise even than Eliot's first "Prelude:"

> December, mortal season, crusts
> The dark snows shuffled in the street,
> And rims the lamp with sleet.
> The beggar, houseless, chill, and thin,
> Leans to the chestnut vendor's coals,
> The cart creaks off which trails the winter bush,
> And the thick night shuts in.

This is surely very close to the vein of Shakespeare's "When icicles hang by the wall" or Blake's "When silver snow decks Susan's clothes / And cold jewel hangs at th' shepherd's nose."

Like Bogan, she exhibits a single character; herself, quite probably; and we see her chiefly as engaged in the exquisite contemplation of the phantasma of her thought. "Twilight Revelation" is typical of her art:

> This hour was set the time for heaven's descent,
> Come drooping toward us on the heavy air,
> The sky, that's heaven's seat, above us bent,
> Blue faint as violet ash, you near me there
> In nether space, so drenched in goblin blue
> I could touch Hesperus as soon as you.
>
> Now I perceive you, lapped in singling light,
> Washed by that blue which sucks whole planets in,
> And hung like those top jewels of the night,
> A mournful gold too high for love to win.
> And you, poor brief, poor melting star, you seem
> Half to sink, half to brighten in that stream.
>
> And these rich-bodied hours of our delight
> Show like a mothwing's substance when the fall
> Of confine-loosing, blue, unending night
> Extracts the spirit of this temporal.
> So space can pierce the crevice wide between
> Fast hearts, skies deep-descended intervene.

Here a perception transmuted by imagination generates all; she sees twilight, not as we do, as simple twilight, but as the descent of the heavens, as the actual incursion of outer space into the earth's atmosphere. And thus her lover, near her as he is, seems remote "in nether space"; "so drenched in goblin blue," so "washed by that blue which sucks whole planets in," that he is remote as a star. She feels him, thus, "too high for love to win"; he is, moreover, seen as but a brief and transitory thing among the perduring stars, even as he is momentarily transfigured by the light which he shares with them; and all the time of love, rich as it is, seems suddenly insubstantial as a moth's wing. Thus, she muses, between even the most closely-bound hearts, the skies intervene; and twilight has become a portent both of the brevity of love (for merely by setting it against the eternal, we see that it is not) and of the essential isolation of the human soul; this whatever lovers feel or say.

Notice that all the imagery is of the same order as, and is a consequence of, the first image; and the moment we imagine the first, we enter into her own thought, strikingly original as it is, and feel as she does, in perfect sympathy with her. Identification and sympathy or empathy are not so general in art as theorists have tended to claim; they result only when the artist has brought us perfectly into the frame of mind of his character and set forth the cause or object of emotion precisely as the character apprehends it. In Miss Bogan's poetry, for instance, the effect depends upon our considering the poetic character as distinct from ourselves; Miss Adams, conversely demands identification. This is one reason why she uses more imagery than Bogan; she must at all times make us see things as she sees them, to carry us with her.

It is a reason, too, why she depends upon suggestion, rather than implication. Implication can operate only when we are familiar with consequences; where interpretations and consequences are very unusual, we cannot infer to any great effect. I doubt, for example, whether many of us—if any of us—would have been able of ourselves to see twilight as "heaven's descent" in the sense in which Miss Adams does, and whether any of us would have been able to intuit from it, as she does so easily and naturally, the transience and loneliness of love, together with the poignant beauty of that transience and loneliness. Suggestion is another matter; our minds can be led along a given course, familiar or unfamiliar, by the evocation of certain ideas in certain conjunctions. When Bogan makes us feel the still brightness of the court, it is by implication, and we can reduce it to syllogism: *if* the mirrors "gaze" and the parquet shines with unbroken tranquility, *then* the chambers are deserted, and so on. But compare that with the following lines from Adams's "The Rounds and the Garlands Done":

> Day that cast the lovely looks is sped,
> And from the turf, circled with white dew,
> The lovers and the children are gone;

Leaving the wreath, the bouquet fresh, looped up with grasses.
All the golden looks are spent,
And the time of the rounds and the garlands done.

Here we feel that we are looking upon the earth of the Golden Age, or at least that of some eternal pastoral; the sunlight was surely not ours, but that which shines in the poems of Sappho, in "Daphnis and Chloe," or in Sidney's "Arcadia." But the poet has neither said nor implied that it was; she has merely suggested it by a few cunning phrases; and her magic is so subtle and immediate that we must make a special effort to realize that perhaps, after all, she was talking about a scene in a park.

Indeed, her words bring to mind almost constantly the customs, beliefs, arts, and sciences of an older day; they cast, thus, a light which half brightens, half obscures in shadow the immediate reality. These excerpts call to mind old customs, for example:

> Then, tatter you and rend,
> Oak heart, to your profession mourning . . .

> "Of my father's father I got a proud steed,
> And a barb of my father I took". . . .

> The loss was twenty jewels worth . . .

These, surely recall an old cosmogony:

> Cast on the turning wastes of wind
> Are cords that none can touch or see. . . .

> . . . older than the golden sun
> And his measure trod with night.

The following, again, recall Renaissance sculpture and pre-Renaissance painting:

> There marble boys are leant from the light throat,
> Thick locks that hang with dew and eyes dewlashed,
> Dazzled with morning, angels of the wind,
> With ear a-point for the enchanted note.

> . . . so at the innocent lady's feet
> The blond, the young, delicate ones of heaven,
> Stare at the pretty painted skies.

If her thought is in an older age, her language shows the same deliberate archaism. It has been called Elizabethan; as a matter of fact, it is not; yet there is this much truth in calling it so, that she reminds one more of the Elizabethans and of certain metaphysical poets— Traherne and Marvell especially,—than of anyone else, even such

astute imitators of the Elizabethan and Jacobean as Darley and
Beddoes. It would be absurd to condemn her on this account, and I do
not suppose that any sensible person ever would; perhaps nine-tenths of
the greatest glories of English poetry are written in some sort of
artificial language. The real question is whether her diction is effective
or not; and her successes are so overwhelming that there is no doubt
that it is.

All this archaism has the same function: to remove any sense of
immediacy which might produce violent emotion, and to address the
gentler instead; that is, to soften and transform emotion much as time
itself does. The wilder emotions are produced by immediacy, the
gentler by remoteness; the *Iliad* sets us in the very midst of its events,
ancient and half-mythical as they were, and excites emotions of one
kind; the "Eve of St. Agnes" places its events far back, and evokes
emotions of the other.

But there is this point, too, as far as the archaism of her ideas is
concerned: that ideas function very differently in poetry from the
manner in which they do in science or philosophy. In the latter they
have value as they are adequate or true, and as they have logical
consequences of some value; in poetry they have value as they affect
imagination and emotion. For ideas have an imaginative and emotional dimension as well as an intellectual one; Dante's notion of Hell is
a sublime and terrifying one, whether it be true or false, and poets of
our own day (Millay, for one) have continued to use the idea of the
planetary atom, discarded though it is by science, because of the sheer
magnificence of the notion that our universe could thus consist of an
infinity of worlds within worlds, a thought, as Emerson says, "to
dwindle our astronomy into a toy." Donne and Milton similarly used
worn-out conceptions of science purely for their emotional effect. The
question of when philosophic or scientific thought becomes poetic
material—a question often raised since the early nineteenth century—
seems to me to have a very obvious and certain answer; it does so
whenever the emotional qualities of thought can be actualized.

In an age of startling poetic innovations, neither Miss Bogan nor
Miss Adams has been thought of as an innovator. I think they have not
quite had their rights in this matter. In the matter of versification
alone, each has made important advances. Bogan broke up the "tight"
and regular stanza forms with some very original variations, while
retaining the general effect of strictness and regularity, and she also
contrived, in "Summer Wish," for example, a distinctly modern
development of blank verse, highly plastic and serviceable. Adams's
innovations in versification are too numerous and too subtle to discuss
here; I shall bluntly say, at whatever risk of exciting indignation, that
no poet of our day, not even Yeats, can be said to have a finer and
more delicate ear.

The question of how much of the work of these poets will last is a natural and unavoidable one; it is also a futile one. The only guarantee an artist can have against fortune lies in the integrity, soundness, and discipline manifest in his art. That Miss Bogan and Miss Adams possess this guarantee is, I should say, beyond question.

THE POETRY OF
MARIANNE MOORE

On reading Miss Moore's latest volume (*Like a Bulwark* [New York: Viking Press, 1956]) I was struck once more by certain characteristics which distinguish her work from the greater part—perhaps one should say, the mainstream—of contemporary poetry. Her poetry has been considered, universally and quite justly, as unique in our time; and while she is as "modern" as anyone writing today, she cannot be linked plausibly with any modern movement. I suspect that the reason for this is that, despite T. E. Hulme's famous prediction, in 1913, of a classical age in poetry, and despite the willingness of many to take that prophecy as fact, we are still in a romantic period; and that Miss Moore is one of the very few major poets of our era who can reasonably be called classical. Romanticism and classicism are tricky terms, of course; I mean simply that her work belongs in a tradition which began with the *Satires* and *Epistles* of Horace. This is a matter of resemblance, and it is very important. Despite T. S. Eliot's *Homage to John Dryden,* and the less formal honors he has paid to Pope, Johnson, and others, I cannot believe him "classical"; he resembles Keats, Shelley, Tennyson—even Swinburne—far more than he does Dryden or Pope.

It is not easy to describe briefly the tradition which I have in mind. Perhaps it can best be done in terms of a single distinction. The greater part of poetry, whether narrative, dramatic, or lyric, depends upon what might be called the principle of the extraordinary. The poet invents some action which involves an extraordinary crisis, serious or comic, in human affairs, or invents extraordinary characters, or deals with the human soul in extraordinary states of passion, imagination, intellection, or perception. The extraordinary is selected to begin with, or techniques of amplification or depreciation are used to make

Reprinted from *Chicago Review*, vol. 11, no. 1 (Spring 1957).

something extraordinary. Tragedy and comedy, epic and mock-epic, almost all forms of lyric, depend upon this principle.

But there is an order of poetry which does not. It deals neither with extraordinary events nor with unusual psychic conditions, but with ordinary matters and normal mental conditions. It may involve images, but it presents sensation undistorted by emotion and imagination; its images are objective and accurate—true in terms of what we commonly experience, or if not, truer than that. It may involve imagination, but it excludes all imagination that leads to the fanciful and implausible, all imagination undisciplined by reason. It is always intellectual in character, always exhibits reason as in full control, and the intellectual element in it is never magnified to profundity; whatever profundities may be involved, they are never presented as such, but rather as general opinion, or at most, as a kind of sublimated common sense. It shuns all obvious artifice, and remains so close to ordinary discourse that its artifices can hardly be detected. It is a poetry of personal discussion, and a great part of its value consists in the value of the person who is discussing.

The eleven poems of *Like a Bulwark* belong, like Miss Moore's earlier work, to this tradition. What is most remarkable about them—more remarkable even than the infallible and enormous skill which they exhibit—is Miss Moore herself. Her poems are all of a certain kind, but within that kind they are of bewildering variety. The variety comes from the abundance of objects contemplated and the abundance of things found in them. The similarity comes from the fact that the poet never dramatizes, never impersonates, is always herself, and—intent on what she contemplates—keeps herself in the background. It is not that she is impersonal; she is aware that if poetry is to be something like conversation the conversation ought not to be primarily about oneself. The character that underlies her work is, nevertheless, clear, and it is one of many virtues. She is honest, just, prudent, shrewd, urbane, witty, fastidious, courageous, and a great deal beside; we know her to be so, not because she makes any attempt to convince us, but because the feelings and opinions to which she gives voice, and the manner in which she voices them, could only have origin in one of that nature.

These virtues are rare enough in themselves and rarer still in combination; but what is even more rare is a quality of mind which I find difficult to describe. Perhaps one might call it an imagination with more precision than sensation because it is governed by an intellect more precise than either. By this very odd expression I mean that she deals repeatedly with the hardest of all things to imagine: the fact perfectly known, or known, at any rate, far more perfectly than most of us know it.

A few images, selected at random, may make this clear. Here is a porcupine:

> as when the lightning shines
> on thistlefine spears, among
> prongs in lanes above lanes of a shorter prong . . .

Here is the racehorse, Tom Fool:

> You've the beat
> of a dancer to a measure or harmonious rush
> of a porpoise at the prow where the racers all win easily—
> like centaurs' legs in tune, as when kettledrums compete;
> nose rigid and suede nostrils spread . . .

Here is a dancer:

> Entranced, were you not,
>   by Solidad?
> black-clad solitude that is not sad;
>   like a letter from
> Casals; or perhaps say literal alphabet—
> S soundholes in a 'cello
> set contradictorily; or should we call her

> *la lagarta?* or bamboos with fireflies a-glitter;
> or glassy lake and the whorls which a vertical stroke
>   brought about
> of the paddle half-turned coming out.
>   As if bisecting
> a viper, she can dart down three times and recover
>   without a disaster, having
> been a bull-fighter . . .

Notice that comparisons are involved in each of these; in each comparison something is sharply and cleanly seen in itself, as by a rare eye; it is compared to something else, seen sharply and clearly by that eye; and the resemblance is striking, but only a rare mind would have seen it. A resemblance as difficult to see as in a metaphysical conceit— one of Donne's, say; but these are no conceits. The resemblance in a conceit is paradoxical and must always be argued; resemblance here, once pointed out, is self-evident. And these are no fictions, but facts; facts, however, fully and more perfectly revealed. It would seem, on first sight, that nothing could be deader than facts about ordinary things; to see the dead fact brought alive in this fashion is to witness something as astonishing and miraculous as the blossoming of Tann-haüser's staff. One has the constant sense, in reading her, of having the scales fall from one's eyes; the world that is revealed seems new, but one knows that it was always there.

Miss Moore's poems never reveal her in any emotional situation, but we infer a capacity for deep—though never violent—emotion. They never exhibit her at the point of some dramatic moral choice, though, as I said, her character is manifest. She is always relaxed, composed, serene; the evenness of her voice is inflected only lightly, and chiefly by her excitement at what she perceives. She is always in complete control of herself.

The structure of her poems is intellectual, but it is not that of deductive argument. Rather it is an association of insights which culminate almost invariably in a final insight. The principal devices of her technique are ones which force us to those insights; which force us, that is, to see what she sees.

"Tom Fool at Jamaica," for instance, begins thus:

> Look at Jonah embarking from Joppa, deterred by
> the whale; hard going for a statesman whom nothing
> could detain,
> although one who would not rather die than repent.
> Be infallible at your peril, for your system will fail,
> and select as a model the schoolboy in Spain
> who at the age of six, portrayed a mule and jockey
> who had pulled up for a snail.
>
> "There is submerged magnificence, as Victor Hugo
> said." *Sentir avec ardeur;* that's it; magnetized by feeling.
> Tom Fool "makes an effort and makes it oftener
> than the rest" . . .

The poem is somewhat like a little essay on what makes the champion; we have just been made to see, in the instance of Jonah and the schoolboy's jockey, that the incredible and unforeseen must happen, and that consequently none can become a champion by seeking infallibility. Championship lies in "submerged magnificence"—the ability for "the extra spurt when needed." What has made us see this? The fact that we have had to contemplate Jonah, the jockey, and "submerged magnificence." Jonah is perfectly familiar to us; but he is nevertheless unfamiliar as an instance of a system foiled by the unforeseen. The jockey pulling up for a snail might signify many things; but the drawing must be interpreted in a given way if the paragraph is to be understood. And "submerged magnificence" is a puzzling phrase; we understand it best, perhaps, when we ask what its opposite would be, and realize that it has just been dealt with.

Marianne Moore is a difficult poet, but not an obscure one; on the contrary, she is extremely clear, and our difficulty comes from her insistence that we think and think well at every point in her poems. To miss once is almost certainly to miss again in what follows, and perhaps also to fail to see the full significance of what has gone before. This is no fault of hers, but of ours; she is purely the artist, concerned with saying what she has to say as quickly and effectively as possible. She does not enlarge, she does not digress, and she does not make obvious transitions; as a highly civilized person, she assumes the intelligence of her audience. She is, moreover, not concerned with saying something characteristically, but with saying it rightly; in consequence she is frequently satisfied with quotation, when the quotation hits the mark. She includes nothing unnecessary; she never pads to fill out a pattern. She is willing to leave a sentence unfinished when the reader can finish it for himself, to use a phrase only, when it says what a sentence might, or a word only, when it says what a phrase might. One can gain some notion of her strict economy, of her positive mercilessness with what is beautiful in itself but not part of the whole, by comparing the first published versions of her poems with later ones. "The Steeple-Jack," for example, has thirteen stanzas in its first version (*Poetry*, vol. 40, no. 3 [June 1932]); seven in the version of *Collected Poems*. Look at the exquisite stanzas deleted, and learn something about art. It must have cost blood.

The innumerable subtleties of her art—indeed, of her prosody alone—would demand, as they say, a treatise. I have tried only to suggest what gives me particular joy in her work. In the words of another and quite different poet, it is "the fine delight that fathers thought."

THE POETRY OF
WALLACE STEVENS

Wallace Stevens has been thought of as primarily a poet of ideas, and his poems have been discussed chiefly as forms of philosophic statement. Viewed as a philosopher, he is no more satisfactory than T. S. Eliot: his ideas are few, his problems are among the most hackneyed ones of epistemology and metaphysics, his doctrines are equally familiar, and his arguments are unconvincing. We begin with what is surely one of the most original and, within the limits he has sought to impose on himself, rich and various poets of our day, and end up with a philosopher who, to say the least, does not possess these qualities. This startling transformation of a good poet into a bad philosopher suggests that criticism has gone off the rails somewhere, or perhaps was headed in the wrong direction at the start.

Stevens is a poet of ideas, if you will, but in poetry ideas function very differently from the way in which they do in science, philosophy, or ordinary discourse. Ideas have an emotional as well as an intellectual dimension. The faculties of the mind are distinguishable in thought but not in fact; they are involved in constant and subtle interplay, whether or not we respond with the whole fabric of the soul. When Milton sets Hell before us, he does not merely cause us to connect certain ideas; he plays powerfully upon our emotions, and he does so not merely through ideas but through images which he summons up in our imagination.

Perhaps the human mind cannot conceive ideas without framing images, or entertain images without conceiving ideas; but we tend to disregard one or the other, according to whether our concern is intellectual or emotional. In science the image exists for the sake of the idea, and is unimportant except as it conveys or fails to convey the idea; in poetry the opposite is true. For example, if you think of a *triangle*, you make a mental picture of it; if your concern is intellectual, it does not matter what sort of triangle you picture, red or blue,

Reprinted from *College English*, vol. 16, no. 7 (April 1955).

small or large, right, scalene, or equilateral, for you disregard the special character of the image and go on to the idea. But if your concern is with ideas in their emotional aspect, the image is more important than the idea, for what we actually imagine affects us more powerfully than something we merely conceive. Indeed, emotions are produced in us far more frequently by sensation and imagination than by ideas in themselves; the latter affect us only when we have some settled emotional or moral attitude toward them.

An idea need only be clear and adequate; an image must be emotionally potent; it must evoke at least pleasure or pain, and through the special character of its pleasurableness or painfulness it evokes particular emotions. Ideas can be connected affirmatively or negatively, but images cannot; whatever the imagination contemplates, it contemplates as conjoined. Thus when Stevens tells us that pears are not nudes or bottles or viols, the intellect understands that they are not, but the imagination sees them as if they were, and has its own moment of dominion. Finally, whereas the rational operations of the intellect can be stated as argument, the processes of the imagination cannot; they can be stated, if at all, only in terms of interaction between images and emotions. For example, I am in a gloomy frame of mind, and my imagination supplies one dismal image after another; or I entertain a series of cheerful images and become cheerful.

I discuss these matters at some length because they are, I think, crucial to an understanding of most poetry, and of Stevens's poetry in particular. A poet of ideas he may be; but I can think of no one else who seems to suffer so badly from logical paraphrase. For he operates chiefly through images, and it is these images we must study if we are to grasp his poems. Perhaps I can make all this clear by considering an early and simple, yet in many respects typical, poem, "Life Is Motion":

> In Oklahoma
> Bonnie and Josie
> Dressed in calico
> Danced around a stump,
> They cried,
> "Ohoyaho,
> Ohoo,"
> Celebrating the marriage
> Of flesh and air.

In its logical aspect, this poem can be viewed as proof by example of the thesis stated in its title. Poetically, however, truth of thesis or adequacy of proof is here unimportant. What is important is that a certain image is presented in a certain way, and that our emotions are affected accordingly. If we examine the image which arises in our minds, and then examine the poem, one of the first things that strikes us is that the image is much more complex and full than the poem, and that a good deal of it has no logical justification in the poem. We imagine two little girls, in an ecstasy of joy; they wear quaint, stiff, "dutchy" dresses homemade out of calico flour sacking; they cry out shrilly as they dance with clumsy abandon around a stump, against a background of farm land. We cannot logically prove all of this from the poem. Oklahoma contains cities and oil-fields as well as farms; Bonnie and Josie may as well be the names of old women as of little girls; dances may be graceful as well as clumsy, and so on. Yet I daresay no one would imagine here two decrepit old women or two languid sirens moving against a background of buildings or oil fields.

We ought not to read anything and everything into poetry; but also we ought not to concentrate on the bare words of a poem and leave out what the human intellect, imagination, and emotion are likely to make of them. Look at this poem line by line, and see what the imagination does at each point. The first two lines contain no images, but they do contain elements that may modify images. The third line gives us an image of two little girls in calico; the two little girls are suggested by feminine diminutive names, simply because that is our most immediate association with such names and because nothing conflicts with it, and "Oklahoma" now joins with "calico" to suggest homemade dresses of print flour-sacking. So far the imagination sees them side by side, motionless and without particular expression; the fourth line sets them in motion, arranges them at opposite sides of the stump, fills them with joy, and summons up a farm background. The fifth tells us merely that they cried, and although Mr. Empson would doubtless tell us that "cried" may also mean "wept," the imagination is in full course, and such a meaning never enters our heads. Indeed, their shrill, meaningless, and vigorous cries are necessary in the next two lines because silence here would disturb the image of childish joy which is being built up in our minds. The last two lines suddenly, surprisingly, give us the cause of the dance, and we understand why the cries had to be meaningless, even barbaric: the joy they express is ageless and primitive, the joy of life itself, of life which is motion.

Simple as it is, this poem is rigorously contrived. Its lines cannot be rearranged, for instance, even where their grammar would allow; they are ordered to steer the imagination upon a certain course, to make it do certain things and to keep it from doing certain others. Words of less determinate association appear first: "Oklahoma" and "calico" give us country, but at "stump" farm country springs up; "dance" gives us motion, but the rhythm of the line gives us the character of the dance. Substitute "round" for "around" and the line smoothes out to suggest a more measured and graceful motion; "around" gives it a hopping character.

The poem consists of an image and an insight. The image had to be only definite enough to convey a certain impression, and the poet had two problems with it: to give materials which the mind could supplement so as to form, on its own, that impression, and to suppress any element—of the pathetic or the ridiculous, for instance—which could disturb that impression. That is, the girls had to be presented as joyful with no special reason for joy, without being in the least made pathetic or absurd. We frame an image which we view with amused indulgence, just such as we should feel if we saw the girls in reality; at that very moment we are given insight into the cause of the girls' behavior —an insight which immediately changes our attitude toward them. They are no longer simply two quaint little girls having a good time; they are embodiments of an eternal and mysterious energy and joy. The insight is the poet's, to be sure, but his art makes it ours also, because we are forced to interpret the metaphor of "the marriage of flesh and air" in order to arrive at it.

Consider another typical poem, "The Emperor of Ice-Cream":

> Call the roller of big cigars,
> The muscular one, and bid him whip
> In kitchen cups concupiscent curds.
> Let the wenches dawdle in such dress
> As they are used to wear, and let the boys
> Bring flowers in last month's newspapers.
> Let be be finale of seem.
> The only emperor is the emperor of ice-cream.
>
> Take from the dresser of deal,
> Lacking the three glass knobs, that sheet
> On which she embroidered fantails once
> And spread it so as to cover her face.
> If her horny feet protrude, they come
> To say how cold she is, and dumb.
> Let the lamp affix its beam.
> The only emperor is the emperor of ice-cream.

This differs from the foregoing in that whereas in the former we had, in the perception of the two girls, the cause of the poet's state of mind, we have here the effects of it: he says what he says because he feels revulsion at the conventional notion of the dignity of death, the old idea that Death is the king of kings, the only true emperor. On the contrary, life is king; it stops for no one; and let no one pretend that it stops for the dignity of death. The notion that death dignifies poor as well as rich is absurd; here is the poor old woman, dead; what is her dignity? These reflections, and the feelings which they evoke, impel him to utter a series of orders as cynical and brutal as the real attitude of the living toward the dead. First of all, the wake is the thing, and the dead person merely gives occasion for it; the funeral is unimportant. Indeed, the first stanza is so far from containing any hint of death that it might deal with preparations for a rather dubious party. We become aware of a death only with the word "face," well on in the second stanza. "Concupiscent curds" are to be prepared rather than the funeral baked meats and custards; the "wenches" are to don, not mourning, but their usual dress, and they do not desist from work through grief, but "dawdle"; the boys are to bring, not bouquet and wreath and flowers sedately boxed, but flowers in old newspapers. A crude and vulgar life goes on despite the corpse in the bedroom. In the second stanza the poverty of the dead woman is intimated by the cheap dresser with missing knobs, her age by her "horny feet." She is to be covered, not with a white sheet, but one on which she had once embroidered fantails (probably fan-tailed and gaudy-colored birds), even though it may be too short; she is covered, not out of decency, but for a gayer reason. Suppose her feet protrude, they can only indicate how little she has to do with the warm and noisy life going on in the kitchen.

I have said that these poems are typical of Stevens's art. We may now consider generally what that art is. In the first place, "Life is Motion" and "The Emperor of Ice-Cream" are not "about" two little girls and a dead old woman. Girls and woman are present in these poems, not as characters proper, but as objects of someone's thought, although they occupy the center of the stage, and his thoughts and feelings are intimated only through what is said about them. That "someone"—possibly Stevens himself—is the constant character, however fantastically disguised at times, of Stevens's poetry: even in "Sunday Morning," the poem is not about what a woman thinks, but about what someone thinks and feels about what she thinks. Let us suppose, for simplicity's sake, that that character *is* Stevens.

I think there are no poems involving an exciting external situation, or the drama of a tremendous moral choice, or violent and immediate passion. On the contrary: he seems perpetually aloof, always at one remove at least, not only from the feelings of others but from certain ones of his own. People seem to exist for him only as matter for contemplation, along with natural objects and objects of art; indeed, he is likely to respond to these latter more directly. He sees, not individuals, but the collective soldier, the collective hero, the collective man (see for example "The Death of a Soldier," "Examination of the Hero in Time of War," "Chocorua to Its Neighbor"). He assumes various persons, it is true, but only as a manner of speech, and never as true dramatic impersonation. He remains the detached spectator, chiefly, even of his own emotions; it is as spectator, not as participant, that he is moved when he is moved. His pleasures and pains are those of the exquisite connoisseur, rather than the fundamental ecstasy and anguish of the human soul in itself. Look at the way in which he handles the Crucifixion in "Lunar Paraphrase": he is concerned with it only as an artistic arrangement to serve as a metaphor for November moonlight.

His activities are mental only, but they hardly cover all that may happen even in the mental theater. They are not as rational as they appear, and the poetry is not strictly philosophical poetry; you would never be able to state the argument of it as you might that of any page of, say, Lucretius. Perhaps one might call these activities a dialectic of the imagination, playing perpetually on the diverse relations of things, ideas, images, and emotions. Sometimes he takes a thing or an idea and relates it to a series of intricately connected images producing different emotions; sometimes he holds a mood or an image constant and relates it to different objects and ideas; but it is these which are his concern, and indeed there is hardly a permutation or combination of these that he has missed. It is no accident, thus, that he often writes in forms which approach those of music: the theme with variations as in "13 Ways of Looking at a Blackbird," "Nuances on a Theme by Williams," "Sea Surface Full of Clouds," and "Variations on a Summer Day"; the suite, as in "Like Decorations in a Nigger Cemetery," "Examination of the Hero . . . ," and the "Extracts from Addresses to the Academy of Fine Ideas"; and even the fugue, as in "The Pure Good of Theory" and "Description without Place." In all this, his philosophic materials—his problems of whether the knower is ever identical with the known, whether the world is the same for all or different for each, whether language can express reality or extend sensation, and so on—are but a single element. Yet all these elements are only the colored bits of glass and angled mirrors of the kaleidoscope which is his imagination; it is the innumerable images which form and dislimn that hold our interest, and, I suspect, Stevens's. It is these that produce his thought and emotions, and it is in these that his thoughts and emotions find ultimate expression; witness "Life is Motion" and "The Emperor of Ice-Cream," respectively.

Divorced as Stevens's work is from the human drama as it is usually conceived, the images themselves are tremendously "dramatic," as we say a picture of the ocean, of clouds, of still life, or even an arrangement of colors is dramatic. Visual imagery predominates in his work, and he is amazingly successful with it; often he seems to see objects as a painter would, and then to realize them in words. He seems aware of this himself: his titles frequently suggest those of pictures "Bantams in Pine Woods," "Landscape with Boat," "Sea Surface Full of Clouds", and he can refer to Corot for an autumn evening, to Franz Hals for a cloudscape. One almost looks for the signature of Cezanne under "Study of Two Pears," of Renoir under "Poems of Our Climate." There is perhaps no quicker way to poetic shipwreck than by cataloguing colors; yet Stevens triumphs in this difficult business again and again. He knows how to heighten colors and set them against a contrasting background, as in "rouged fruits in early snow"; how to modify them sharply and effectively, as in "blunt yellow," "dense violet"; even how to suggest them without mentioning them (note how many colors spring to mind in "The Emperor of Ice-Cream," though none is mentioned). He knows the importance of light and shade ("The shadows of the pears / Are blobs on the green cloth") and the influence of atmosphere on objects (observe how bright the tigers are in "tigers in red weather"). And he can draw upon a palette whose colors range from the stark, gaudy flatness of circus posters to such luminous transparencies as "the dove with eye of grenadine" and "Triton dissolved in shifting diaphanes / Of blue and green. . . ."

These are only snatches. See what he can do in a few lines:

> Our bloom is gone. We are the fruit thereof.
> Two golden gourds distended on our vines,
> Into the autumn weather, splashed with frost,
> Distorted by hale fatness, turned grotesque.
> We hang like warty squashes, streaked and rayed. . . .
>
> Last night, we sat beside a pool of pink,
> Clippered with lilies scudding the bright chromes,
> Keen to the point of starlight. . . .

He achieves such startling triumphs, however, not because he is a painter, but because he is a writer. Someone—I have forgotten who—once praised a passage in a story by Aubrey Beardsley because it described a fountain so elaborately that a sculptor might easily have executed after it. He was badly mistaken. Painting and "painting in words" are very different things. The colors of the imagination are brief, imagined lines and planes can bear only the simplest relations to each other, and the poetic image can never have the precision of the painted one. Twenty artists executing even the most precise image in poetry would end up with twenty very different pictures. Imagination must deal with elements so simple and so few that they can be supplemented and synthesized instantly. Stevens is well aware of this; he has analyzed forms and simplified them into their essential lines and planes, to the point where they can be done in a few bold strokes. He can, thus, set before us the diagrammatic starkness of a steeple and a chimney stack in a "morbid light" with a single comparison: the scene is like "an electric lamp / On a page of Euclid." Where objects are more elaborate, he knows how to force the reader to construct them step by step, as in " Study of Two Pears" and "So-and-So Reclining on Her Couch."

Marvelous as his visual images are merely as pictures, one misses their real force unless their other aspects are taken into account. Images, I have remarked, are related to ideas, they produce ideas and are produced by ideas; they produce emotions and are produced by emotions. Now, we tend to make, from habit or convention, certain definite connections between a given idea and a given order of imagery, and between a given emotion and a given object of emotion. For example, the ancient Greeks and the medieval Christians had strikingly different imaginative conceptions of, and emotional attitudes toward, the idea of death, as their funeral statuary shows. I cannot discuss these connections here except to say that they have profound roots in the whole character of a society; they involve beliefs and attitudes which concern what is true or false, good or bad, beautiful or ugly.

An artist can use this preestablished switchboard, so to speak, just as it is, or he can change the connections. Dickens used the switchboard as it was to depict the criminals in *Oliver Twist;* Dostoevski altered it in *Crime and Punishment.* There are similar readjustments possible in emotional reaction. For example, we tend to compare something which we think beautiful with something else which we also think beautiful; La Forgue obtains a startling effect by violating such conventional categories in his comparison of the autumn sun to saloon spittle or a ripped-out gland, and so does T. S. Eliot in his famous comparison of evening to an etherized patient. When the moral and emotional categories are violated in this fashion, the startled reader is likely to find the poetry which does so shocking, ridiculous, what you will; at the very least, unintelligible.

A part of Stevens's force lies in that he has never respected such categories too greatly. For one, he has always distrusted the kind of emotion which was the stock in trade of those who thought that poetry "should be simple as a cry from the heart"; consequently he finds grounds for mockery in such emotions, even when he feels them deeply. His bitterness in "The Emperor of Ice-Cream," his determination to violate the convention of respect for death, is based upon knowledge that the convention is hypocritical, and upon his own very real respect. Again, in "Le Monocle de Mon Oncle," deeply in love, he mocks himself and his beloved as being too old for such emotion. The image of them as grotesque squashes, in the passage cited earlier, is so much a caricature as to be unintelligible, perhaps, unless we recognize the attitude from which it springs. Indeed, he has a whole string of devices for handling emotions which offend his sense of reticence or decorum; he translates them into comic terms, gives them partial or cryptic statement, or utters them through a mask. Thus "The Revolutionists Stop for Orangeade" appears to contain his *ars poetica,* but it satirizes the poetic revolution in which he was most earnestly involved as a mixed Hispano-American-cum-Italian revolution; "Like Decorations in a Nigger Cemetery" is a sort of autumn journal in which his (frequently profound) moods of the season are given cryptic intimation, and mocked in the title, which apparently means as oddly-assorted a collection of memorials as one finds in such cemeteries; in "Chocorua to its Neighbor" he makes the mountain speak for him.

More than anything, it is the collapse of belief in our day—beliefs religious, ethical, political, metaphysical, even aesthetic—which moves him. His satire strikes at what he thinks false, but he is also intent on finding what can be thought true; thus his notion of poetry as the supreme fiction constructed to replace abolished belief, and of the imagination as the architect of that fiction. There has been much talk about his later poems as being especially philosophic and difficult. I should say they are neither. Between them, two poems, "To One of Fictive Music" and "The Man with the Blue Guitar," state nearly the whole body of ideas treated in his later work; the pieces in his first volume, *Harmonium,* contain every literary device he ever uses; and his enterprise is not so much philosophic as personal. I should say that it amounts to inventing imaginary objects of emotion, since the older objects of emotion can no longer be believed in as worthy of it, and since, after all, he feels strong need for such emotions. If what was formerly thought divine or heroic can no longer be believed in, one must invent something divine or heroic, because one must believe in the heroic and the divine.

The real source of whatever difficulty there may be in his poetry— aside from his frequent use of foreign words, of old words, and of his famous invented cries of *hoo, ric-a-nic,* and so on—lies in the fact that he is primarily a poet of images. Images, merely by *themselves,* can (1) force the mind to supplement, rearrange, and augment, (2) produce other images, (3) cause inferences, (4) induce emotions and trains of emotion. Ideas must be collocated into propositions and arguments, must be related by signs of transition, coordination, and subordination, but images need not; and because Stevens is aware of this fact, he uses aphoristic and epigrammatic methods, even shorthand notations such as the fragmentary sentence and the isolated and disjunct phrase. This is likely to puzzle the reader who expects signs of logical relation, and who seeks to turn the poem into rational meanings. Images as such are not logically but psychologically related; and to look for rational meanings in them, as Stevens himself once pointed out, is to destroy their imaginative and affective value. Again, the reader who looks for explicit instruction—such as is frequent in the older poets—as to what emotional or moral attitude to take is likely to be distressed; but the image, if efficiently constructed, contains its own stimulus; one has merely to contemplate it, and to feel. Properly read—that is, read without expecting him to do what he will *not* do—Stevens is seldom obscure; almost invariably he gives us the materials we need if we are to feel as he wishes us to.

However he is read, he *should* be read; for he has one of the most exquisitely fastidious minds of our age. Any contact whatsoever with it, perfect or imperfect, is certain to be exciting and valuable. In one of his latest poems, calling himself Ariel, he remarks "Ariel was glad he had written his poems"; whoever reads him will be glad also.

THE POETRY OF
DYLAN THOMAS

There is some evidence that even well-equipped readers have found the poetry of Dylan Thomas difficult; and one would be surprised, considering the nature of his work, if the case were otherwise. It is, in the first place, work characterized by unusually powerful and original conceptions, formulated in symbols difficult in themselves and complex in their interrelations. Secondly, what we may call the "dramatic presentation" of his poetry—roughly, the whole body of clues by which a reader determines who is speaking in the poem, to whom, of what, in what circumstances—is full of deliberate, even studied, ambiguity. Again, an even greater ambiguity, and even more studied, pervades his language, to a degree where it—the first thing we have to go by, in any literary composition —seems to exploit all the possibilities of the formal enigma. Finally— although this is not a matter of poetic structure but of historical accident—Thomas is working in a tradition not likely to be familiar to his readers.

Much has been said, by Miss Sitwell and others, about the grandeur of Thomas's "themes"; however, since no artistic work was ever good or bad simply by virtue of its dealing with a certain theme, I presume that what these critics have in mind is the *constituted* theme—what the poet has made of it, not what the theme in itself is—or, in a word, the conception governing the work. The artistic excellence of a work is dependent upon whether the conception itself is of value, and upon whether it has so dominated the whole construction of the piece as to be fully realized in it and enhanced by it. When Thomas's power of conception is at its height, when it masters all the elements of the poem, something like sublimity results; when the conception is merely odd, fanciful, or otherwise trivial, or when his handling of it obscures, distorts, or otherwise fails to manifest itself, he fails.

Reprinted from *Poetry*, January 1954. Copyright 1954 by The Modern Poetry Association.

"The Ballad of the Long-Legged Bait," to take one of his best poems
as an example, has as its bare theme the notion that salvation must be
won through mortification of the flesh. A common enough notion; but
in the fiery imagination of Thomas the process of purification becomes
the strange voyage of a lone fisherman; the bait is "A girl alive with his
hooks through her lips"; she is "all the wanting flesh his enemy," "Sin
who had a woman's shape"; and the quarry sought is no less than all
that Time and Death have taken, for since Sin brought Time and
Death into the world, the abolition of Sin will restore all that has been
lost. With the death of the girl, the sea gives up its dead, as foretold in
Revelation 20:13; Eden returns, "A garden holding to her hand / With
birds and animals"; and the sea disappears, accomplishing the prophecy of Revelation 21:1 ("and there was no more sea"). In the terrible
actuality of the voyage we never guess its essential fantasy; "the whole /
Of the sea is hilly with whales," "All the fishes were rayed in blood,"
and most beautifully:

> He saw the storm smoke out to kill
> With fuming bows and ram of ice,
> Fire on starlight, rake Jesu's stream;
> And nothing shone on the water's face
> But the oil and bubble of the moon . . .

As in these last lines the storm is given the menace, the fury and power
of a kind of supernatural warship, firing "on starlight" until nothing
shines but "the oil and bubble of the moon," so the theme of the whole
poem is given the emotional power of its legend: the subduing of
sensual desire becomes mysterious and cruel as the immolation of the
girl, the salvation takes on the beauty and mystery of the resurrection
of the dead and the past from the sea.

Similarly, "Fern Hill" and "Poem in October," luminous with all the
weathers of childhood; "A Refusal to Mourn the Death, by Fire, of a
Child in London," apprehending the child's death in its relation to the
whole universe (all creation is spanned, awesomely, from beginning to
end, in the first stanza, and the last carries us back to the "first dead");
the "Altarwise by Owl-light" sonnet-sequence (surely among the
greater poems of our century): all these are founded upon conceptions
possible, we feel, only to a man of great imagination and feeling. On
the other hand, such pieces as "Shall Gods Be Said to Thump the
Clouds," "Why East Wind Chills," and "Ears in the Turrets" rest upon
trivialities; their themes are conceived with too little imagination, and
with too little relation to humanity, to leave us anything but indifferent.

Thomas the poet has much less range than Thomas the prose-writer.

The poet is the greater, but the prosewriter assumes far more characters and enters into far more moods and shades of moods. The poet is a single character, and he is a poet only of the most exalted states of mind—the most exalted grief, joy, tenderness, or terror. Such lofty art demands great energy of thought and feeling, and all the accoutrements of lofty style; but when the lofty conception is lacking, energy becomes violence or plain noisiness, the tragic passions become melodramatic or morbid, ecstasy becomes hysteria, and the high style becomes obscure bombast. When the bard is not the bard, the bardic robes may easily be put off; not so the habitual paraphernalia of his art. When Thomas is not master of his tricks, his tricks master him; he is then capable, quite without any artistic point so far as I can see, of calling the dead Christ a "stiff," of having Jesus say, "I smelt the maggot in my stool," or of devising such fake nightmares as " 'His mother's womb had a tongue that lapped up mud.' " In his good work or his bad, his devices remain the same; it is their employment that differs.

The point in employing any literary device is that in the circumstances it discharges its function better than any other. Metaphor and simile, for instance (if we leave aside their instructive function of making the unfamiliar known in terms of the familiar), have two principal functions in poetry: either they isolate a quality or qualities by indicating something else which has them, or they serve as an indication of thought, feeling, or character; and it is thus that poet controls the feelings and ideas of his reader. When Enobarbus says that Cleopatra's barge "burnt" on the water, its fire-like brilliance is singled out; when Hamlet calls the world "a rank, unweeded garden" he manifests his state of mind. Both kinds fail, of course, if no real or fancied resemblance can be found to justify the analogy; but the former kind fails in its special function when the qualities isolated are, either in kind or degree, insufficient to produce the idea which must be grasped or the emotion which must be felt; and the latter kind fails in its special function when it fails to identify thought, feeling, or character.

When, in the passage cited earlier, Thomas gives us the storm conceived in all its power, presented in metaphor which discloses fully that conception, he succeeds wonderfully in the first kind; when he makes rain into milk from "an old god's dugs . . . pressed and pricked," he fails miserably in it. "In the groin of the natural doorway I crouched like a tailor / Sewing a shroud for a journey" is an excellent simile of the second kind, for it is a sharp index of the frame of mind of one who sees the womb itself as preparation for the grave; but "my love pulls the pale, nippled air / Prides of tomorrow suckling in her eyes" can hardly be said to identify the state of mind of the lover, or to offer any vision of his beloved with which we might reasonably be expected to be sympathetic.

I have already mentioned Thomas's dramatic and linguistic obscurity. The former is usually a relatively simple matter; for instance, appropriate titles would have made clear that "Where Once the Waters of Your Face" treats of a sea-channel gone dry, that "When Once the Twilight Locks No Longer" is the Spirit talking of man's death-dream, that "Light Breaks Where No Sun Shines," "Foster the Light," and "The Force That Through the Green Fuse Drives the Flower" are all variations on the macrocosm-microcosm theme, and that "If My Head Hurt a Hair's Foot" is a dialogue between an unborn child and its mother. There is no more point in such concealment, I think, than there would be in a dramatist's concealing the characters and the assignment of speeches in a play. Similarly with "the white giant's thigh"; if, as Thomas is alleged to have said, all is clear to one who knows that the "thigh" is a landmark on a Welsh hill, the reader should have been informed in a note; any effect which depends upon accidental ignorance can never be permanent, and is not worth trying for.

Yet if these obscurities are faults, those who damn Thomas's and much other contemporary poetry simply on the ground of its obscurity are badly mistaken. This amounts to legislation; whereas the artist is properly bound by no law but the dictates of the individual work. Moreover, it is always necessary for the literary artist, in the simplest lyric or the most extended narrative or play, at times to conceal and at times to disclose, in order to effect surprise and suspense, the subtlest shading of emotion into emotion, and the most delicate or vehement degree of emotion. It is precisely in the manipulation of language to these ends that Thomas, at his best, shows himself a master; consciously or unconsciously, he is in the tradition of the great Welsh enigmatic poets of the fourteenth century, and he seems to have learned or inherited all their art. He is particularly master of the sentence artfully delayed and suspended, through many surprising turns, until its unexpected accomplishment, and also of the mysterious paraphrase which, resolved at its conclusion, illuminates the whole poem. He is at his best in the latter in the magnificent "Sonnets"[1]; at his worst, perhaps, in "Because the Pleasure-Bird Whistles," but the latter illustrates his procedure more clearly. "Because the pleasure-bird whistles after the hot wires" means "Because the song-bird sings more sweetly after being blinded (with red-hot needles or wires)"; "drug-white shower of nerves and food" means "snow," snow being seen both

1. I have commented upon these at length in a book called *The Poetry of Dylan Thomas* (Chicago: University of Chicago Press, 1954).

as the "snow" of cocaine-addicts and as manna from heaven; "a wind that plucked a goose" means "a wind full of feathery snow"; "the wild tongue breaks its tombs" and the "red, wagged root" refer to fire; "bum city" refers to Sodom, "bum" meaning simultaneously "bad" and "given to sodomy"; the "frozen wife" and "the salt person" are of course Lot's wife; and so on.

He becomes easier to read if one is aware of his linguistic devices. He is fond of ambiguous syntax, and achieves it sometimes by punctuation, as in "O miracle of fishes! The long dead bite!" which leads us to think both expressions are phrases, whereas the last is a sentence; sometimes by lack of punctuation, as in the first three lines of "A Refusal to Mourn," where hyphenation would have clarified everything, thus: "Never until the mankind-making / Bird-beast- and flower- / Fathering and all-humbling darkness"; sometimes by delaying the complement in phrase or clause, as in the first stanza of "Poem in October," where many words intervene between "hearing" and its infinitive object "beckon," and many again between "beckon" and its object "myself"; sometimes by setting up apparent grammatical parallelism where none in fact exists, as in "talloweyed," which is a compound adjective, and "tallow I," which is adjective modifying personal pronoun. He is not merely fond of puns, but of using them to effect transition; thus in the "Sonnets" a pun on "poker" makes the transition from sonnet 4 to the imagery of sonnet 5.

Thomas exhibits astonishing variety in his statement of similitudes. Most commonly he uses compound expressions with metaphorical implications, as in "lamb white days" (days innocent as a lamb is white) or in "And a black cap of jack- / Daws Sir John's just hill dons," where the hill capped with jack-daws is seen as a judge donning the black cap for the pronouncement of the death-sentence. He is fond, too, of confusing the reader as to what is metaphorical and what is literal; for example, "Where once the waters of your face" leads the reader to suppose "waters" metaphorical and "face" literal, whereas the reverse is the case. He sometimes offers an apparently impossible statement, whether taken metaphorically or literally, and then indicates its metaphorical meaning much later; for example, in "Our Eunuch Dreams" "one-dimensioned ghosts" seems impossible, even though he is talking of images on a movie screen; it is only when he speaks of the photograph's "one-sided skins" that we understand "one-dimensioned" to mean a façade merely, something having no farther side. He is much given to various kinds of implied but unstated metaphor; for example, the storm-warship metaphor, where the warship is given only by implication, and again in "the stations of the breath" where he effects metaphor by substituting "breath" where we expect "cross."

It is difficult to say whether he has progressed much or not. There are extraordinarily fine poems in all his phases; but as he eliminates the faults of one period, he acquires new ones in another. His first poems are sometimes unnecessarily obscure through terseness; his later, sometimes obvious and verbose. In his earlier work the thoughts and emotions are sometimes too complex for lyric treatment; in his later, too simple for the elaboration he gives them. It is difficult, too, to say how he may develop; we must be grateful for the genius already manifest, and for the rest, have faith in the poet, a faith by no means without firm foundation.

————

I wrote the above when Dylan Thomas was still a living man. I should like to pay him the tribute of letting it stand exactly as I wrote it; for I meant it as a candid examination of his art which should result in a fuller exhibition of his genius.

2

INTERPRETATION: TWO ON *HAMLET*

HAMLET AND THE
HERMENEUTICS OF DRAMA

I n the present condition of *Hamlet* studies, it is almost useless to offer one more interpretation of the play. Enormous as the mass of interpretative commentary is, its variety is almost commensurate with its quantity. Hardly a speech, a character, or a detail of the plot but has posed numerous problems; hardly a week passes but new problems are discovered; and the solutions proposed are more numerous than the problems themselves. What is more, problems, methods, and solutions of the most fantastic order seem often to be given an authority equal to or even greater than that of the most solid scholarship, as if the criteria on which authority depended were novelty and ingenuity rather than cogency of proof. Critical commentary upon the play is in a similar condition, as one might expect; for criticism rests upon interpretation, and variant interpretations can scarcely lead to identical analyses and evaluations. Unless we are to pursue knowledge only to find confusion, some instrument must be discovered which will serve as laws of evidence, to permit the distinction of the unsound from the sound: laws of evidence, however, which are specifically relevant to the problems of imaginative literature, as distinct from laws of evidence that would be relevant if such problems were transformed into other problems of life or nature.

We must confine our discussion here to problems of hermeneutics simply, in their relation to the interpretation of a dramatic text as such; and if we are to determine what is specifically relevant to these, we must bear in mind that—although the interpretation of a text requires interpretation of character, thought, action, passion, expectation, criteria, and fact—the interpretation of a text is distinct from the

Reprinted from *Modern Philology*, vol. 61, no. 3 (February 1964).

I gratefully acknowledge the invaluable assistance of Professor Richard McKeon, whose suggestions and criticisms benefited me greatly.

interpretation of nature or truth, or experience or fact, and of value or feeling. We must recognize, in other words, that there is a difference between action, passion, thought, and character as these appear in drama and as these appear in nature; and that this difference entails a corresponding difference between their interpretations.

And we must set further limitations. We must exclude critical considerations, since these are by nature posterior to those of interpretation. By the same token, if we are to consider interpretation itself, we must also exclude textual and linguistic problems, which are by nature prior to those of interpretation: that is, we must assume that a text has been determined and that the meanings and the syntactical connections of the words contained in it are not in question. In fact textual and linguistic problems are in reciprocal relation with those of interpretation, for matters of what is to be read and of what it signifies obviously influence interpretation, and conversely; but we cannot inquire simultaneously into different disciplines based upon different principles.[1] For our purposes there is a point where interpretation begins as well as a point where it ends. We shall assume that it begins where textual and linguistic matters leave off, basing itself upon these, and that it ends where literary criticism proper begins, based upon it in turn.

All interpretation is in its essence hypothesis. However certain we may feel about it, it never permits of absolute demonstration, for it concerns an individual thing, and demonstration of the individual is impossible. It permits of probability proofs only, and the highest "certainty" that it can reach is that of being beyond reasonable doubt. When it concerns anything made up of parts, it is in addition a complex hypothesis, entailing subhypotheses as to the parts; and when it concerns any very extended work, such as a novel or a play, it is a very complex hypothesis indeed, entailing subhypotheses not only as to the parts, but also as to their interrelation with each other and with the whole. Now, clearly the complex hypothesis is dependent for its probability upon the relative probability of the subhypotheses which make it up. It is like a compound proposition, the truth value of which is determined by the truth values of the propositions which make it up: the compound proposition "Hamlet was sane and Ophelia was mad" cannot be more probable than its constituents "Hamlet was sane" and "Ophelia was mad."

Indeed, when stated, complex hypotheses such as the interpretations we have in mind take the form of compound propositions; and when

1. The principles and problems of interpretation remain identical whether a good text or a bad is chosen, and whether the language of it is properly or improperly construed. Interpretation is thus a discipline distinct from textual criticism and linguistics.

we examine their constituents, we discover that they consist of propositions of a very different order. There are, first of all, basic propositions, such as "Horatio informed Hamlet of the Ghost," and "Polonius advised Laertes." Second, there are what we will call inferential propositions, since they are the products of inference. Thus, "The ghost lied" is inferential, for this is an inference from "Claudius was innocent," which in turn is an inference from "Had Claudius been guilty, he would have reacted to the dumb-show." Finally, there are evaluative propositions: "Hamlet was noble-minded" or "Eminently pleasant traits can be found in Claudius."

These are quite different statements; they differ in terms of *what they are about.* Basic propositions are about facts or occurrences; the evidence for them is that these facts or occurrences exist or occur in the work. If the proposition "Polonius advised Laertes" is disputed, we can establish it only by reference to the work—not by citing some other proposition. A basic proposition may be a highly compound one, but all of its constituents must then be basic ones. "Laertes advised Ophelia and Polonius advised Ophelia" is a compound basic proposition only if its constituents are basic.

Inferential propositions are about facts and occurrences *implied* by basic propositions; the evidence for them is the basic propositions as related to them by inference. "Hamlet was sent to England" is inferential. It happens to be true; but to prove its truth, we must cite basic propositions which imply it. Conceivably it might have been directly displayed to us as fact; but it is left to inference instead. The evidence that Hamlet was sent to England is that—to put it succinctly —Hamlet and everyone else in a position to know agree that he was; this succinct statement involves a number of basic propositions from which we infer.

While formally all inference is necessary in the sense that the premises necessitate the conclusion, there are four sorts of conclusions which may be drawn—assertoric, necessary, probable, or possible— according as the premises themselves involve propositions of these four kinds. A conclusion can never be stronger than the premises upon which it depends; thus probabilities can never establish necessary propositions, and possibilities can never establish probabilities.

Evaluative propositions are a subclass of the inferential. Their characteristic is that they have predicates qualifying an action or an agent—"Hamlet treats Ophelia brutally," "Hamlet is noble"—and the qualification always involves reference to a standard of some kind. Evidence for them therefore always consists in part of basic and inferential propositions, in part of some standard, established as appropriate, to which these are referred. If I say, "Claudius's counseling of Hamlet (I, ii) is a kindly act," the evidence for this is more complicated than it may seem. Claudius's speech must first be interpreted as an act—for he is not merely *saying* something, but *doing* something by saying it. Second, the act must be considered in all its known circumstances. The circumstance of motive, for example, may force a complete revision of the conception of the act itself: Claudius may not be really advising Hamlet, but *commanding* him *under color of advising* him. Finally, the circumstances weighed, a standard of kindness must be selected as appropriate, and the act referred to it. The evaluative proposition is the ultimate resultant.

The evaluation of character is still more complicated. The proposition "Claudius is kind," for instance, depends upon consideration of the totality of his actions, all of which must be evaluated and then employed as data from which the character of Claudius must be inferred. Character can never be observed directly; it is a potentiality which must be inferred from its actualizations.

It should be clear, then, not merely how evaluations may be established, but also at what points they are subject to attack, as well at what points differences of evaluation may originate. Besides these, differences may arise through the mistaking of an evaluative proposition for a basic one. For example, "Hamlet delays" is often treated as basic, for although it obviously involves reference to a standard of how rapidly he should have acted, a standard is seldom discussed.

All kinds of propositions—basic, inferential, or evaluative—may be true or false or probable or whatever; a proposition is not true or false because of its kind. At the same time there is a risk of error in proportion as the process is complicated. In this respect, an evaluation is more likely to be in error than an inference, for it involves inference, and an inferential proposition is more likely to be in error than a basic one, for it involves basic propositions. Again, basic propositions must form the foundation for any inference, or there will be no guaranty that discussion is in any way related to the work; and inferential propositions in turn form the immediate foundations of evaluative ones. In these terms, there is a difference between them in priority and authority, but such differences relate to their truth only as they relate to their subject matter and evidence.

However, much of the present confusion in *Hamlet* studies may be attributable to the confusion of these kinds; therefore, it is not due simply to the fact that they are employed. Indeed, inspection of *Hamlet*, or for that matter any other work of imaginative literature, will quickly assure us that in it certain data are afforded, and that inferences and evaluations based on these are demanded if the work is to have its effect. We cannot react to a work unless we evaluate the characters and their actions, and we cannot evaluate these unless we can infer what they are. It is precisely in these terms, therefore, that we can construct—very generally—a statement of what a perfect interpretation is. It is one which is absolutely commensurate in its basic, inferential, and evaluative propositions with the data, the implications, and the values contained within the work. That is, its basic propositions will be statements point for point correspondent with the data afforded by the work; its inferential propositions will state precisely what is implied in the work; its evaluative propositions will concur, both in values and in the evaluated, with the values proposed in the work. As a hypothesis its structure will correspond exactly with the work, part for part and as a whole; and it will contain no more or less than is warranted by the work.[2]

If we may assume this account of "perfect interpretation" as, very generally, true, we must say that it is too general to be useful, unless we can discover what we mean by "warranted by the work" and other expressions just used. What things in a work, we may ask, constitute data, and how do they warrant basic propositions? How can we know when and what specific inferences are warranted? Similarly, when are evaluations warranted also?

We have been speaking of the interpretation of imaginative works in general; if we are to be more specific, we must specify in this instance by limiting discussion to drama. The questions just raised now become questions of what means are available to the dramatist, whether to afford data or to warrant implication or evaluation. These problems in no wise involve the dramatist's intention, for that is generally something that must be inferred from the work, and so the argument would be circular; they rather involve what the dramatist has *done* in a given work. To put this figuratively, if there is anything like a grammar and syntax of drama, we can discuss what a drama *means* without reference to what the dramatist may have meant, just as we can discuss what a given sentence in fact means apart from what someone meant to mean by it.[3]

The analogy between language and the body of dramatic devices is less far-fetched than it may seem, and deserves investigation. Consider what drama can do. It has subjects (e.g., "Hamlet," "Claudius") and predicates ("is advising," "is meditating"), and it can combine these affirmatively or negatively. If we grant that there are such things as problem plays and propaganda plays, drama can question or com-

2. In consonance with my earlier assumptions, I omit here any consideration of the possibility that historical or other arguments involving matters external to the work may be required to effect proof. These are not propositions about the work as such; and if appropriate and sound, would have the effect of subarguments establishing the structure commensurate with the work.

3. Mrs. Malaprop's utterances mean one thing while she means another, and we discover what *they* mean first. From these we conjecture her real intent. It is possible that there are Mrs. Malaprops of the drama.

mand; in other words, interrogation and the imperative are possible in it. Certain subjunctives are also possible, for example, the subjunctive contrary to fact: for example, "Horatio would have killed himself, had Hamlet not stopped him," "Had Hamlet but acted as Laertes and Fortinbras did, the event would have been different." Limitation and generalization are possible in it; that is, it can attach a certain predicate to *some* or all of its characters. It can qualify predicates, and indicate tense, as "Hamlet killed Polonius *mistakenly*" and "Hamlet *will be told* of the Ghost," "Horatio *has not betrayed* Hamlet." It is obviously capable of emphasis. It as clearly permits conjunction and separation: for example, it can indicate that something happens *because* of something or *after* something, and that when something was happening, something else was happening; obviously, therefore, it must have devices comparable to causal and temporal conjunctions. It can also *prove* as well as *imply*. It even permits of "figures of speech" in its own way: for instance, personification and comparison. The proof of all this, besides the examples given, is that all commentators, however diverse, assume that drama can convey things; therefore there must be a means of conveying them. Thus another statement of correct interpretation might be that it is an exact "translation" of "dramatic language" into actual language. Conversely, the dramatization of a narrative involves translation of the language of the narrative into the "language" of drama: a problem of how this can be "said" on the stage.

We are not discussing the actual employment of language *as* language in the drama, it should be clear; there is nothing remarkable in the fact that language should be able to convey what language can convey. Certainly language is used to narrate and describe in plays as it is in anything else. Here there is simply a problem of meaning. But when language is used as it is in some parts of narrative and in certain lyric poems and generally throughout drama, we must go beyond meaning, as I have argued earlier, and deal with the speech as action; not merely with the "significance" of what is said but with the "significance" of someone's *saying* it. If this is so, it is clear that the whole sphere of the dramatist is action; and our problem becomes one of how action can convey what it evidently does. And if we can state the "vocabulary and syntax" of action, we shall be in a better position to interpret it.

Experience generally provides us with syntheses; but language in itself is analytic. Experience gives us, let us say, a man running; language distinguishes between the man and his running, giving each a separate name, and then artificially couples these together again to say "the man is running," in order to express the synthesis. Because it fragments experience after this fashion, it must give successive expression even to attributes which are simultaneous in fact. As it proceeds in its course of distinction, it develops two kinds of expressions: those resulting from the distinctions, and those which indicate how the former are to be connected and correlated. The "language" of action, on the other hand, reverses this process. It does not give us "Hamlet is speaking," but *Hamlet-speaking*. Attributes that language can express only successively, action can render simultaneously, if they are not incompatible; for action is a synthesis. To put it generally, to ask *why* we have the various forms which language develops is to answer the question of *how* action "speaks," for the principles by which experience is converted into language are identical with those involved in the syntheses of action. For example, in experience one thing happens at a later time than another; to express this in language we utilize such an expression as "after"; action expresses a thing which is "after" another by *having it happen afterward*, in the way of experience itself. Or, in experience we have man-talking-loudly; language separates out and reconnects, to say "A man is talking loudly"; action presents this in turn as *man-talking-loudly*. So much for the "syntax" of action, generally; insofar as the conveyance of meaning is concerned, the problem of the dramatist is simply to construct an object in which the attributes manifestly appear.

Everything that is conveyed, even by language as such, is conveyed either directly or indirectly; and this applies to the "language" of action as well. Compare the arts: in painting, for example, a plane surface may convey the impression of mass or space, though these involve a third dimension which a plane surface cannot have. *Directly* a plane surface may represent only another surface; but it is possible for it to represent mass and space *indirectly*, that is, by *implication;* for it can represent the effects of distance (gradual diminution in size, loss of detail, occlusion of one object by another, etc.), and these are *signs* which *imply* distance. On the other hand, musical tones cannot possibly represent a human figure, for they have no position in space, nor can they imply any determinate position in space.

This consideration leads us into the "vocabulary" of the dramatist. As we examine it, we see that it is the inverse of that of the actor in certain respects. The sphere of the actor is physical action; that of the dramatist, verbal action. Whenever the properties of the medium are identical with the properties of the thing presented or conveyed, direct representation is possible; otherwise, indirect representation only is possible. The actor works with physical action: bodily motion, gesture, facial expression, utterance. Bodily action can represent directly any motion possible to the body, and so on for the rest; whatever else these represent, they must represent by implication. The dramatist, on the other hand, cannot do this. Where any physical action is involved, he can either imply it or stipulate it in a stage direction, in which case he is simply falling back upon the use of language as language—not language as action. For example, "And lay your hands again upon my sword" implies that that action has taken place; whereas such a direction as "(*Dies*)" or "(*Exit*)" uses language as language. Any verbal action is directly possible for the dramatist, on the other hand; whereas the actor can only *imply* such things by the tones of his voice, etc.

While no doubt a play is fully realized only in performance, we must discuss the written play, for that is or should be the foundation of performance, and it is this alone for which the dramatist is solely responsible. Besides, performance rests upon interpretation. Now, a verbal action, although it is performed by speech, is not the same thing as the speech: a given speech of some length may contain a number of different actions, or a number of speeches may constitute a single act, or speech and act may coincide.

It is hardly necessary to argue that in reading a play we frame opinions and conjectures about the characters, their actions, passions, fortunes, and the interconnections of these, and that we evaluate these in various ways as well; and that whatever we do is always supposed to have some foundation in the play. Some of these opinions, conjectures, and evaluations remain true throughout the work; others turn out, as we read, to be false, and are modified or exchanged for others; and alterations depend upon what is gradually revealed to us by the play. If it is correct to suppose that drama conveys primarily by verbal action, and conveys that alone directly, conveying everything else indirectly, that is, by implication, it follows that such action is the very center of everything else, and the foundation of all opinion and conjecture. And since actions themselves are subject to conjecture and evaluation, there must either be some actions or some aspects of action which are not thus subject; otherwise the foundation itself will rest upon nothing.

If by *saying* something it is possible to *do* something, and this deed arises from the meaning of what is said, then what we are looking for may be called *the first actualization of meaning* or the *first apparent form* of the verbal action. This is not necessarily the same as the *real nature* of the action; but it remains a thing done, regardless of what constructions may be placed upon the doing of it. Examples may indicate what I mean. The first words in *Hamlet* are Bernardo's "Who's there?" If we say that this is an interrogative sentence and that the meaning of it is such and such, we are still within the confines of grammar; if we say, "Bernardo questions," we are stating an action, but not properly, since this question in these circumstances is something other than a question; what Bernardo is in fact doing is *challenging*. Now, it is possible that Bernardo is really doing something else while apparently challenging; but it remains the case that he is doing it under the appearance of challenging, and challenging is the first apparent form of the action. Thus in act V, when Claudius calls for drink, he is really preparing to poison the cup; but the first apparent form of the action—though we know perfectly well what he is up to—is requesting drink.

In the strictest sense, the basic proposition *of interpretation* is a literal proposition stating the first apparent form of any verbal action in the work.[4] It always has the agent as its subject and the action as its predicate. Furthermore, that predicate is always a definition of the action, and is immediately convertible with it. For example, to utter a particular demand in certain circumstances is to challenge, and anyone who utters such a demand is challenging; conversely, anyone who challenges must make a particular demand in certain circumstances. This is not necessarily a matter of grammatical form; for example, Francisco challenges in return, with "unfold thyself." While one expression is interrogative and the other imperative, and while there is some difference in meaning as sentences, they are precisely the same as actions, although one is authorized and the other not.

Basic propositions of interpretation are, as I said, immediate, in the sense that they do not rest upon other propositions of interpretation, but upon the immediate conversion of speech into action. Since action is not the same as speech, the unity and completeness of the one is not the same as the unity and completeness of the other. A single speech in drama may contain several actions, or several speeches may make up a single action. For example, Francisco's first speech contains both a refusal to answer a challenge and a counter-challenge; on the other hand, two of Laertes's speeches to Ophelia (I, iii) make up a single act of admonition. An action is "one" either in the sense that it is indivisible as such, that is, does not divide into constituent actions, or is divisible into actions which are specifically identical with each other and with the total action which they make up, or, though not specifically identical with each other, constitute a whole action when taken together. Thus Francisco's refusal is simple and indivisible, and would be so if it were stated in many words instead of one—it does not divide into parts which are refusals. Laertes's single admonition may be

4. Basic propositions are about facts and occurrences, and therefore treat of more than verbal action. Some things that are not or cannot be directly witnessed can be represented by implication. The basic proposition in these instances always predicates the indication; this implies an inferential proposition interpreting the indication. Thus we *witness* Laertes' crying out (IV, v); we *infer* that he is in anguish. The statement of what we witness is the basic proposition. Where the inference is a very obvious one, as in this instance, we are not always aware that inference is involved; it is, nonetheless.

Basic propositions of this sort are tested like those of verbal action. Others derive directly from the meaning of the language as language. The proposition of verbal action is, however, primary, as most closely associated with dramatic form, since drama is impossible without verbal action, except as mere pantomime.

divided into parts, but these are all acts of admonition, and in their
totality are admonition; the King's persuasion of Laertes to assist in the
plot against Hamlet (IV, vii) is a single action as a whole, though made
up of different actions as parts. A single action is always continuous,
either in the sense that its parts follow in immediate succession, as
when the act is contained within a single speech, or in the sense that
interrupting speeches do not disrupt the process of the action as such.
The King's act just mentioned is single, although interrupted by
Laertes's answers.

An action is complete when it realizes its first apparent form as a
single act, or when all the parts that make it up have realized their first
apparent forms. An incomplete speech—in the sense that the character
does not get to finish what he is saying—may still, thus, constitute a
complete act; for example, someone may protest without finishing his
protest. It seems thus that all these would yield basic propositions,
whether simple ones or conjunctions. (I assume that a conjunction here
is not inference but mere summary of the basic propositions.)

Where the act itself is incomplete, it cannot yield a basic proposition, since its form must be determined by inference. An act may also
be ambiguous, in the sense that it is not clear whether the agent is
doing this or that; such acts will not yield basic propositions. Certain
actions—quarreling, for instance—are not possible to a single agent;
but they are collectively predicable in a basic proposition of their
subjects if there are basic propositions stating that each participated.
Outside of entering into a collective action of this sort, or into a whole
action of the kind mentioned earlier, while also performing an act
which is a part of these, it is hardly likely that two different verbal
actions can be performed simultaneously, unless we take different
consequences into account, for example, Edmund's simultaneously
deceiving his father while incriminating his brother in *King Lear;* but
that is rather inaccurate statement. Two different physical actions may
of course be performed simultaneously, or a verbal action may be
performed simultaneously with a physical one; but I can think of no
examples of verbal acts performed simultaneously by the same agent.

Not every speech is an action; for example, Laertes's "Do you see
this, O God?" (in IV, v) is not an action except in the sense that he says
it; it is simply an outcry which indicates his anguish. But Hamlet's "O,
what a rogue and peasant slave am I" *is* an action of self-condemna-
tion. Ambiguity of a speech, moreover, does not necessarily result in
ambiguity of action unless the ambiguity gives support to two different
actions.

All basic propositions, whether simple or compound, and whatever
their kind of predicate, may be tested for truth by examining them to
see whether their predicates are definitions convertible with the

statement of the action or actions, as I have explained before. The predicate, furthermore, must never contain a metaphor, for all metaphors involve ambiguity; and it must also never involve any term of evaluation, that is, anything that involves a judgment of the action. Thus an act of Hamlet's cannot be described as, for instance, his acting as an "ambassador of death," for that is a metaphor; and Claudius's acts cannot immediately be described as "kind." Neither of these can possibly state the nature of the act performed.

Once true, a basic proposition remains true even though the action should turn out to be other than it seems; for what it states is not necessarily the "real" nature of the action but its first apparent form. When the real nature of the action is different from that of the apparent one, it must be inferred; that is, the statement of its nature is an inferential proposition; for clearly it cannot be witnessed. The reader of a play is in some sense a witness of the things involved in basic propositions, and these will be part of what he will actually witness in a faithful performance of the play. He may be deceived by appearances; but that the appearances are of a certain order and afford a basis for interpretation is hardly open to doubt. That an action is not what it appears to be, however, clearly cannot follow from its appearance; it must therefore be inferred.

Acts differ from each other in terms of their particular conditions or circumstances; and these are, generally, the agent, the act, the person or thing on which the act is done, the purpose, the result, the instrument, the manner, the time, and the place. But there are further specifications of some of these. For example, the agent may have acted by chance, or he may have acted by compulsion, or natural causes may have been responsible; and in these cases the action is involuntary, as not due to the agent himself. On the other hand, actions due to the agent himself and voluntary proceed from habit, from reasoning, anger, or desire. Again, in the matters of time and place we must consider whether the action was done in private or in public, and all the matters that may be associated with these: for instance, if something is said in public, whether friends or enemies were present, and what the characters of these were, and so on.

Some of these circumstances are substantive, that is, constitute the act as an act of a particular nature; others are incidental. Fratricide, manslaughter, murder, and accidental killing are different acts constituted by different circumstances, although all are forms of killing; the circumstances which constitute them are their substantive circumstances, and all others are incidental, important as they may be in determining emotional responses to the act. Evidently, then, any construction of the nature of the act which goes beyond its first apparent form depends upon the revelation, prior or posterior to the act itself, of substantive circumstances different from those constituting the first apparent form. Since that revelation itself is the effective factor, we need not consider here the dramatic method by which it is accomplished.

Physical actions, when not stated in stage directions, are necessarily implied; they are implied either by the speech itself, as in "The king rises," or by the verbal action, as in Hamlet's violent wresting of the poisoned cup from Horatio. Even in these matters, there is a difference between what is actually implied and what merely seems plausible. For example, the conjecture that the arras rustles or that Polonius peeps from behind it in III, ii may be plausible; but it is not implied by anything in the speeches; rather it results from the supposition—false, in point of fact—that there is nothing in Ophelia's conduct which might make Hamlet suspicious. There is a similar difference between what the text warrants and such striking pieces of stage business as a brilliant director might invent. The actor's delivery of the speeches is determined by the same considerations: that is, it is either implied by the speech or the act, or it is not warranted by the text itself.

Character and emotion can be represented only by implication, and hence can only be stated in inferential propositions. Character, as I employ the term here, is not moral character as good or bad—for that involves evaluation—but the potentiality of the agent for action of a certain kind, in whatever kind of action; or to put it differently, it is what determines the necessity or probability of a given action in terms of *its* agent. Character in this sense is clearly reciprocal with action; that is, we may infer character from an act or infer an act from character, although in the nature of drama, as we have seen, action is prior. Character is inferred either through probabilities or signs, as these arise either from the character himself or from other characters. In the case of the character himself, we base inferences on his actions, including speech, his emotions and the things which generally are shown to give him pleasure or pain, and any similar indications. We infer by probability when, for instance, we infer that he is envious since he has been shown to be ambitious, and because the ambitious are generally envious; we infer by sign that he is envious because he has been exhibited as envious of a certain individual. Emotions are inferred in the same way: that is, we infer that he is angry because the kind of thing which has been done to him generally produces anger, or we infer that he is angry because he exhibits the signs of anger.

When we infer from probability, we must remember that plays are not based merely upon natural probability; certain things are probable by convention in certain forms at certain times, and certain others are probable as postulated by the dramatist. Conventional probabilities always entail historical argument, for example, that in plays of a certain period mothers may recognize their grown offspring, parted from them in infancy, by maternal instinct alone. Postulated probabilities are exemplified by any attributes arbitrarily assigned to a character, for instance, invulnerability, superhuman strength, mysterious powers of mind, or whatever; from these it follows that the spear will not wound, and so on. Hence probability inferences must be based upon probability as it is *within the work*, not as it is in nature.

The same caution applies to inferences from signs. Signs are either natural or conventional or peculiar to the work; thus weeping is a natural sign of grief, passing the hand before the face in a Nō play is a conventional sign of weeping, and in particular plays a special mannerism may be assigned to a given character to indicate that he is in a certain emotional state. Signs are either infallible or fallible, as they completely prove something or only tend to indicate it. For example, having a very high temperature is an infallible sign of illness; but weeping is a fallible sign of grief, since one may also weep for joy and other reasons. Here, again, we must distinguish fallible and infallible as the work dictates.

Since character is thought to be something over and above mere circumstance, the constructed conception of character must be in a sense abstracted from circumstance. That is, it must not rest upon what is done in a single instance, but what is done consistently. At the same time, circumstance must always be borne in mind; a given individual may act in one way consistently toward his friends, and in another way consistently toward his enemies, all consistently with his character. The consistencies which underlie apparent inconsistencies will be the basic constituents of the character. The character of the individual may also change in the course of the piece, and there should be consistency underlying these changes. Similarly, the relations between the persons of the drama may alter; consistency must be sought here as well. It is perfectly possible that the dramatist himself has been inconsistent; but we can only discover this by seeking consistency.

Inferences as to the character of a given person in the drama are based also upon the actions, emotions, and statements of others. In such cases, the process of inference is similar, except that here everything must be qualified by the consideration of the characters of those who provide the basis, together with their particular relation to the character of the person in question. It makes all the difference whether we are considering the account, let us say, of friends or enemies, and whether these are possessed of information and are men of good sense and good character. And there are differences of value which are consequent upon these considerations: a grudging admission of virtue coming from an enemy is worth more as testimony than the enthusiastic encomium of a friend, and condemnation by a friend means more than condemnation by an enemy. Similarly, the testimony of someone who has been deceived is of less value than that of someone who has been fully informed: we can hardly accept the statements of those whom Hamlet is trying to deceive by feigning madness as proof that he is really mad.

Events past or future, the interrelations of character, and other things must also often be established by inference. Questions of past and future fact involve the same considerations of cause with, of course, differences of time. Thus, if the power and the motive to do something both exist, it will be done unless something interferes; if it has been done, they did exist. If the process of doing something has begun, the thing will be done unless prevented; if the thing has been done, the process existed. Off-stage actions supposedly happening simultaneously with events shown on stage involve the same considerations.

In general correct inferences depend upon three things: recognition of when inference is required (i.e., of what implies); recognition of the type of inference required (i.e., by what type of probability or what type of sign); and recognition of what inference to draw (i.e., of what is implied).[5] It should be obvious that inference can never exceed its materials, and that unless inference is determinate, its conclusion cannot be determinate, however "plausible" on other considerations it may be. Action, character, emotion—whatever is being inferred— cannot exceed the data supporting them or be derived except by the appropriate methods of inference.

Evaluative propositions—from one point of view the most complicated of all—are from another the simplest to discuss. Primarily the problem is one of what standard is to be involved. Standards are either general or special or particular. A work may assume, for instance, a universal standard of morality; or one which is assumed in a given time, or a given culture, or a given class of work; or it is one established by the work itself. In the last instance it is one held by the best

5. Probabilities and signs, as these occur in the work, provide matter for minor premises permitting inference. Both predicate a middle term of a subject which is the agent; in both, the problem is to find a major term predicable of the middle, to permit construction of a major premise. Their difference lies in the relation of major term to middle: in signs, the major is a cause of which the middle is an effect, in probabilities the major is an effect of which the middle is a cause. Since causal relation is crucial here, the grasping of a causal correlative constitutes recognition of sign or probability as such. Both are tested in terms of their causal correlatives as probable consistently with the probabilities of the work.

Signs which separately are fallible may in conjunction with other fallible signs constitute an infallible sign, i.e., by constituting a complex sign with a unique reference. For example, pallor is a fallible sign of fear, since many conditions may produce it; but conjoined with other signs it may make up an infallible composite sign of fear. Also, a fallible sign may be confirmed by an infallible sign justifying the same inferential proposition.

person—judged by the work—or the better persons, or by all. The standards of any or all of these persons may be open to objection, but that entails *criticism of the work,* which is no part of interpretation; from the standpoint of *interpretation* it is proper to accept the standards of the work itself. For example, it is one thing to judge Hamlet's speeches to Ophelia in the Mousetrap scene as vile, obscene, and ungentlemanly in the extreme by one's own standards, quite another to judge them as Ophelia evidently judges them; still another, to judge them in terms of Hamlet's motives in uttering them. In brief, from the point of view of interpretation, standards of the work are prior; failing these, one falls back upon the conventional standards of a given time, culture, creed, and so on; failing these, upon general morality.[6] As with moral standards, so with any other; any proposition which involves reference to a standard is an evaluative proposition.

Standards may, however, shift in the course of the work, one supplanting another, just as inferential propositions may supplant others. How is the "true" one to be ascertained, in that case? This question is involved in the larger problem of what determines truth— or the nearest approach to truth—in interpretation. If, as we have seen, it is not the form of the proposition advanced, what is it?

We know about something finally and completely when we know it, not in part merely, but as a complete whole. Thus knowledge of any particular process becomes more complete and certain as the process itself approaches completion. Now, a play is always a process; even when it does not depict a process of action—that is, of consequences following upon an act—it must necessarily involve a process of revelation. As a process of revelation, it may be thought of as posing a series of questions, composing one fundamental question. These are all gradually answered—sometimes only tentatively to begin with, but completely and finally answered at the end, and their answers constitute the answer to the fundamental question. In a consequential action, for example, each event raises the question of what will follow upon it, which of various possibilities will be realized; the actual realization of the consequence answers this question, to pose in turn the question of what will succeed it. Thus the entire plot of *Oedipus Tyrannus* may be seen as answering one fundamental question—of

6. The moral evaluation of an act necessitates consideration of its cause. It makes all the difference whether an act is done willingly and knowingly; willingly but through ignorance of principle; by constraint or by ignorance of the fact, and in the latter case, whether repented of or not; or whether, although the origin of action is in the agent, the act would not be chosen were it not for the circumstances: e.g., the choice of the lesser of two evils. Praise and blame, pardon or the refusal of it, clearly depend upon these considerations. If, for example, we assume that Hamlet is mad, we cannot discuss his moral character; he does not know, in that case, what he is doing, and he is not morally responsible, and his actions cannot indicate his moral character.

what will be done about the plague in Thebes; and this question divides into many constituent questions which in their successive solution establish the answer to it. The constituent questions are not abstract or retrospective, but concrete and prospective; that is, they are about particular actions, and actions that will be done. The answer to each of them, thus, is the doing of a particular action; and the whole action constitutes the complete answer to the fundamental question. The statement in words of that complete action as a complete and unified whole is a proposition supported by all other propositions. In the same way, the final answer to constituent questions derives its authority from the fact that it represents a complete constitutive part of the whole structure. The warrant of truth, thus, is that a complete action has been completely revealed, whether by direct representation or implication.

No constituent question is left unsolved in a complete drama. Any question left unsolved in the final answer to the fundamental question is not a question relevant to the drama. For example, while people naturally tend to wonder who the Matchseller is in Harold Pinter's *A Slight Ache*, the play affords no evidence, and the question is irrelevant to the drama; the action does not consist in his actions but in what other people do in consequence of his presence. It is perfectly possible that a director may have to pose and answer such a question to obtain a unified performance, and that an actor may have to do so in order to play the part; but it is not a question warranted by the drama itself. The greater part of such questions, however, arise from the confusion of the action of drama with real action, and its agents with real agents, and the consequent treatment of them in terms of such sciences as would be appropriate to real actions and real agents; or from conversion of the work into something other than it is—into an action of the author, for instance, as T. S. Eliot does in *Hamlet and His Problems*. Such questions are "insoluble" because they are irrelevant: the very posing of them involves unwarranted speculation; and because it does not involve sound interpretation in the first place.

A question of interpretation, then, is one posed by the action of the work itself, and answered by it. The question, for example, of whether the Ghost of Hamlet's father informed him correctly is a proper question of interpretation because Hamlet himself has doubts about it—doubts which both prevent him from following one course of action and lead him to pursue another—that of removing these doubts; and it is answered by a series of actions answering the constituent questions of whether a ghost existed, whether it was the ghost of Hamlet's father, whether it informed Hamlet, and whether what it said was true. The existence of the ghost is established on the evidence that it was seen by several persons on several occasions; that an educated man, completely skeptical of ghosts, saw it and was convinced; that we ourselves witnessed it; that it continued to manifest itself to others; that it was not only seen but heard, and we ourselves heard it. How might the dramatist have cast doubt on its existence, had he wished to? He might have had it vouched for by one man only, and that a habitual liar or a superstitious fool; it would have failed to reappear; and so on. He has done none of these; all the evidence is on one side, and the answer is established. What proves the ghost to be that of Hamlet's father? It is recognized as such by everyone who had seen the elder Hamlet, including the son himself; it identifies itself as that spirit. Again we must ask what Shakespeare would have done to throw doubt upon the point; he has done nothing. In the same way, the giving of information is verified insofar as the dramatic situation permits; and the truth of it is borne out by the king's behavior at the play—witnessed by Hamlet, Horatio, and ourselves—the king's confession at prayer, and the queen's acknowledgment in her chamber.[7]

Questions with answers thus unequivocally supported might seem beyond all controversy; yet unfortunately it is such as these that make up a large part of the commentaries on Hamlet. The problem of Hamlet's sanity is conspicuous among them, although every dramatic device is used to establish Hamlet's sanity, and none to throw doubt on it. If problems are to be solved, if interpretations are to be provably sound, it must be by some such instrument as I have adumbrated here. The alternative is an endless succession of free improvisations on Shakespearean themes.

7. It should be noted that the action does not merely supply the materials for propositions but also determines their modality. At the beginning, an action presents as possibilities or probabilities many things which in the course of the action become impossible or improbable, and possibilities also become probabilities and, on their realization, necessary, for whatever has happened was necessitated. This must be taken into account in framing propositions, for it involves their truth: what is true at one point in the action may not be true at another, and what was possible at one point may be impossible or necessary at another.

"MIGHTY OPPOSITES":
REMARKS ON THE PLOT OF *HAMLET*

I have often wondered what a student would suppose *Hamlet* to be like, as a play, if he were never permitted access to the text or to a performance but forced instead to read the entire body of criticism and commentary upon it. That huge mass of discussion, full of interpretations, hypotheses, and judgments so diverse, so dissonant—could he penetrate it to gain some notion of the play about which it centered? I fear he could not; and while some may take such diversity of comment as a mark of the richness of the work, I take it rather as a mark of the irresponsibility of commentators. It seems to me a test of the soundness of critical discussion that it should give an accurate idea of the work it discusses; a body of criticism which does not do so must be in proportion unsound.

The extreme variety of interpretation seems to be due principally to two causes. The first is that critics have, by and large, failed to establish proper controls in failing to distinguish adequately between facts, inferences, and value judgments, and hence between warranted and unwarranted inferences and value judgments. The second is that in the history of its discussion the action of the play was first reduced to Hamlet's actions only and then Hamlet was taken out of the play, to be explained and analyzed as a real rather than a fictional person, in terms of natural rather than artistic considerations. In consequence interpretation and discussion were extended far beyond the relatively narrow limits of matters appropriate to tragedy. In counteracting the first of these causes, we may clarify what happens in individual scenes; in counteracting the second, what happens in the plot as a whole.

In establishing what occurs in individual scenes, we may pass over the question of the reality of the Ghost. Every device accessible to a dramatist is used to assure us of his reality, including permitting us to see and hear him, and the play offers no foundation for doubt on the

Reprinted from *Studies in Theatre and Drama: Essays in Honor of Hubert C. Heffner* (The Hague: Mouton, n.d.)

matter. There are, however, three important questions concerning the Ghost, and to fail to resolve them properly is to risk gross errors of interpretation. These are the problems of precisely what accusations the Ghost makes, of what he asks Hamlet to do, and of whether his statements are true and his demands just.

The Ghost makes two accusations. No one in his senses can mistake the first: in clear language and in full detail the Ghost charges Claudius with having poisoned him and with having given out a false report of the manner of his death. The second accusation, however, offers some difficulty because of its ambiguity, and its exact nature must be determined by inference. It involves Hamlet's mother, and its ambiguity is such that it might refer simply to her "o'er-hasty marriage." Indeed, a good many critics have so understood it, and in consequence pondered problems of Hamlet's inadequate motivation and excessive emotion. The charge can in fact mean three different things: that Gertrude married improperly in marrying her husband's brother, and that too rapidly; that she committed adultery with Claudius prior to the death of the elder Hamlet; and that she not merely committed such adultery but was implicated in the murder as well. Now, the first interpretation is clearly untenable. It is preposterous that the Ghost should inform Hamlet of what he already knows all too well (there needs no ghost come from the grave to tell him this) and that Hamlet should respond to such stale news with shock and indignation ("O most pernicious woman!"). The metaphor in which the charge is couched is worth noting:

> But virtue, as it never will be moved
> Though lewdness court it in a shape of Heaven,
> So Lust, though to a radiant angel linked,
> Will sate itself in a celestial bed
> And prey on garbage. (I, v, 53–57)

The analogy involved here is identical with that in Iachimo's charge of adultery in *Cymbeline,* I, vi, 47 ff.:

> The cloyed will,—
> That satiate yet unsatisfied desire, that tub
> Both fill'd and running,—ravening first the lamb,
> Longs after for the garbage.

The point is put bluntly and literally by Hamlet (V, ii, 64): "whor'd my mother." The second and third interpretations are thus the only reasonable ones; the latter is Hamlet's own until the closet scene.

We have, then, a prince whose king and father has been murdered, whose mother has been seduced by the murderer, possibly even induced to participate in the murder, whose throne has been usurped by the murderer, whose father's ghost has returned to demand vengeance, who is "prompted to [his] revenge by Heaven and Hell"; and we may well wonder at critics who can manage to doubt whether Hamlet has "the motive and the cue for passion" and who never progress beyond Gertrude's first and erroneous conjecture that Hamlet's behavior is in response to his father's death and her o'er-hasty marriage. Indeed, the whole point of the play is that with such extraordinary motivation, Hamlet does not act.

What sort of action is required of him? It is no simple command that the Ghost gives. Hamlet is to avenge the murder and, apparently, the adultery ("Let not the royal bed—"). The manner of revenge is evidently left to his choice, with the provision that he is not to taint his mind nor contrive against his mother. For a man like Hamlet, in Hamlet's circumstances, the execution of these demands is no easy task. Hamlet is no Iago, who "for mere suspicion . . . / Will do as if for surety." He must be certain of the justice of his cause, to kill even a man whom he detests as much as he does Claudius. He must determine what act of vengeance is appropriate and just. He must keep the foul grounds for vengeance in mind in order to act, and if he does keep them so, how shall his mind not be tainted? He must dwell upon the crime of uncle and mother and take vengeance upon one but leave the other to Heaven. Surely there is much here to "puzzle the will."

Finally, are the Ghost's statements true, and his demands just? The demands are just—according to the conventions of the play—if the statements are true; that they are true is attested, so far as the murder is concerned, by the King's aside in III, i, 48 ff., by his behavior at the play, by his very explicit statement of his crime as fratricide, as well as his reasons for committing it, in the prayer-scene. It has been offered in objection to this view that the King does not react to the dumb-show, but this objection fails to account for the passages just mentioned and the fact that he *does* react to the play—indeed, it is his recognition of the image of his crime that sends him to remorseful prayer. The accusation of adultery is confirmed by Gertrude's response to Hamlet's charge in the closet scene (III, iv, 66–67), a charge employing a metaphor in basis the same as those already cited from the Ghost's speech and from *Cymbeline*. Her aside in IV, v, 177 ff. offers further evidence. In addition to his accusations, the Ghost claims to be the spirit of Hamlet's father. Hamlet may doubt the truth of that, and presently does, but we may not.

Since, then, the Ghost speaks truth, we may bend his remarks back upon act I, scene ii to understand it in retrospect. In the light of what we now know, what kind of court is this? It is a court in which deception rules, in which seeming and being, appearance and reality, that within and outward show, have no necessary relation to each other;

in which, consequently, nothing and no one can be surely trusted, and in which, consequently, one must plot and spy, pose and lie. This fact is the very axis of the play: all actions, Hamlet's as well, turn upon it. We are not given this fact fully in the scene, but we are given a good part of it. The first fifteen lines of the King's opening speech contain a pack of lies. The elder Hamlet obviously was not a "dear" brother, for Claudius murdered him. Since he did murder him, there was no such thing as "an auspicious and a dropping eye," etc. Moreover, Claudius's counsel to Hamlet, which has so greatly impressed Wilson Knight, is in fact an attempt to get Hamlet to doff his mourning because it reminds him of his crime. Beneath the guise of kindly counsel, the King's real feelings are betrayed by his indignation:

> But to perséver
> In obstinate condolement is a course
> Of impious stubbornness, 'tis unmanly grief.
> It shows a will most incorrect to Heaven,
> A heart unfortified, a mind impatient,
> An understanding simple and unschooled.
> For what we know must be and is as common
> As any the most vulgar thing to sense,
> What should we in our peevish opposition
> Take it to heart: Fie! 'Tis a fault to Heaven,
> A fault against the dead, a fault to nature,
> To reason most absurd. . . .

This is strong language, considering that the "fault" rebuked is grief for a beloved king and father "but two months dead."

Furthermore—why does Shakespeare show us the granting of Laertes' request—something we might readily have gathered from scene iii—if not to underline the refusal of Hamlet's? And why is Hamlet not permitted to return to Wittenberg, where he would be well out of the way and might wear all the mourning he chose without troubling anyone? Is it simply that since Gertrude desires her son to be near her, the King in honeymoon fashion indulges her desire? Or is it that Hamlet must be kept where he can be watched? Again, when Hamlet pointedly accedes to his mother's request rather than the King's, Claudius accepts the snub as "a loving and a fair reply"; can he possibly think so?

These last points need not be labored; there is other evidence in abundance of the hypocrisy, lying, distrust, and spying prevalent at the court. Act I, scene iii presents us with a brother advising a sister not to trust her lover, the sister in turn advising him to follow his own precepts about chastity, the father giving counsel to the son upon whom he will later set a spy, and finally, the father also advising the daughter not to trust her lover. Act II, scene i shows us the father setting the spy upon his son; the spy is to lie in order to uncover the truth. Much that is subsequent in the play is illustrative of how one may "by indirections find directions out."

The discrepancy between seeming and being, pretense and truth, constitutes, as we said, the axis of the play. Rosencrantz and Guildenstern pretend to be Hamlet's friends to forward the King's aims; Ophelia pretends to be alone; the players are to be used as a pretended entertainment of Hamlet, with the real purpose of sounding him; the Queen pretends to be alone in her closet; the voyage to England is a pretended mission; the final duel is a pretense. The note is struck with Hamlet's first long speech: "Seems, Madam! Nay, it is." Indeed, the whole speech is a development of the opposition. The note is struck many times thereafter; in Hamlet's first soliloquy, in which he compares his mother's apparent love for her husband with her real lack of it; in the themes of scene iii, as we saw; in the first five lines of Hamlet's speech to the Ghost in scene iv and in Horatio's words, lines 69–74; in "my most seeming-virtuous queen," "one may smile, and smile, and be a villain," and "put an antic disposition on," all within scene v. We may perhaps leave this point; to cite all of the instances would be to cite a great part of the text.

In the uncertainties of this court, Claudius and Hamlet are at stalemate. Claudius can do nothing to Hamlet beyond keeping him at court. Hamlet is loved by the people and by Gertrude, a circumstance that keeps Claudius from overt action even when he has the best of reasons for it (IV, vii, 9 ff.). At this point, although he may be annoyed by Hamlet, he has no reason whatever for action; he needs only to pretend a paternal affection. Hamlet, in turn, however much he despises Claudius, must suppress his real bitterness and disgust; however much he may be sickened by a world of sham and pretense, in which solemn vows and shows of affection are meaningless, he can do nothing but hold his tongue and wish for the release of death. He is, moreover, alone and friendless until the advent of Horatio; there is no one to whom he can unburden his heart. Can he trust Ophelia when his mother's professions of love could so quickly be proved hollow? (It is this thought, doubtless, that underlies his behavior toward Ophelia as she describes it in II, i.)

At the outset, then, Hamlet and Claudius are in equilibrium and inert. Even with news of the appearance of his father's ghost, Hamlet can at most merely "doubt some foul play"; till he definitely knows something, his soul must "sit still." It is only when the Ghost informs him that he is in a position to act. And here he makes his first mistake. He has two courses open to him: action immediate, direct, and open, taken without thought, or action calculated—and therefore delayed, and therefore needing to be kept secret. He chooses the latter. It is not strange that he should have, in view of his nature, and indirection is a plausible course in a court so full of indirection. What would have happened had he chosen the former? We are shown what would have happened in the episode of Laertes's assault on the palace; indeed, the chief function of the episode is to illustrate this, for Laertes might have been brought to conspire with the King in a dozen different ways. The King is but shakily set on his throne. Laertes is merely a noble, his father was merely Lord Chamberlain, his actions are founded on mere rumor and suspicion, and yet he is able immediately to raise a mob of followers who wish him for king—a mob so considerable and formidable as to overcome the palace guards and win into the very presence of the King. How would it have been then with Hamlet, a greatly beloved prince, with a King for his father, with witnesses at hand to attest to the appearance of his father's ghost?

But Hamlet chooses calculated action, which implies secrecy, which implies plots and stratagems, as well as pretense. His basic stratagem is of course feigned insanity; we see him considering it tentatively in I, v, and he puts his plan into effect in the interim between Acts I and II. In feigning he is simply playing the favorite game of the court, and using it to turn the tables, so to speak. Why insanity? Thus ran the old story, of course; but Shakespeare never follows a story simply to follow it. In truth we do wrong to the piece by raising the question; it is an essential detail to alter which would be to alter everything else; everything else is predicated upon it, it is a donnée. Even so, Shakespeare has done something to establish its probability. Clearly it was suggested by Horatio:

> What if it tempt you toward the flood, my lord,
> Or to the dreadful summit of the cliff
> That beetles o'er his base into the sea,
> And there assume some other horrible form
> That might deprive your sovereignty of reason
> And draw you into madness? Think of it.
> The very place puts toys of desperation,
> Without more motive, into every brain
> That looks so many fathoms to the sea
> And hears it roar beneath.

There is no doubt that these words made a great impression upon Hamlet. The expressed distrust of the Ghost becomes the reason for his initial delay and for his decision to use the play as a test. While the play is certainly a test of Claudius's guilt, it is primarily a test of the genuineness and veracity of the Ghost, which Claudius's reaction simply confirms. The question whether

> The spirit that I have seen
> May be the Devil, and the Devil hath power
> To assume a pleasing shape. Yea, and perhaps,
> Out of my weakness and my melancholy,
> As he is very potent with such spirits,
> Abuses me to damn me.

is resolved with

> I'll take the ghost's word for a thousand pound.

Although the feigned madness is properly treated as a donnée, there are certain advantages in the pose for one in Hamlet's circumstances; perhaps they are worth considering even though they have no warrant in the text. To act naturally while possessed of such knowledge and purpose as he has would be very difficult, as Chambers and others have observed, and the merest slip would expose him to suspicion; the pose obviates both the difficulty and the risk. More importantly, the mad are without rational purpose; what better disguise for a man with a purpose? Even more importantly, the mad are in a certain sense free, in that they may do anything and everything at any time and cannot be called to account for it, whereas the sane may be forced to explain actions dictated by reason.

Of the assumed madness we are shown—with one exception, the fight in Ophelia's grave—the verbal rather than the physical side. That there was a physical side we know; the King remarks that neither "the exterior nor the inward man / Resembles that it was" (II, ii, 6-7) and speaks of him as "Grating so harshly all his days of quiet / With turbulent and dangerous lunacy" (III, i, 34), and there are other indications. We have nothing to support this, however, in the represented actions—nothing of Saxo's and Belleforest's antic heroes. Shakespeare's Hamlet does not besmear himself with filth and ashes, sharpen sticks and hooks, pretend to be a cock in the Queen's chambers, or cut Polonius's body to pieces, boil them, and feed them to the hogs. Yet physical manifestations of "madness" there undoubtedly were; although they are part of the plot, they are not part of the scenario, that is, are not represented on stage.

This raises the question of what other parts of the plot may have gone unrepresented; for the moment, however, we must look into Hamlet's madness as it is set before us. Consider all of Hamlet's speeches throughout the play. There is no hint of madness in any of the asides, in any of the soliloquies; there is none in his speeches to Horatio or any other whom he trusts. To whom are his "mad" speeches addressed? To his enemies or to those whom he does not trust. In what does his "madness" in those speeches consist? In actual excess of rationality, in sheer brilliance of wit, in passages of thought connected by a threat so subtle as to escape detection by inferior minds. Speeches between which we can see no connection we assume to be disconnected; so it is with those who think Hamlet mad. Sometimes—very seldom—they have inklings of the connection, like Polonius in II, ii, 211 ff., or Claudius in III, i, 171-172. But the connection is always present. Hamlet uses the device of deliberate misunderstanding, based upon puns or other equivocations, to balk questions:

Pol.   What do you read, my lord?
Haml. Words, words, words.
Pol.   What is the matter, my lord?
Haml. Between who?

He uses fantastic paradoxes and sophistries:

Haml. ...Farewell, dear mother.
King. Thy loving father, Hamlet.
Haml. My mother; father and mother is man and wife, man and wife is one flesh, and so, my mother.

He uses "metaphysical" conceits, as in this passage where he is simply capping conceits with Rosencrantz and Guildenstern:

Haml. ... were it not that I have bad dreams.
Guil. Which dreams are indeed ambition, for the very substance of the ambitious is merely the shadow of a dream.
Haml. A dream itself is but a shadow.
Ros.   Truly, and I hold ambition to be of so light and airy a quality that it is but a shadow's shadow.
Haml. Then are our beggars bodies, and our monarchs and outstretched heroes the beggars' shadows.

Notice, moreover, the concealed argument, which is a *reductio ad absurdum* of the position advanced by Rosenkrantz and Guildenstern. He "cannot reason?"

He uses in addition irony, innuendo, a kind of super-Euphuism with Osric—in brief, every conceivable device to frustrate the inquisitive.

How can this be real madness? Those who think Hamlet really mad do so because they import their own definitions of madness into the play, as some think him merely neurotic or perfectly sane because they import their own definitions of neurosis or sanity. All of this is completely illicit. The play defines one test of madness for us:

> Bring me to the test,
> And I the matter will re-word, which madness
> Would gambol from. (III, iv, 142-4)

This is a test that Hamlet certainly can pass.

Moreover, the feigned madness of Hamlet is sharply contrasted with the real madness of Ophelia. Her thought consists only in short passages of association, centering chiefly on the two recurrent themes of death and faithless love. Compare Lear, who is also mad; in his mad period there is the same shuttling back and forth between fixed themes. Compare Othello when his passion drives him to the brink of madness; you will find the same thing. But Hamlet—if we are to abide by the evidence of the play—is sane. That "wounded name" which his dying voice asks Horatio to clear can involve only three things: his "madness," his killing of Polonius, his killing of the King; and that name can be cleared only by explanation of his real sanity, of his motives for pretense, of what occasioned his killing of both men.

Hamlet, then, must be considered sane. But, as we saw, he made a wrong choice at the beginning; had Laertes (or shall we say, Macbeth or Hotspur) been in his shoes, we should have had a one act play. He is a bookish man, as the metaphors of his first speech after encountering the ghost make clear, as, indeed, his writing in his tables makes clear, for he records the unforgettable. He is a thoughtful, deliberative man; he can act, indeed, but—at first—not without thought. It is a great irony of the play that his first commitment to the Ghost is

> Haste me to know't, that I, with wings as swift
> As meditation or the thoughts of love
> May sweep to my revenge.

It is precisely meditation and thought that forbid him haste. Shakespeare's major tragic figures fall into error, not through flaws, but through their virtues. A man of virtue is thrown into circumstances in which his virtue is his undoing. Hamlet is being asked, most solemnly, to do something in opposition to his fundamental nature; he responds in accordance with his fundamental nature. What a difference there is between that "Haste me to know't" and, at the end of that very scene,

> The time is out of joint. Oh, cursèd spite
> That ever I was born to set it right!

We may spend too much thought upon this question, however, for it is not the true question of the play. The question is not one of *delay because of*—and this is where most critics have gone astray—but *delay as cause;* that is, of what happens *in consequence of delay* when action should have been immediate. Hamlet later learns this:

> Rightly to be great
> Is not to stir without great argument,
> But greatly to find quarrel in a straw
> When honor's at the stake. How stand I then,

> That have a father killed, a mother stained,
> Excitements of my reason and my blood,
> And let all sleep. . . .

In his major works Shakespeare has the convenient habit of stating clearly and repeatedly the basic probability of his play. He states it in the speech of the Player King:

> I do believe you think what now you speak,
> But what we do determine oft we break.
> Purpose is but the slave to memory,
> Of violent birth but poor validity. . . .
>
> What to ourselves in passion we propose,
> The passion ending, doth the purpose lose.
> The violence of either grief or joy
> Their most enactures with themselves destroy.

He states it again when Claudius speaks to Laertes:

King. Laertes, was your father dear to you? . . .
Laer. Why ask you this?
King. Not that I think you did not love your father,
But that I know love is begun by time,
And that I see, in passages of proof,
Time qualifies the spark and fire of it.
There lives within the very flame of love
A kind of wick or snuff that will abate it.
And nothing is at a line goodness still,
For goodness, growing to a pleurisy,
Dies in his own too much. That we would do
We should do when we would; for this "would" changes
And hath abatements and delays as many
And there are tongues, are hands, are accidents,
And then this "should" is like a spendthrift sigh
That hurts by easing.

Hamlet himself is made to state it in the soliloquy of III, i; a soliloquy which, despite general opinion, cannot possibly be a meditation on whether he ought to take his own life, for he has dismissed that question in his first soliloquy. It is instead a meditation on the way in which thought ("conscience") can baffle all enterprises, even great ones; and the point is argued from two examples, the first of which has nothing to do with suicide but with the problem of whether to remain passive or to take action under misfortune and of which is the nobler course. The second, while it involves suicide, is in perfectly general terms: even with the inducement of release from an intolerable life men hesitate to kill themselves for fear of unknown consequences (it is

the generality of the consideration, incidentally, that permits Hamlet
to speak of the "bourne" from which "no traveller returns" despite the
fact that he has seen one return). The conclusion is very clear:

> Thus conscience doth make cowards of us all;
> And thus the native hue of resolution
> Is sicklied o'er with the pale cast of thought,
> And enterprises of great pitch and moment
> With this regard their currents turn awry
> And lose the name of action.

We have now worked out some of the chief difficulties of individual
scenes; the rest may be made clear as we proceed. Suppose we put
Hamlet back into the play, and back into his proper role in the play.

Hamlet and Claudius have generally been treated as static figures in
static relation. This is of course the consequence of abstracting them
from the play, so that all acts and changes become merely evidence of
traits entering into a description of character; all kinetic elements
become, as it were, telescoped into stasis, and plot becomes merely the
gradual revelation of something which is itself stationary. To see how
this violates the play we need only to consider their respective speeches
in succession. At the beginning Claudius—though his speeches are
untrustworthy, as we saw—is prepared to be gracious to Hamlet, and
publicly acknowledges him as his "son" and successor to the throne.
When we next see him, in II, ii, he has been sufficiently troubled and
puzzled by Hamlet's "madness" to send for Rosencrantz and Guildenstern. He is by no means content with Gertrude's conjecture that its
cause is "no other but the main"; he wishes to discover whether it is
"aught to us unknown," and grasps eagerly at Polonius's hypothesis.
When this hypothesis is disproved, he begins to doubt the madness
itself ("what he spake, though it lacked form a little / Was not like
madness") and fears that what Hamlet is hatching in his mind "will be
some danger." It is at this point that—no longer wishing Hamlet to
remain at court—he devises the plan of the voyage to England. When
Polonius proposes the interview with the Queen, the King agrees, for
"Madness in great ones must not unwatch'd go." Struck to heart by the
image of his crime in the play scene, he realizes that his secret is
known, reacts with fear, fury, and remorse, and prepares the document that is to send Hamlet to execution in England. After the death of
Polonius he expresses his feelings toward Hamlet in the soliloquy which
closes IV, iii: "like the hectic in my blood he rages." We need go no
further; that there is change is manifest.

The changes in Hamlet are, quite naturally, far more various and
extensive. There are, to begin with, all of his changing relationships to
other personages of the play. Horatio he seems to trust increasingly: if

his confidence in I, v, is somewhat qualified (though this may be due to the presence of others), by act III, scene ii, two months later, he has told Horatio at least something of the Ghost's words and of the circumstances of the murder, and now asks aid in ascertaining the King's guilt (59–62); shows further trust in IV, vi; has confided all by V, ii, 80, including the matter of his mother's adultery (l. 64); and ultimately entrusts Horatio with the telling of the whole story. In his relationship with Ophelia Hamlet moves from distrust on purely general grounds—from, that is, a mere generalizing on his mother's inconstancy ("Frailty, thy name is woman!") to distrust founded on particulars in III, i. The long perusal of her face during his visit to her chamber seems to be the effect of a desperate hope that she is as true within as she is fair without (compare the "Ha, ha! are you honest? . . . Are you fair?" of III, i), and his sigh seems to indicate abandonment of that hope. There is no need to suppose with Coleridge and others that some stage-business betrays the presence of the King and Polonius in the "nunnery" scene, nor is there any indication that Hamlet detects it. Hamlet cannot trust her and so must play the madman. He does so from his very first words to her; it is only in his soliloquy that he speaks tenderly. She gives him particular grounds for distrust in this scene, for while she reproaches him with unkindness, it is she who has denied him access; furthermore, though pretending to read and meditate, she has come provided with all the gifts he has given her. Rosencrantz and Guildenstern he obviously views with increasing distrust. He greets them cordially enough at first, but either suspects or has learned that they were sent for. Once he has brought them to admit that they were summoned, he seems briefly to trust them, for he is apparently at point to reveal the secret of his madness (II, ii, 396) when Polonius interrupts. They must have revealed his selection of the play, perhaps even his interpolation of a speech, to Claudius; otherwise the King's great "choler" and being "much offended" with Hamlet is unintelligible. If so, the "choler" itself would show Hamlet that they had betrayed him. At any rate, he voices his distrust in the recorder passage; later, he would trust them as he would "adders fang'd"; ultimately, he can dismiss his engineering of their deaths with "they are not near my conscience." Laertes he seems to have no great connection with at first. His fury in the graveyard he explains himself ("sure, the bravery of his grief did put me / Into a towering passion"), and it is understandable in view of his preoccupation with outward show and "that within which passeth show." He repents and decides to court Laertes's favor. The "Give me your pardon" speech of V, ii has been called hypocritical; what is overlooked is Hamlet's need to persist in his role as madman. If hypocrisy is looked for, it may easily be found in Laertes's ensuing speech. He readily forgives Laertes at the end. In his relationship with Gertrude, finally, Hamlet moves from an initial disgust with her inconstancy to horror at her adultery and possible complicity in the murder. Once he has realized her innocence in the latter and has seen her conscience at work, he entrusts her with the secret of his "madness," offering her both mental and physical proof of his sanity (III, iv, 139 ff.). It must be noted that she never betrays Hamlet; in her narrative to Claudius she conceals much and lies about most of the rest. Hamlet has succeeded in making her feel "those thorns that in her bosom lodge," for she is still plagued by guilt in IV, v, 17-20.

There are also changes in Hamlet himself. He changes in his attitude toward death: it is at first something greatly to be desired; in the graveyard scene he discovers that it has another side; later, it is "that sergeant . . . strict in his arrest," even though it is a way to "felicity" and though to live is to "in this harsh world draw thy breath in pain." He changes in his view of his task: he is first sure that he has grounds for revenge, then doubts his grounds, then confirms his grounds, then seeks for the appropriate act of revenge (the prayer scene), and in between meditates on the "event" or consequence of action. He changes in his view of human action itself. He first sees himself as a solitary agent who must plot; presently realizes that others are plotting against him also, and thinks he must plot more deeply still—"delve one yard below their mines / And blow them at the moon"; and finally, after the English voyage, comes to understand that "our deep plots do pall," that rashness is praiseworthy, that divinity and Providence have a part in all human actions and fortunes (V, ii, 6-11; 48; 230-35) and that "readiness is all." Had he been earlier what he is at this point, he would not have delayed.

Hamlet's actions, thoughts, and feelings are not intelligible by themselves; they can be understood only in the context of the actions of others—in particular, of course, the actions of Claudius. For Hamlet and Claudius are protagonist and antagonist, hero and adversary. The plot of the play is a protracted duel; Hamlet himself recognizes that what he is engaged in is a matter of "the pass and fell incenséd points / Of mighty opposites" (V, ii, 61-62). In this duel Claudius makes six passes, each of which Hamlet meets with parry and counterthrust. These "passes" or stratagems utilize every conceivable instrument against Hamlet: friends, mistress, mother, even Hamlet himself, in that they involve his predilections for drama and fencing and indeed, in the supposed mission to England, his very rank. The stratagems have, to be sure, different purposes, according to the state of Claudius's knowledge; the earliest are merely attempts to discover the cause of Hamlet's madness, whereas the later ones—those which follow on the play scene—have deadly intent.

Each pass produces a situation at once advantageous and disadvantageous for Claudius, as each counterthrust does for Hamlet. Thus the first pass—the use of Rosencrantz and Guildenstern to sound Hamlet—fails in its purpose, and informs Hamlet that the pair are working in the King's interests and that his pose of madness is under scrutiny; on the other hand, it eliminates the easy hypotheses and sharpens the King's interest in causes "to us unknown." Hamlet's counterthrust—in this instance as in the next, the baffling of his interrogators by persisting in his pose—foils Claudius's intent, but it also convinces him of the need for further investigation, and leads him to accept Polonius's proposal to use Ophelia. This device in turn fails, but it permits him to reject the hypothesis that love is involved, to suspect the madness itself, to surmise that danger is involved, and thus to hatch the plan of the voyage to England. Hamlet's counterthrust, if it foils the King, also exposes the Prince to closer scrutiny and hence greater danger; the guise adopted to shift attention from his actions is actually drawing attention to them. The third pass—the stratagem of sounding Hamlet through his amusements—also involves both success and failure: if it exposes the King to Hamlet's counterthrust, the riposte which it provokes reveals Hamlet's knowledge of the murder. At this point the opponents stand on equally firm ground, prepared for action, for while Hamlet has proved the veracity of the Ghost, the King too has found a cause for prompt and definite action. After Hamlet fails to kill him at prayer—another matter of seeming and being, by the way, for the King is only apparently praying—the initiative passes to Claudius. So it is with the other three stratagems and their counter-stratagems: the conversation with the Queen, the voyage to England, the final plot with Laertes, all involve mingled success and failure on both sides.

In a curious way the situations of protagonist and antagonist parallel each other, for each seeks a sure ground for action, contemplates what action should be taken once the ground is established, with the hampering proviso that certain consequences must be averted; each, moreover, is at certain points in possession of knowledge which the other is unaware that he possesses; and, as we just saw, each by his actions produces results both more and less than those looked for. The whole plot, were we to exhibit it in detail, would be seen to be one of extreme complexity; were it fully represented on stage, the play would perhaps be twice its present length.

But Shakespeare does not choose so to represent it; indeed, his extreme abridgment of it in his representation has been at the bottom of many problems of interpretation. We have already observed that Hamlet's physical antics as a madman have been suppressed—for, among other reasons, the very good one that they would have tended to endanger his tragic stature, perhaps even convert him into a comic figure. But many other things are suppressed. What happened—aside from Hamlet's "going mad"—in the interval between acts I and II? What were Hamlet's thoughts and feelings, what were the reactions of others in that period? What led Hamlet to suspect that Rosencrantz and Guildenstern were sent for? What, step by step, produced his increasing distrust of them? Did they betray his selection of the play and his writing of a speech to Claudius? At what point did Hamlet take Horatio into his full confidence? How and when did Hamlet gain knowledge of the projected voyage to England and the "letters seal'd?" Etc., etc.

Not all of this is important; some of it undoubtedly is. But, given full representation of the plot, the melodramatic elements would have swamped the more serious ones. With the internal obstacles of thought and passion obscured—for both Hamlet and Claudius labor against internal as well as external obstacles—the play would have turned into a mere adventure story. It bears some resemblance, in fact, to *The Mark of Zorro*, for Zorro also assumes a pose to disguise his real powers and purposes. Shakespeare, however, forewent the superficial excitements of a savage contest to study the issues, problems, and passions which underlie action. In so doing, he gave his play tragic dimension.

3

CRITICS

LONGINUS AND REYNOLDS

Few are likely to protest the association of "Longinus" and Sir Joshua Reynolds. The work of Saintsbury, Collins, Roberts, Monk, and Henn has rendered it acceptable to consider Longinus important for the history of English aesthetics, and to regard Reynolds as one of the chief instances, or if we except Burke, perhaps the chief instance, of his influence. The circumstantial differences which separate so widely the Greek rhetorician from the British painter appear to be more than canceled, in the general view, by affinities of their artistic doctrines and even likenesses in the spiritual characteristics of the two men as these have sometimes been inferred from their doctrines. "In his *Academic Discourses*," writes John Churton Collins, "Sir Joshua Reynolds, if I recollect rightly, only once mentions Longinus; but, whether consciously or not, there is scarcely one of them in which he does not recall and recall closely the *De Sublimitate*. There is the same noble conception of the character and functions of art, of its relation to the divine, of its relation to nature, of the spirit in which its study should be approached and pursued. There is the same union of the critic and the enthusiast. He speaks of Michelangelo precisely as Longinus speaks of Homer. His definition of the sublime, and his criteria for testing it, are identical with those of the Greek critic. If Reynolds had not studied Longinus with the greatest care and the greatest sympathy, we can only assume that experience, reflection, and genius, operating on similar temperaments, have conducted both these critics independently to the same truths, and inspired them to express themselves in the same language."[1] A. O. Prickard more succinctly says much of the same thing: "Sir Joshua

This essay originally appeared as the Introduction to *Longinus on the Sublime and Sir Joshua Reynolds Discourses on Art*, University Classics (Chicago: Packard Co., 1945).

1. John Churton Collins, *Studies in Poetry and Criticism* (London, 1905), pp. 217–18.

Reynolds draws from our author [Longinus] many of the precepts laid down in the *Discourses,* and often all but quotes his words."[2]

It may consequently be supposed that the object of the juxtaposition here of Longinus and Reynolds is to facilitate the observation of their similarities. Yet the intention is rather the contrary: paradoxically and seriously as well, it may be said that these similars are here placed side by side to encourage a consideration of their differences. For the similarities, it can be argued, are incidental and superficial, while the differences are essential and fundamental. Indeed, the relation in which literary history has placed Longinus and Reynolds affords a striking instance of the tendency of critics to employ similar statements and even similar arguments in the construction of systems sharply different, and of the tendency of literary historians to associate or distinguish critical systems almost exclusively in terms of the doctrines which are held to be characteristic of the systems in question.

The broad "similarities" between Longinus and Reynolds are obvious enough. Much might be added to Collins's observations: both writers are concerned with theories of sublimity in art, i.e., are interested in *qualities* rather than *species* of art; both treat of the faculties requisite to the artist; both hold that great works of art should be taken as communicating inspiration to the artist, rather than as affording models for his strict copy; both are importantly concerned with the faculty of taste; and both propose what is in effect the famous criterion of *quod semper quod ubique.* The list might be indefinitely prolonged; even the remark that Reynolds is frequently paraphrasing Longinus is perfectly correct. There can even be little doubt, moreover, that Longinus influenced Reynolds greatly, whether directly or through the filtration of Boileau. Yet the historical proposition that Longinus influenced Reynolds does not, it should be observed, carry the necessary consequence that Reynolds must be *like* Longinus even in those respects in which he was influenced most strongly. Similarity of statement, moreover, does not always imply a similarity of method, principles, or meaning. Coleridge tells us that he and his friends were struck with the similarity of Hume's *Essay on Association* to the commentary of Aquinas on the *Parva Naturalia,* and indeed Coleridge subsequently unearthed some evidence that Hume knew the earlier work; but the anecdote is pointless except on the supposition that few would be likely to confound the philosophy of Hume with the philosophy of Aquinas. Perhaps it is enough to remark that when philosophic or critical method is reduced to statement, the most opposite philosophers or critics can be brought to coincide, and the most similar to disagree.

2. A. O. Prickard, *Longinus on the Sublime* (Oxford, 1926), p. vi.

If, however, we reflect on the fact that statements can be conclusions from premises, or premises of conclusions, as well as historical events brought about by other historical events—that, in a word, statements may be elements of argument as well as of history—a more fundamental treatment of critical discussion than history or linguistic disciplines may afford appears as a possibility. Such a treatment, in its proper dimensions, could not very well avoid the question of how, in a given system, terms are given their meaning, propositions their truth, and arguments their cogency; indeed, for its proper ground, it would necessarily involve the prior solution of all the most ambitious problems of methodology. In this essay it may suffice merely to suggest some of the possible consequences of such an approach, first by roughly outlining the arguments of the two critics in question, next by considering the respective manner in which their chief problems are formulated, and finally by placing their supposedly similar pronouncements within the contexts thus constructed.

Longinus is concerned with the establishment of an art of which, as an art proper, he considers himself the discoverer; his criticisms of Caecilius, the only predecessor whom he acknowledges, turn on the latter's failure to formulate an art, and, moreover, Longinus's first positive concern is to differentiate the art of the sublime from that of rhetoric, to which it is closely similar in some respects, and to which, apparently, he fears that it may be reduced. The differentiation of the art of the sublime is accomplished in terms of the *author*, the *work*, and the *audience* as these are respectively involved in rhetoric and in the art of the sublime. This triad of terms is fundamental to his inquiry and, in subsequent elaboration, permits the statement of his whole literary doctrine. The art of sublimity differs from rhetoric in that the practitioners of the former are those writers who are held to have the highest intellectual genius; in that the sublime work is characterized by the quality of certain of its parts, whereas the rhetorical work is efficient as a whole; and in that the effect of the sublime upon an audience is involuntary transport, whereas the effect of rhetoric is voluntary accession. The construction of an art of sublimity begins with the effect, as that which is first known; and it proceeds by arguing the qualities which the work must possess in order to produce such an effect, and, these determined, by deriving from them in turn the qualities requisite to the author of sublime works. It is through discovery of these latter qualities, i.e., of the author, that the statement of technical means—i.e., means for the acquisition of these qualities— is possible; and possession of these qualities, given a natural power of expression, carries with it, as necessary consequences, sublimity of discourse and the transport of audiences. These qualities, moreover, are not peculiar, in Longinus's view, to writers and speakers,—they are the distinguishing marks of men "who almost approach the god"—and they can be illustrated by reference to Ajax and Alexander as well as to Plato and Homer. When possessed in a high degree, therefore, they might be said to be transcendental virtues which, reflected in speech, lend to language their loftiness and thus over-whelm audiences; like the virtues, they depend in part upon natural capacity, in part upon practice, and demand liberty as their essential condition. Consequently, the province of the art of sublimity becomes, for Longinus, the sphere in which such virtues bear on language.

The fundamental question which Longinus raises, it should be noted, concerns not one, or several, but all of the arts of discourse, since the effect of *ekstasis* is produced, not merely by poets or rhetoricians, but by historians, philosophers, and prophets as well. To raise such a question is to commit oneself to one of two possible answers: either the cause of such an effect is, whether single or complex, common to all the arts of discourse, or the cause differs for each art. Longinus's differentiation of sublimity from rhetoric deter-mines the question in favor of the former alternative; for if the art of rhetoric of itself does not effect *ekstasis*, clearly it is in virtue of some other principle that rhetorical works at times achieve the sublime. This raises the question whether such a principle is natural or artificial; and Longinus consequently addresses himself to prove that an art of sublimity is possible. His conception of an "art" may be gathered from his proof of the existence of an art of sublimity: an art is some system or method, supplementing or improving natural means to a given end, and communicable by instruction. If art is so conceived, the require-ments which the framer of an art must fulfill are, as Longinus remarks, twofold: (1) he must state what the sublime is (and it is this which affords the matter for the first part of his treatise, the sublime being defined ultimately and most precisely in terms of its five sources [*pēgai*]), and (2) he must state the means by which it may be achieved (and it is this question which is resolved in the latter part of his work). Caecilius, according to Longinus, had failed to produce an art, since in respect of the first requirement he had defined sublimity only by example, and since he had omitted the second requirement entirely.

Unlike Edmund Burke, who finds the sources of sublimity in qualities of the subject-matter of art, Longinus finds them in the faculties of the author. In each case the discovery results from the argument rather than from any other cause: if we differentiate the emotions of the audience, as Burke does, in terms which permit natural as well as artificial objects to be considered as their causes, the qualitative differentiations in the objects are responsible for the qualitative differentiations in the emotions; i.e., the source of the sublime is in the subject-matter, not in the art; if, on the other hand, we are concerned like Longinus with an effect which, although it is similar to certain effects produced by natural objects, is itself a peculiar consequence of speech, the source must lie within the art and thus, given the other Longinian determinations, in the human faculties relative to discourse.

The basis for the five sources of the sublime is fairly obvious. Given a subject, conception, passion, and expression are requisite; the third of these, however, is threefold, for expression deals with words, and words can be considered either as signs, simple or combined, or merely as sounds. Words considered as signs can be taken non-syntactically or syntactically; in the former case they appear as constitutive of such modes of discourse as question, prayer, oath, etc. (i.e., figures of thought, since such modes are prior to and independent of any syntactical consideration); in the latter case they appear as constituted of grammatical elements (i.e., figures of language, such as asyndeton, hyperbaton, polyptoton, etc.); Longinus includes both under the head of Figures, the third source of the sublime. If words are regarded as simple, two possibilities again result: signs may literally signify, when the choice of words becomes one of synonyms, or signs may involve comparison, when the choice of words becomes one of tropes and metaphors. These are problems strictly of diction, and their solution affords the fourth source of the sublime. Finally, words may be regarded as sounds constitutive of harmony and rhythm; this is synthesis or composition in its narrowest sense, if differentiated from the other sources, or if considered relatively to them, composition in its broadest sense.

Since sublimity is not a function of the whole discourse, and hence not of its form, there can be for Longinus no derivation of criteria from the definition of a literary species or kind, after the manner of Aristotle; and since, again, discourse is held sharply separate from its subject-matter, there can be no derivation of criteria from the subject-matter, after the manner of Plato. Of a possible tetrad of terms—*subject-matter, author, work,* and *audience*—only two remain, the author and the audience; and Longinus employs both to provide criteria for the working artist; the artist is to imagine how Homer and the other great wits would have written in his stead, i.e., how they would have operated as artists, and he is also to imagine how they would have reacted as his audience. These touchstones are substitutes for the true, but to the working artist somewhat inconvenient, criterion of time.[3]

The span of years over which the *Discourses* of Reynolds were delivered has led some commentators to consider them either as

3. For a more detailed analysis of the argument of Longinus see pp. 161–89.

fragmentary and occasional, or as evincing progressive alterations of Reynolds's original position. However, while it would undoubtedly be excessive to claim that the program of their construction had been completed before the delivery of the First Discourse in 1769, it is well to remember that a philosophic system derives its unity, not from the time of its utterance, but from the compendency of its parts; and that while it is possible to interpret these addresses as exhibiting an increasing adherence to or defection from Reynolds's earliest doctrines of art, it is equally possible, and perhaps preferable, to regard them as evincing logical rather than historical development.

The problem with which Reynolds is concerned is the education of the painter; and unlike Longinus, Reynolds differentiates the phases through which the artist must pass in the development of his faculties, and discovers them to pose different problems requiring different methods of solution. The stages through which the artist passes are three in number, as determined by the most general differentiation of the parts of painting, and are formulable in terms of the powers of the student which are characteristically developed in a given stage, and in terms of the nature of his instructor. The first stage is, in Reynolds's phrase, the "grammar" of the art, "a general preparation for whatever species of the art the student may afterward choose for his more particular application;" and it includes drawing, modelling, and coloring. It is, in his view, a period involving "implicit obedience to the rules of art," and the student is strictly cautioned against any transgression of this apprenticeship; during this period, the instructor is a particular master. The second stage, "still a time of subjection and discipline," is one in which the student, now empowered of expression, amasses a stock of ideas for expression; and in this period it is his business "to learn all that has been known and done before his own time;" his master now "is the Art itself"; and whereas the earlier stage had required submission to a single master, the second, requiring submission to *all*, thereby demands submission to no particular one; that is, imitation of the manner of no one painter must shut out "the variety and abundance of Nature." The third stage frees the student "from subjection to any authority, but what he shall himself judge to be supported by reason." Of the artist in this stage Reynolds says:

Confiding now in his own judgment, he will consider and separate those different principles to which different modes of beauty owe their original. In the former period he sought only to know and combine excellence, wherever it was to be found, into one idea of perfection: in this, he learns, what requires the most attentive survey and the most subtle disquisition, to discriminate perfections that are incompatible with each other.
He is from this time to regard himself as holding the same rank with

those masters whom he before obeyed as teachers; and as exercising a sort of sovereignty over those rules which have hitherto restrained him. Comparing now no longer the performances of Art with each other, but examining the Art itself by the standard of nature, he corrects what is erroneous, supplies what is scanty, and adds by his own observation what the industry of his predecessors may have left wanting to perfection. Having well established his judgment, and stored his memory, he may now without fear try the power of his imagination.

In this stage "Nature herself is not to be too closely copied," for "the mere copier of nature can never produce anything great"; rather, Reynolds remarks, "The wish of the genuine painter must be more extensive; instead of endeavoring to amuse mankind with the minute neatness of his imitations, he must endeavor to improve them by the grandeur of his ideas; instead of seeking praise, by deceiving the superficial sense of the spectator, he must strive for fame, by captivating the imagination."

The entry of the term *imagination* into the discussion permits Reynolds both the statement and the solution of his two leading problems—the problems connected with the highest excellence in art and those connected with the highest sensibility to art, or in a word, the problems of the grand style and of taste, for imagination is involved in both since it, rather than perception, discovers to the artist the abstract Beauty which is the leading principle of the grand style, and since it, rather than reason, is the principle of taste. The term as Reynolds uses it, one must note, carries none of its ordinary, and none even of its usual philosophical, meanings. The artist who is ready to try the power of his imagination is liberated from Nature, but not in the sense that he is free to follow whimsy, to depict the monstrous and impossible, or to transcribe celestial visions. What Reynolds opposes to Nature (i.e., the particular objects of sense) is not a supernal perfection but "a perfect state of Nature"; the ideal Beauty is achieved by the artist who "corrects nature by herself, her imperfect state by her more perfect." The ideal, thus, is earthly; "This great ideal perfection and beauty are not to be sought in the heavens, but upon the earth. They are about us, and upon every side of us." Nor is the artist the possessor of mysterious and celestial gifts; rather, says Reynolds, "his eye being enabled to distinguish the accidental deficiencies, excrescences, and deformities of things, from their general figures, he makes out an abstract idea of their forms more perfect than any one original; and what may seem a paradox, he learns to design naturally by drawing his figures unlike to any one object." Whereas for Longinus the sources of the sublime lie in human faculties, for Reynolds it is the subject-matter, as constituted by the imagination, which communicates enthusiasm to both artist and spectator, and which guarantees the great effect. "When a man once possesses this idea in its perfection, there is no danger but that he will be sufficiently warmed by it himself, and be able to warm and ravish everyone else."

The principle of general ideas informs not only the sphere of exercise of the artistic faculties—the departments, that is, of the art—but the faculties themselves, i.e., invention, composition, expression, coloring, and drapery. Indeed, a comparable principle of generalization obtains for each term of the tetrad of terms upon which Reynolds constructs his theory; for "as the painter, by bringing together in one piece those beauties which are dispersed among a great variety of individuals, produces a figure more beautiful than can be found in nature, so that artist who can unite in himself the excellences of the various great painters, will approach nearer to perfection than any of his masters;" comparably, the "fire of the artist's own genius, operating upon these materials which have been thus diligently collected [by imitation], will enable him to make new combinations, perhaps superior to what had been ever before in the possession of the art," i.e., the work itself abstracts from the accidents and deficiencies of works which served it as models; and finally, taste itself may be regarded as an abstraction from particularities and accidents of judgment, for of the two parts of taste the one relates to "the general idea of nature," the other "does not belong so much to the external form of things, but is addressed to the mind, and depends upon its original frame, or, to use the expression, the organization of the soul; I mean the imagination and the passions." Thus, whether we speak of subject-matter, artist, work, or spectator, the general is opposed to the particular, and this opposition is fundamental not only to the definition of each of these terms, but to the hierarchy of values from which Reynolds derives his criteria. Moreover, the general is connected with the general, the particular with the particular, from term to term of the tetrad; i.e., the highest faculty of the artist is related to the highest subject-matter, the highest excellence of the work, and the highest taste, and so on.

With this much as a crude background, we may more concisely examine the two critics in terms of their diverse formulations of their principal problems and in terms of the consequences which follow on their formulations. Longinus poses the question of what causes underlie an effect which the greatest works of all literature achieve. Since, as we have remarked, Longinus views himself as the founder of the art, and since the effect proceeds from no one of the linguistic arts, prior instances of the sublime must have been due chiefly to the extraordinary greatness of the artists, i.e., must have been due to nature, for the greatest proficiency in an art cannot extend beyond the art itself. To make sublimity due chiefly to nature is not to preclude the possibility of an art of the sublime, but it is to assign to art the secondary role of insuring the efficacy of natural powers, or of imitating their efficacy in producing an effect which is the natural consequence of naturally great men employing a natural medium of communication. If, however, the causes of an artistic effect reside solely in the artist, the artist becomes the subject-matter of art; consequently Longinus's dialectic reduces the tetrad of subject-matter, author, work, and audience, to a triad. Moreover, once the sublime has been defined, the audience may be dropped out, since sensitivity and experience, the qualifications of a proper audience, reduce to the qualities of the work, in the observation of which the audience is sensitive and experienced. Again, since powers of discourse are assumed to be natural, Longinus need not examine the phases of development of the artist, as Reynolds does, for that is a matter of art; thus the dialectic can reduce ultimately to a play between those faculties of the artist which can affect his discourse and the work itself. Since the faculties must be over and above any faculty of the specific literary arts, they appear as thought, feeling, and three general powers related to speech; and since the sublime subject-matter is in effect the author himself, the work expressing that subject-matter is regarded as containing signs or reflections of the greatness of the author. Thus "great style is the shadow of a great soul"; and it must be observed that this famous remark is no isolated dictum produced by a flash of insight, but the necessary consequence of the structure of an argument.

Whereas Longinus sets up a single end and inquires how the means of any literary art may be addressed to it, Reynolds considers a single art, differentiated from other arts in terms of its medium, but consisting of diverse skills, styles, and effects, and having diverse subject-matters. If art is considered as the totality of faculties exerted on a given medium, the problem of genius as such—i.e., of extraordinary natural capacity as such—disappears, for even the genius works by rules of art; the problem of the nature of the artist, thus, becomes the problem of the nature of the art, and artists may be differentiated and evaluated only in terms of the parts of the art in which they are competent. Reynolds's problem, thus, is the education of the painter in any department whatsoever of painting. Since the medium is viewed, not according to whether it is "natural" for men to paint, but according to whether skill can be taught or acquired, skill in the use of the medium is first in the order of education, for not only all other practice, but also all other instruction, presupposes it; and the nature of the competency involved in this stage determines the proper instructor—in this instance a particular master, for anyone who has mastered the rudiments of art may impart them to others. All three stages of instruction derive ultimately from the conception of the work of art, for if the work is conceived as a beautiful expression of something, we may distinguish the means of expression, the expressive use of the means, and the subject-matter; the last, it should be noted, is itself constituted by art. Since the subject of painting at its highest not only is produced by, but also in its expression in the work affects, the imagination, the fundamental terms of the dialectic become a tetrad; for the subject-matter of high art is not particular nature, but nature conceived as perfect by the imagination, and judged as beautiful by taste, so that the faculties requisite to the artist are clearly defined. Similarly, taste itself is developed by art. In brief, Reynolds views subject-matter, artist, work, and, in the sense we have suggested, spectator too, as amenable to art.

In the light of the foregoing argument, it is clear that Longinus and Reynolds are not only dissimilar, but quite unrelated to each other. They do not deal with the same critical problem; they make different assumptions; and they pursue different methods of argument. Longinus views the products of several arts in terms of a single effect; Reynolds views all the effects of a single art. Longinus conceives of the powers of the sublime speaker, including the "gift of expression" as natural; for Reynolds the "language," even, of painting is taught by art, and in general all the powers of the great artist are developed by art and are reducible to art. The effect of *ekstasis*, for Longinus, is dependent upon a greatness in man which is comparable to a greatness in Nature, in the Ocean and in Aetna; the effect of enthusiasm which proceeds from the grand style is for Reynolds the effect of a beauty which is peculiar to the arts. For both, as Collins observes, the sublime "strikes like a blow"; but for Longinus this is proof that sublimity resides in the part, for Reynolds that it consists in the whole, of the work of art.

Indeed, it might be said that they are never so far apart as when they are saying nearly the same thing. When both remark that rules of art are not incompatible with genius, they sound alike; but one may remember that neither the term *art* nor the term *genius* means the same for both. When they speak of sublimity, for that matter, they mean different things; for one defines it ultimately in terms of human faculties, the other in terms of abstract beauty. When one says "the soul is raised by true sublimity, it gains a proud step upwards, it is filled with joy and exultation, as though itself had produced what it hears," and the other echoes it with "the mind swells with an inward pride, and is almost as powerfully affected, as if it had itself produced what it admires," the reader can scarcely be other than astounded at the apparent similarity; but Longinus is defining the nature of the sublime, whereas Reynolds is speaking of how the artist can "learn to invent"; and much might be learned by asking why the British writer uses the word "almost," and why the Greek does not. Nor is Michelangelo to Reynolds as Homer to Longinus, after all: that imagined artistry and imagined criticism of the great which Longinus recommends is for Reynolds appropriate only to the artist in the second stage; the finished artist is emancipated from "subjection to any authority, but what he shall himself judge to be supported by reason," and he stands "among his instructors, not as an imitator, but a rival." Nor do Longinus and Reynolds similarly conceive of genius. For the rhetorician, genius without invention would be incomprehensible. The painter writes: "The greatest natural genius cannot subsist on its own stock: he who resolves never to ransack any mind but his own, will soon be reduced, from mere barrenness, to the poorest of all imitations; he will be obligated to imitate himself, and to repeat what he has before often repeated."

WILLIAM EMPSON
CONTEMPORARY CRITICISM
AND POETIC DICTION

The last quarter of a century has seen the rise, in England and America, of a new critical movement. Its mere longevity would perhaps entitle it to some importance in the eyes of future literary historians; but that importance is guaranteed and augmented by the esteem which it has won, and by the distinction and persistent fame of the persons who are regarded as its chief practitioners. The "New Criticism," as this movement is called by both its friends and its foes, seems to be almost universally regarded as having at last brought literary study to a condition rivaling that of the sciences. It has, we are frequently told, established itself upon principles the scientific character of which is assured by the fact that they are drawn from such sciences as psychology, biology, anthropology, linguistics, economics, and so on, in their most modern development; it has led, according to its proponents, to an unparalleled accuracy and minuteness in the treatment of texts, and in the employment of terminology and critical techniques; it has, we are assured, an over-all if not specific unity of method, as well as a doctrine sufficiently established to permit a list of "heresies" and "fallacies"; finally, and best of all, it not only can discuss more and explain it better than the outworn criticisms which it supplants, but it is still, like the sciences, in a happy condition of growth.[1]

Mr. William Empson is among the principal exponents of this movement, and it might almost be said that where he is mentioned, it is mentioned, and where it is, he is. Nor is this extraordinary; in certain

Reprinted from *Modern Philology*, vol. 47, no. 4 (May 1950).

1. I do not, of course, imply that every one of these views is held by every critic, and with equal conviction and enthusiasm. But I have taken pains to construct a statement which should convey as fully as possible, and without too great inaccuracy, the general attitude which the New Critics assume toward their criticism. See John Crowe Ransom, *The New Criticism*, preface; William Elton, *A Glossary of the New Criticism* (Chicago, 1949), pp. 3–5; Robert W. Stallman, "The New Critics," in *Critiques and Essays in Criticism* (New York, 1949), p. 506.

respects it can be said that he has produced it, and it, him. His prestige, briefly, is enormous; his theories, never too vigorously assailed, have gained wider acceptance with the years, and his particular interpretations of texts are regarded as pretty near exhaustive and definitive. The recent republication of one of his principal works, *Seven Types of Ambiguity*,[2] as a "classic of modern criticism," affords us an occasion to examine the critical method of Mr. Empson and, in that connection, of the New Criticism as well.

I

For Empson, as for his master I. A. Richards, poetry is simply an aspect or condition of language; it is therefore definable in terms of its medium; it is language differentiated from other language by a certain attribute. Richards first proposed that this distinguishing feature was ambiguity, and occupied himself with exhibiting the complexities of response which ambiguity engenders; Empson has followed by enumerating seven kinds of ambiguity.

The term "ambiguity" here does not carry its usual meaning. Ambiguity as Empson conceives it is not the mere possession of double meaning; an obvious pun or a patent irony is not ambiguous, for instance, "because there is no room for puzzling";[3] although such expressions when less obvious are called ambiguous "even by a critic who never doubted their meaning" since they are "calculated to deceive at least a section of their readers."[4] Nor is ambiguity simply concision, nor the quality of language which produces mixed emotions; it is, rather, "any verbal nuance, however slight, which gives room for alternative reactions to the same piece of language."[5] The important point here is that of alternative reactions; Empson illustrates his meaning by remarking that a child might view the sentence "The brown cat sat on the red mat" as part of a fairy story or as an excerpt from *Reading without Tears.*[6]

The ambiguities are types of "logical disorder," arranged as stages of advancing disorder,[7] or, what is apparently the same thing, "in order of increasing distance from simple statement and logical exposition."[8] The seven types, then, are kinds in which (1) "a detail is effective in several ways at once," (2) "two or more alternative meanings are fully resolved into one," (3) "two apparently unconnected meanings are

2. William Empson, *Seven Types of Ambiguity*, 2d. ed. rev. and reset (New York: New Directions, 1947).

3. P. x.

4. Ibid.

5. P. 1.

6. P. 2.

7. P. 48.

8. P. 7.

given simultaneously," (4) "alternative meanings combine to make
clear a complicated state of mind in the author," (5) "a fortunate
confusion" is present, "as when the author is discovering his idea in the
act of writing or not holding it all in his mind at once," (6) "what is
said is contradictory or irrelevant and the reader is forced to invent
interpretations," and (7) "full contradiction" is present, "marking a
division in the author's mind." These kinds are general and have
subdivisions; the first, for example, divides into "comparisons with
several points of likeness," "antitheses with several points of difference," " 'comparative' adjectives," " 'subdued' metaphors," and
ambiguities of rhythm, or, as Empson puts it, "extra meanings
suggested by rhythm."[9]

One of his best-known passages is in illustration of "comparison with
several points of likeness," and is a good example of his method in
operation:

There is no pun, double syntax, or dubiety of feeling, in

> Bare ruined choirs where late
> the sweet birds sang,

but the comparison holds for many reasons: because ruined monastery
choirs are places in which to sing, because they involve sitting in a row,
because they are made of wood, are carved into knots and so forth,
because they used to be surrounded by a sheltering building
crystallized out of the likeness of a forest, and coloured with stained
glass and painting like flowers and leaves, because they are now
abandoned by all but the grey walls coloured like the skies of winter,
because the cold and Narcissistic charm suggested by choir-boys suits
well with Shakespeare's feeling for the object of the sonnets, and for
various sociological and historical reasons (the protestant destruction of
monasteries, fear of puritanism), which it would be hard now to trace
out in their proportions; these reasons, and many more relating the
simile to its place in the Sonnet, must all combine to give the line its
beauty, and there is a sort of ambiguity in not knowing which of them
to hold most clearly in mind. Clearly this is involved in all such
richness and heightening of effect, and the machinations of ambiguity
are among the very roots of poetry.[10]

The broad theory underlying Empson's method seems to be as
follows. Poetry uses language, and language is meaningful and communicative; hence poetry is communicative. In analyzing communication, there are three possibilities: one may speak about what happened
in the author's mind, about what is likely to happen in the reader's

9. These quotations have been extracted from the analytical table of contents,
pp. v–vi.
10. Pp. 2–3.

mind, or "about both parties at once," as involved in the communication itself.[11] The first two kinds of discussion, according to Empson, make the claim of knowing too much; "the rules as to what is conveyable are so much more mysterious even than the rules governing the effects of ambiguity" that the third possibility is best. Hence in the main he talks about the third, although he is by no means, he says, "puristic" about this.[12] Apparently the poet communicates ideas, like everyone else, and the reader is affected by these ideas according to their kind; the poet, however, would seem to be a poet, not in virtue of the emotional quality of his ideas, but in virtue of the devices of ambiguity which he consciously or unconsciously employs. Moreover, the effects *proper* to poetry are not the emotions evoked by the ideas; rather, since ambiguity is the essence of poetry, the process of reading is a process of "inventing reasons" why certain elements should have been selected for a poem, as in the passage just quoted, and the peculiar pleasure derived from poetry is produced by the mental activity in response to these ambiguities.[13] It is, to use Empson's own word, a pleasure of "puzzling," apparently different from the pleasure afforded by riddles, charades, and anagrams in that these latter involve matters emotionally indifferent.

The method of interpretation which rests upon this theory is, as we might expect, one reducing all poetic considerations to considerations of poetic diction, and one reducing all discussion of diction, even, to problems of ambiguities. The method might be described as the permutation and combination of all the various "meanings" of the parts of a given discourse, whether these parts be simple or complex; out of the mass of "meanings" so found, Empson selects those which "give room for alternative reactions," i.e., which satisfy the fundamental condition of ambiguity. The instrument by which he detects the possible meanings of words is the *Oxford English Dictionary;* although it is seldom mentioned by name, its presence everywhere is neither invisible nor subtle. Its lengthy lists of meanings seem to have impressed no one so much as Empson. Apparently he reasons that, since poetry is language highly charged with meaning, the poetic word must invariably stagger under the full weight of its dictionary significances. Since the mass of significances achieved by permutation and combination is often very great, and since ambiguity is so extensive a principle

11. P. 243.

12. P. 235 n.

13. "Two statements are made as if they were connected, and the reader is forced to consider their relations for himself. The reason why these facts should have been selected for a poem is left for him to invent; he will invent a variety of reasons and order them in his own mind. This, I think, is the essential fact about the poetical use of language" (p. 25; see also p. 57).

of selection, the discovery of the main meaning or meanings of a passage often becomes for Empson an embarrassing matter. At such points he invokes the aid of rather general and often highly dubious historical, ethical, and psychological propositions about the poet and the audience. I suspect that such propositions are mainly conveniences for him; he does not, at any rate, worry too greatly when he finds they are false.[14]

The resulting interpretation is not always so prettily fanciful as the remarks on the Shakespearean sonnet may suggest; fanciful it is always, indeed, but the method of "permutation and combination," as I have called it, is a mechanical method, and it is capable of all the mindless brutality of a machine. Witness the treatment of a famous speech of Macbeth:

> If it is an example of the first type [of ambiguity] to use a metaphor which is valid in several ways, it is an example of the second to use several different metaphors at once, as Shakespeare is doing in the following example. It is impossible to avoid Shakespeare in these matters; partly because his use of language is of unparalleled richness and partly because it has received so much attention already; so that the inquiring student has less to do, is more likely to find what he is looking for, and has evidence that he is not spinning fancies out of his own mind.

As a resounding example, then, there is Macbeth's

> If it were done, when 'tis done, then 'twere well
> It were done quickly;

(double syntax since you may stop at the end of the line)

> If th' Assassination
> Could trammel up the Consequence, and catch
> With his surcease, Success; that but . . .

words hissed in the passage where servants were passing, which must be swaddled with darkness, loaded as it were in themselves with fearful powers, and not made too naked even to his own mind. *Consequence* means causal result, and the things to follow, though not causally connected, and, as in "a person of consequence," the divinity that doth hedge a king. *Trammel* was a technical term used about netting birds, hobbling horses in some particular way, hooking up pots, levering, and running trolleys on rails. *Surcease* means completion, stopping proceedings in the middle of a lawsuit, or the overruling of a judgment; the word reminds you of "surfeit" and "decease," as does *assassination* of hissing and "assess" and, as in "supersession," through *sedere*, of knocking down the mighty from their seat. . . .

14. See, e.g., p. 21 n.

He continues this at some length, concluding: "The meanings cannot all be remembered at once, however often you read it...."[15]

Such a passage as this needs only attentive reading to make manifest its utter absurdity; but then that very absurdity in a fashion protects it, and gains a certain credence for it; it is so absurd that we in a measure believe it, merely because we are loath to believe that anything could be so absurd. To escape such spurious persuasion, we must, I think, forcibly remind ourselves of the facts. We are actually being asked to believe that the speech actually *means* all these various things; that Macbeth, trembling on the brink of murder, and restrained only by his fears of what may follow, is babbling of bird-nets, pothooks, levers, trolleys, assessments, lawsuits, and what not; and all this on the shadowy grounds that the *OED*, or whatever dictionary, lists alternative meanings for "trammel," "surcease," and "assassination," and that poetic language is ambiguous. This is a wrenching of a text if I ever saw one; what is worse, it is a wrenching to no rational purpose. The remark about "double syntax" is typical; for there is no double syntax in

> If it were done, when 'tis done, then 'twere well
> It were done quickly...,

for if you pause at the end of the line, as Empson suggests, you leave an unaccounted-for and absolutely unintelligible residue in the next line; and as a matter of fact you make nonsense, anyway, of the first. In short, the "double syntax" here owes its existence only to the supposition that poetry is necessarily ambiguous.

There are many other marvels of interpretation: at one point Empson not only confuses Macbeth with the witches, but the play itself with *King Lear;*[16] in *Hamlet*, the line "In the dead vast and middle of the night" is made to suggest a personification of Night as one of the terrible women of destiny, on the grounds of possible puns (*vast: waste: waist, middle* of night: *middle* of body);[17] and Crashaw's translation of the *Dies Irae*, on equally compelling grounds, refers to the defecation of God—hence the poet, "to find an image for the purest love ... falls back on sexuality in its most infantile and least creditable form."[18] But one of the most common results of Empson's procedure is that poets appear to him unintelligible, or, to use his own word, "muddled." For example, Shakespeare's sonnet 16, with which I imagine few readers have found difficulty, is "muddled."[19]

15. Pp. 49–50.
16. P. 18, par. 3.
17. Pp. 96–97.
18. Pp. 222–24.
19. P. 57. The sonnet is analyzed on pp. 54–56.

These things of course result, as I have said, from the theory of
ambiguity; and one would suppose that a principle so ruthlessly
applied would be of absolute force, especially since it is the "essence" of
poetry. But as a matter of fact, Empson is not quite willing to credit it
with as much authority as he demands from it. An ambiguity, while it
can be "beautiful,"[20] is "not satisfying in itself, nor is it, considered on
its own, a thing to be attempted; it must in each case arise from, and
be justified by, the peculiar requirements of the situation."[21] "On the
other hand, it is a thing which the more interesting and valuable
situations are more likely to justify."[22] This is an admission, I take it,
that ambiguity is not even in Empson's view the *principle* of poetry,
since its propriety or impropriety is determined by something else—an
unanalyzed thing vaguely called "the situation." Rather, it is a sign,
and by no means an infallible sign even for Empson, that an interesting
and valuable situation is involved. (The statement even of that much
is, by the way, left undefended and unsupported by Empson, although
his whole position depends upon it.) And he seems to discuss the
sign—ambiguity—rather than the "interesting and valuable situation"
of which it is a sign only because the sign is "less mysterious."[23] In
short, he appears to be in the position of many of the ancient theorists
who sought to discuss the elevated style; the style itself evaded their
formulations, but since it predominantly involved certain tropes, the
tropes might be analyzed, although, it was recognized, the mere
production of tropes would not constitute elevation of style.

Indeed, Empson is really a tropist *manqué*, and the seven types are
really tropes, as can be seen from the fact that the regular tropes fall
under his divisions; the first type, for instance, includes metaphor and
antithesis, and the subclasses are clearly subclasses of tropes. But there
are certain important differences between the types of ambiguity and
the ancient tropes; the types are not nearly so comprehensive; they do
not offer nearly such clear distinctions between figures of language;
they are not organized upon nearly so clear a principle; and, what is
most crucial, they are not nearly so useful. The main difficulty with
the tropes, as they were generally treated, was that, in Samuel Butler's
phrase, "All a rhetorician's rules / Teach nothing but to name his tools";
that is, their treatment was not sufficiently functional; but they did offer
a precise and exhaustive distinction, at their best, between kinds of
grammatical devices. Hence, once a trope has been identified, one is in a
position to inquire how it has been used, and thereby arrive ultimately
at judgments of value. Empson's types, however, do not even permit the

20. P. 235.
21. Ibid.
22. Ibid.
23. P. 243.

distinction of the device; I fear that only Empson can find instances of them, and even he is sometimes unsure.[24]

But indeed to deal rigorously with Empson's ideas, to attempt to state them clearly, to demand precision and adequacy of proof for them, is in a sense to be very unfair to him. It is unfair, perhaps, even to inquire into his exact meaning. As a matter of fact, I am not sure that he means anything exactly. He is constantly offering statements; but there is not one—even of his cardinal doctrines—which he is willing to stand by. It would appear that he is offering a method of verbal analysis based on ambiguity; but he is not quite sure what he means by "ambiguity."[25] It requires certain conditions; but these conditions are not always satisfied by his examples.[26] His first definition of ambiguity was that it "adds some nuance to the direct statement of prose." But, he continues, "this begs a philosophical question and stretches the term ambiguity so far that it becomes almost meaningless." Even his new definition "is not meant to be decisive but to avoid confusing the reader; naturally the question of what would be the best definition of ambiguity . . . crops up all through the book."[27] Elsewhere, he remarks in a footnote: "Effects worth calling ambiguous occur when the possible alternative meanings of word or grammar are used to give alternative meanings to the sentence"[28]—but this would disallow much of his own practice, for he constantly confounds potential with actual meaning, as in the examples we have just considered. The real truth of the matter is, I suspect, in the following sentence: "Apart from trailing my coat about minor controversies, I claimed at the outset that I would use the term ambiguity to mean anything I liked, and repeatedly told the reader that the distinctions between the Seven Types which he was asked to study would not be worth the attention of a profounder thinker." And he remarks, briefly afterward: "I have tried to clear the text of the gratuitous puzzles of definition and draw attention to the real ones."[29]

After such admissions it is almost improper to remark what is nevertheless plain to behold. Empson is not sure of the types of ambiguity; for instance, he is not sure that the first type *is* ambiguous.[30] He is not sure of the principles of classification. He is not sure that his method is useful to poets—on the contrary, poets ought to

24. E.g., "The fundamental situation, whether it deserves to be called ambiguous or not. . ." (p. 2).

25. See preface to the 2d ed., pp. vii–xv.

26. E.g., p. 214, par. 2.

27. P. 1. n.

28. P. 70 n.

29. Preface to the 2d ed., pp. vii–viii.

30. P. 2.

avoid ambiguity[31]—nor that it is of too much use even to readers, for, he says, they need not remember or apply it.[32] In short, it would seem that his only safeguard against complete and utter refutation is his slipperiness of statement and his ability to insist that any counter-argument, any refutation, does not affect his ideas, but is merely a criticism of his expression.

These traits might seem to convict him of sophistry also; but they are rather a clue to the interpretation of his work. He is pointing to a problem; whatever we may think about his statement and treatment of it, the problem itself undoubtedly exists: what kind of minute and precise discussion of poetic language is requisite in order to make manifest the subtleties of genius and art? His principal difficulty is that contemporary criticism, for reasons that we shall examine later, affords no devices by which such a problem can be handled. In fact, it cannot even be accurately stated; for instance, the only alternatives to his theory which Empson can conceive are the theories of "Pure Sound" and of "Atmosphere," as he calls them;[33] since neither of these is tenable, he pursues his own course. He seems utterly innocent of any knowledge of the history of criticism; as a consequence, he is a victim of the collapse of the theory of art in his own day. Possessing no clear or adequate poetic principles, he nevertheless has his intuitions, and he must use language to express these. If the language permits the concept to shine through, well and good; if not, one must alter the language. Recognizing that poetic language can be enormously effective, he supposes that this is due to denseness of meaning; and since denseness of meaning implies ambiguity, one must discuss ambiguity.

It is, indeed, on this topic of Meaning, so crucial to his system as well as to that of Richards, that his confusions are least manifest and most serious. Perhaps most serious of all is that between meaning and implication or inference.

The discrimination of four conditions of meaning and inference may perhaps clarify this issue. First, meaning may be present without inference, or, if inference is present, it is based wholly upon linguistic or other semantic matters—for example, if language is involved, upon the meanings of words and upon syntactical laws. Meaning here is the simple resultant of the significant powers of words and of their combinations; the meaning of what Empson calls "direct" statement or expression is of this order. Inference, if present at all, is here minimal; from what a child knows, for instance, of the elemental parts (word-meanings) and of types of construction (attribution, predica-tion, etc.) he may infer the meaning of the primer sentence. This

31. Pp. 235–36.
32. P. 256.
33. P. 8.

would be simple part-whole inference, and wholly linguistic in character; if the child fails to infer the whole, he is reminded by analysis into parts and types of construction. Sentences which have a meaning of this order may be of infinite grammatical complexity; they will still be direct or simple in meaning, since the meaning is the resultant only of verbal signs.

But secondly, meaning may be the resultant of more than verbal signs. It may, that is, result from inferences based on the character or purpose of the speaker, the manner of delivery (e.g., facial expression, gesture, etc.), our presupposed knowledge or opinions of the subject, the situation, and many other circumstances; and—while such inferences are frequently unrelated to the meaning, or do not affect it—frequently also they serve to modify, emphasize, or even contradict the meaning of the words uttered. For instance, irony, as we now conceive it, is possible because we can infer from something over and above the verbal expression that the expression means the opposite of what it says. Sentences affected by such inferences never mean quite what they say; however simple their form, their meaning is never a simple resultant of the verbal expressions.

Thirdly, meaning, if it is produced by inference, also produces inference which is not, however, part of the meaning. Not every inference which can be drawn from a fact is *meant* by the sentence which states the fact. An axiom of geometry does not, in its statement, *mean* every theorem which can be drawn from it. Similarly, a sentence is in itself a fact, but inferences drawn from that fact are no part of its meaning. For example, if a certain sentence is possible, it is inferable that language is possible; but the sentence itself—say, Empson's "The brown cat sat on the red mat"—does not, as he thinks, *mean* "Language is possible" or "This is a statement about a cat."

Fourthly, inference is possible quite apart from meaning. If I see a bloody ax and infer that something was killed with it, no question of meaning is involved, for all arbitrary signs are absent; a fact implies a fact, even in the absence of language and meaning.

Now while Empson talks of meaning and implication, he makes no effective distinction between these four cases. All are equally "meaning" for him. The cat-sentence does not have merely its obvious meaning (case 1), but it *means* that it might have come out of a fairy story or a primer (case 2) and that it is a statement about a cat (case 3). The confusion would not be so serious, perhaps, if it did not carry with it his commitment to dictionaries. As one can readily see, dictionary meanings are absolutely determinative, if anywhere, only in the first case; and they grow less and less so, until they are not involved at all in the last case.

The confusion becomes particularly important when Empson is

talking of the Meaning of Poetry. For strictly speaking, a *mimetic* poem, an imitation—and he is mainly concerned with poems of this kind—has no meaning at all. It is a certain kind of product, like a picture, a symphony, or a statue; like an ax, a bed, a chair; it has no more meaning *as a poem* than these have.[34] It is a fact; from that fact we may make inferences, to which we respond emotionally and about which we make judgments; but it means nothing; it is. In short, to speak of the "meaning" of a poem is to confuse meaning with the implication of a fact.

Presumably, however, Empson means the diction of the poem when he speaks of poetry. In that case he confuses the diction with the poem; but his question may be very readily answered. In the broadest sense, what the diction means, precisely, is the poem itself.

The importance of these distinctions, which at first sight may seem pedantic and useless, is that they lead, so far as poetics is concerned, to a distinction—a very important one for the problems in which Empson is interested—between *lexis* and *praxis*; between speech as meaningful and speech as action. What the poetic character says in the mimetic poem is speech and has meaning; his *saying it* is action, an act of persuading, confessing, commanding, informing, torturing, or what not. His diction may be accounted for in grammatical and lexicographical terms; not so, his action. And the profundity and complexity in poetry which so much interests Empson is due primarily to action and character, which cannot be handled in grammatical terms, rather than to diction, which can. That profundity is only in a small degree verbal, in the sense that verbal analysis will yield the whole of it; and even then it is very, very seldom a matter of verbal ambiguity. Shakespeare's profoundest touches are a case in point. "Pray you, undo this button" and "The table's full" are profound, not as meaningful verbal expressions, but as actions permitting an extraordinary number of implications, in that they are revelatory of many aspects of character and situation. We shall not explain them by jumbling the dictionary meanings of "button" and "table," but by asking, among other things, why Lear requested the unfastening of a button and why Macbeth thought the table was full. This is true even in lyric poetry: the "Once more" of "Lycidas," for instance, has no profound verbal meaning; it is affecting because it implies the repeated suffering of bereavement.

The theories of Richards and Empson illustrate a tendency, very prevalent among critics who rate diction as important, to rate it as

34. I trust that these statements will not seem to make me a member of what Empson calls the "cult of Pure Sound" and that they will give no encouragement to slovenly and irresponsible reading. I do not imply here that the attempt to discover meaning should be foregone, but that more than meaning is involved in poetry. The ensuing discussion will, I hope, clarify the somewhat terse statement here.

entirely too important. In the order of our coming to know the poem, it is true, the words are all-important; without them we could not know the poem. But when we grasp the structure we see that in the poetic order they are the least important element; they are governed by everything else in the poem. We are in fact far less moved by the words as mere words than we think; we think ourselves moved mainly by them because they are the only visible or audible part of the poem. As soon as we grasp the grammatical meaning of an expression in a mimetic poem, we begin drawing inferences which we scarcely recognize as inferences, because they are just such as we habitually make in life; inferences from the speech as to the character, his situation, his thought, his passion, suddenly set the speaker vividly before us and arouse our emotions in sympathy or antipathy; our humanity is engaged, and it is engaged by humanity. But where we can draw no such inferences, where no such impression of humanity is conveyed, we remain largely indifferent in the face of the finest diction. These inferences, moreover, largely determine our interpretation of the language itself; we recognize a pun or an ambiguity when we see a human reason why the character should deal in puns and ambiguities, and not when the dictionary lists a variety of meanings.

We do indeed say the character must be so-and-so *because* his words are such-and-such, as well as that the words must be such-and-such *because* the character is so; thus at first sight diction and the other parts of the poem seem mutually determinative; on closer inspection, however, we see that *because* has a different sense in each case, since it refers to a cause of a different order. The words are a cause of our conjecturing the character; the character is a cause of the words being said. We can see this even if we are speaking merely of words and meaning: the words are a cause of our knowing the meaning; but the meaning is the cause of the words in their selection and ordering.

If the words, then, are not what is primarily responsible for the effect, purely verbal interpretation, however essential, will not explain poetry, any more than stringing fine diction together will constitute it. Indeed, even Empson in a manner admits this; for he tells us that ambiguity must be justified by the "situation"; but he makes the fatal error of supposing that, because the situation is not something verbal, it is therefore outside the bounds of poetic consideration. As a consequence of this, he defines the poetic pleasure itself much too loosely; that pleasure is not, as he thinks, a logical pleasure produced by puzzling over the relation between statements; it is a pleasure produced by a play of emotions aroused in us by an exhibition of the actions and fortunes of men. Inference is indeed involved, and carries a pleasure of its own; but inference is only a necessary condition, and not a sufficient cause, of the poetic pleasure.

This looseness of treatment might seem to broaden the scope of Empson's inquiry; but it tends rather to restrict. He can conceive of metaphors, for instance, only as comparisons based upon real similarity; the more real likenesses present, the better the metaphor; the better the metaphor, the better the poem. His treatment of "Bare ruined choirs" is an instance. What he misses entirely is the governance of metaphor by thought, of thought by character, of character by action. For a metaphor is not simply a figure of diction in poetry; it is also someone's thinking, significantly, that something resembles something; it is the thought, that is, of a certain character in a certain situation, and it is significant of these things. The best similitudes are not always good metaphors in a given poem, and the best metaphors are not always good similitudes.

In short, something is missing in all this; and what is missing is the nature of poetry.

II

Empson's theory, then, deals only with a single part of poetry, and that part the least important one poetically; indeed, only with a single attribute of that part, and one only vaguely and supposititiously attached to poetry, for ambiguity is neither peculiar to poetry nor universal to all, or to the best, poetry. Moreover, his treatment even of that attribute is so limited as not merely to send inquiry in the wrong direction, but also to preclude proper explanation and supplementation of whatever truths it may, as a system of discussion, contain. Nor are these faults peculiarly Empson's; they abound everywhere in the New Criticism, and, for that matter, in contemporary criticism generally. Scrutinizing the New Criticism as a whole, I do indeed find that "unity of method" which Ransom, Elton, and others have claimed for it;[35] I find it also in contemporary criticism generally; and on examining that method, I find it directly responsible for all the faults I have noted.

Contemporary criticism seems, for a variety of reasons, to have broken with the past, and to have begun afresh upon a discussion of principles. Such a venture required a new determination of the subject matter of criticism and reopened the question of the nature of poetry, thereby giving rise to an indefinite number of definitions and hypotheses. The principal reason for the rejection of preceding theories was the belief that these were incommensurate, and incapable of being made commensurate, with the growth of poetry in our time, having been, it was supposed, founded upon conceptions of poetry entirely too narrow and limited. The new criticism was to comprehend all that has

35. Ransom, *The New Criticism*, preface, p. x. While, strictly speaking, Ransom is speaking of R. P. Blackmur, he is clearly discussing him as a representative instance of a New Critic.

been called "poetry," to discover its true nature and determine methods of its proper criticism and construction. A second important reason stemmed from the advances made in certain sciences which might have some bearing on poetry; psychology, for instance, was thought to have advanced considerably and to possess new techniques and hypotheses that applied immediately both to the creative process of the artist and the emotional responses of the audience.

Commendable as these motives may be, the task of establishing and developing the principles of art is a formidable one always, even for the philosopher, and in this instance it was complicated by certain difficulties. Chief among these was the absence of any clear, fruitful, and widely accepted metaphysics, epistemology, philosophy of science; a discipline, call it what you will, capable of articulating and organizing the arts and sciences, establishing and criticizing their principles and methods, and, in short, settling the broader and more general questions which the pursuit of any department of inquiry must involve. How seriously this lack has affected contemporary criticism may be seen by anyone who takes the trouble to note the frequency of metaphysical questions, as well as the infrequency of happy solutions to these, in any critical discussion which seeks, nowadays, to rise above the mere particulars of art. Definitions are made by men who know neither what a definition is, nor how it is constructed, nor what it is for, and methodology is discussed by men who would be hard put to it to say what method is. The excellent amateur of poetry has become a sadly amateurish philosopher. But the fault in this instance must be laid at the door of the philosophers.

A second difficulty lay in the fact that the term "poetry," or its equivalents, had from antiquity been applied to a great number of things of widely different natures. The attachment of a name to something is, after all, only the reflection of an opinion of likeness; and custom had quite naturally extended the application of the name of poetry, not merely to poetry itself, but to anything that involved the use of poetic devices such as verse, rhyme, ornamental diction, etc. Now, it is impossible to have a single art, science, or discipline unless some homogeneity can be found in the subject matter; and criticism was thus faced with the impossible task of finding homogeneity among heterogeneous things: that is, of finding a common principle among things that had no common principles, and of finding a single definition that should state the common nature of things that had no common nature.

Criticism had to find points of likeness among an accidental accumulation of things of diverse natures, which had been called "poetry" because in accidental respects they resembled it; and likenesses it found; but these were *accidental* likenesses, as one might expect under the circumstances. Even where the characteristic selected was itself a necessary condition of poetry—as, for example, the use of language—there remained the difficulty of discerning in what special respects it was related to the nature or essence of poetry. Language functions very differently in the epigram, the didactic verse-treatise, and mimetic tragedy; if you call all of these "poetry" and inquire into the nature of poetic language, you will end up with some description which, because it must be common to all of these, will be very general, and will shed little light upon the special functioning of language in, say, mimetic tragedy. Moreover, it was in the nature of the case that certain of these characteristics, being very general, should turn out to be common to things which were obviously not poetry, in any of the accepted senses, at all. For example, language is common to all the things called "poetry"; but nothing is more evident than that scientific prose, for instance, is very different from poetry, although it too is language; it must therefore be differentiated from poetry—but what is the proper differentia? You decide, at this point, that scientific prose is bare, poetic diction ornamented; or the latter is more highly charged with meaning than the former, or something of the sort; and if this does not sufficiently distinguish it, you proceed further, through differentiae of the differentia, until definition is finally achieved. Despite the fact that the definition was founded on a characteristic accidentally found in common among an accidental collocation of things, you will now, if you are a typical modern critic, consider that you have stated the nature or essence of poetry.

These "definitions" are not necessarily false, in the sense that they attribute to poetry characteristics which it does not have; but they are certainly not definitions; they certainly do not state the nature of poetry. The accidental characteristics of things, and hence the possible comparisons in terms of these, are limitless; thus an infinite number of definitions of the same thing can be generated in this fashion, all equally valid, since they are based upon and warranted by precisely the same procedure of definition. If so, they are equally "essential"; but—which of these "essences" is the *essence?* An examination of the construction of these definitions will disclose in every instance that the definition has a minimum reference to the object defined, for it touches only a certain attribute which is itself not shown to be essential to the object; all the rest is provided by the apparatus and mechanism of comparison. In short, these "definitions" are at most indications of the light in which the object "poetry" is to be viewed.

But may not these definitions even in that case have some value? Doubtless they may, as devices for permitting the discussion of a subject the nature of which is unknown, and where they function so, they are unexceptionable. It is frequently the case that, before we can state the

nature of a thing, much preliminary discussion is needed: the properties, even the accidents, of the subject must be considered in order to
be dismissed; and even when erroneous definition results, no great
harm is done, for inquiry is still in progress; definition serves as matter
for inquiry, and not as the basis of inquiry; it is itself examined and
tested, it does not as yet fix and determine the whole approach to the
subject. The definitions proposed by contemporary criticism do not,
however, function thus heuristically; instead, they operate as a basis
for proof, as principles of demonstration; and as such they are sources
of misreasoning and error, and hinder rather than foster further
discussion. It is one thing to suppose tentatively that poetry is language
characterized by ambiguity, and then to inquire whether this characteristic is common to all poetry, whether it is peculiar to poetry,
whether it accounts for all that poetry is and does; it is quite another
thing to employ it to insist that any interpretation of poetry must turn
upon ambiguities, and to twist the language of *Macbeth* into a
meaningless and tasteless muddle, merely because, according to the
definition, poetry must be ambiguous. It is the reverse, not merely of
science, but also of sense, to erect a hasty guess into a principle of
method, so that, far from being tested by the data, it tests the data by
itself, silencing all adverse testimony, and forcing assent where it
should itself yield to correction.

If the definitions of contemporary criticism are thus not strictly
definitions, the hypotheses which are framed to support or supplement
them are also not strictly hypotheses. In Empson's case, for instance,
the definitive property of poetry, ambiguity, rests upon the hypothesis
that there is a connection between ambiguity and interesting or
valuable situations; that is, if poetry deals with interesting and
valuable situations, and these tend to involve ambiguity, poetry must
involve ambiguity. Such a hypothesis does not really give the *cause*, for
it does not state why the *thing* is such-and-such; it is merely a *reason*, a
ground of belief, stating why the theorist *thinks* the thing is so. It is not
a poetic principle; it is the rationalization of an opinion. Even if the
opinion and its ground were not false, however, both would still be
inappropriate, for the terms in which they are couched are much too
general: neither ambiguity nor a concern with interesting and valuable
situations is peculiar to poetry. Moreover, even if they were appropriate, they would be falsely reductive; ambiguity, when it is present
in poetry, is present through a variety of causes, and not simply
through the fact that a certain kind of situation tends to involve it.

The hypotheses of contemporary criticism are not, as a matter of
fact, hypotheses in any technical sense at all; they are rather a sort of
postulate. We may distinguish, I think, three sorts of hypotheses: the

heuristic, the demonstrative, and the nameless kind that serves both functions. The heuristic hypothesis is the first principle of a given science, used as a basis for inquiry into more general principles; thus dialectic, according to Plato, "uses hypotheses not as first principles, but as genuine hypotheses, that is to say, as stepping stones and impulses, whereby it may force its way up to something that is not hypothetical, and arrive at the first principle of everything."[36] The demonstrative hypothesis is a first principle in a given science, without which scientific knowledge in that particular sphere is impossible. Both of these imply completed inquiry within the given science; the third kind, which is hypothesis in the sense intended in modern science, implies no such completion; it is a tentative principle, a supposition either of "fact" or of the cause of a "fact." Obviously, the hypotheses of contemporary criticism are not hypotheses in the first two senses; nor are they hypotheses in the third sense, although they have the same function as the tentative suppositions of modern science, viz., to explain facts or other hypotheses, or to render them consistent and compendent. For the true hypothesis, in this third sense, is character-ized by reciprocal implication; as Descartes remarks, the facts must imply the hypothesis, and the hypothesis must imply the facts; and these are conditions which the modern critical "hypotheses" fail to satisfy. Empson's hypothesis, for instance, satisfies neither condition: it neither implies the data nor is implied by them. A canvass of interesting and valuable situations will not show that they "tend to involve ambiguity"; conversely, even if they did, this would prove nothing about individual instances, for a statistical attribute of a large class ("tend to involve ambiguity" is of this order) does not belong, affirmatively or negatively, necessarily or probably, to any subclasses of that class.

The characteristic hypotheses of contemporary criticism tend, finally, to have two salient characteristics which vitally affect the systems based upon them. First, they are inadequate; second, they are preclusive of supplementary hypotheses which might compensate for their inadequacies.

A very little discussion will, I hope, make this clear. All poetic theory is a form of causal explanation; and such explanation must comprise all the causes requisite to make a thing what it is. Unless the causal account is complete, the explanation is inadequate; if it is insisted upon as adequate, if it is claimed to account for the whole and not merely for the part, it is also preclusive. The theories of the early Greek physicists offer an example. Thales, for instance, thought to account for the phenomenal universe in terms merely of its material cause, the principle of water; but, as numerous philosophers have pointed out,

36. *Republic* vi. 511.

this would at most account for the substrate; it does not explain the distinctive forms which water assumes as rain, cloud, ice, or snow, nor the motive forces which cause water to assume such forms, nor the functional organization of animate things; it offers only one principle of explanation where several are required.

Modern criticism is very much in the condition of Thales.[37] It may be divided into two principal kinds: criticism based upon hypotheses concerning the medium of poetry, and hence given to the explanation of poetry as language, or language of a certain kind, and criticism based upon hypotheses concerning the subject matter of poetry, and hence given to the explanation of poetry as myth, as knowledge, as experience, or something of the kind. The first seeks to establish some distinction between poetic language and language in any other form or use. Thus Richards opposes poetry to scientific discourse, finding the latter ordered to clarity and the former to ambiguity, the latter informative and the former emotive;[38] Yvor Winters opposes poetry "to other kinds of writing," finding that poetry takes special pains with the expression of feeling";[39] John Crowe Ransom opposes poetry to unmetrical and unrhymed language, finding poetry a "compromise" between "meaning and meter";[40] but the end result is largely the same; in each case the nature of poetry is ultimately determined solely by the critic's hypotheses as to the nature or functions of language. All these statements contain a measure of truth; but they are inadequate as hypotheses. If tragedy, comedy, epic, and lyric be poetry, how shall they be described as distinctive species of language? Upon what special properties of language does each depend, so that, once these are determined, we shall have a given species of poetry? Is the difference between drama and narrative a difference of language? Are the differences between the large and complicated actions of epic and the small and simple of lyric, the differences between tragic and comic action and character, the differences between the emotional effects of tragedy and those of comedy—are all these differences of language? Can we account for any differences of poetic language without taking into consideration such differences of poetic form as these? As a matter of fact, is there any attribute of poetic language which cannot also be found, and that abundantly, in other forms of discourse?

These positions are like arguing that ice is ice because it is water; they are attempts to derive the form from the matter. All such

37. See R. S. Crane, "Cleanth Brooks; or, the Bankruptcy of Critical Monism," *Modern Philology*, 45 (1948): 226–45.

38. Richards, *Principles of Literary Criticism* (New York, 1930), p. 267.

39. Yvor Winters, *The Anatomy of Nonsense* (Norfolk, Conn., 1943), p. 12.

40. Ransom, *The New Criticism*, pp. 294–95. But see the whole final chapter, "Wanted: an ontological critic."

argument runs, obviously, in the wrong direction; it would infer the design of a house from the shape and weight of the bricks. No product is what it is simply because its matter is such-and-such; its matter is indeed a necessary, but not a sufficient, condition of its existence and nature. A saw, for instance, is not a saw because the steel determined it should be. The reverse is the case; I wish to cut the fibers of wood a certain way: I must therefore have a blade of a certain kind; it must therefore be made of a substance capable of assuming a certain shape, and hard enough to retain that shape; hence the steel. And, if I am to give a complete account, I must talk not merely about the steel but about the form given it, and how it was given it, and the function of cutting.

The hypotheses concerning subject matter take a variety of forms: poetic fiction is set against truth, or poetic truth against other truths; certain concepts or orderings of concepts are opposed to others, imaginables against credibles, and so on. The principal position is that poetry is myth, or at any rate closely related to myth; it is currently fashionable, numbering among its proponents Maud Bodkin, Robert Penn Warren, nearly all of the psychological and political critics, and the critics who talk of "symbolic structure."[41] Superficially various as these hypotheses are, all are based, like those concerned with the medium, upon a simple dichotomy between what is poetic and what is not. With a little translation, the objections against the linguistic theories also apply to them.

Indeed, the subject-matter hypotheses and the linguistic hypotheses are fundamentally the same, being only separate developments from the same general hypothesis: viz., that all discourse is differentiable in terms of subject matter and style. This supposition, which may be traced at least as far back as the Ciceronian distinction between *res* and *verba*, has proved less profitable and more influential than any other single proposition in the history of criticism. To apply it to poetry is to assume that poetry of whatever kind is a form of discourse, and to suppose that poetic organization is necessarily comparable to the organization of any other form of discourse. Such a supposition makes it impossible to differentiate any form of poetry except in terms of characteristics which it has in common with other discourse; it burkes all discussion of important peculiar characteristics of poetry for which there is no analogue in other discourse. That is, it provides no distinctions whereby any kind of poetry—whatever we may mean by the term—may be isolated and discussed as a separate kind.

41. See *Modern Philology*, 45 (1948): 275-79; 47 (1949): 45-64.

III

I have remarked already that the term "poetry" is ambiguously used. On the one hand, it stands for such works as *Hamlet,* the "Ode to a Nightingale," and "Sailing to Byzantium," all of which are imitations; on the other hand, it stands for any works which, although non-imitative, involve devices or characteristics especially associated with mimetic poetry. In this latter sense, philosophical treatises like Parmenides's *On Nature,* Lucretius's *De rerum natura,* Sir John Davies's *Nosce teipsum;* medical treatises like Fracastoro's *Syphilidis;* histories like the chronicles of Geoffrey Gaimar and Wace or the *Dittamondo* of Fazio; ethical works, like Pope's *Essay on Man* and his *Moral Essays* have all been called poetry. The distinction is not one of value, but of kind; witness the fact that the *Divina commedia* belongs to the second class. The works of the first class are of a quite different order, and are constructed on, and hence have to be judged by, quite different principles from those of works in the second.

This distinction, simple as it is, is likely to prove difficult if not repugnant to a twentieth-century mind. Distinctions of kind are nowadays likely to be called "scholastic"[42]—an epithet which means, I presume, that they are pedantic and useless; and, even if that charge be waived, we have become so used to considering poetry a matter of quality, or even of a degree of a quality, that the distinction is likely to seem a wrong one. Surely, one may say, the *De rerum natura* has more in common with *Hamlet* than with the *Critique of Pure Reason* or the *Essay Concerning Human Understanding;* obviously it ought, therefore, to be considered as poetry rather than as philosophy, especially since the philosophic content is quite incidental, in the view of most readers, to the beauty of the poetry; hence, if kinds are to be distinguished, they must be distinguished on different principles. The proper distinction, however, is not one of kind but of quality transcending all such schoolmasterly distinctions of kinds; one finds poetry in any kind of composition if the *poetic quality* is present.

This skeleton of argument underlies, I am sure, much of modern criticism; and it is by no means pointless or baseless. The objection that no one has yet defined the poetic quality is scarcely a fair one, and the objection that investigation of a quality common to all literature cannot produce sound or fruitful criticism is patently absurd; great critics, Longinus, Sainte-Beuve, and Arnold among them, have done just that. The weaknesses of contemporary criticism are not due to this position but to inept treatments of this position; to the position itself

42. The latest instance occurs in an article by Murray Krieger, "Creative criticism, . . .," *Sewanee Review,* 58 (1950): 41.

perhaps only two rejoinders can be made. First, the legitimacy of inquiring into a quality common to all art, if granted, does not imply the illegitimacy of inquiring into the distinctive characteristics of each art; and second, inquiry of the first kind cannot provide such knowledge as the second kind would provide. Inquiry into a common quality as such cannot of itself provide knowledge of distinctive qualities. Qualitative criticism can at best tell the poet how to construct, the critic how to judge, poetry generally; it can scarcely give information for the construction and judgment of a poem of a given kind. In short, in so far as the problems of constructing and judging the various kinds of poetry are the same or similar, qualitative criticism may be useful; but in so far as these problems differ, it is useless, and may sometimes be pernicious.

It has, for instance, a dangerous tendency to bring about the discredit of principles perfectly valid within a given sphere of art, simply because they are not universally valid. The result is to make most literary theories and judgments curiously unstable, and to make the surviving principles, supposedly universal to a whole art or group of arts, few and very far removed from any particular artistic problems. Art is not composed wholly of universal and absolute principles; if we look at the whole range of art without prejudice, with absolutely open eyes, it is not difficult to see that universality and validity are not necessarily connected. Certain principles underlie all art; others apply only to the temporal, or only to the spatial arts; others apply only to certain arts below these, and so on; but a principle is not less valid in a certain art merely because it happens to be specific to that art, and is invalid in any other. Yet, if we look at the history of criticism, we can readily see that many of its revolutions and counterrevolutions have turned precisely upon this confusion of validity with universality; false universalization—the elevation of something to absolute truth and force when it had only conditional truth and force—and a false demand for universality—the insistence that a principle could not hold for anything unless it held for everything—are the offspring of this confusion; and have time and again thrown criticism into chaos.

Criticism is likely, in the course of its development, to provide many propositions of conditional truth only, and to forget, because such propositions fitted the conditions exactly, that they were only conditionally true. In this fashion many a convention became a rule, many a rule a principle. Such tyranny usually brings revolt; but those who revolt tend to forget, in turn, that if what is conditionally true is not so absolutely, the false conditionally is also not false absolutely. The Three Unities, after long tyranny, have been utterly destroyed as false; but with them was destroyed the little measure of truth which they as doctrines contained. Not every play, it is true, need confine its action within one day and one place; but it is also true that the actions of certain plays would have been much more effective if they had been so confined. The theory of genres has been demolished; but what was true and useful in it perished along with what was false and dangerous. Criticism has been either wholly general or wholly particular ever since; and its present plight, indeed, is in great part due to its lack of such *specific* principles as might have eventually developed out of the theory of genres.

A second dangerous tendency of qualitative criticism is that in emphasizing the common poetic quality it is likely to blind us to the great variousness of poetry. We need, I think, to consider only the two major branches of poetry mentioned above to realize that their differences of kind must be respected if they are to be properly constructed, interpreted, or judged.

Greek epic and drama are mimetic poetry; despite their origin in ritual and myth, they require no reference to these in order to be intelligible and effective. Whatever the mythical origin of an Odysseus, an Achilles, or an Orestes, these are characters simply, and must be interpreted as such; neither they nor their actions and fortunes require allegorical interpretation; whatever symbolic significance they may have possessed as myth they have lost as materials of poetry. Plato, it is true, practiced the allegorical interpretation of poetry which Theagenes and Anaxagoras are said to have initiated in Greece; but he did so clearly as a consequence of his philosophic approach, rather than as a consequence of any characteristics of Homer and the dramatists, and doubtless the case was the same with his predecessors.

Such interpretations indicate, not the inherent necessity of interpreting epic and dramatic poetry as allegory, but the tendency to interpret them so when in their literal interpretation they conflict with doctrine. When the Christian doctrine arose, pagan poetry, literally interpreted, conflicted both with its theological and its moral teachings; and those who sought to defend such poetry were forced by the nature of the case, not only to interpret it allegorically, but also to insist that allegory was the essence of poetry. Moreover, if poetry was to be brought into accord with doctrine, it had itself to become doctrinal, and hence didactic. It is not surprising, in these circumstances, that poetry came to be thought of as didactic allegory.

Didactic allegory presents many superficial resemblances to mimetic poetry; but the differences between them, while perhaps few and obscure, are fundamental. Didactic poetry, whether allegorical or not, must always either propound a doctrine or determine a moral and emotional attitude toward a doctrine in such a way as to command action in accordance with it. The didactic structure must always, therefore, involve explicitly or implicitly some pistic or argumentative element: either the poem argues the doctrine directly, or the argument is left to the reader, as in the case of parables and fables. Argument of some form, however, is always involved; and, whatever form it takes, it inculcates either knowledge or action. In this respect it resembles either the theoretical or the practical syllogism. The principle of didactic poetry, therefore, is its doctrine or thesis, in the peculiar acceptance, theoretical or practical, required for it. Everything in the work mediately or immediately exists and has its peculiar character in order to enforce the doctrine; for instance, the argument itself exists only to prove the thesis, and is absolutely determined by it. Such poetry is, of course, really a kind of dialectic or of rhetoric; and it is not surprising that ages which gave themselves over to such poetry should have identified poetry with rhetoric or dialectic in their critical treatises.

Didactic allegory, as a branch of this kind of literature, comes about when the argument is given a particular metaphorical turn. Like fable and parable, it depends upon the possibility of extended metaphor, which in turn depends upon the possibility of discovering multiple analogies between a thing and its analogue, not only as wholes, but as wholes corresponding part for part. The salvation of the soul, for example, can be allegorically represented as a journey because like- nesses can be found not merely between salvation and a journey, but also between the stages of salvation and the stages of a journey. The metaphor or symbol may, moreover, be an action, and as such be narratively or dramatically represented. It then bears, to a superficial view, a close resemblance to a plot—particularly to the episodic plot; and readers who are unaware of, or uninterested in, its metaphorical import are quite likely to disregard the import and become interested in the action for its own sake, treating it, consequently, as if it were a plot. *The Faery Queene* and *Pilgrim's Progress* are very commonly read in this fashion, as romances rather than as allegories. Anyone who wishes to read them so, purely for the excitement and pleasure which they produce, of course may do so; but he is reading them only in part, and for the sake of certain qualities of that part which are incidental to the primary intention; and if he proceeds to judge these works as romances, to complain that the "plot" is not as effective or that the characters are not as convincing as might be, he is being unreasonable: he is insisting that because a work happens in part to conform to his accidental interest, it should conform to his interest wholly. For the action of an allegory is quite different from a plot. Its characters and incidents are determined, like those of a thesis-novel, by the doctrine to be urged; the only difference is that they are metaphorical whereas the thesis-characters and -incidents are literal and instantial. The characters very generally represent the subjects, and the incidents the predicates, of the doctrinal proposition; such is the case, for example, in the *Divina commedia*. They exist because the doctrine exists and because it must be presented in a certain way; they are what they are because the doctrine has certain characteristics. The allegorical incident happens, not because it is necessary or probable in the light of other events, but because a certain doctrinal subject must have a certain doctrinal predicate; its order in the action is determined not by the action as action, but by the action as doctrine; and whatever emotional quality and force it may have is determined rather by the emotional attitude which the doctrine must inculcate toward a certain object than by the context of action in which it occurs. Allegorical characters are what they are because we must view virtue or vice or whatever is involved in a certain light; not because we must adopt a certain attitude toward agents and patients if the action is to affect us in a certain way. Such poetry is a mode of statement; everything in it is representative of parts of discourse.

The construction of such mimetic poetry as epic, tragedy, and comedy is very different; these are ordered, not to a doctrine, but to a plot. And the construction of a plot is very different from that of an allegorical action. A plot is not a string of interesting incidents, but a system of incidents so constructed as to give us a specific pleasure by arousing and allaying our emotions. It is not, like allegorical action, complete because it completely expresses a given doctrine, but because, as action, it resolves those issues out of which it has begun. It does not, like allegorical action, seek to inculcate certain moral attitudes by arousing our emotions; on the contrary, it makes use of our moral attitudes to arouse our emotions. It does not engage our interest and emotions in particulars of the action in order to instruct us generally; on the contrary, it instructs us about particulars of the characters and actions in the poem in order to engage our emotions and interest in behalf of these very characters and actions. Whereas didactic poetry assumes that if we can be made to feel a certain way in the presence of certain objects we shall be able to make certain moral distinctions, mimetic poetry assumes that if we make certain moral distinctions we shall feel a certain way in the presence of certain objects. Didactic is antecedent to the formation of moral character; mimetic, subsequent. The former assumes that the reader is imperfect and requires to be perfected; the latter, that the reader is perfect and may enjoy a virtuous pleasure.

The characters in plot are present because an action, if it is to effect emotion, must be morally determinate and hence must involve agents and patients of a determinate moral cast; or because they are convenient to the effective representation of that action. The incidents in plot occur because they are necessary or probable, or because they increase the emotional effectiveness of the work. We are not required in mimetic poetry, as we are in allegory, to ask what the characters or the incidents stand for; we are required to interpret the characters only as men and women, and the incidents only as fortunate or unfortunate, and seriously so or not. Mimetic poetry is not statement; doctrine appears, not as something urged, but as something assumed, and chiefly as what the poet assumes to be necessary or probable, or to be evocative of this or that emotion or moral attitude.

The language of didactic allegory is always many-meaninged or "polysemous," as Dante called it, because the things for which the words stand always stand for something further. The language of mimetic poetry, however, is ambiguous only when plot, character, thought, or the exigencies of representation demand that it be so. Hence these forms must differ even in the analysis of their language.

Custom has given these kinds of poetry the same general name; and perhaps courtesy requires that we should withdraw it from neither. But we need not therefore be misled by the name to suppose that these kinds are the same and to be given the same treatment. The critic who reads the *Divina commedia* as if it were mimetic poetry is likely to feel severely rebuked if he ever encounters the Epistle of Dante to Can Grande della Scala; for the poet makes clear that he is writing a scholastic treatise. The critic who, on the other hand, reads mimetic poetry as allegory commits the converse fault of Fulgentius, whose *Continentia Virgiliana* contains interpretations as far-fetched as any in our contemporary mythologists.

IV

There are no necessary differences between poetic diction, as diction, and the diction of any other kind of composition. There are no devices of language which can be pointed to as distinctively poetic; any other kind of composition may utilize metaphor, images, rhythm, meter, rhyme, or any of the "devices of poetic language," and poetry may utilize any of the devices associated with any other literary kind. We talk properly, therefore, about poetic diction as "poetic"—whatever we may mean by poetry—not when we deal with a given order of diction, but when we talk about language in its poetic employment. It is true that in given poetic works the language is markedly different from language in nonpoetic functions; but in any properly constructed work, these differences are brought about, not by any fixed rule of poetic language, but by the functions which the language serves. Whether we refer to didactic, mimetic, or other forms of poetry, language can never be the sole issue, it can never even be the principal issue of poetic analysis. Language is always merely a medium, a material, never a form. Even in the extreme case of Arthur Machen's hero,[43] who wrote meaningless verses purely for their sound, diction is subsidiary; in this case rhythm and melody were formal. If, therefore, we must always talk about poetic diction in terms of some principle over and above language, it follows that discussions of poetic diction must differ, to some extent at least, in accordance with the different principles on which different kinds of poetry are composed.

It might seem at first sight that any such discussion must turn on tropes and figures;[44] but in fact it need not, and perhaps it should not. Important as tropes and figures may be, they are devices with many possible uses, and consequently the mere fact of their employment cannot tell us much about their actual function in given works. Moreover, most if not all of them are capable of being used for quite different, in fact opposite, ends, especially when they are used in combination. A metaphor indicates likeness; but a metaphor coupled with irony indicates difference. Furthermore, tropes and figures have been so repeatedly arranged in impressively exhaustive classifications that we are likely to be given two false impressions: first, that they are really complete and cannot be added to, because it is "against logic" that anything should be added to an exhaustive division; secondly, that their uses or functions have also been exhaustively treated. The first impression is false because it takes no account of development and growth; the second impression is false because poets are inventive, and because new uses for old devices and old uses for new devices are among the things they invent.

Discussion ought therefore to proceed, not from devices to functions, but from functions to devices. In the remaining pages of this essay I shall try to illustrate how language functions in relation to some of the most general aspects of mimetic form. In order to do so it will be necessary first to consider what might be called the general mechanism of such form; that is, how it is constructed and how it ŏperates.

The vicissitudes of literary criticism have made it almost impossible to convey a notion of mimetic form by the simple enumeration of such names as tragedy, comedy, epic, and lyric; for these have all been applied to nonmimetic forms. Furthermore, if the names of literary kinds have broadened in meaning, they have also narrowed in other respects; for example, the name "poetry" itself is today denied to the types of narrative and dramatic prose, although these were commonly regarded as poetry, and their authors as poets, until the early

43. In *The Hill of Dreams*.
44. Cf., e.g., W. K. Wimsatt, Jr., "Verbal Style: Logical and Counterlogical," *PMLA*, 65 (1950): 5–20, and the earlier articles by the same writer cited ibid., p. 13, n. 13; also Maynard Mack, " 'Wit and Poetry and Pope': Some Observations on His Imagery," In *Pope and His Contemporaries: Essays Presented to George Sherburn* (Oxford, 1949), pp. 20–40.

nineteenth century. On the whole, therefore, it is safer to say that mimetic forms include *some* tragedies, comedies, epics, lyrics, novels, short stories, and so on. Differ as they may from each other, all of these have in common the fact that they present to us some spectacle of human happiness or misery, of actualized virtue or vice, or of pleasure and pain; that is, some human action or suffering. It is to the effective emotional presentation of this action or suffering that they are ordered as to a principle; that is, the action or suffering is the part which is chief, which gives form to the work, and to which all else is ordered. By that human spectacle, if I may call it thus, they evoke emotion in us. This is not to say, with Maud Bodkin and others, that they evoke emotion by the reference of their action to one or more generalized myths; on the contrary, they affect us by their particular representation of their respective objects; we react, not to man, but to Oedipus and Hamlet, and to these as presented by Sophocles and Shakespeare, and not to these as detached from the poems in which they are found. Our basic human nature of course underlies our reactions; but the capacity for moral or merely sympathetic emotion is a capacity only; what we actually feel is what is actually called forth by the poet through his representation of objects capable of so affecting us. We feel, both in art and in life, what we are capable of feeling; but we feel a given emotion only when there exist the proper conditions for that emotion; otherwise we should suffer all emotions simultaneously and continually.

The emotions are states of consciousness attended by pleasure and pain; their exciting causes are our opinions; for instance, we grow angry when we think we have been offended, fearful when we think we are in danger, and we do not feel these emotions unless we have these opinions. But emotions do not result merely from the operation of an exciting cause upon our basic human nature; the same exciting cause may produce different and in fact opposite emotions in different persons, or even in the same person at different times. Emotion is also a product of the frame of mind in which we are—of, that is, our disposition as determined by what we have experienced and felt—and of our moral character. Moreover, our opinion is twofold: we opine about persons and about the occasions on which they do or suffer something. There are, therefore, three factors in any emotion: our disposition, the person, and the occasion; for instance, we feel angry when we are disposed to be angry, with persons capable of arousing our anger, when the occasion for anger arises.

We feel a given emotion precisely when these three factors have been brought to concur; the history of the emotions invoked in us by a mimetic poem is precisely, therefore, the history of such concurrences effected by the poet through his imitation. Thus the analyst who would know what the audience is feeling from time to time in the course of a poem—in so far as their emotions are controlled by the poem—must follow the line of such concurrences, taking them of course in their proper sequence.

Most broadly, our emotions are determined by the object which is imitated; e.g., in tragedy, by the action. But, while the object is thus the foundation of what we feel, our emotions are very much modified by the particular manner in which the incidents and characters are disclosed to us; in fact, what we feel at a given moment is much more particularly determined by the manner of representation than by the object. Finally, the words employed by the poet modify still further the emotions produced in us by object and manner, and determine even more particularly what we feel. What we feel concerning the object of imitation, in short, is dependent upon the devices of disclosure which reveal that object to us.

Language is the device of disclosure in most mimetic poetry; in theatrical productions it is of course supplemented by the spectacle and sometimes by music (only, however, when the music interprets what is happening or may happen.) But it would be a mistake to suppose that language can be adequately analyzed as an instrument of disclosure merely by talking about its *meaning*. I have already distinguished, in the first part of this essay, between speech as action (*praxis*) and speech as meaningful (*lexis*); to neglect that distinction is, I think, to blind one's self to a great deal of the poetic mechanism. Most of what is termed "meaning" by critics and poets is not meaning at all, but implications of character, passion, and fortune derived from the interpretation of speech as action. Unless the meaning of the words is grasped, we cannot, to be sure, grasp the nature of the speech as action, but when we grasp the nature of the speech as action, we make inferences—which, as I have argued, are not *meanings*—as to the character and his situation; we perceive an object which is the principal cause of our emotions in poetry.

How far language as diction affects us can be seen if we consider that, from one point of view, the causes of emotion in mimetic poetry fall into four classes: (1) the precedent context, not of words merely, but of the action as a whole up to a given point; (2) the particular speech-action, together with its implications; (3) the speech as diction; (4) ornament. The "Pray you, undo this button" speech of Lear affects us, according to this division, (1) because the whole person has, up to this point, excited certain emotions with respect to Lear and his fortunes, and has left us in a certain frame of mind, (2) because the plea sets before us his utter helplessness, his anguished hope to save Cordelia, the bitter repentance implied in that hope, and so on, (3) because the diction simply and starkly expresses that plea, and (4) because the ornament—in this case, the rhythm merely—affects us as well. Of these four classes of emotional causes, only the last two depend upon the particular choice and arrangement of words. A translation good enough to permit the operation of the first two would not be greatly inferior; indeed, the principal difficulty of translations, even in lyric poetry, is not so much that the translator fails in respect to the last two, as that in his efforts to achieve a certain literary manner or a certain rhythm, or even to give the literal meaning, he fails to preserve the significance of the speech as action; he loses the passionate anger, or the fright; he loses the characteristic marks of nobility or meanness; he translates the meaning only, or the style, or the rhythm.

It is speech as action which plays more powerfully upon our emotions; it provides us with the signs from which we infer such things as plot, character, and thought, the most powerful elements in the work; but the signs which it offers us are natural, and not arbitrary, signs. The signs by which we infer from speech that a man is, say, frightened or resolute, or of this character or that, are not fixed by any convention of language; they differ no more from one tongue to another than weeping in Africa differs from weeping in Alaska, or a groan in Italy from a groan in Spain. And much of the "richness" of poetic language is due to this aspect of it. Much of what is currently discussed as "meaning" is this implication of the speech as act.

A great deal, then, of suspense, surprise, and emotion is effected by something other than diction; nevertheless, diction can enhance these, and on occasion even generate them itself. It is this aspect of poetic language—of diction as diction—that I wish particularly to examine. Its problems are problems of word-choice and word-arrangement; they can never be solved without reference to conventional signs, although they can be discussed generally apart from a given language. The problem of diction is not one of how a frightened man, say, would talk, or of how, more generally, speech serves as an indication of character, passion, or situation; it is one of how, given all such determinations of the speech, words as words may prove most effective. As I have said, this is in one sense the least important part of poetics, for the words are determined by everything else in the poem; in another sense, it is the most important, because the words are all we have to go by, they alone disclose the poem to us. The effectiveness of what they disclose must be kept distinct from their effectiveness as instruments of disclosure; the "startling statement" in drama is startling because it discloses something startling, usually, not because it is startling as a matter of words and their arrangement; but what the words disclose can be effective only if the words are effective in their disclosure of it.

But while disclosure is the general function of the words, what is disclosed must be disclosed properly and in the proper order. Language is a temporal medium; its parts are not coexistent, like those of a spatial medium, but successively existent; when one part is existing, one has ceased or will come to exist; its effects can never have the simultaneity of the effects of color and line in a painting. Moreover, the object imitated in mimetic poetry is always an activity, however minute; even a mood which is momentary is not something static and timeless; hence the object is temporal, too. Consequently the activity must be remembered, if it is to be seen as a whole and have its whole effect; the language must be such as to permit this. This means that certain parts of the action must be rendered vivid, to have their full and proper emotional force, while others must be dimmed; language can produce such vividness or lack of it by the direction of our attention. Again, all arts that have temporal media, since they cannot exhibit everything at once, involve anticipation, as the spatial arts do not, since they present everything to perception simultaneously; and where anticipation is present, we have also suspense and the unexpected, since our anticipation can be played upon and can be surprisingly foiled. It is clear, therefore, that language can be artfully used to conceal or half-conceal. Finally, since language can be pleasing in itself, it has an ornamental function in poetry as well.

While language, then, has, strictly speaking, the general functions of disclosure and of ornamentation, it is useful to treat it under more special heads which follow from the foregoing argument. The mimetic poet, like any other, may be said to have seven subsidiary aims, with respect to language; I call them subsidiary because this essay has made it obvious that they could not be principal. These aims are disclosure, partial disclosure, concealment, direction of attention, evocation of suspense, production of the unexpected, and ornament. What must be disclosed, concealed, etc., belongs to the parts of poetics which deal with plot, character, and thought, and cannot be analyzed here; our present concern is simply the functioning of language as meaningful with respect to these aims.

Disclosure is at a maximum when language is as concise and clear as possible. There are two kinds of concision in language: one is obtained by the use of as few words as possible to express the meaning, while nevertheless expressing the full meaning; the other by expressing only part of the meaning, leaving the rest to inference. Thus the use of enthymeme for syllogism is concise in the latter way; and the famous Lacedaemonian dispatch "Dionysius in Corinth" is of this order. The implication involved here is different from the implications of character, etc., by speech as action in that what is implied is *meaning*, whereas the implications of speech as action are derived from meaning. For instance, the full meaning of the dispatch is "If you attack us, you will be served like a similar aggressor, Dionysius, who was also a great king and is now living, an exile and a private citizen, in Corinth." With the meaning clear, the speech may now be interpreted as an act of defiance implying the moral qualities of the Spartans. Concision is possible also apart from language, when an act is a concise sign, i.e., one which has many implications; and poetic concision is greatest when both language and action are concise. For example, the "Who's there?" of *Hamlet* is not only concise as diction; the fact that the wrong man challenges shows tension, fright, doubt whether the sentinel on duty had suffered some unknown misfortune, an expectation of some foreign and possibly hostile presence, etc. The particular devices for obtaining concision of diction when the meaning is fully expressed vary according to the linguistic structures of the various languages; in general it may be said that such languages as have the same syntactical elements (e.g., the same parts of speech) tend to permit the same abridgments; thus asyndeton is possible in all tongues having conjunctions; and similarly such languages as form their words in the same way permit of the same devices of compounding several words into one. Concision of diction where only part of the meaning is expressed varies similarly with the language; it is also based, perhaps more importantly, on expectation and on logical implication.

Clear language is not language which raises no problems—for example, a scientific fact raising numberless problems may be clearly expressed; indeed, if language when clear never raised problems, questions could never be clear. It is, rather, language which raises no problems as to its meaning for those adequately acquainted with the tongue in which it is couched, however many and however profound the problems arising when its meaning is grasped. Anyone who thinks clear language is possible thinks that it consists in using clear words clearly; and in fact, generally speaking, that is all there is to it. But it is useful to analyze further, especially since the devices of ambiguity and indirection depend upon such analysis.

Whether we think of language as evocative, as evoking concepts, or as significative, as standing for something, the possibility of language depends upon a certain condition: the condition that the powers assumed for language by the speaker in his act of speech—whatever the extent and nature of such powers—should not also simultaneously be denied by the speaker, as evinced by the mode of utterance. I do not mean that he may not decide a given expression is inappropriate or incorrect, or change his mind, or reveal his true opinion by offering us an apparent statement and then withdrawing it; I mean that since language consists of arbitrary signs, which have only such powers as we assign them, the speaker cannot at once assign and refuse to assign them. This is different from the principle of contradiction; the principle of contradiction is not the source of this condition, but a consequence of it; indeed, operates only when certain powers of language are assumed. This fundamental condition is the linguistic warrant, without which language is impossible as language, although it may produce effects in us merely as sound. When it is really violated, lack of clarity does not result because there is no language to be clear; but apparent violations of it result in lack of clarity. Such apparent violations occur when any unit of speech seems to negate itself, either openly, as in oxymoron and paradox, or covertly, as when the things stated do not constitute oxymoron, paradox, etc., but imply them. An example is Donne's analogy of a woman's virtue to a snake's venom. All of these apparent violations relate to the conditions of clarity, and not those of language.

The conditions of clarity itself can be seen if we consider that it is dependent upon three things: the words, the syntactical arrangements, and the relations of sentences. Clarity is produced by the words in so far as they are prime, immediate, commensurate, consonant, and familiar. Words are prime if their use does not suggest that they are not being used in their first literal meaning; for example, "dog" or "animal" are both prime as applied to the beast on the hearthrug. Any word is capable of ambiguity; but conversely, any ambiguous word is capable of being made prime. Words are immediate if they do not in themselves require any special calculation before they yield their meaning; thus the "not-not-not man" of logic-books is not immediate because it requires a calculus of negations, and Eliot's "polyphilo-progenitive" requires etymological calculation. In general no word is immediate unless it is intelligible as a synthesis. This is merely a distinction between simple and familiar compounds on the one hand and unfamiliar compounds, such as coined words, on the other; and it is different from the question of being prime—once we have calculated what "not-not-not man" means, nothing leads us to suppose that it is not prime. Words are commensurate when they are neither too general nor too particular for the thing they stand for; thus "animal" or "Socrates" is incommensurate with "man." Words are consonant if they belong to the same order or level of discourse, in that they contain, as words, no implication of incompatible or inconceivable predication or attribution. For example, a pejorative word used to denote something admirable is used inconsonantly, and is unclear since we have to wonder about its use. Words are familiar when they not only are commonly employed, but are used in their customary grammatical functions, i.e., qua parts of speech; for instance, if a given word is commonly used as a noun and rarely as a verb, it is not wholly familiar when it is used as a verb.

Clarity is produced by syntactical arrangement when amphibology is absent, when grammatical construction is familiar, when the order is the common order, when the material sequence is observed, when predication and attribution are immediate, when the sentence is unified and complete, when the sentence form is primary, when the rhythm is appropriate to the emphasis, and when the sentence is of the proper magnitude. Not all of these need explanation. By observing the material sequence I mean such things as observing the natural order of events; for instance, Shelley's "I die, I faint, I fail" does not observe the material sequence. By immediate predication or attribution I mean that the predicate or the modifier lies adjacent to the subject to which it attaches. Thus parenthetical expressions of any length between subject and predicate produce lack of clarity. By unified sentence I mean one which connects matter which ought to be connected. For example, "She mourned his death and subsequently became very proficient in athletics" is not a unified sentence. By primary sentence form I mean the posing of a question in the interrogative, a statement in the declarative form, and so on. By proper magnitude I mean that the sentence should not be so long that the beginning is forgotten before the end is reached.

Clarity is produced in the relations of sentences when the proper signs of subordination, co-ordination, and transition are employed; when the material sequence is observed; and when the whole correlation (the paragraph) is unified, complete, and of the proper magnitude. Sentences are related to each other in four ways: additively, qualificatively, antithetically, and inferentially; they either add fresh information, qualify what has been said, oppose each other in some way, or are related as parts of an argument. Question and answer and command and compliance are not separate relations, but types of additive relation. The interrogative sentence always presents a subject and demands an attribute, or presents an attribute and demands a subject, or presents both and demands to know their connection; the answer adds the missing point, just as a blank is filled in a questionnaire. The compliance similarly adds information. Clarity results from the relations of sentences when grammatical signs make explicit, in any doubtful cases, which of the four relations is involved; this is particularly necessary when the words or the syntactical arrangements have not been clear.

In general, language is clear in proportion as it requires fewer mental operations to derive its meaning, however many mental operations may result from the meaning once it is known. Hence clear language never involves any misdirection of the mind of hearer or reader, except as this is caused by the tongue in which it is couched; hence language is clear in proportion as it follows normal expectation in all things, for we are not misdirected if what follows is what we expected, whereas any unexpectedness necessitates readjustment; hence familiar words in familiar arrangement are always clearest, since familiarity determines expectation. Language which follows expectation can always be more concise than other language, without sacrificing clarity; for we need only occasional indications that we are on the right track.

It is far from true that ambiguity is the essence of poetry; on the contrary, poetic language should always be as clear as possible, not in the absolute sense, but in the qualified one of maximum clarity consistent with the requirements of the individual poem as a whole. That is, there should be no *unnecessary* misdirection of the reader; and in this respect the greatest poetry is not "puzzling" or unclear, but amazingly clear. Indeed, it would seem that in proportion as the *implications* of the language increase in number and in importance, the language itself is clearer; compare the later poetry of Yeats.

Clarity is not, however, always consistent with the maximum effectiveness of the poem. If everything were disclosed as quickly and clearly as possible, interest, suspense, and surprise, and indeed the poet's whole control of our emotions, would be minimized, and the emotional force of poetry would be greatly lessened. In proportion as characters and situations are made vivid to us, they exert more powerfully their peculiar emotional force, and they can be disclosed too rapidly to be vivid. We are, for instance, more vividly aware of the vice of a man when we realize that we were mistaken in the supposition that he is virtuous, and we are more vividly aware of virtue which we have misjudged; our reaction in each case is proportional to our vivid awareness. Interest and suspense must diminish once we know all, and surprise is impossible when only the expected happens. Hence, obviously, the poet must, if merely upon these grounds, conceal some aspects of his subject, and misdirect us in our interpretation of it; and, although language is not the only instrument of concealment and misdirection, it is nevertheless an important one.

All of the points involved in disclosure, as analyzed above, generate devices of partial disclosure and concealment. An example or two must suffice here. Partial disclosure is produced by vagueness, among other things; and vagueness is produced most generally by the incommensurateness of terms, by ambiguity either of terms, syntax, or sentence-relation, and by altering circumstances within the poem. All but the last are clear; I mean by it such phenomena as are produced when a verbal expression changes meaning as the poem advances, not because of verbal ambiguity as such, but because of changing circumstances, just as "King of England" may now mean one man, now another. This is different from ambiguous prophecies such as those in *Macbeth*. The powerful effect of vagueness in inducing suspense and otherwise

augmenting attention and emotion is admirably exemplified, as Coleridge has observed, by Shakespeare's treatment of the ghost in *Hamlet;*
it is first disclosed to the audience as a "thing" which "appears," has
appeared before, and may momently be expected to appear again,
then as something that may be fantasy, as something that might not be
believed, then as a "dreaded sight" twice seen, and as an "apparition";
after such verbal preparation the ghost appears, and that unexpectedly.
This is indeed, as Coleridge says, "admirable indefiniteness," and it is
particularly effective since the prior discussion has induced a certain
frame of mind in the audience. Complete disclosure here, by the use of
the word "ghost," would have ruined the effect. The vagueness of the
incommensurate word is not necessarily a matter of generality; for
instance, T. S. Eliot achieves many effects by the use of words more
specific than his meaning, e.g., the proper names which turn out after
all not to have an individual reference. In general it may be said that
the poet must disclose as much of his subject, and only so much, as is
requisite to produce the opinion and frame of mind on which the
desired emotion depends; and obviously language can help or hinder in
this.

Since emotions are produced, not from mere opinions, but from
opinions actively entertained, and since this active entertainment
results from the focusing of our attention, clearly the direction of
attention is of great importance. It is achieved in many ways: by the
mere mention of something where other things are left unmentioned;
by repetition; by the repeated omission or avoidance of the obvious
word where the whole context insists upon it; by implication, especially
when the premise given is dull, but the conclusion implied is shocking
or startling, or vice versa when the conclusion is given; by treatment on
a larger scale than that afforded other things, provided that the scale is
not so large as to weary the attention; by use of suspense and surprise;
by understatement, overstatement, or irony; by changes of style, as
from the circumlocutory to the terse; and by images and metaphors.

Only a few of these require explanation. Omission of the obvious
word can be achieved by breaking off the grammatical member short
of the word, or by substituting an incommensurate or an inconsonant
word; or, what is rather a matter of invention than of diction, by
substituting attributes for subjects, antecedents for consequents, and
so on. The chapter called "The grindstone" in *A Tale of Two Cities,* for
example, directs attention to the bloodiness of Paris not merely by
repeatedly using the word "blood," but by naming attributes of blood
such as redness and imparting them to the whole scene. Attention is
produced by the unexpected in various ways, and especially when the
whole meaning is reversed so that, for example, a compliment becomes
an insult. Thus the speech of the elder Yeats at the Abbey Theatre:

"This Ireland, this land of saints—plaster saints"; and thus John Barrymore's declining of an invitation: "I have a previous engagement which I shall make as quickly as possible."

Suspense and the unexpected are of course based upon disclosure and concealment; nevertheless not everything concealed or disclosed produces these. The matter disclosed or concealed is of course the primary determinant, and it must be matter which engages interest and anticipation; but this granted, suspense and surprise may nevertheless be enhanced by the diction. Broadly speaking, we are in suspense until we have found the meaning of any discourse that engages our attention, merely because of the nature of language as temporal; but suspense can be artificially produced by delaying what we wish to know; hence, by stopping the sentence short of the informing word, or by using vagueness at the point that should inform, e.g., paraphrasis, especially where the paraphrasis resolves the familiar into the unfamiliar, so that we are delayed by having to conjecture (cf. Stefan Zweig's "wooden wedge affixed to a hollow tube" for "rifle"); by interruption of predication through apposition, parenthesis, and so on; by oxymoron, paradox, and the other devices that rest on apparent contradiction (for we must pause to consider how "rash timidity" or "drunken sobriety" is possible); by extension of the grammatical parts, e.g., making an attributive adjective into a predicate or a relative clause, etc.; by giving the facts in such order that knowledge is incomplete until the last (e.g., by saying "There, in the drawer, lay a shiny cylinder . . . fitted with a needle, the tip of which was still stained dark brown" instead of "There . . . lay the hypodermic syringe which had been the instrument of murder"). In general, suspense will be produced by every device of diction which delays the discovery of meaning.

An image is a verbal expression capable of conveying a conception of the form either of some sensory presentation or of some bodily feeling. Images therefore derive from three sources: the "common sensibles," which are perceptible to all senses or more than one, such as magnitude, motion, rest, figure, and number; the external sensibles, e.g., an object of vision; and bodily feelings such as pain, heat, cold, pressure, fatigue, tension, etc. As our perceptions are limited—we do not, for instance, see all that is presented to the eye—so images are limited; an image must not therefore be a complete depiction, but the formula of an *aperçu*. An image, moreover, must consist of parts (a subject and its attribute, as the minimum); yet the statement must be concise enough so that all details fuse and operate as one perception. Such a synthesis is impossible if the elements are too many or too indeterminately related to each other. For instance, a contemporary novelist takes several sentences to say that a man's face was composed of V's, which effects nothing despite the elaborate statement of how it was so composed, because the V's have to be imagined in various positions and because the memory cannot retain them all; a second description of the man as "a blond satan" conveys a better picture, but it is still not really an image. For an image must be distinguished from a mere description of an object; otherwise every descriptive catalogue would be full of images; and it is also different from a word effecting a picture, or every concrete noun would be an image. What distinguishes the image from ordinary description is that it effects a mental representation such as a particular perception might, with a speed as nearly approaching simultaneity as words permit. Thus it must consist of elements readily conceivable and simultaneously conceivable as what a single perception would present; any change of point of view or other condition of perception is fatal: Coleridge was right in rejecting "the furrow followed free," because this necessitated a change of place. The novelist mentioned above speaks of a speeding car appearing to one of its passengers as "a tan streak beneath us"; this similarly refuses to synthesize into an image. From what has just been said about the content of an image, it follows that the diction of an image should be clear, concise, and "heightened." By "heightened" language I mean slightly exaggerated; the words should suggest a color clearer or brighter than would apply to the real perception, since mental images are necessarily fainter than real perceptions; this increases vividness.

"Vivid images" are commonly confused with images of vivid things; but a vivid image is so because of its depiction and not its object. Thus the imagery of Yeats's early poems is vivid although it depicts dim things like "moth-like stars" and "glimmering moths." Obviously images should always be vivid; whether the things they present should be made vivid is another question. Poets frequently try to gain a kind of spurious vividness of imagery by the insertion of words like "bright" and "vivid," but this is, on the whole, bad; anyone can make vivid imagery of that sort. The effect of imagery ought to be more like that of dramatic presentation than of narration; we must feel as though we are seeing or hearing, not as though someone were describing something to us. The "brightness" should be brought out by an accurate word, or implied, or suggested by metaphor. Images are made more vivid by contrast or by the inclusion of an uncommon or unexpected element, just as objects themselves are—for instance, Wallace Stevens's "rouged fruits in snow." Vividness results also from the selection of an unusual object—cf. Eliot's "jeweled unicorns draw by the gilded hearse"—or from an unusual perception of it; this is, however, a matter of content. Much more might be said; perhaps it will suffice here to say one thing further: that while good images do not necessarily make a good poem, bad ones can damage a poem greatly.

Aristotle has distinguished four kinds of metaphor; we may supplement his remarks by observing that such metaphors as he calls "proportional" divide into the simple and the complex, according as the likeness on which the metaphor is based is in terms of a single attribute or several. For instance, "pearl-pale hand" is simple, whereas "angelic hair" is complex; the former sets only a certain pallor before us, whereas the latter suggests sheen, delicacy, length, color, etc. Complex metaphors give us either a mere conjunction of attributes or a correspondence of whole with whole and part with part. The latter is exemplified in the famous analogy, in Ecclesiastes, of the body to a citadel, in the comparison of the body to a castle in *The Faery Queene*, and of the state to a body in *Coriolanus*.

There are three elements in every metaphor: perhaps we may call them the referent, or thing analogized, the analogue, or thing to which the referent is analogized, and the continuum, or ground of likeness, whether in fact or thought, which permits the analogy. A metaphor is clearly stated as metaphor when these are explicit, and when the grammatical indications of similitude are present or easily understood. But a metaphor to be clear as metaphor must be something more than the clear statement that something resembles something in a certain respect; it must be intelligible as a likeness. A metaphor can never be false; it must be true, either in that the analogy is real, or in that someone in a certain condition might think it real. Hence a metaphor can be "difficult" in three principal ways: through omission of one of its elements, through unclear statement grammatically, through apparent falsity. Difficult metaphor always produces suspense, and is useful for forcing inference; that is, the difficulty produces curiosity which impels the reader to infer; the inference involves delay, and thus suspense. When one element of the metaphor is suppressed, a riddle always results: for example, "Why is a snake's venom like a woman's virtue?" Curiosity, and therefore suspense, are heightened when the things involved are seemingly disparate, and heightened even more when seeming paradox is involved, as in Donne's metaphor just mentioned; for the comparison of a snake's venom to a woman's virtue implies that good is like bad.

When the continuum is a sensible quality, the metaphor is bound to be easy; where it is not, it always involves some difficulty. Anyone knows that the sun is like a lamp in respect of light; but why a flea is like marriage, or why lovers resemble compasses, is another matter. The metaphysical metaphor takes referents and analogues with no apparent continua; or states the continua last.

When both referent and continuum are suppressed, or only vaguely intimated, the metaphor becomes a symbol; what we speak of as "symbolism" is, so far as diction is concerned, merely the employment of symbolic metaphor. When even the symbol is ambiguous, either because it involves the unfamiliar use of the familiar, or because it has been vaguely or partially stated and must be clarified by the context, suspense due to metaphor is at a maximum. Eliot's "little old man" is an example; for when we have translated *gerontion* into that, the familiarity of the expression keeps us from realizing that it is a symbol.

Many other kinds of metaphor may be distinguished; among them what might be called the "correlative metaphor." Hart Crane's "adagios of islands" is of this kind. This type makes an attribution to the correlative of one of the terms of the metaphor, rather than to the term. For example: *motion of ship: motion of adagio music;* the motion is now transferred to the correlative, i.e., to that with reference to which the ship moves; hence *adagios of islands.*

Among kinds of unexpected metaphor, there is the kind which unites terms commonly united, so that the likeness appears trite; a new continuum is involved, however, in the light of which the metaphor is suddenly vivid and startling.

Again, there is what I shall call the "subsumptive metaphor" or the "subsumptive symbol." This is a general metaphor comprising many metaphors as its parts, and uniting all; the Platonic process of "combination" must be used in order to produce such metaphor. It is particularly powerful because of the dialectic which it entails. The magical mythology of Yeats's *Vision* involves it, and Eliot's Wheel is of the same order.

Somewhat akin to metaphor is the use of words which, while not constituting metaphor, have metaphorical suggestion, either determinately suggesting some analogue, or leaving the analogue vague. For instance, "The train glided out of a hole in the mountain and slid into a dark wood" suggests a serpent determinately, although without real metaphor, for these are perfectly literal attributes. Use of more general attributes in the instance would render the analogue indeterminate, but have the effect of metaphor still. This is very useful for producing "atmosphere."

Many other developments of diction are, like these last kinds, fairly new; the study of diction, even as tropes and figures, may scarcely, therefore, be regarded as completed; and still less the investigation of its complex uses in relation to the various kinds of poetic ends.

THE ARGUMENT OF
LONGINUS'S *ON THE SUBLIME*

T he brief and fragmentary treatise Περί Ὕψους presents the spectacle, not too uncommon in literature, of a major critical document which has gained assent—in this case almost universal assent—to its statements while the arguments which developed and guaranteed those statements have gone nearly unexamined. Since its publication at Basel by Robortello in 1554, and more particularly since Boileau's translation a hundred and twenty years later, the treatise has been frequently edited and translated, admired and eulogized, cited and discussed; but the quality of sensibility for which it has been chiefly esteemed, and which has won for it innumerable and illustrious admirers, seems unfortunately to have discouraged logical analysis. Twentieth-century commentators on the work, from Churton Collins[1] to Mr. J. W. H. Atkins[2] seem to have written with Gibbon's famous remark in mind and consequently to have been occupied chiefly with the insight, the enthusiasm, and the originality displayed in the treatise; and while these preoccupations have in their turn produced eloquence and insight, as well as some excellent outlines and précis, they have as often led to the neglect and, in Saintsbury's case at least, even to the deprecation of the dialectical apparatus which underlies the work.[3]

Yet Longinus, if, indeed, he was the author of this treatise, exhibits on every page a concern with problems which could scarcely have arisen in a random discussion wherein literary enthusiasm was the solitary guiding principle of the critic; and even to grant, as numerous commentators have done, that the work presents clearly marked divisions, amid the ruins of which some fragments of an argument may

Reprinted from *Modern Philology*, vol. 39, no. 3 (February 1942).
1. Churton Collins, *Studies in Poetry and Criticism* (London, 1905).
2. J. W. H. Atkins, *Literary Criticism in Antiquity* (Cambridge, 1934), 2:210 ff.
3. George Saintsbury, *A History of Criticism and Literary Taste in Europe* (New York, 1902), 1:159, 161–62.

still be discerned, is to offer insufficient explanation of the portions of the manuscript which are still extant. The eleven manuscripts of the work have been the object of much learned scrutiny from a philological point of view, but even in the collect they scarcely present, by the methods of consideration possible to grammarians, anything like an adequate representation of the whole treatise. As a consequence two courses, the pursuit of both of which has been sufficiently exemplified, have been open to the scholar operating on purely grammatical principles: either the lacunae might be made the subject of learned lamentation, in the absence of further manuscripts, or the text as we have it might be called in question on the basis of philological arguments of varying direction and cogency. To the literary historian yet another course is open: the topics with which Longinus is concerned may be treated as the conventional topics of Greek and Roman writers on rhetorical theory, and questions of their order and even of the manner of their discussion may be answered in terms of the practice of earlier, and not infrequently even of later, rhetoricians.[4] The objection to both the grammatical and the historical solutions is properly, not that either approach is inferior or that distinguished efforts have been wanting in either, but that, in terms of what Longinus himself says, as I have suggested, many questions of importance remain unanswerable. The first page of the treatise, for example, presents to us an author who is pre-eminently concerned with method, for the criticism of Caecilius rests upon methodological grounds and the major preoccupation evinced by the introductory remarks is with the precepts according to which a technical treatise must be constructed. Again, the discussion of whether an art of sublimity is possible[5] becomes transformed, if we regard it as a matter of convention, into a servile and meaningless imitation of other and more philosophic inquiries; and, in like manner, topics of discussion throughout the treatise become unimportant and ineffectual, sometimes indeed wholly unintelligible, efforts to conform to a literary tradition. To such a place of unimportance, thus, we should have to consign the criticism of the *Odyssey*, the discussion of faultlessness versus faulty grandeur, the chapters on pettiness, and the discussion of literary decadence which closes the portion of the work which we have; and, similarly, numerous minor passages would become intrusions into a

4. Mr. Atkins's explication seems to me to be chiefly of this sort.

5. Sec. ii. For this essay I have chiefly used the text and Latin translation of Benjamin Weiske (Leipzig, 1809) and the text and English translation of W. Rhys Roberts (Cambridge, 1899). Most of the translated phrases which occur in the essay have been taken, however, from the translation of A. O. Prickard (Oxford, 1926). Since this essay does not depend upon genetic questions, such as that of the authorship of the treatise, I have chosen to refer to the author simply as "Longinus," whatever his actual name may have been.

work which, in the judgment of many critics and scholars, would have been better without them. In the general disregard, then, of the logical schematism of the work, the *Peri Hypsous* has become an aggregation of fragments, important chiefly for the extraordinary "insights" which they contain; and those passages wherein the power of insight seems to have failed, or wherein the author does not make his judgments intelligible, may be dismissed—by the author's own canon as expressed in sections xxxiii–xxxv—as faults which cannot dim the grandeur of the whole.

In opposition to these methods of consideration and as a possibly convenient auxiliary to them in the problems which they pose, a third approach might be suggested. While the treatise is doubtless of striking philological and historical interest, it is, nonetheless, as Longinus himself points out, a treatise on a certain kind of literary art, that is, it is a practical treatise expounding certain means as conducive to a certain end; as a consequence, unless the citation of means is to be regarded as purely arbitrary and dogmatic, the treatise might be exhibited as a reasoned structure, that is, as an argument, and considered wholly in that light.

The treatment of the work purely as a reasoned structure would turn, it goes without saying, on questions at most only equivocally connected with those ordering other methods. Indeed, it would be proper to lay down at once a series of postulates governing the procedure. In the first place, we may assume that any argument whatsoever—provided, of course, that it is strictly argument—comes about through the necessity of resolving some question and that the argument proper terminates, as having achieved its end, when that question is really or apparently resolved. Second, since the resolution of a question is the end of argument, it is clear that the question must be expounded solely from the text as from the only proper clue to the meaning and that the argument itself must be regarded at all times as the means by which, previous knowledge mediating, the end is achieved. In the third place, since in any extended inquiry a problem contains a series of subproblems, the argument must be divided according to these in its primary divisions, and into further subdivisions, if these have subsidiaries. In the fourth place, we may assume that every device—distinction, definition, example, analogy, quotation, etc.—is used deliberately and that the use of every such device is to be explained in terms of the necessity of the end and to be noted as a sign of what the author considers to be demonstration. Finally, the order of the text as a whole is to be explained in terms of demonstration as the author conceives it, that is, in terms of his method. It may be objected to such a proposal that the resultant analysis would depend wholly on the assumption that Longinus had indeed constructed the treatise with this particular end in view. The objection must, of course, be accepted; but the grounds of its acceptance would make it clear that it is acceptable not as an objection but as a general comment concerning any mode of consideration and interpretation of a work whatsoever. Any mode of grammatical analysis must depend on the assumption that the work in question was composed according to grammatical principles; any mode of historical consideration must rest, likewise, either on the assumption that the writer was to an extent shaped by his times and his admirations, consciously or unconsciously, or on the assumption that some relation, however tenuous, is traceable between the writer as a historical entity and certain other historical entities. Similarly, it is true, the philosophical analysis of the work must be based on some assumption appropriate to the mode of consideration, since no method proceeds *ex nihilo*; but it must be added that it can scarcely be dangerous or groundless to assume that philosophic works would be ordered to a philosophic end or that this treatise in particular is composed upon principles which alone—if we except sheer accident—could have given it the character which it is universally conceded to possess.

The treatise *On the Sublime* is an inquiry into the methods by which a certain quality of literary composition may be achieved. The question which it seeks primarily to answer, thus, is a question which neither Plato nor Aristotle nor the "scholastic" rhetoricians of Greece and Rome would have indicated as a principal question even in the study of literature. For Plato, rhetoric and poetics are arts which are occupied with the construction of semblances of the truth; and since the semblance is most perfect when its maker is one who knows what the truth is, the ultimate questions of poetic and rhetoric transcend the limitations of these arts and fall under dialectic, for they must involve knowledge—a problem which is properly to be treated by the dialectician alone. Thus in the *Ion* the true poet, and in the *Phaedrus* the true rhetorician, is ultimately he who knows, i.e., the dialectician; and those who are rhetoricians and poets merely, like Lysias and Ion, are men in possession merely of the elements of their arts and, in sharper statement, indeed possess no art whatsoever. The question posed by Longinus is, therefore, for Plato, at best an elementary one; for Aristotle, on the other hand, it would have been an impossible one, since Aristotle's method entails a distinction between rhetoric and poetics and involves, even within these, a specialized treatment dependent upon a distinction into kinds. In such a method the question which Longinus poses as the primary question of his art consequently would not have been answerable as a generality; even in specific treatment, on the other hand, it would not have served as the subject matter even of an opusculum and in its reduction to the Aristotelian method would have been relegated, perhaps, only to the discussion of appropriate and impressive stylistic in the third book of the *Rhetoric*. Lastly, for the "scholastic" rhetoricians of Greece and Rome, the question of sublimity is posed never as an end but as a question relevant to the various means—more specifically, to the different kinds of styles—of rhetoric; and, while for these rhetoricians the question would have been one of greater importance than for Plato or Aristotle, it would have been, nonetheless, specifically a rhetorical problem, and its solution would have consisted in the enumeration of stylistic devices—chiefly the "figures" of rhetoric—which are constitutive of the elevated style. Whereas Plato draws a distinction between literary kinds and transcends it, whereas Aristotle discriminates among kinds of works and uses this discrimination as a principle of his treatment of them, and whereas the scholastic rhetoricians find their primary distinctions among rhetorical ends rather than among kinds of means, Longinus obliterates ultimately all such distinctions of kinds and end and makes the focal point of his inquiry a certain quality discriminated from among other qualities of composition. A treatise so ordered is distinct in method from these other treatments; and the statements which are employed in the prosecution of that method cannot be compared directly, without a precarious shift of meanings, to the statements which arise out of such variously opposed treatments as those of Plato, Aristotle, and, let us say, the author of the *Ad Herennium*.

The criticism of Caecilius with which the treatise opens is significant of Longinus's awareness of the problems which a literary treatise, as a practical work, would involve. The criticism turns on two main issues: first, the earlier treatise had been too low and had failed especially in the omission of vital points; second, it had failed to give readers sufficient assistance in accordance with the proper first aim of every writer. While the generality of the statement of these censures allows a certain latitude of interpretation, the exemplification of Caecilius's errors, together with the positive precepts immediately laid down for a technical treatise—a treatise stating the various means to a practical end—perhaps makes the import of the criticism sufficiently clear. There are two main rules, Longinus tells us, for a practical treatise, the first dealing with the end aimed at, the second with the means toward that end: first, the end must be made evident, and, second, specific means to its achievement must be indicated; and it is a mark of Longinus's concern with the practical that the first question, which is a theoretical one, should be adjudged less important in the present treatise than the second, which is a practical one. By both these precepts, Caecilius has utterly failed: with respect to the first, he has sought to define the sublime by the mere collection of instances of sublimity; this is useless, either for a theoretical or for a practical inquiry, inasmuch as in the first consideration it does not provide a definition of sublimity and so affords no knowledge, and, in the second consideration, it does not afford such knowledge of the end as will permit the enumeration of the various means directed toward it. Sublimity is known instantially to all men of education and taste; and to write after the manner of Caecilius, thus, "as though we did not know," is to fail to construct an art of the sublime. With respect to the second precept, Caecilius, we are told, "unaccountably passed over" the indication of the means. Hence the earlier treatise has neither theoretical nor practical value.

Even from these earliest remarks, the ordering of the treatise, i.e., the principal division of its problems, can be seen clearly. Any art approached in this fashion must have three primary problems: clarification of the end aimed at, enumeration of the means to this end, and demonstration that the means are actually conducive to the proposed end. Since art involves purpose, the end must be known in some manner to the artist, or else his operations will be only vaguely purposive, if purposive at all; since any art affords instruments to its end and since not all instruments are appropriate to a given end, the appropriate means must be designated; and, since the efficacy of the art depends upon whether the instruments are actually efficient of the end, the connection of means and end must be demonstrated. The consideration of the end is clearly prior in a practical inquiry, since the means are determined by it; and we know the means when we know the causes of the end, so that what in a theoretical inquiry would be the causes would become in a practical inquiry the means; and to know the means as causes, third, of a given end is to know that the means are indeed efficacious of that end. The main body of Longinus's discussion, therefore, turns on these three problems: from the end of section ii to section viii he treats of the end of the practical inquiry, i.e., of sublimity and its opposites, together with the causes of all these; from section viii to the lacuna occurring in section ix, he deals with the demonstration of the means as conducive to sublimity; and the remainder of the work is given over to a discussion of the means and the divers problems which they entail.

Before these questions can be asked or answered, however, certain preliminary problems must be solved. Longinus has already treated, in his first paragraph, of the rules by which a technical treatise must be regulated; he must now ask, also, whether an art of the subject matter he proposes is in fact possible. To ask whether an art is possible is to pose two fundamental problems: it is, first, to ask whether the object produced by the art has existence (and Longinus is concerned with this question from sec. i. 3 to sec. ii) and, second, to ask whether there are

modes of artificial production of that object (and this question occupies
the extant whole of sec. ii). The object to be produced must first of all
be something which can exist, for there could obviously be no
production of what cannot exist; and in this proof of the existence of
the object Longinus finds it necessary only to select from among
admittedly existent psychological phenomena. These phenomena have
as their immediate cause literary works; but it will be necessary to
distinguish these from the phenomena caused by rhetoric, or the art of
the sublime will not itself be distinct from rhetoric and, indeed, would
be subsumed by it as a part under a whole, thereby precipitating the
inquiry into an enumeration of the usual rhetorical devices. Consequently, to avert this danger, Longinus distinguishes his proposed art
from rhetoric,[6] with which it might be so easily confused, and in his
distinction he introduces the triad of terms—author, work, and
audience—which constitute the fundamental framework of his argument. With respect to the author, sublimity is that which has
constituted the greatest poets and prose writers in their high place and
given them their fame; with respect to the audience, the effect of
sublimity is transport (ἔκστασις) and not persuasion (πειθώ); and the
former differs from the latter in that it is stronger than persuasion or
the incidental pleasure attendant on persuasion, for the audience is
powerless to resist ἔκστασις, although πειθώ may be resisted; and,
finally, with respect to the work, the excellences of rhetoric are
contextual, that is, they emerge from the whole and are temporal,
whereas the virtue of sublimity is that it emerges from the part and is
instantaneous. Since there are psychological phenomena answering to
this description, as, according to Longinus, all men of education and
taste are aware, since there are productions of the kind described, and
since there are men who are designated as the greatest writers, it is
evident that sublimity has been proved to exist.

Next it is necessary to show that modes of artificial production exist
by which sublimity may be generated, inasmuch as not every existent
object is the product of art. Since Longinus assumes that man can
produce literary works which have the quality of sublimity and that
hence the quality exists, the argument[7] reduces to two questions which
form the center of a dispute as to whether sublimity is produced, since
produced it clearly is, by nature or by art and to a third question as to
whether in any case its modes of acquisition are teachable. The import
of these problems is clear: the first objection, that genius is innate, i.e.,
natural, and that the natural is spoiled by art, is countered by the
statement that nature itself is systematic; were this not so, the present

[Marginal handwritten notes: Tate balances ω. / νόησις ω. / ἔκστασις. / Often is more observant.]

6. i. 3-4.
7. ii.

art would be impossible, since art must be an improvement upon nature; there are no arts of doing badly what nature can do well. The second objection, that nature is sufficient, elicits Longinus's response that even in genius it is insufficient, since genius falls into faults, exemplified fully in the later discussion, if left to itself without the controls of science; were this not so, again there would be no possibility of an art of the sublime, since there would be only a natural basis of sublimity and since there are no arts for doing what nature does adequately and infallibly. But, says Longinus, nature is to art as good fortune is to good counsel; and as good fortune is annulled where good counsel is wanting, so is genius annulled by lack of art. The third objection, that production of the sublime is unteachable, is removed by an argument which turns on the very possibility of making the judgments which led to the first two objections: if those who argue against the possibility of an art of the sublime can make such objections, then, since these statements concerning sublimity themselves fall under art and not under nature, they serve to substantiate the existence of the art, and, since they are preceptual, the production of sublimity is teachable. Hence, by all considerations, there is possible an art of the sublime.

Since an art of sublimity is possible, Longinus now takes up the problems of the art itself; and the fundamental triad of terms signifying author, work, and audience makes possible an argument of considerable clarity and power. In the order of composition the genius (author) composes a work which has a certain literary quality of sublimity (work) and which effects ἔκστασις in hearers or readers (audience); the order of inquiry into the technique of composition, however, is the reverse of this; for we begin with a sensation in ourselves, as audience, which we recognize to be ἔκστασις. Inquiring into the cause of this sensation, we find it to be a certain quality of sublimity in the work; but, while this is perhaps explicative of our sensation, we can at this stage say nothing concerning the manner in which a work must be composed. Consequently, we must inquire beyond the work into the faculties of the author which permitted its composition; and when we have achieved a statement of these, we have only to ask how these may be acquired or cultivated to answer the question of how the sublimity of a work may be achieved or the ecstasy of an audience effected. The manner in which the terms of the triad may be employed is clear: the dialectic moves in the one direction or in the other across the triad, using a reaction of the audience to define a fault or virtue of a work, a quality of the work to illustrate a faculty of the author; and what warrants this motion, primarily, is that our sensibility distinguishes ἔκστασις from any other effect of discourse upon us and that we know ourselves to be moved to ecstasy by a literary work produced by a human agent. To argue in this manner, Longinus is well aware, is ultimately to analogize author, work, and reader; but the legitimacy of the procedure can hardly be called in doubt, particularly when we recall that the statements in the work which have gained most general assent—such statements as "the effect of sublimity is not persuasion but transport"[8] and "sublimity is the ring of a great soul"[9]—constitute the very foundations of the argument. So analogizing, however, Longinus has made it impossible to discuss separately the various literary kinds; there can be here no theory of tragedy, of comedy, epic, or comic-epic and no theory of rhetoric, since sublimity may be found in all these and in philosophic and historical literature as well and since it results from the nature of neither one nor another of these kinds of literary production but from the faculties of the agent who produced these. So analogizing, too, it is impossible to escape the consequence that the foundations of the art must be stated in psychological terms; this, however, scarcely affords a foothold for objection, since it means merely that Longinus, in answering the question of how the sublime is produced, has chosen to answer it in terms of human character and faculties rather than in terms of the characteristics of a literary work or of the literary devices which must be employed. We may deny the analogy constituted by the triad, we may demand an answer in other terms; but the argument of the treatise itself could be called in question only if we insist on affixing other significances to the terms which Longinus employs or on asserting that the study of literature involves totally different questions.

The text resumes, after a lacuna amounting to two pages of the Paris MS 2036, in the midst of a discussion of the faults into which unassisted genius may fall. Fragmentary as the whole treatise is, however, one perhaps need not despair of the intelligibility of the work; a careful consideration of the direction and method of argument and of the assumptions involved in the critical judgments affords excellent ground for some restoration of the lacunae, at least to the extent of reconstructing the argument. In the case of this—the first—lacuna, the missing argument can be reconstructed by an analysis of the most immediate problems of Longinus, and the reconstruction is supported by the resumption of the text itself. The argument has begun, let us remember, with an inquiry into ἔκστασις, a term falling under the audience-term of the triad; and the term itself has been defined, since a mere selection was intended, only by reference to a term in some way its opposite, persuasion, this term being taken also in the sense of an affection of the audience. This treatment by opposites is characteristic

8. ii. 4.
9. ix. 2.

of the method of the entire treatise; sublimity itself is defined, at one stage, by contrast with opposite qualities of style, and the causes of sublimity are contrasted with the causes of these opposites; truth is held up against fiction, impeccability against sublimity, and the treatise closes, in fact, with an analysis of the mean style which parallels the analysis of the sublime and with an inquiry into the degeneration of contemporary writers. It is clear, therefore, that Longinus must have argued, from effects upon an audience contrary to that of ἔκστασις, toward qualities of style contrary to that of sublimity, since, indeed, we find him discussing, after the lacuna, exactly such qualities of style; and since the warrant for the existence of sublimity depended upon the audience's sensibility of a certain kind of passion, viz., ἔκστασις, it is clear that, if the treatise is consistent, the existence of the opposite qualities must have rested upon the same basis. For there are no topical terms (i.e., terms central to the discussion) which do not fall under one or another term of the triad of author, audience, and work; and since explication of qualities of style in terms of the author would be impossible, inasmuch as the argument has not yet reached that stage of development, and since explication of qualities in terms of kinds of works would likewise be impossible, inasmuch as no discrimination of kinds has been made—for, as we remarked, sublimity is a term predicable of any kind of work—therefore explication must have been made in terms of diverse effects upon the audience. And this is shown, furthermore, by the fact that the discussion, when it resumes, presupposes such discrimination of effects. On the grounds of these four arguments, then, such discrimination must have been made.

If this is so, we may attempt to reconstruct the discrimination; and this may be done either by considering the procedure of the previous argument or by asking what the resumption of argument presupposes. First, in the former manner, we may note that since the discrimination is of effects upon the audience and since one known effect is that of ἔκστασις, which is defined as an irresistible moving of the souls of the audience, and since the other effects are the opposites of these, the opposites must therefore have in common the general characteristic of nonmovement in that special respect; and since ἔκστασις is literally a being-put-out-of-place so that, as Longinus later remarks, the audience is as one with the speaker, it follows that the opposite effects will differ specifically in that they are different kinds of movement away from that unity with the speaker. How they differ specifically may be discerned from examination of the text when it resumes:[10] Longinus is discussing three vices of style, two of which arise from certain relations of the passion of the speaker to the subject matter of the work, one of

10. iii.

which arises from a lack of relation of his passion to the subject matter. Given a subject matter which lends itself to sublimity, the passion of the speaker may exceed the subject, and so the style will be turgid; or fall below it, and so the style will be frigid; or be unrelated to it, i.e., inappropriate to it, and so *parenthyrsus* results. If the classification of vices of style is on this principle, it is exhaustive; and there seems, consequently, no reason to suppose that parts of the classification are missing. The different opposites of ἔκστασις, therefore, would be effects upon an audience corresponding to each of these stylistic vices. In one sense, then, they are various kinds of indifference to the speaker; but they will be diversely attended, as special kinds of boredom, by risibility, mere contempt, and the confusion resulting from a display of unintelligible emotion.

It must be noted that Longinus has now moved in his discussion to a treatment of stylistic qualities; yet, from the resumption of the text at section iii, his discussion of them is still in terms of sensibilities of the audience, and properly so: at this stage qualities of style can be discussed only through their effects, that is, either by naming the effect as contempt, risibility, etc., or by providing examples of stylistic viciousness which indicate the intended effect by actually inducing it in the cultivated and sensible reader. The author enters into the discussion not as one possessed or not possessed of the sources of sublimity but as one who aimed at sublimity and in some way missed in each case; and his introduction depends upon the necessity for illustrating his failure—a failure in art, in the strictest sense, since the intention of sublimity is actually present—to achieve that unification of author and audience which is ἔκστασις. The audience must feel what he feels—hence the statement of stylistic vices, in terms of passion as related to subject, becomes at this stage the only possible statement. When the vices of style are made clear in this manner, their cause can be stated, although not as yet with respect to the causes of sublimity, since sublimity itself has not yet been defined; and so Longinus remarks, in section v, that the general cause of these vices is a craving for intellectual novelties. The reason why no other vices of style have been treated becomes clear when we recognize that this is an exhaustive division, *given a sublime subject;* other vices would fall outside an art of the sublime, as not resulting from an intention of sublimity; but these may be confused with sublimity itself because, as he remarks, they are "thus intimately mingled with it," since sublimity is aimed at.[11]

Longinus has treated the opposites of sublimity in order to exhibit what constitutes failure in the art and what is to be avoided; and he

11. v.

has treated these vices before he has dealt with sublimity itself because sublimity is more readily located, as a kind of mean between these various extremes which are more easily apparent to sensibility—the latter being still his chief point of reference—than would be sublimity. Now, following his precedent treatment he turns in section vi to a discussion of sublimity itself. For him sublimity permits neither of definition by example (as his criticism of the "instances of the sublime" provided by Caecilius would indicate) nor, on the other hand, of a purely theoretical statement; this is a practical problem, and hence discourse will not serve as a substitute for experience, for "judgment of style is the last and ripest fruit of much experience."[12] Now, if mere experience, on the one hand, or mere theoretical discussion, on the other, cannot provide knowledge of the sublime, there is a third way by which such knowledge may be achieved; and that is by means of an amalgamation of the two into touchstones for the sublime. Hence Longinus enumerates the signs or notes by which we may know whether or not a given work has true sublimity; drawing an analogy between true and false greatness in general, Longinus is enabled, first of all, to state his criteria in terms of proper and improper admiration and, proceeding thence, to adumbrate the sublime in terms of the character of admiration which it excites. The soul is elevated by sublimity to joy and exultation;[13] the reader feels an identification with the author, for the soul feels "as though itself had produced what it hears";[14] hence what does not elevate at all would not even be false sublimity, and that which elevates only temporarily and has a diminishing force forever after is false sublimity, while that which has a permanent force and which provides a perpetual nourishment for the soul is the sublime itself. Hence it is that transport which is impossible to resist and which establishes itself firmly in the memory and which always leaves material for fresh reflection. Since the sublime would have these characteristics, the most certain attestation of sublimity would be the discovery of its universal appreciation; thus the *consensus gentium* constitutes, for Longinus, an unquestionable test, since it abstracts from any possibility of individual error.[15]

The provision of these touchstones makes possible the recognition of individual works as instances of the sublime, on the one hand, and a knowledge of the nature of the sublime, on the other. Hence, since we now know what the sublime is, in something other than a merely instantial mode, we may know what its causes or sources are, and so state its nature causally. Thus Longinus, in section viii, passes to a

12. vi.
13. vii. 2.
14. Ibid.
15. vii. 4.

consideration of the sources of sublimity, to their enumeration and demonstration as exhaustive and discrete; and in so doing he completes his fundamental triad of terms by now stating sublimity in terms of characteristics of the author—that is, in terms of what the author must *be* in order to produce sublimity. That this is the case is clear; for Longinus is careful to use predicates which are strictly predicable only of a human subject: "having power of expression,"[16] empowered with great (full-bodied) conception,"[17] "having passion,"[18] etc.; and his treatment of them, moreover, is precisely as human characteristics, for his preliminary classification of them is according to whether they are innate or acquired.[19]

The manner of derivation of the five sources is not explicit in the treatise; consequently, the enumeration of the sources has not infrequently been called in question, and sometimes, even, their importance for the treatise has been minimized. Saintsbury remarks:

> No nervous check or chill need be caused by the tolerably certain fact that more than one hole may be picked in the subsequent classification of the sources of ὕψος. These attempts at an over-methodical classification (it has been said before) are always full of snares and pitfalls to the critic. Especially do they tempt him to the sin of arguing in a circle. It cannot be denied that in every one of the five divisions (except, perhaps, the valuable vindication of the quality of Passion) there is some treacherous word or other, which is a mere synonym of "sublime." Thus in the first we have ἀδρεπήβολον, mastery of the ἄδρον, a curious word, the nearest equivalent of which in English is, perhaps, "stout" or "full-bodied," as we apply these terms to wine; in the fourth γενναία, "noble," which is only "sublime" in disguise; and in the fifth ἀξίωμα καὶ διαρσις, of which much the same may be said.[20]

If we may overlook in this statement what is merely dogmatic—as, for example, the curious carping that an art or method of achieving sublimity is somehow at fault for being methodical—we may concentrate on the principal issue of the objection, i.e., whether there is any circularity of argument. Longinus has been asking the causes of sublimity here, as in section v he discussed the causes of failures in sublimity. Since the fundamental triad of terms must be in alignment with a term signifying the subject matter which is sublime, the basis for an enumeration of five sources, and of only five, is fairly obvious. Sublimity of subject matter is not achieved by art, or there would be a

---

16. viii. 1.
17. Ibid.
18. Ibid.
19. Ibid.
20. *History of Criticism*, I:161–62.

fundamental tetrad rather than triad; since, given a sublime subject, an author must first conceive it, secondly feel concerning it if it is excitative of passion, and thirdly express it, it is clear immediately that the sources would, at first sight, involve conception, passion, and expression. But the third factor is complex: since expression deals with words, words can be considered either as signs, simple or combined, or merely as sounds. If we consider words as signs in combination, we can regard them nonsyntactically, as constitutive of such modes of discourse as question, prayer, oath, etc. (in which case we have *figures of thought*, since such modes are prior to and independent of any syntactical consideration), or we may regard them syntactically, as constituted of certain grammatical elements (in which case we have *figures of language*, such as asyndenton, hyperbaton, polyptoton, etc.); and Longinus groups these two under the head of Figures, as his third source of the sublime. On the other hand, words may be regarded as simple, and here again there are two possibilities; all grammatical distinctions being dropped out, the problem is reduced to the imposition of signs for things and their qualities; and the imposition may be strict, i.e., literally stand for the thing, when the problem reduces to a choice of synonyms, or it may involve a comparison when the matter is one of a choice of tropes and metaphors. These problems are problems strictly of diction for Longinus, and their solution establishes the fourth source of the sublime. Finally, words may be regarded as sounds constitutive of rhythms and harmony; and he so treats of them under the head of σύνθεσις.

If, indeed, there is a circularity here, the whole argument collapses; but Saintsbury's charge of paralogism falls a little oddly on our ears. It is difficult to see how an argument from effect to cause could involve a circularity, even though apparently synonymous adjectives be applied to both cause and effect; for example, there is nothing wrong with the statement that it takes a human being as cause to produce a human being as effect. In an alternative statement, we might simply say that Longinus's derivation of the sources depends upon the possibility of identifying the human faculties which make a literary work of a certain quality possible; and though for Longinus the soul of the great writer reflects the sublime subject and the work reflects the soul and the mind of the audience ultimately reflects the work, the similarities which the analogical argument discloses, and upon which, indeed, it depends, are not to be confused with such circularity as would vitiate syllogistic procedure.

The insistence of Longinus, in section viii, that Caecilius is in error in his enumeration of the πηγαί, or sources of sublimity, suggests, since the attack has a rational basis, that he regarded his own statement of them as defensible; and the nature of its defense may be reconstructed, perhaps, despite the length of the lacuna in section ix, without exceeding the evidences of that defense which the extant portions provide. The latter portion of viii, for example, indicates through the objections posed to Caecilius the general character of the dialectic which would be used to establish any one of the five sources as actually distinct means conducive to sublimity. If Caecilius has omitted passion, Longinus argues, it is either because he has identified passion with sublimity or because he has not thought it conducive to sublimity. In the first case, he is in error because, if passion is inseparable from sublimity, then what is passionate must also always be sublime, and conversely; but both this consequence and its converse can be seen to be false, as well from an examination of works as from an examination of the faculties of orators.[21] In the second case, Caecilius is in error because "nothing attains the heights of eloquence so certainly as genuine passion in the right place."[22] The argument establishing the existence of any one source, thus, would turn on whether the "source" in question was distinct from any other and whether in fact it was a source at all. It is probable, therefore, that, since such questions have been raised, they will be answered; and undoubtedly the missing section in ix must have been devoted, in great part at least, to the settling of just these questions with respect to the remaining sources. The extant portion of section ix before the lacuna bears out this hypothesis: for Longinus proceeds to argue in it, first, that great conception is distinct from any of the linguistic sources, since "without any utterance a notion, unclothed and unsupported, often moves our wonder, because the very thought is great"[23]—the example of Ajax's silence entering in as proof of this proposition—and, second, that greatness of conception is actually conducive to sublimity because "great words issue, and it cannot be otherwise, from those whose thoughts are weighty";[24] and the text is interrupted as Longinus is apparently proving this proposition also by example, in all likelihood the speech of Alexander to Parmenio which is reported in Arrian.[25] The third question which would be pertinent to each source—whether it permits of acquisition, since otherwise it could not fall under art—has likewise its answer in this section: even though, as Longinus has already remarked, great conception and passion are primarily natural, means for their development and cultivation may be indicated.[26]

In a similar manner, the missing portion must have treated of the

21. viii. 2–3.
22. viii. 4.
23. ix. 2.
24. ix. 3.
25. *Exp. Alex.* ii. 25.2.
26. ix. 1.

remaining sources; and the character of the argument may be outlined. Once great conception and passion have been shown to be sources, Longinus has completed his treatment of those topics which would be common to all arts; the remaining discussion enters as resulting from the means. Since the treatise is concerned only with literary sublimity —although, as Longinus frequently remarks,[27] the ὕψος, in a wider sense, may be found in any of the other arts, painting, sculpture, architecture, music, etc.—and since conception and passion are independent of words,[28] it is necessary to consider how sublimity is achieved through the use of words, peculiarly; and, as we have seen, Longinus accomplishes this by considering words in connection with thought, the figures of thought resulting; next, by dropping out thought and considering words in relation to one another, the figures of language so resulting; next, by considering isolated words in their application to things, so that the problems of word choice emerge for solution; and, finally, by considering the word as a collocation of syllables, thus opening the questions of rhythm, and as an aggregation of letters, thus raising the problem of harmony, both rhythm and harmony being parts of the problem of *synthesis* or *compositio*. The power of expression, Longinus says, must be presupposed;[29] it is natural and does not fall under art; the latter three sources are not a substitute for it but grow out of it as special determinations of the exercise of that power. This presupposition made, however, it is impossible to attack Longinus's treatment of the verbal sources; since they arise from a consideration of the ways in which words may be employed, there must be a separate verbal faculty for each such employment; in the case of Figures, mere use of figures does not constitute sublimity,[30] although a proper use of them is conducive to that end, so that a consideration of figures falls clearly within the art, but as a means; hence it falls among the sources, but it is a source distinct—on the one hand—from great conception and passion because these are primarily natural, whereas skill with figures is acquired, and because these are independent of words, whereas skill with figures is not, and—on the other hand—from diction and synthesis, although both of these involve words and are acquired faculties, because, as we have seen, different aspects of words are the object of each; and Longinus defends these distinctions by pointing out again and again[31] that works fall short of the sublime or achieve it by failures or successes in one of these respects or another and that authors who are skilful or

27. E.g., xvii. 3; xxxix.3.
28. viii–ix.
29. viii. 1.
30. xvii. 1.
31. See, e.g., x. 4, 5, 6; xvi. 2–3.

inept in certain respects are not necessarily so in all. These matters are ascertainable by sensibility alone: "it is mere folly to raise problems over things which are so fully admitted, for experience is proof sufficient," but he does not therefore refrain from argument.[32]

The resumption of the text[33] reveals Longinus in the midst of a development of the means by which greatness of conception, as the first source of the sublime, may be achieved; and the first means, from various indications of the context, is by the direction of the author's mind toward great objects, so that, if true greatness be truly and completely ascertained, a commensurate greatness of conception must needs follow. The various indications of which I speak may be briefly stated. First, that this section falls within the means would be arguable, even if the problems of the treatise and their manner of treatment were less evident than they are, from Longinus's statement (x. 1) that we may pass on to consider any "further means"; and, second, that all this is relevant to greatness of conception may be seen from the close of xv, in which he remarks that that topic may now be considered as closed. If this section is relative to μεγαλοφυές (or ἀδρεπήβολον) then, the quotations here must be taken, not as striking instances of hyperbole or other verbal devices, but as examples of noetic magnificence; it is the *conception*, here, which interests the critic and not the words. His first treatment of conception is in terms of the gods as its object; his second in terms of heroes; and conception is evidently subjected to two criteria: the first, truth; the second, completeness. Thus Homer is praised for his conceptions of Strife, of the horses of the gods, of theomachies, of Poseidon, and of Ares, in so far as he realizes the loftiness of deity, i.e., the truth about the gods; he is blamed, however, when the gods are conceived as in any way less than they actually are, as, for example, when "he presents to us woundings of the gods, their factions, revenges, tears, bonds, sufferings. . . ."; for then "he has made the gods men."[34] On similar grounds Hesiod is condemned and Moses is praised;[35] and the assignment of the *Odyssey* to a lower place than that of the *Iliad* depends precisely on these considerations as well; and what we have here is no "instinctive, unreasoning terror" of the Greek at the "unknown Romance," as Saintsbury phrases it,[36] for the objection is not that these are myths but that they are myths which could not possibly be true of their subjects. The criticism which appears in this section has been frequently censured; but the censure is hardly justifiable on logical grounds.

32. xxxix. 3.
33. ix. 4-5.
34. ix. 7.
35. ix. 5, 9.
36. *History of Criticism*, I:163.

Longinus is saying that if you wish to nurture your soul to great conceptions you must contemplate great objects—gods, heroes, the majesty of nature, etc.—and that your conception will not be great if you fail to conceive the greatness of your object, i.e., if you fail to form a true and complete conception; for a true and complete conception of a great subject would necessarily be great. Thus the "dreams of Zeus" which occur in the *Odyssey*—"the stories of the wine-skin, of the companions turned by Circe into swine," and the many marvelous episodes of a similar nature—might well be the fantasies of the gods, they are certainly excellent literature; but they are hardly true and complete conceptions either of gods or of heroes, and they are therefore hardly sublime. Both the *Iliad* and the *Odyssey* are by Homer and are marks of his transcendent genius; but the former is "a throng of images all drawn from the truth," while the latter is "a wandering among the shallows of the fabulous and incredible."[37]

Next, according to Longinus (sec. x), "since with all things are associated certain elements, constituents which are essentially inherent in the substance of each," the writer who would gain greatness of conception must select and integrate these essentials. The meaning of this statement becomes clear if we consider the context. Greatness of conception is cultivated by the true apprehension of great objects, as we have seen; but, given a sublime subject matter of which the author has conceived, not all of its aspects are equally responsible for its sublimity, and hence it is the business of the writer to select those aspects which are most responsible and to integrate them in such fashion as that in which they are integrated in the object itself. Thus, for example, a storm is terrible, and hence sublime, inspiring fear and awe; however, not all its characteristics inspire these feelings, but only such as relate to its power and danger; hence the writer must choose those most relative and unite them in such manner, in his mind, that they are not scattered conceptions but "the form and features of that peril."[38] The integration must be present because it is the integration of the characteristics in the object itself which inspired such feelings as were peculiar to it; without such unification, the various conceptions would not induce a feeling comparable to that caused by the object. The *Ode to Anactoria* is praised for such selection and collocation; considering still the conception as opposed to the diction, Longinus remarks that the subject matter—"love-madness"—has been well treated, since Sappho has chosen to speak of those effects, physical as well as intellectual, which are the essential symptoms of love frenzy.[39] On the other hand, Aristeas of Proconnesus is blamed for the evident

37. ix. 13.
38. x. 6.
39. x. 1–3.

and just reason that the details of seafaring which he enumerates are hardly those by virtue of which the sea itself is sublime—seasickness, which forms the climax of his description, scarcely gives the impression of sublimity; and though Aristeas has talked around that painful subject by saying that the sailors' "inward parts, even, are tossed terribly to and fro," the trick is purely a verbal one, and so the description is more embroidery than sublimity.[40] Similarly, Aratus, in saying that "only a tiny plank keeps off bitter destruction," is not sublime[41] because he is merely verbalizing also; in all cases of sailing, a few planks keep off death, but there is no terror here because those planks are generally sufficient; the sea itself is not a source of terror at all times, but only when it rages; and so the device of Aratus constitutes an attempt to rhetoricize, to falsify a quite normal situation. One must understand Longinus as still speaking of *conception;* on that ground, the passage is bad; on a purely verbal ground he might have considered it excellent.

Again, the writer may achieve sublimity by the accumulation of vast detail, with the assurance that this multiplicity of detail will tend to give any subject importance and also to bring out whatever effects would be caused by that subject itself. The second mode—the mode of selection and integration—is conducive to sublimity in that the writer seeks those aspects upon which the effect of the subject depends; in this, the third mode, the effect depends, in so far as it is mere amplification, strictly upon number; as Longinus remarks, amplification always implies quantity and abundance. We may adumbrate a subject either by stating its essential characteristics or by enumerating at large its characteristics both essential and accidental; for in fact the thing itself so presents itself to us, as a mixture of the essential and accidental. It matters not how we effect this quantitative expansion, Longinus tells us; there are numberless varieties of amplification; we may either work through the topics or commonplaces or exaggerate (in the sense of forming a conception which exceeds the thing or fact or event) or emphasize, or do any one of ten thousand things; in any case, the writer must dwell upon the subject with accumulation and insistence, building always toward sublimity. If the subject contemplated is in truth a great subject, sublimity will be reached in this manner; if not, a merely rhetorical amplification will result; and Longinus is careful here, as throughout the treatise, to discriminate between a device in its merely rhetorical use and the same device as a means of achieving sublimity; he finds it necessary, indeed, to redefine amplification, lest it be thought synonymous with the sublime itself and lest, consequently, the art of the sublime be collapsed into an art of

40. x. 4.
41. x. 5.

rhetorical amplification. Like other modes of achieving sublimity, amplification is only conducive to sublimity, not identical with it; nor is Longinus so incautious as to omit a demonstration of this point. The comparatively brief lacuna which occurs at this place in the text interrupts both the demonstration and the exposition of its significance; but here, for once, the main lines of the discussion are not destroyed. When the text resumes,[42] Longinus is discussing, clearly enough, the properties of diffuseness (which would be achieved by amplification) and intensity.

So far, in his treatment of μεγαλοφυές, Longinus has considered the author as contemplating the great subject in order to formulate great conceptions; and, as we have seen, he has shown that the author may attempt either to formulate a conception commensurate with the sublime subject or to select and integrate those characteristics upon which its sublimity depends or to enumerate at large until the multiplicity of conceived detail approximates the real fulness of the thing. Following section xii, however, he suggests two other modes by which greatness of conception may be achieved. First, if the sublime authors, e.g., Homer, Plato, Demosthenes, etc., have attained sublimity by greatness of conception, so that their thoughts were commensurate with great subjects, it follows that, if an author can make his thoughts commensurate with their thoughts, he likewise will achieve greatness of conception; thus, greatness of thought can be attained by the imitation of great authors.[43] Longinus is not speaking of the reproduction exclusively of tricks of style; he says explicitly, "Therefore even we, when we are working out a theme which requires lofty speech and greatness of thought" must call to mind the performances of great authors;[44] and the analogy of this sort of literary inspiration to the Pythian vapors makes his meaning completely clear; if we are not able to achieve greatness of thought by contemplating the thing itself, we may contemplate instead those authors whose thoughts were stretched to its stature, as "even those not too highly susceptible to the god are possessed by the greatness which was in others."[45] And he gives the author touchstones again, formulating them in terms of the fundamental triad of author, work, and audience: in composing, the author is to consider Homer and the great ones as composing in his place, knowing them as he does through the medium of their works; in judging his work, he must regard them as his audience, and, further, he must ask how the ages to come will esteem his composition.[46]

42. xii. 3.
43. xiii. 2.
44. xiv. 1.
45. xii. 2.
46. xiv.

Second, if we neither contemplate the object directly nor contemplate it through the contemplations of others, we may invent, we may imagine;[47] where our knowledge is partial and incomplete, we may piece out what is missing by imagination, and the examples which Longinus uses seem intended to illustrate invention out of whole cloth, as in the case of the sane Euripides imagining madness,[48] or of detail only, as in the ride of Phaethon in *Iphigenia in Tauris.*[49] According to Longinus, there is a difference between the application of imagination in poetry and in rhetoric, the latter being limited by what is known to be true and what is thought to be probable. This much done, Longinus remarks that his treatment of the "sublime effects which belong to great thoughts, and which are produced by the greatness of man's soul, and secondarily by imitation or by imagination" has been adequate.

Longinus now[50] passes on to a discussion of the Figures, postponing his treatment of passion for reasons which will be indicated later in this essay. As he remarks, there are infinite kinds of Figures; dividing them into Figures of Thought and Figures of Language, he mentions in the former class adjuration (or apostrophe or oath), questions and interrogations, in the latter class, asyndeton, hyperbaton, polyptota (including all departures from the normal usage of case, tense, gender, person, and number), and periphrasis. Figures by themselves, Longinus tells us repeatedly, do not constitute sublimity; thus any merely rhetorical definitions of the Figures are insufficient to indicate their use toward effecting sublimity, since such definitions are only recipes for the construction of the Figures themselves, without consideration of the context of their use; consequently, in his treatment of the Figures, Longinus is careful always to include some statement of the literary circumstances in which they would effect sublimity and of those in which they would not. Adjuration or apostrophe, for example, is an oath, discourse involving a solemn appeal to something sacred to witness that a statement is true or that a contract is binding; the rhetoricians tell us merely to swear by those names which are most sacred; "but," says Longinus, "it is not the mere swearing by a name which is great; place, manner, occasion, purpose are all essential";[51] and the rhetoricians have failed in their prescriptions because they have treated these variables of place, manner, occasion, and purpose as constants. Thus, though both Demosthenes and Eupolis swore by Marathon, so that in a sense their oath is the same, the apostrophe of the latter is merely that, whereas the apostrophe of the former is at once an

47. xv.
48. xv. 2–3.
49. xv. 4.
50. xvi.
51. xvi. 3.

assurance resting upon oaths, a demonstration, an example, a eulogy, and an exhortation.[52] His point, of course, is extremely well taken; indeed, any other statement would have been irrelevant or insufficient, since the sources stand related to sublimity as means to end.

While a formula of the constitution of a Figure is necessary therefore, so that the orator may know what it is and hence be able to construct it at will, he must also know what effect it produces; consequently, throughout his treatment of the Figures, Longinus states the effect of each Figure, so that we may know whether it is conducive to the proper end. Questions and interrogations, thus, "reproduce the spontaneity of passion" and give intensity and vehemence and conviction to the discourse, "drawing the hearer off until he thinks that each point in the inquiry has been raised and put into words without preparation, and so it imposes upon him."[53] Asyndeton, wherein "the words drop unconnected and are, so to speak, poured forth almost too fast for the speaker himself," gives "the impression of a struggle, where the meaning is at once checked and hurried on."[54] Similarly, hyperbaton "is the surest impress of vehement passion"; the hearer fears that a failure of both syntax and logic is imminent, and, since this is a sign of vehement passion, he is persuaded that the discourse is an instance of vehement passion.[55] And thus Longinus treats also of the other Figures. The principal determinant throughout is the tendency of the audience to reason from the consequent; and, although Longinus never makes such explicit reference to the tendency as Aristotle (*Poetics* xxiv), all the instances which he mentions are plainly arguments from signs.

Concerning the choice of words, next, Longinus clearly lays a basis for selection. Certain words are noble and beautiful, while others are inferior;[56] a similar distinction, as he remarks particularly in xxxv, may be made among things and also among thoughts. Thus the primary determinant in the choice of words is the necessity of maintaining a correspondence between these hierarchies; and, while the choice of grand words is necessary for noble composition, the words must be accurate as well; and, like Quintilian, he likens the choice of a grand word for a thing of lesser stature to the fastening of a large tragic mask upon a little child.[57] An unfortunate lacuna occurs at this place, apparently just as Longinus was about to say that in poetry, however, which like fiction is less bound by probability than rhetoric or history, these restrictions do not always apply. Doubtless he proceeded to treat

52. Ibid.
53. xvii.
54. xix.
55. xxii.
56. xxx.
57. Cf. Quintilian vi. i. 36.

of the various possible permutations of the central terms of his discussion here; if we take only two elements—words and things—then two principles emerge; since the hierarchies, verbal and real, must correspond and since the effect is to be one of greatness, one must use the grand word as well as the right word, and the choice of diction thus becomes merely a choice of objects of discourse. But this solution of the problem of word choice—one common enough in the history of rhetoric—is too simple for Longinus; it will do as a preliminary consideration, but one must also take into account the element of thought; and since it is possible that a low conception may be entertained of a great thing and conversely, several consequences emerge; in tragedy, for instance, Longinus would have been likely to argue, since the effect is to be one of grandeur, the characters are lofty, and their thoughts must consequently be lofty, even where the object of thought is common or mean; hence, too, their discourse must be lofty—even bombast is admissible in tragedy, he has said earlier, provided it does not degenerate into tasteless rant. On the other hand, vulgar words, as he is remarking when the text resumes,[58] may be preferable to ornamental language, may be used with an effect which is not vulgar when sheer accuracy and credibility are concerned.

Longinus's treatment of metaphor, trope, and simile under word choice, unconventional as it is, is consequent upon his careful separation of the sources. Since all grammatical collocations would fall under the Figures, word choice deals with the selection of names for things, thought being an intermediary term: now words either stand for things strictly and literally or they do not, in which case they are either metaphors, paraboles, similes, or hyperboles. The differences obtaining between these (although they are in a sense akin) may be seen by an examination of the schematism which has developed them. On the one hand, Longinus clearly ranks words and things; on the other, within this hierarchy, words must either stand for what they strictly mean, and hence for what is like or different, or not. Hyperbole, thus, results, as he says,[59] when words exaggerate the thing in terms either of excess or of defect by likening it to what is more than it or less than it; the other tropes result when, although a comparison is involved, inasmuch as something is likened to what it is not, it is strict, i.e., is not of a greater to a less or of a less to a greater; and the distinctions between these are apparently that metaphor is absolute comparison, inasmuch as the name of the thing is actually substituted, whereas παραβολαί and εἰκόνες are not, these differing in turn from each other in that the former is in terms of difference, the latter in terms of likeness. Were the differences stated in grammatical terms—that is, in terms of the

58. xxxi.
59. xxxviii. 6.

grammatical particles employed in the case of simile, for example—
simile, parabole, and hyperbole would have fallen under the Figures
and would have been statable merely as formulas in consequence of
this; but to state the problem as one of signification, as here, is to
permit the choice of words to depend on the imposition of names and
to introduce again the variable factors of place, manner, occasion, and
purpose—which again would appear as constants in a merely rhetorical formulation—as determinatives of the choice of diction. And in the
problem of word selection, as elsewhere, Longinus is insistent that
metaphor, simile, parabole, and hyperbole are always means, never
ends; the device must be dependent upon the use, never the use upon
the device; to provide mere recipes for the formulation of rhetorical
devices, without clear indication of the variable literary circumstances
in which they would be appropriate, is, in effect, to constitute them as
ends not means, so that the work becomes not a final unity but an
aggregation of ends; and since, for Longinus, the use is always statable
in terms of the audience—a certain effect of ἔκστασις in the hearers—
the unity of a work is properly stated not in terms of the work itself or of
exclusively literary formulations but in terms of the unity of effect
upon those reading or hearing. Consequently, Longinus remarks that
there are no literary regulations as such governing the use of such
devices as metaphor;[60] the proper determinant is the passion of the
author, since whatever numbers and kinds of metaphors would appear
appropriate to him in his passion would also appear appropriate to an
audience to which that passion has been communicated; and Longinus
is scornful, consequently, of the apparent decision of Caecilius that
the number of metaphors to be applied to a single object should not
exceed two or three.[61]

   The treatment of synthesis,[62] finally, offers but little difficulty. In his
first mention of this source of sublimity,[63] Longinus had remarked that
synthesis included all the others; however, in his actual treatment of
the source, it appears solely as a topic dealing with the arrangement of
words into harmony and rhythm. While at first sight there seems to be
a contradiction here, the contradiction is readily resolved from an
examination of the contexts of the discussions. Synthesis—the arrangement of words—presupposes thought, passion, the Figures, and the
choice of words, and in a mere enumeration of the sources would be
stated, therefore, as the consummation of all of them, as inclusive of all
of them in the sense that any literary work may be ultimately regarded
as a certain arrangement of words. If, on the other hand, one deals

[margin handwritten note: His actual treatment was presented in two earlier books.]

60. xxxii. 4.
61. xxxii. 8.
62. xxxix.
63. viii.

with the sources as means, expounding what is proper to each source, then synthesis appears only as the arrangement, rhythmic and harmonic, of words which have already been selected as a consequence of all the other artistic operations.

Longinus's argument concerning the importance of synthesis is a simple analogy; words considered merely as sound and incorporated into harmony and rhythm are to musical tones similarly incorporated as the effect of the former to the effect of the latter; then, if we recall what is superadded to words by their significance and recall also how tremendous is the effect of music, we may gauge adequately the effect of the arrangement of words. Hence, section xl points out that synthesis is the ultimate collocation, in which all the sources meet.

The remainder of the extant treatise is given over, first, to a consideration of how literary works fall short of sublimity[64] and, second, to a consideration of the causes of the lack of sublimity among the authors of Longinus's time.[65] The first topic need scarcely be discussed; as Longinus remarks, "there is no present need to enumerate by their kinds the means of producing pettiness; when we have once shown what things make writings noble and sublime, it is clear that in most cases their opposites will make them low and uncouth"; and Longinus proceeds to treat them in reverse order to that of the sources of sublimity, going no further, however, than the choice of words. The second consideration enters into the topic importantly; if the times constrain the artist to the point where he cannot operate, then rhetorical tuition is useless; hence the artist must be demonstrated to be a free and independent agent. And, as he shows, in any failure of art it is the artist and not his time which is at fault, so that art remains a permanent possibility. At this point the extant treatise concludes, with a broken transition to the topic of the passions.

Unfortunate as the loss of the remaining discussion is, it cannot and need not be accepted as a permanent mutilation of the text. Since, as this essay has doubtless made clear, passion is one of the important determinants as well as a source in itself of literary operation, it follows that there must be some specification of the conception of passion if the *Peri Hypsous* is to appear as an intelligible technical treatise. And further, although we have no part of the promised treatise on the passions, we have in the text ample reference and comment on the subject of the passions from which Longinus's treatment of passion might be reconstructed, in sufficient part to render the technique of *Peri Hypsous* operable at least, although perhaps not sufficiently to permit a reconstruction of his entire theory of psychology.

Happily we have in section xx a definition of passion; it is a rush and

64. xli–xliii.
65. xliv.

commotion of the soul;[66] its contrary, calm, is a rest, a stasis of the soul;[67] and, although Longinus explicitly says that "passions are many, nay countless, past the power of man to reckon,"[68] so that an attempt to achieve their complete enumeration would clearly be useless, the text nevertheless furnishes us not only with many examples of the passions but with some indication of their causation and determination, their course, their symptoms, and their ordering. Pity, joy, fear, grief, pride, wonder, awe, hate, disgust, love, reverence, inspiration, madness, persuasion, ecstasy, suspicion, anger, indignation, jealousy, patience, shame, laughter, weeping, and envy constitute a partial list, and one more than adequate for our purposes; and Longinus's comments concerning those which are directly mentioned by him make it evident that, first of all, every passion has a cause—a cause which is its object. Since passion is a motion of the soul, then either the soul itself is the cause of motion or something external to the soul; but it is clear from Longinus's statements that something external to the soul is the cause, as peril of fear, safety of confidence, the gods of awe and reverence, the mean and vicious of disgust, etc. And it is clear, further, that passion admits of degree, since Longinus speaks frequently of vehement passion and since such statements constitute an admission of the possibility of degree. Further, it is clear that not every passion has the same object, since Longinus remarks that certain things excite terror, certain things disgust, and that not every object excites passion in the same degree, since he says also that one thing may be more terrible than another. It follows, therefore, that the object is by nature determinative both of the kind and of the degree of the passion which it excites. Hence, as he says, passions are infinite in number, since the objects are causative of unique effects. His remark concerning laughter, that "it is a passion, a passion which has its root in pleasure,"[69] provides the determination of the degree of passion; for, if pleasure is a root of passion, then pain must be a root also; and it follows from what has been discovered so far that every object is capable of inducing passion in so far as it is capable of inducing a motion of the soul attended either by pleasure or by pain and that the degree of passion which it induces would be proportional to the amount of attendant pain or pleasure. It would not be difficult, once this much is known, to construct definitions of at least the more familiar emotions, since the extant text provides ample illustration of Longinus's method of framing definitions; but perhaps this will be unnecessary if we remark that each such definition would state that the passion in question is an agitation

66. xx. 2.
67. Ibid.
68. Ibid.
69. xxxviii. 6.

of the soul, accompanied by pleasure or pain, and slight or great in proportion to that pleasure or pain, attended by such and such symptoms, the moving cause being something which in such and such a fashion is capable of inflicting pain or inducing pleasure.

Further, Longinus clearly ranks objects as high, common, or low; now, since it is possible that any object is capable of inducing passion and since passion is determined in kind and degree by the object, it follows that passions themselves must be capable of similar classification to that of objects; hence as high, common, or low; and this is borne out by his statement in section viii that wretchedness, annoyance, and fear are passions of a mean order. They are such because they cannot properly be caused by the highest objects; what is itself good in the highest degree must naturally cause, in the highest degree, those passions which are highest; for example, love, reverence, and awe are passions which are properly excited in us to the highest degree by the gods; but disgust, pity, or annoyance they could not properly cause.

It is clear, furthermore, that for Longinus the soul has both an active and a passive principle, since the soul is capable of thought and since thought cannot here be passion, for if it were passion, it could not be reckoned as a distinct source of sublimity. And this is clear also from his statement that men have the power to be good and to think elevated thoughts;[70] for this would be impossible if the soul were passive only, and, indeed, it would be impossible for the soul to initiate any action whatsoever; hence, on the same grounds, an active principle of the soul is implied by the very possibility of an art of anything. If, then, there is this active principle, then either it governs the passive, or the passive governs it, or they govern reciprocally, or both are ruled together by some other thing. But this last is impossible; for if the active is governed by something further, there is no active principle; but we have seen that there is. Now passion can be known to be unseasonable or excessive or defective, while thought can be known to be false; and in whatever principle the criterion rests there must also be governance; but passion cannot know anything. It follows, then, that the active principle must be the ruling principle. Hence reason must rule appetite and passion, and, when it so rules with all propriety, virtue results. But in such cases as those in which passion and appetite gain the upper hand and either become dislocated from their proper objects or become excessive or defective, in these vice or madness must result.

The gods are passionless;[71] heroes are distinguished from common men in that they suffer a passion different either in kind or in degree from that which common men undergo, for the heroic passions have higher objects; thus the anger of Ajax arises from no common cause

70. xliv.
71. ix. 8.

and exhibits itself in no common fashion, and similarly the fear of an
Ajax is not of death but of a death which is unheroic.[72] Sublimity of
passion, then, must be of this heroic order; but its evocation is
ultimately dependent upon thought, noble passion resulting where
thought itself is noble, and ignoble passion where thought is mean. The
noble mind, if not passionless like the divine, is at least free of the
meaner passions because it is averted from the objects which call these
forth.

So much for the reconstruction of Longinus's theory of the passions;
it remains to observe the consequences of such a theory for the
Longinian art of the sublime. The method would now appear to be
perfect and complete. Certain things are by nature sublime; by nature
man is capable of recognizing them as sublime and of loving them with
an eternal and invincible love, for nature determined man to be no low
and ignoble animal; admitted into the universe in part as spectator,
in part as participant, and driven by his love into rivalry and
competition with the supremacy of the marvelous, the great, and the
beautiful, he fulfils the function which these in a manner appoint him;
and, although human understanding is limited and wonder results
when marvels surpass human thought, in a sense also the mind grows
beyond its ordinary bounds, so that "for the speculation and thought
which are within the scope of human endeavor, not all the universe is
sufficient."[73] The nobility of man's thought, then, finds its warrant in
these sublimities, and thought itself is the warrant of all else; for it
determines passion, and thought and passion together, in literary
endeavor, determine the use of all literary devices and guarantee their
success.

Consequently, the artist must himself be sublime in soul if he is to
reflect the sublime; if he is led by the love of pleasure or the love of
money, he becomes little and ignoble. Like a corrupted judge he
mistakes his own interest for what is good and noble, he admires his
mortal parts and neglects to improve the immortal, and he becomes
eventually the prisoner of his passions.[74] And the ignoble man, the
slave, cannot produce what is admirable; "the true Orator must have
no low ungenerous spirit, for it is not possible that those who think
small thoughts fit for slaves, and practise them in all their daily life,
should put out anything to deserve wonder and immortality."[75] But
"great words issue, and it cannot be otherwise, from those whose
thoughts are weighty";[76] and literary greatness is to be estimated not

72. ix. 10.
73. xxxv. 3.
74. xliv. 5.
75. ix. 3.
76. Ibid.

by mere freedom from fault but by the greatness of the spirit reflected in the words as in a mirror. Art thus in a sense is a double discipline, being both moral and aesthetic; but its literary function is ultimately only to provide some suitable medium which the spirit of the writer transcends and illuminates. So the spirit of the writer be sublime and the mirror of words present an adequate image, hearers who are properly prepared cannot fail to be stirred, for words carry "the passion which is present to the speaker into the souls of the bystanders, bringing them into partnership with himself";[77] and the admiration of men for what is truly great is "as it were, a law of nature," failing only when men have sunk beneath their natural state or have not reached their proper development.[78]

The topic of the passions is not treated with the other sources because the passions are not, like them, open to voluntary acquisition; they are per se passive movements of the soul, hence cannot be initiated by the soul itself; but in the properly controlled spirit they are mastered by reason; and it is only then that, moving among higher objects which contemplation has discovered and provided, they form an important factor in sublimity. Passion alone, Longinus tells us, is not enough to effect sublimity, for not all passion is sublime; indeed, the soul wherein passion reigns deteriorates from its nobility. But, although reason must master passion for sublimity to obtain, the acquisition of that mastery is not an aesthetic, but an ethical, problem; there is no skill of the passions; and in so far as there are quasi-literary means for their control, the means must be found in elevated thought.

It should appear from this discussion that the term "sublimity" can scarcely be taken as referring to a mere elevation of diction, for to take it in this sense is to regard a literary work as a mere arrangement of words and to collapse all the sources of sublimity into those which are merely verbal, and perhaps all of these, even, into synthesis alone. The treatise of Longinus affords every evidence that he sought to avoid such a reduction and that hence the word should not be taken in its merely stylistic sense but should receive its definition in terms of that communication of nobility which is made possible by the perfection of the human soul and of art, and which receives its answer in the wonder and admiration of all men.

77. xxxix. 3.
78. xxxv.

in terms of (26 times)

THE POETIC METHOD OF ARISTOTLE:
ITS POWERS AND LIMITATIONS

N o especial recognition," writes A. E. Taylor, "is given in Aristotle's own classification to the Philosophy of Art. Modern students of Aristotle have tried to fill in the omission by adding artistic creation to contemplation as a third fundamental form of mental activity, and thus making a threefold division of Philosophy into Theoretical, Practical, and Productive. The object of this is to find a place in the classification for Aristotle's famous *Poetics* and his *Rhetoric*. But the admission of the third division of Science has no warrant in the text of Aristotle, nor are the *Poetics* and *Rhetoric*, properly speaking, a contribution to Philosophy. They are intended as collections of practical rules for the composition of a pamphlet or a tragedy, not as a critical examination of the canons of literary taste."[1]

The problems touched upon in the passage just cited are important, for they involve the entire scheme of the Aristotelian sciences and the role of poetics within that scheme, and even raise the question whether the treatise on poetics is of philosophical character. They bear directly, therefore, on the whole matter of Aristotle's poetic method; and they illustrate not merely how questions of the powers and limitations of a method are dependent upon interpretation of the method but also how that interpretation, in turn, is dependent upon our interpretation of the larger scheme. With all respect to A. E. Taylor, I should like to look into these problems a little. I shall do so by considering (1) what knowledge, especially scientific knowledge, meant for Aristotle; (2) how, consequently, the subject of an art would be handled by him; (3) how all these considerations affect the structure of the *Poetics*; (4) the consequent powers and limitations of his poetic method.

For Aristotle, all animals are capable of knowledge in some sense; the character of that knowledge, however, varies according to the

Reprinted from *English Institute Essays* (New York: Columbia University Press, 1951).
1. A. E. Taylor, *Aristotle* (London, n.d.), p. 19. See also pp. 88–90.

object of knowledge, the nature of what is known, the faculties involved, and the end of the knowledge. Thus, all animals have at least one sense, that of touch, which tells them about the tangible,[2] and those with more senses have additional channels of information.[3] But the knowledge provided by sensation is of the fact alone, and is instantial only;[4] that is, it is knowledge, let us say, that this particular flame is hot, but not that flame generally is hot or why flame is hot. Some animals have memory, and so can supplement present sensation by past sensations; and man, moreover, is capable not merely of supplementing present sensation by past but also of unifying memory so that several memories of the same thing have a single effect; this capacity Aristotle calls *empeiria*, experience. Experience is also knowledge of a kind, and is similar to art and science; but art and science are, strictly speaking, produced out of experience, rather than identical with it. For experience is knowledge of individuals, while art and science are knowledge of universals, and although in reference to action and production (the sphere of which is the individual) men of experience alone succeed better than those who have theory without experience, experience provides knowledge of the fact, but not of the cause of the fact, whereas artistic and scientific knowledge is of the cause.[5]

But scientific knowledge is not constituted simply by knowledge of universal and cause. Sensation, which gives particular information, is not scientific, but neither is intuition; if reference of individual to universal were all, intuition would be scientific knowledge, induction would be the solitary scientific process, and science would consist of scientific principles only. We moderns tend to classify the sciences as inductive or deductive; Aristotle thought that all sciences are both, in the sense that principles achieved through induction are utilized to demonstrate, through causal reasoning, the inherence of attributes in a subject.[6] Hence, for him scientific knowledge is a matter neither of mere generality nor of mere specificity, but is knowledge of cause as appropriate to (or, we might say, as commensurate or simultaneous with) the inherence of attribute in subject.[7] For example, the figure *ABC* has its internal angles equal to a straight angle; it has this attribute, not *qua* this individual triangle of wood or *qua* plane figure or *qua* isosceles

2. *De anima*, iii. 12. 434b 13-15. In order to avoid multiplying references I shall merely give the first that comes to mind, except when there is a special point in doing otherwise.

3. *Analytica posteriora*, i. 18. 81a 36.

4. *Physica*, i. 5. 189a 7; *Met.* i. 1. 981b 10 ff.

5. *Metaphysica*, i. 1. 980a 21-981b9; *An. post.* i. 13. 22 ff.; 31. 87b 27 ff.

6. *Loc. cit.*; see also *Phys.* i. 1. 184a 9 ff.; *An. post.* i. 1. 71a ff.; ii. 19.

7. *An. post.* i. 13. 15 ff.

triangle, but simply *qua* triangle, and the cause is the appropriate cause of the inherence of this attribute in the subject (triangle), in which it inheres primarily.[8] Based on this conception, the subject matter of a science is neither determined by a subject simply, nor by an attribute or group of attributes simply, but by a subject as possessing certain attributes which inhere in it primarily. Thus, for Aristotle science is not single and all-comprehending; there are several different sciences, according to the inherence of different attributes in different subjects through different causes, and these sciences must necessarily differ in their principles.[9]

In a very general sense the methods of these sciences will be the same, for all will depend upon principles intuitively derived from experience of particulars, and all will be concerned with proof, via cause, of the inherence of attributes in a subject;[10] but more specifically their methods will differ, for as subjects differ, attributes and proofs of their inherence will differ:[11] not all causes will be relevant,[12] not all definitions will be constructed in the same way,[13] directions of proof will differ,[14] principles will differ in number and accuracy,[15] demonstration will be inappropriate to inexact subject matters concerned with probabilities,[16] probable reasoning will be inappropriate to exact subject matters concerned with necessary attributes,[17] and so forth. Again, not all questions relating to a given object are relevant to the science of that object, but only those which relate to that object as falling under a single universal. For example, not all questions relating to geometric figures are geometric questions, but only those which form premises for the theorems of geometry or its subaltern sciences, such as optics.[18] A single object, poetry, let us say, can fall under a whole variety of sciences, but not all questions raised concerning it are "poetic"; some will be metaphysical, some ethical, some political, and so forth. Distinguished as the sciences are in this general scheme, they have also a basic communion, for all are connected through the common axioms of demonstration and the common disciplines such as dialectic.[19]

8. Ibid., i. 9. 76a 3 ff.
9. Ibid., i. 9. 75b 37 ff.; i. 10. 76a 37 ff.; i. 28. 87a 38 ff.
10. Ibid., ii. 19. 100b 1–18.
11. Ibid., i. 32. 88a 17-88b 29.
12. *De an.* i. 1. 403a 25-403b 17.
13. *Phys.* ii. 2.
14. *Met.* vii. 7. 1032a 25; *Phys.* ii. 9. 200a 15.
15. *An. post.* i. 27.
16. *Nicomachean ethics*, i. 3. 1094b 23–27.
17. 1094b 28.
18. *An. post.* i. 7 75a 37-75b 20; i. 12. 77a 40 ff.
19. Ibid., i, 11. 77a 26 ff.

We have, thus, a body of sciences distinct from each other in subject matter, problems, and methods, but still interconnected. Aristotle divides the sciences into three groups, the theoretical, the practical, and the productive, or "poetic," sciences; he not only makes this division explicitly a number of times (although Taylor has strangely failed to find warrant for it),[20] but makes many correlative distinctions, such as the numerous ones between "knowing," "doing," and "making,"[21] and as a matter of fact the very foundations of his method demand this primary distinction.[22]

The theoretical sciences—metaphysics, mathematics, and physics— differ in certain respects but are alike in that they involve necessary propositions and have knowledge as their end. In the practical sciences of ethics and politics, knowledge is subordinate to action—one knows what virtue is in order to act virtuously[23]—and in the productive sciences, which are the arts, whether useful or fine, the end is neither knowledge nor action, but the product to be produced. As the practical sciences are less exact than the theoretical, so the productive are less exact than the practical; for sciences are more exact as they involve fewer elements[24] and are less dependent upon other sciences[25]—thus, arithmetic is more exact than geometry—whereas the practical sciences derive many propositions from the theoretical, and in turn the productive derive propositions from both theoretical and practical sciences.

The *Poetics* is so sharply determined in its problems and method by the fact that it is a treatise of productive science that we may well occupy ourselves briefly with some considerations concerning the scope and structure of such science. In the first place, is scientific knowledge of poetry possible? Not, we must answer, if it is a matter of the accidental or the incidental. There is no science of the accidental for Aristotle:[26] science is concerned only with what happens always or for the most part, with what is necessary or probable;[27] hence, to ask whether a science is possible is to ask whether some subject can be found in which attributes inhere, and that not accidentally. Hence, poetic science cannot center in the artist or the producer; for, although

20. E.g., *Met.* i. 1. 982a 1; vi. 1. 1025b 21, 1025b 26; ix. 2. 1046b 3.

21. *Nic. eth.* vi. 4. 1140a 1; also 3. 1139b–4. 1140a 24.

22. Since art is distinct from theoretical science (ibid., vi. 3) and since making and acting are different (1140a 16), and since these distinctions go back radically to the distinction of the sciences in terms of causes, which in turn rests on the subject-attribute-cause formulation of scientific knowledge, the very pivot of the Aristotelian philosophy.

23. Ibid., i. 3. 1095a 5.

24. *An. post.* i. 27 87a 33.

25. *Met.* i. 2. 982a 25 ff.

26. Ibid., vi. 2. 1026b 24-1027a 28.

27. *Met.* vi. 2. 1027a 20-21.

art has a natural basis in man, nature does not produce art, and artistic activity is not a necessary attribute of man. Again, the activity itself cannot serve as the subject, for it does not contain its principle in itself; it is for the sake of the product and is determined by the product. The distinction between doing and making is precisely that in doing the activity contains its own end (Happiness, the end of virtue, is an activity and not a quality for Aristotle), whereas in making the end is a product produced over and above the activity—that is, the productive action is for the sake of the product. The ethical and political sciences are possible because ethical and political activities contain as principles their own ends; but a science of artistic capacity or activity, apart from consideration of the product, is not. We are left, thus, with the product itself as a possible subject.

Moreover, according to Aristotle all art is concerned with coming into being, that is,

with contriving and considering how something may come into being which is capable of either being or not being and whose origin is in the maker, not in the thing made; for art is concerned neither with things that are or come into being by necessity nor with things that do so in accordance with nature, since these latter have their origin in themselves.[28]

What is made by the artist is neither the form nor the matter, but the *synolon*, the *concretum*. For instance, the sculptor makes neither the marble which is his material nor the human form which he gives it, but the statue, which is the human form imposed upon marble; and the ironworker makes neither the iron nor the spherical form, but the iron sphere, a *concretum* of form and matter.[29] In art a form in the mind of the artist is imposed upon his medium, to produce the artistic composite;[30] and the productive process may be divided into two parts, which are, as it were, of contrary direction. The first proceeds from the form to be produced to the first thing which can be produced; this is reasoning. The second proceeds from the first thing which can be produced to form itself; this is making.[31] For example, if a shoe is to be produced—a certain kind of composite—then parts must be stitched or nailed together; but first there must be the requisite parts, and these will have to be cut and prepared, and so forth back to the first thing that can be done. All that leads up to the first thing that can be done is reasoning; but the process from the terminus of the reasoning to the final production of the form is making. Now art according to Aristotle

28. *Nic. eth.* vi. 4. 1040a 10–16 (Oxford tr.).
29. *Met.* vii. 8. 1033a 23-1033b 11.
30. 7. 1032a 32.
31. 1032b 15 ff.

is a state concerned with making, involvoing a true course of reasoning; and it is precisely this reasoning universalized, the rationale of art or production, which is in a sense scientific knowledge of the productive kind; the reasoning part, that is, not the making part; for the latter is not knowledge, but production in accordance with knowledge, and it depends rather upon skill and experience. By "course of reasoning" Aristotle means, naturally, not the psychological processes of the individual artist, for these are incidental to the individual and cannot be formulated, but the course that would be followed in correct, true, and appropriate reasoning about making a given product. Since the arts propose not merely productions but excellent productions—the sculptor, for example, seeks to make not merely a statue but a good statue—such reasoning will have to include not merely the "nature" of the thing intended but its "excellence" as well.[32]

The scope of any productive science, therefore, is the rational part of production centering in, and indeed based upon, the nature of the product; and the structure of such science may be described as hypothetical regressive reasoning, taking for its starting-point, or principle, the artistic whole which is to be produced and proceeding through the various parts of the various kinds to be assembled.[33] The reasoning is hypothetical because it is based upon hypotheses: If such and such a work, which is a whole, is to be produced, then such and such parts must be assembled in such and such a way; and if the work is to have excellence as a whole, then the parts must be of such and such a kind and quality. The reasoning is regressive because it works backward from the whole, which is to exist, to the parts which must have existence previous to that of the whole. Since the reasoning is based upon a definition of a certain whole as its principle and since that definition must be arrived at in some fashion, any productive science must consist of two main parts: inductive reasoning toward its principle, and deductive reasoning from its principle.[34] One part must make possible the formulation of the whole; the other must determine the parts according to that formulation.

On examination, the *Poetics* clearly follows this general pattern. Chapters i–v are concerned with establishing the definition of tragedy, which is given in chapter vi; chapters vi–xxii resolve tragedy into its proper parts; chapters xxiii–xxiv offer a treatment of epic based upon that of tragedy; and the final chapters conclude with critical problems relative to both forms.

The definition on which everything centers, thus, is no mere statement of the meaning of a term or name, as we ordinarily think of

32. *Poetics*, i. 1447a 10: εἰ μέλλει καλῶς ἕξειν ἡ ποίησις.

33. *De partibus animalium*, i. 1. 639b 24 ff.; *De generatione et corruptione*, ii. 11. 337b 14 ff.

34. *Supra*, n. 6.

definition today;[35] it is a statement of the nature of a whole produced by a certain art; and it is introduced, not merely to clarify meanings a little but much more importantly, to serve as the principle of the art and hence as the basis of all reasoning. And because it is a definition of a thing produced by art, it must differ sharply from a mathematical or physical definition. Mathematical definitions treat forms as abstracted from matter and hence do not include the matter;[36] I do not, for instance, include "brazen" or "wooden" or anything of the sort in my definition of sphere or cube. Physical definitions—dealing with natural things—must include matter;[37] for physical things are composites of matter and form; hence physical terms, as Aristotle repeatedly reminds us, are like the term "snub"—for "snub" involves not merely nose or merely concavity, but both—a nose (matter) which is concave (form).[38] The things of art—also composites—must also be defined through matter and form. But natural things have a natural matter and are in a natural genus, whereas artificial things are not; hence, while natural things are defined by a two-part definition consisting of genus (matter) and difference (form), artificial things must be defined by enumeration and differentiation of the various causes which make them what they are. These will still group themselves into two parts, matter and form: the one part will state what has been organized as matter; the other will state the working or effect or power (dynamis) which is their form. For, as Aristotle says, things must be defined through their working or power;[39] thus, a definition of a hand as a certain organization of bones, veins, and tissues would be incomplete, for it would leave out manual power, which is the form of the hand and the end to which these elements are organized, and such a definition would fit a dead hand as well, although a dead hand is really a hand in name only.[40]

The argument leading to the definition may be stated as follows. Assuming that certain arts are imitative (and this is strictly assumed, not proven, for it is not a proposition which belongs to poetics, but to some other science), specific forms of these arts must be specific forms of imitation. To imitate implies a matter or medium (means) in which one imitates, some form (object) which one imitates, and a certain way (manner) in which one imitates. Thus, considered as imitation, every imitation must involve means, object, and manner, and therefore imitations must differ as they involve different means, objects, or manners. Hence, in chapter i Aristotle differentiates a certain body of

35. *An. post.* ii. 10. 93b 28–94a 3.
36. *Met.* vii. 10.
37. *Phys.* ii. 2.
38. 194a 4–6.
39. *Pol.* i. 2. 1253a 24.
40. See, e.g., *Met.* vii. 10. 1035b 25; *Meteōrologica*, iv. 12. 398b 26.

arts which involve related media (words, rhythm, tune) according to specific differences of the media involved; in chapter ii, according to objects imitated; and in chapter iii, according to the manners of imitation. As he shows,[41] no one of these lines of differentiation is sufficient to discriminate a given art; according to manner alone, comedy and tragedy are indifferentiable; according to object alone, epic would be indifferentiable from tragedy; while according to the means alone, the imitative poet is not distinguishable from the scientist who writes verse treatises. All three lines of differentiation must therefore be used simultaneously; no one is peculiar, but all three collectively are peculiar, to a given art.[42] These lines of differentiation are in fact causes, in the technical sense in which Aristotle speaks of causes as the answers we give when we are asked "Why is this thing what it is?"[43] For if we are asked, let us say, "Why is this thing a tragedy?" we respond, "Because it is in a certain medium, because it imitates a certain object, and because it does this in a certain manner."

Yet this causal account is still incomplete; for, to continue the example, tragedy is not really owing to these differentiations, although if they did not exist, tragedy would not.[44] A saw, for instance, does not exist simply because of a certain shape and material, although without these the saw would not exist. They are conditions of its existence, and necessary ones: but the saw exists primarily because it has a certain function, sawing. And the existence of tragedy results primarily from its effect or power; these other things are for the sake of that. Compare the case of the saw just mentioned. Why is a saw designed as it is? To effect cutting in a certain way a certain shape and material are required, and an artisan must compound them. This fourth, or final, cause must be found for the various arts under consideration; chapters iv–v are devoted to it. Since for Aristotle what each thing is when fully developed is its nature, and since the nature of each thing is its end and is best and self-sufficient,[45] he achieves the final cause by recounting the origin and development of poetry. This is a history in terms of the successive final causes which imitative poetry has had; each phase involves a different final cause, and in each that cause is shown as governing the other elements of poetry.

Thus, in the first phase, human instinct for imitation for the sake of the pleasure and knowledge derived from it, whether we ourselves

41. *Manner*, 1448a 25 ff.; *object*, 1448a 7 ff.; *means*, 1447b 17 ff.
42. *An. post.* ii. 13, esp. 96a 32. See also 96b 15–24, and for important remarks on differentiational procedure, *De part. an.* i. 2–4; and *Met.* vii. 12. On species, see *Met.* x. 8.
43. *Phys.* ii. 3; ii. 7; *Met.* v. 2; vii. 17; *De part. an.* i. 1. 639b 12 ff.
44. *Phys.* ii. 9. 200a 5-200b 10.
45. *Politica*, i. 2. 1252b 32 ff.

imitate or merely observe imitations, is the originating cause; and since
man has also an instinct for tune and rhythm, it is natural that
imitation in words, melody, and rhythm should result.[46] But instinct is
perfectly uniform and consequently cannot account for variation in
poetry; and in the second phase, in which poetry diversifies, as poets
imitate either noble or ignoble actions and characters, the cause of the
diversification lies in the moral nature of the imitator himself.[47] In the
third phase, forms desirable in themselves are developed; here we have
art proper.[48] Poetry thus passes through phases in which its functions,
or final causes, are instinctive, ethical, and artistic. In the first the
means is developed;[49] in the second, objects of imitation are differentiated, and the means is adjusted to these;[50] in the third, manner is
developed and, art forms such as comedy and tragedy having now
come into being are improved and perfected by alterations and accom-
modations of their parts.[51] Taylor, among many others, has said that
Aristotle's theory of *katharsis* was intended to answer Plato's charges
against poetry;[52] but it is much more accurate to observe that Plato
never conceives of poetry as developing into this third phase and that
Aristotle's proper answer lies here: it is one thing to imitate the low and
vicious through inclinations of one's character; quite another to imitate
them for artistic purposes.

The causal account now complete, Aristotle "collects," as he says,[53]
the four causes into the famous definition. The specific problem is now
to discover what parts, of what kind and number, are requisite for a
whole of the sort just defined. If tragedy is dramatic in manner, there
must be spectacle; if the means are as described, there must be diction
and music; and if the object imitated is an action of a certain kind
(*spoudaios*, or serious), there must be plot and hence (since action is
discriminated in terms of character and thought) character and thought
also. But a whole, for Aristotle, does not simply have a certain number
of parts but has them in a certain ordering; one part will be determined
by another until the principal part is reached, which determines all.[54]
Consequently, to determine this ordering he establishes the relative
importance of the parts, arguing that plot is the principal part, the
"soul" of tragedy; and one may observe in passing that those who

46. *Poet.* 4. 1448b 4–24.
47. 1448b 25.
48. 1449a 5 ff.
49. 1448b 24.
50. 1448b 26–32.
51. 1449b 10–31.
52. *Aristotle*, pp. 88–90.
53. ἀπολαβόντες.
54. *Met.* v. 26, esp. 1024a 1 ff.

attack this view have never answered the arguments here and, perhaps, have never quite conceived of plot as it is here conceived.

If tragedy is a whole, and if plot is its primary part, and if a whole has its characteristics according to its primary part, plot must be investigated; for if that is not whole and entire and beautiful, the tragedy also will not be. Aristotle's treatment of plot is governed by three primary considerations: that it, too, is a whole, and a whole of a certain kind; that it is to be a beautiful whole; and that it is to have a certain effect or function. Plot is a whole of the sort that has beginning, middle, and end; has its parts complete and ordered; is not only of some magnitude, but of a magnitude such that it is beautiful; has a certain unity, in this instance a unity achieved by conjuction; and is continuous. Moreover, since actions, as continuities, are simple or complex according as they are or are not differentiable into distinctive parts, plot also must be simple or complex, the latter kind having as its parts reversal, discovery, or both. These matters, resulting from the specification of metaphysical doctrines of "whole," "part," and so forth to the case of plot, occupy chapters vii–xi. But plot is not merely to be whole and beautiful, but is to have a particular effect or power (upon the emotions); the true form of the tragic plot, thus, is precisely to have this effect; hence, Aristotle examines the nature of the tragic protagonist and the tragic deed, which are the conditions of the tragic effect (chapters xiii–xiv). Development of these conditions brings the treatment of plot as principal part to a close, and the remaining parts are discussed in the order of their importance. Finally, since tragedy includes the parts of epic, epic can be dealt with in terms of its similarities or dissimilarities to tragedy, and the two forms can be compared, and critical questions organized and resolved.

The method of the *Poetics*, thus, is precisely the method of productive science or art as Aristotle conceives it, and as such determined by the entire body of the philosophy of which it is a part. The degree of this dependency can be seen in the fact that, as Aristotle brought all his doctrines of method to bear on the subject matter of poetry, it was necessary in the foregoing analysis to explain his procedure by reference to most of his extant works. A more thoroughgoing analysis would, I believe, establish that dependency more clearly and fully, and would clarify Aristotle's procedure proportionately; conversely, apart from such consideration of the philosophy as a whole, not merely the argument of the *Poetics* but even the doctrines, indeed, even individual concepts, such as those of imitation, plot, and katharsis, become unintelligible.

In order to illustrate this last point, as well as to exhibit some further aspects of Aristotle's method, let me briefly consider the case of plot.

Aristotle's conception of plot is unique in the history of criticism, and in the innumerable discussions of "plot" from his day to our own, his conception is never again attached to the term *mythos* or any of its synonyms, such as *fabula, argumentum, argumento, favola, fable,* fable, plot, *Handlung,* and the like.

Critical discussions of "plot" since Aristotle have turned, I think, on several different conceptions. First, "plot" sometimes has the meaning of the material, whether historical or legendary, which is given poetic treatment; in this sense the various Oedipuses and Fausts are said to have the same plot. Plot often means a tissue of metaphorical or exemplary events or actions used as a vehicle for didactic statement. Thus, we have all heard of the "plot" of *The Faerie Queene* and the "plot" of Richardson's *Pamela,* although the former is really sustained allegorical metaphor and the latter a series of *exempla;* and in ages when poetry is conceived of as didactic only—for example, in the greater part of the medieval period—this meaning becomes the principal, if not the exclusive, one. Plot has meant the sequence of events simply, without regard to the moral agencies involved in the actions; this is the sense in which you tell the "plot" of a movie, and in this sense *Romeo and Juliet* and "Pyramus and Thisbe" (in *A Midsummer Night's Dream*) are said to have the same general plot, although one is serious and the other comic travesty. Plot can mean such events as are narrated, or as are represented upon the stage; this is the sense, I think, in which most European critics of the sixteenth and seventeenth centuries employed the term. Finally, there is "plot" in the sense of a string of occasions invented, *ficelle*-fashion, for the manifestation of character and thought and even the use of special diction. This is the conception which Ortega y Gasset entertains when he speaks of plot as a mere spine, skeleton, or armature, something as arbitrary as the string upon which we string beads.[55] I submit that these conceptions of plot are not equivalent to Aristotle's, that they stem from conceptions of poetry very different from Aristotle's, and that, even if plot should appear as important in any of them, it would hardly be in the sense in which Aristotle thought of plot as important.

Aristotle was not concerned with everything which we should call poetry, and was concerned with some things that we should no longer call poetry. It will not do even to say that he was concerned with tragedy, epic, and comedy, for the significance of these terms has altered since his day. He thought of epic as the *Iliad* and the *Odyssey* and whatever had the same form—not as the sort of epic that Aratus and Nicander were to produce; of tragedy as poetry similar to the *Oedipus* of Sophocles, not to the *Oedipus* of Seneca or *The White*

55. See, for example, Ortega y Gasset, *Notes on the Novel,* pub. together with *The Dehumanization of Art* (Princeton, 1948), pp. 65, 82, 87–88.

Devil. While he says repeatedly that the arts imitate nature, he means that the causes and productive processes of artificial objects resemble those which nature would have evolved had the products been natural and not artificial; he does not mean that all artificial objects are imitations in the sense in which he thinks tragedy is an imitation.[56]

In brief, he had observed that certain kinds of art had developed to a stage at which they were produced and appreciated for their own sake; that these forms happened to be (he uses the verb *tuxanousi*) imitative of human actions, in the sense that they simulated human actions, and that not simply, but human actions of different kinds, as serious or ludicrous, affecting us differently according to such differences of kind. The point is not that everything which has been or might be called poetry imitates human action, but that certain forms of poetry undoubtedly do; and it is these that he is discussing. Now, if actions are serious or ludicrous according to the degree in which they involve happiness or misery, and if happiness and misery are functions of the moral characters of the persons involved, the imitative action, or plot, cannot consist of events simply, or actions simply, but of activity of a certain moral quality, such that it produces a particular emotional effect; that is, the kind of action includes the kind of moral choice made, just as the moral choice includes the kind of reasoning and moral principles upon which the choice is made. Plot, therefore, in such imitative forms, is a system of morally differentiated activities or actions; as such, it is indubitably the primary part of such constructions, since it actualizes and completes and gives form to all the other parts, which are related to it as matter to form. But it is primary only in this conception of it, and only in this conception of poetry; and these conceptions are in turn dependent upon the whole body of the Aristotelian philosophy. To separate them from that philosophy is to lose not merely their scientific justification but their very significance as well.

What, then, are the powers and limitations of Aristotle's poetic method? I think that after a fashion we have been discussing them all along. There are some limitations which are almost invariably brought out—that the *Poetics* is a fragment, that portions of that fragment present certain textual difficulties, that Aristotle could have been cognizant of only very few literary forms and of these only to the degree of development which they had reached by his day, and so forth. I regard these "limitations" as trivial. Any philosophic method worthy of the name is not one which produces merely passive results, but one through which we may actively inquire, prove, and know; and if Aristotle offers a genuine philosophic method, anyone truly possessed of that method will be able to supply these deficiencies, real or supposed, with

56. *Phys.* ii. 8. 199a 8–19. Note Aristotle's careful statement at *Poet.* 1447a 13–16.

the authority of the master himself, for the authority should derive, not from the person, but from the method.

But there are two other kinds of limitation, much more real and important, although neither impairs the soundness of method or of doctrine. One stems from the method of the *Poetics* proper, the other from the general method of Aristotle; both originate in the fact that to adopt a given method is to be able to do certain things and not to be able to do certain others. The *Poetics* cannot be viewed, without serious distortion, as exhausting all questions pertinent to the arts, or even to all of the poetic arts. Of the problems which confront artist or critic, some are peculiar to the individual work, and, as accidental, are not amenable to scientific treatment. Some relate to the artistic faculty or process, some to the psychology of audiences, some to the social and political functions of art, some to the nature of what is imitated, and so forth; while Aristotle can handle such questions, it cannot be under poetic science, but under some other science or faculty. We can grasp something of these limitations, I think, by reflecting on a single point which I do not remember anyone ever to have made about the *Poetics:* that while the center of everything here is imitation, Aristotle in fact never tells us how to imitate; never tells us how to make likenesses of this or that action, this or that character. He tells us that characters must be likenesses, but never how to give them likeness—as he tells us that actions must be necessary or probable, but not how to make them necessary or probable. In fact he presupposes all such things, as he does the natural capacity, skill, and knowledge of the artist, and they do not enter into the art of poetics as he conceives it, although inevitably they must go into the making of any poem. In the *Poetics* he is concerned only with the nature of the forms at which the artist must aim and the causes of success and failure in terms of these. The treatise is not a treatise of the whole poetic art or craft, but of as much of it as can be scientific knowledge of a kind; indeed, it is only the beginnings and principles even of poetic science, for it must be extended to keep commensurate with the generation and development of new forms. To sum up on this point: from the modern point of view the primary limitation is the scope itself of the *Poetics;* and to see that, you have only to look at the first and last paragraphs of the work, in which Aristotle respectively states and restates his program of problems, and ask yourself whether these questions exhaust all the possible questions of art.

As for the kind of limitation arising from Aristotle's general method, that is, that of his philosophy itself: I mean by this that he is limited, precisely as every philosopher is limited, by the questions which he raises, by the kind of solution he requires for them, and by the devices of inquiry and proof which he employs; and since, as I have already suggested, such limitations are necessarily inherent in any single philosophy, it is our part to be aware of the limitations and of the powers of any one system. This is a view of which I cannot attempt to persuade you in a moment or two; let me therefore make a few large statements, more in illustration of my meaning than anything else.

Let me say that by this second half of the twentieth century I think that we should have learned a few things about philosophy, and about criticism too, since that is also philosophy. We should have learned, for instance, that every philosophy is limited by the problems which it raises and that every philosophic problem is limited by the terms in which it is couched. We should have learned, after all the labors of logicians, that there are many different ways of making propositions and that there are many senses of the terms "truth" and "falsity." We should have learned, after the many kinds of proofs and demonstrations offered to us, that there are many kinds of valid logics, as there are many valid geometries and algebras; and we should be wise enough to conclude that perhaps there are many "valid" philosophies. We should be too wise to accept any one philosophy as exhausting the whole of truth, and too wise to conclude that therefore every philosophy is false or that we must make a patchwork of philosophies without consideration of the diverse methods which they entail. We should, in short, be wise enough to consider the diverse valid philosophies only as instruments, all with various powers and limitations, and valuable relative to the kinds of questions to which they are directed.

The conception of mimetic poetry which underlies the *Poetics* is that in these arts the center and principle of all is human beings doing and experiencing things which are humanly interesting and affecting. For Aristotle that humanity is prime: that happiness or misery, that activity serious or laughable, every other part of the poem must serve to set before us as powerfully and vividly as possible; and every part must be as beautiful in itself as it can be consistently with the whole. Insofar as they permit scientific treatment, questions proper to the synthesis of such objects are the whole concern of the *Poetics;* as new forms of mimetic art emerge, the theory can be extended to cover them as well— provided that the extension is by one who has sufficient knowledge of and skill in Aristotle's method. In this sense Aristotle can be said to have developed not only a permanently true but also an indefinitely operable poetic method. But we cannot legitimately expect it to solve all problems that might be raised concerning all forms of art; especially when the questions posed, the answers demanded, and the method postulated are of an order alien to Aristotle's own.

4

CRITICAL THEORY

A LETTER ON
TEACHING DRAMA

Dear Fred:

So you have to teach drama, and want advice. Well: do you mind if I just jot things down anyhow, as they come into my head?

First of all, remember what so much of contemporary dramatic criticism seems to have forgotten: a play is a play. It is not like other literature, in which everything is imagined; it is something *acted out*. Think what this means. The novelist is simultaneously producer, director, actors, scene-designer, orchestra, even; the dramatist is not, he is only a dramatist. Remember Hume's distinction between impressions and ideas? Well, the dramatist has to work with impressions, whereas all other poets (of course I call the dramatist a poet!) work with ideas. That is, he proposes to affect his audience through their *sensations* first of all, whereas other writers operate through the imagination. Hence the dramatist is less dependent upon words than any other poet; he has first of all to construct a scenario of impressions. Don't tell me about Shakespeare and his wonderful language; that's beside the point. Fact is, he knew that the essential thing is to invent something that would be powerful pantomime, without a word said. That is the difference between Shakespeare and Stephen Phillips. (Forget about Knight—he really thinks drama is lyric poetry—which it hain't.) Impressions are more vivid than ideas; what the audience perceives in a stage production will always overcrowd mere images of the imagination. Corollary: a play cannot be read in the sense in which fiction is read; for the reader must always construct the real performance in his mind. That is why it is difficult to judge a play by reading it; fine plays sometimes read poorly, and bad plays sometimes read very well.

In radio drama, everything is done by the ear; hence the radio dramatist has to figure out very carefully *what would have been most vivid in a stage production*, and assign his most vivid images to that, so that it will predominate in the imagination.

What is a dramatic action? I hear you asking. An action, I reply,

Reprinted from *Chicago Review*, vol. 11, no. 2 (summer 1957).

which has its most appropriate and powerful effect when it is realized through external signs. Some things cannot be dramatized at all; for instance, when Henry James demanded that the actors in his play "simply *look* as if they had had tea," without the use of napkins, macaroons, tea-cups or anything, he was asking an impossibility. Some things can be dramatized, but are less effective, or produce effects of a different order when they are dramatized; for instance, Becky Sharp's actions really can't be dramatized accurately because her character and motivations are contrary to those which we infer from her external behavior. Another thing, *tempo;* the writer of fiction has great freedom with time, he can span centuries in a phrase, or stretch out a short incident to great length; but the dramatist has to hold pretty closely to the pace of real action. (What about *accelerated* time, you ask, as in Wilder's *The Long Christmas Dinner* or *The Skin of Our Teeth?* Answer: the *incidents* keep the pace of real action; certain dramatic *conventions* imply the passage of time, just as the dropping of the curtain implies the passing of it.)

Plot: it should be distinguished from a number of things with which it is often confused.

a. It is not the argument or a summary of a play, however detailed that may be. A plot is always aimed at some definite emotional effect, whereas bare summary never precludes the possibility of opposite emotional effects. For instance, the argument of Pyramus and Thisbe in *A Midsummer Night's Dream* closely parallels the argument of *Romeo and Juliet;* but it's comic, not tragic.

b. Plot isn't a bare system of events in abstraction from character, for the same reason. This may afford materials for the plot, but the plot is always something made by the poet.

c. It also isn't myth or legend or story or a series of historical happenings. A glance at all the various Oedipuses will reveal that whereas the same legend is used in all, different plots result.

d. Plot is not simply action; that is, all plot is action, but not all action is plot. Action is often used in didactic works as "proof" of a thesis, and such action is not plot. For example, the action of the *Divina Commedia* is proof, not plot. There are three ways in which action can function as proof in didactic works; even when the action is recognized as didactic, these are often confused, so I'll give them: (1) The type of action in which the characters are understood as individuals; the audience is expected to generalize from them. This is inductive proof, or the *exemplum;* the action of the *Divina Commedia* is of this sort; so are *A Doll's House, Hedda Gabler, Ghosts.* (2) The type of action in which the characters are generalities or classes or universals and the audience is expected to particularize from them. This is deductive proof, and such actions are strictly allegorical. Examples: *The*

Faery Queene, Pilgrim's Progress, Everyman, etc. (3) The type of action in which the relation of didactic action to the thesis is neither as individual to general nor general to individual, but analogical. This is the form of the parable, fable etc. These kinds are simple kinds and can be combined in various ways, so as to appear together in a single work. Since all proof must be either inductive or deductive or analogical, this division is exhaustive.

To come back to plot:

e. it is not mere intrigue or "conflict," although post-Elizabethan theorists often make it synonymous with the former, and nineteenth century theorists often equate it with the latter.

f. it is also *not the representation*. The dramatic representation is what is seen on the stage. That this is different from plot can be seen from the following considerations: the representation may begin before or after the beginning of the plot; e.g., *Hamlet* begins long before the initiating incident of the action (the information of the Ghost); that of *Lear* begins almost immediately before the initiating incident, while the representation in *Oedipus Rex* begins after the initiating incident. Again, parts of the plot, however important, may be omitted from the representation (i.e., are "off-stage); and again, parts of the representation may not be parts of the plot at all, e.g., Act I of *Othello*, etc.; these are "protatic" parts, to introduce the characters and set them in a given light, and generally give the information required for a proper emotional reaction to the plot.

WHAT PLOT IS: A system of *morally determinate actions* (or in cases where characters are purely passive, as in Schicksal Dramas, reactions.) It is one in the sense that, whatever its magnitude and complexity, it has been integrated into one system; complete, in the sense that the action ends by resolving those issues out of which it has developed (another way of saying this is that the consequences of the initiating causes have been exhausted). Morally determinate—determined by a given moral character of the person in the play, and thus also determining a given moral response on the part of the audience.

Points to discuss with respect to plot:

Magnitude of action: We can distinguish four kinds of action (apart from consideration of emotional effects).

1. Action (or reaction) of a single character in a closed situation. This does not occur in drama, but is the "action" of most lyric poetry— "Lycidas," Keat's odes, "Sailing to Byzantium," etc. A "closed situation" is one in which there is no external intervention in the action. For example, whenever a messenger enters, or a new agent, the situation is "opened" in the sense that more causes have now been added to the action, to affect the consequences; but in a closed situation the character operates without such external intervention, except

at the beginning, perhaps, or at the end; thus Keats's "Ode to a Nightingale" has the bird's song start the train of meditation, and the bird flies away at the end; but the action is the train of thought of the poet.

2. Two or more characters in a closed situation (call this a "scene" ...). It is the form of Theocritean idylls, Virgil's Eclogues, and pieces such as Browning's "The Bishop Orders His Tomb ..." (N.B. the latter is a *monologue in representation*, but in fact the characters interact, so it belongs here.) Some short stories and one-act plays are of this order.

3. A series of "scenes" centering about one principal event; call this the "episode." For example, the actions of *Heart of Darkness*, *The Secret Sharer*, Arnold's *Schrab and Rustum*, etc.

4. The "grand plot" proper, where a series of episodes are integrated into one system of action. All of Shakespeare's plays have this kind of action.

Lines of action: all action is either linear or polylinear. E.g., *Othello* is linear, *Lear* is bi-linear (Lear, Gloucester), *Hamlet* is tri-linear (Hamlet, Laertes, Fortinbras). A line of action is a chain of causally connected events involving certain persons, separable from other lines at least in part. Lines of action are either related as contrasting or as similar (they cannot, in a well-constructed plot, be unrelated); they nearly always heighten the emotional effect of the principal line, if they are by-plots or sublines. Thus a comic under-plot in a serious play is contrasting, and the Fortinbras and Laertes lines offer "standards" contrasting with the action of Hamlet himself, while the Gloucester line is similar to that of Lear, paralleling it. The student should be made to determine what line is principal, and what the relation of the other lines is, and what function they discharge in the whole.

Lines of action either converge or diverge or run parallel. If you diagram a plot, and find two or more lines of action starting from a single cause or incident, this is divergence. If you find independent chains of causation concurring in a single effect, this is convergence. If they run along independently, they are parallel. Convergence is principally used in achieving resolution or denouement; divergence in beginning the actions. Threatened convergence is a way of obtaining suspense, when the convergence will materially affect the outcome, and sudden convergence is one way of obtaining surprise. For example, in *Lear*, the points where Albany almost tumbles to the situation; and in *Othello*, where things threaten the plotting of Iago. (I counted some dozen places where the apple-cart was within an ace of being upset.)

Types of incidents: I have already said that incidents of the representation should be distinguished from incidents of the plot (see f above).

But plot incidents themselves should also be distinguished into three classes:

1. the basic incidents of the plot; for instance, in *Othello*, the working out of Iago's scheme ending in the tragic denouement.

2. "factorial" incidents, which are the minor incidents that provide the necessary conditions for the happening of the major incidents; e.g., if Desdemona must be strangled or smothered in bed, she has got to be there, and Othello must enter there, and all that; murderer and victim have got to be brought together.

3. "ornamental" incidents, which are introduced simply to make the action more pleasing; e.g., a progress of the king, in Elizabethan drama, or the introduction of famous historical characters in modern movies dealing with biographical subjects; e.g., in *Song to Remember*, that awful Cornell Wilde job on Chopin, the introduction of characters like Liszt and Kalkbrenner et al.

Make the student distinguish, not only so that he gets a clear idea of what is basic to the plot, but so that he gets some notion of characteristics of a dramatist's handling of the plot itself. A good many value judgments are of course possible here: for example, a bad plot-maker generally has too many factorial incidents; a good one is usually very economical. Moreover, a bad dramatist will multiply his characters unnecessarily, to bring about the happening of the factorial incidents. A good case in point is Bianca in *Othello;* she has about four or five different jobs to do—a bad dramatist would have invented a lot of different characters to perform them. Again, a good dramatist keeps the factorial incidents from being mere continuity and filler by making them interesting and exciting in themselves, but never letting them run away with the main show. They are for the sake of the basic incidents and must always be kept under, without going flat.

Having sketched out the basic incidents, the student can determine their causal connection as necessary or probable by diagramming the action. In such a diagram the basic incidents (and factorial and ornamental) could be related to each other by arrows indicating chains of necessity or probability. "Necessary," in this context, would mean "made inevitable"; "probable" would mean "made more likely than not."

Emotional effect of plot: The whole emotional effect of a work is of course determined by the plot, character, and thought, plus the representation, plus the diction, but the student should be made to think of the effect of the plot in itself. He must think, first of all, of the basic emotional effect of the plot incidents (always, of course, as involving the characters of the play) quite apart from how these are represented; think of how the dramatist has invented or adapted the incidents. For example, Cinthio's tale is mere shilling-shocker sensationalism, a mere crime-story; Shakespeare made *Othello* out of it, sometimes adapting, sometimes omitting, sometimes inventing; what difference did he get in re-making the characters and re-doing the actions? (I take it that the effect he achieves is not mere sensationalism.)

In working a thing of this sort through, I always take the "prime" incident of the basic plot. In tragedy, this is always the tragic deed, in comedy the comic fraud, mistake, or ruse. Now the tragic deed of *Othello* is of course the smothering, under delusion, of Desdemona; this is only sensationally conceived by Cinthio, but is tragically conceived in *Othello*. For the deed to be tragic, it must be an irrevocable action, of great dreadfulness, done by mistake (or some other compulsion), by a person of more than ordinary stature to someone whom he should greatly have cherished; thus, in this example, Desdemona had to be re-conceived, so had Othello, for neither was of the proper moral stature in Cinthio; and since two such lovers would have remained absolutely static (Othello could never have been spontaneously jealous enough to kill her) an outside agency of extreme malignancy and competency had to be invented; thus, Iago. I protest that Shakespeare *invents* Iago; he is there, not because of Cinthio's tale and its ensign, but because of the exigencies Shakespeare had to meet if the action was to be elevated to tragic stature. Now, one works backward from the deed; *if* it is to happen, such and such basic incidents have got to go before; to make these continuous, as well as necessary or probable, the factorial incidents have got to be invented, and so until the web is spun. The student should try to estimate the emotions aroused by each incident, basic or otherwise, as closely as he can. (This is very hard at first, easy later; I shall presently make more suggestions about emotional effects.)

One more rough suggestion about plot: I forgot to tell you, in talking of lines of action, that the student should try to distinguish the lines in terms of magnitude. Thus your lines might be two "grand-plot" lines, or you might have one "grand-plot" line, the principal one, with a sub-plot of only episode-magnitude, and so on. There is room for much discussion, of course, of whether the lines are of the most effective magnitude or not; for example, something very wrong with the Dryden-Lee *Oedipus* (among many other faults) is the "drowning" of the Oedipus-line amid a welter of other stuff, so that it doesn't stand out properly. A plot can also be made of so many separate lines that it is impossible to remember; e.g., Sidney's *Arcadia*. And it can have lines of such length, as well, that it cannot be taken in as a whole (*Arcadia* again.) Or the line can be so short as to fail utterly. For example, Oedipus done this way:

Chorus: We've got this plague because you murdered your father and married your mother.

Oed. Heck. Well I'll just tear out my eyes, then.

Joc. Think I'll go hang myself (Does.)

Chorus: Tough situation. Must be a moral here someplace.

Representation:

Obviously the audience reacts, in proportion as it knows, and in accordance with what it conjectures on the basis of what it knows. Now, the representation has two functions: to supply the audience with information (or to withhold it at certain points) so as to control the emotional reactions, and to set parts of the plot as vividly as possible before them (thus also controlling their emotions, so these two functions meet).

The representation should first of all be thoroughly studied in terms of its relation to the plot. Does the representation begin before the action, and if so, why? Sample answer: *Hamlet,* which requires a full and vivid exposition of the highly complex situation at Elsinore before the ghost's information can mean anything emotionally, naturally has to begin long before; *Lear,* which grows merely out of Lear's quirky way of testing love, in a very simple situation, begins almost immediately before the initiating incident of the testing. Does the rep begin after, & if so why? (This is the principle of *festinare in medias res,* has the effect, when feasible, of great dramatic abruptness and vivacity; it never happens in Shkspr. Similar questions shd be asked about the end. Again: what parts of the represented action are in the plot, what are not; conversely, what parts of the plot are represented, what are not, and of course why, to all this.

One should go into the question of scale of representation. Is a scene "huddled over" (see Olson's Oedipus above) or dwelt on at length? A beautiful case: why does act I sc ii of *Rich III* have to be exactly of the length it is? (I once heard Olivier do it in short form on the radio, and it was awful; you need the slow stages of Anne's persuasion, or it falls right apart, utterly improbable). The scale should be thought of in terms of (a) the length needed to make the thing necessary or probable, (b) to get the audience into the right feeling, (c) to produce the proper amount of suspense or surprise (think of the suspense achieved by Othello before D wakes! and (d) to make the scene fulfill its proper function, and no more or less (a bad writer tries to wring everything dry).

Once all this is worked over, the student should be forced to state precisely what he knows, not only act by act or scene by scene, but speech by speech and part of speech by part of speech, although this somewhat cuts into diction-questions. He should consider each item of information as causing him to frame this conjecture or that, and as affecting his emotions accordingly. Make 'em put a card over the text and slide it from word to word; I do. The subtle dramatist does wonderful things this way with his audience. As these variations in feeling caused by variations in knowledge (and by what is put vividly to the fore, what is under-played) become clear, the student should be made to ask whether the variations enhance the emotional effect, or whether they run off into irrelevancies, etc.

Again, the degree and kind of emotion, produced by representation of the action, shd be roughly diagrammed, peaks for the high excitement, valleys for the low, that sort of thing, with discussion of why.

Also, make 'em discuss what's narrated, soliloquized, pantomimed, etc.

As to characters:

Make the students distinguish between:

a. characters of representation simply. The "protactic" persons of Dryden are of this sort. The "ficelle" character of H. James is a much subtler version of this: a character brought in to elicit a response from a major character which could not otherwise be, or be so effectively, elicited.

b. "factorial characters." E.g., all characters in Othello except Othello, Iago, Desdemona.

c. "essential characters." E.g., Oth, Iag, Des.

d. "ornamental chars."

Make 'em determine the *peculiar* function or functions of a character in a given scene, Stanislavsky-wise.

Make 'em state exactly what kind of character each is, and show what reveals him as such, report of others, own particular speech or actions, etc. Make 'em set each of the speeches of a given character together, throughout the play, and 1) trace the gradual exposition of the character 2) the development of the character (e.g., Macbeth's gradual coarsening) 3) the change of knowledge or affection, etc. in the char (Ex: the speeches of Albany or of Claudius, showing how each gradually "tumbles,") 4) changing relations of other characters to the character on the basis of all this.

Take a given speech, make 'em trace the logic or emotion in it, and explain it through the character and his situation at the moment. Ex: The non-sequitur, highly indicative of Hamlet's character, in the "Now I am alone" solil. A beautiful job can be done of course with things like Antony's oration and the changes in the rabble.

More on plot:

Plot is either simple or complex. Plot is complex if it involves a reversal of fortune and if it involves discovery, e.g., of identity, or of the commission of an act, etc., which materially affects the relations between protagonistic characters (essential characters.) A species of simple plot is the "episodic plot," in which the episodes are strung together without necessity and probability (episodes are always convertible in order in such plots, so one can test thus.) The student shd indicate where discovery & reversal take place, if they do.

The student should analyze the factors of the static situation at the point before the initiating incident, e.g., the situation at Elsinore before the information of the ghost; any other events which determine the course of the action should also be worked out carefully, especially those which lead to complication and resolution. A good way is to ask what would have happened had event X not occurred.

Another good thing is to take an event and work out the way in which the possibilities diminish until the event becomes necessary or probable; e.g., the way in which one mode of escape from assassination after another is eliminated in *Jul. Caes.* until Caesar's assassination becomes inevitable.

Character & Thought, odd hints:

Examine all cases in which a character makes a moral choice, and exhibit the moral rules he assumes or cites in making choice. Relate this to the state of the character's knowledge at the time with respect to situation, persons involved, etc.

Examine all nouns, verbs & epithets in a speech as clues to the character's moral character and state of mind. Metaphors are especially revealing in this way; ask the student what kind of man in what situation & frame of mind would be likely to think this resembled that, or to make this or that comparison. Other figures of speech are also revealing—especially hyperboles. Also the form of the utterance, whether interrogative, declarative, etc.; since these forms are also clues as to what the character thinks and feels. This kind of diction analysis is particularly revealing when, say, two speeches are drawn from the early and late portions of the play, and exhibit a change in the character. E.g., Hamlet's "O that this too too solid flesh (I.ii) with his narrative to Horatio "Up from my cabin" (V. ii).

Must go now. Good luck!

E.

THE LYRIC

$\mathbf{M}$ost of us become acquainted with poetry of one sort or another in our early childhood. At some point in our education we are told about the "forms" of poetry: epic, tragedy, ballad, elegy, pastoral, sonnet, lyric and the rest. And most of us remain content with such supposed knowledge. As a rule we do not reflect on the fact that of these "forms" some, like epic and tragedy, are genuine forms; some, like sonnet and triolet, merely verse patterns; and some, like pastoral and ballad, merely sets of conventions which can be used in varying forms. We talk with confidence about the lyric, as we do about the novel and the drama. We talk about the nature of poetry, the nature of the lyric, of the novel, of the drama. And usually we talk thus with perfect safety, even if we are professional students of literature. It is only when we fall into the hands of a shrewd and persistent questioner that, like the Athenians questioned by Socrates, we come to doubt whether we really know what we think we know. Fortunately or unfortunately, such questioners are rare.

Why should we bother to discriminate literary forms—why bother to define them accurately? Let me admit immediately that for many modes of criticism, for many critical problems, there is no reason whatsoever to bother; for such modes and such problems the questions of specific form are either insignificant or irrelevant. But, on the other hand, there are other modes and other problems for which such questions are crucial. It is sometimes dangerous to talk of things as being the same or alike when they are in fact different. Furthermore, a poet may have a gift for one kind of poetry and not for another; the criteria which are appropriate to one kind may not be appropriate to another; a good judge of one kind may not necessarily be a good judge of another.

Besides, all of us do differentiate, at one level or another—it is only a

Reprinted from *Poetic Theory, Poetic Practice: Papers of the Midwest Modern Language Association*, ed. Robert Scholes (Iowa City, Iowa: Midwest Modern Language Association, 1969).

matter of how general or how specific we wish to be. We talk about poetry, after all; and merely to mention the word "poetry" is of course to differentiate poetry from something else. A great many of us even attempt to define poetry—to say what it is. John Stuart Mill, writing in 1833, observed: "It has often been asked, What is Poetry? And many and various are the answers which have been returned." The question has been asked even more frequently since 1833, and the answers have multiplied in number and variety. We make definitions, none of them satisfactory, and some very bad indeed. Evidently, then, whatever we say, we do think the problem worth thinking about. If it is worth thought, thought ought to be worthy of it. And this our thought has scarcely been.

Consider, for example, the upshot of our various attempts to define the lyric. What is a lyric? A brief poem? How brief? The epigram and the aphorism are briefer; and some lyrics, like Shelley's "Adonais," are very long. Is it a poem of intense emotion? Shall we say the emotion in lyrics is more intense than that in *King Lear?* And in any case, do all lyrics involve intense emotion? What is so intense about "Full fathom five thy father lies?" Is the lyric a poem expressing the poet's innermost feelings? If so, how is it that we recognize as lyrics thousands of poems, the very identity of whose author is unknown to us, let alone his innermost feelings? Conversely, what were Yeats' innermost feelings about old age? He has left us a good number of lyrics on old age, expressing a variety of quite incompatible "innermost feelings." Does, in fact, our recognition of lyric form or the pleasure we derive from it in any way depend upon our reflection on the poet and his innermost feelings? Is the lyric a poem capable of being sung or set to music? *Any* discourse, verse or prose, is capable of being sung or set to music; you could sing or set to music William of Ockham's *Summa totius logicae* if you wanted to, or for that matter, Webster's Dictionary, or the city telephone directory. Well, then: a poem characterized by lyrical quality? That is a vicious circle. Et cetera. I find all such pseudo-definitions senseless trash, the only significance of which is that their makers neither knew what a lyric nor what a definition is. T. S. Eliot, by the way, seems to have felt much as I do, although his distinction between the three voices of poetry is hardly more helpful.

I do not propose in this paper to attempt definitions or the statement of principles or the construction of a poetics. I propose something far more simple, far more modest: to see whether we can establish, so to speak, a geography of the lyric; to delineate its boundaries, so that we may at least know where it begins and where it leaves off. And it occurs to me that a certain kind of procedure might be very useful in this connection. In things that exist by nature we observe that some possess relatively simple, some relatively complex structures. No one doubts that the amoeba is among the simpler organisms, whereas man is among the most complex. It is evident, too, that a greater or less complexity exists also in the poetic arts. The lyric consists of a single utterance, usually brief; epic and tragedy usually involve many characters, in manifold interaction in many incidents, uttering many speeches. Between these extremes, moreover, we find such things as one-act plays, epic episodes, and the like, obviously more complex than the lyric, and less complex than epic or tragedy. It seems that it might be possible, thus, to arrange the structures of poetry, beginning with the very simplest, in the order of increasing complexity, and to see whether we can locate the lyric among them.

What, then, is the simplest form of poetry? While there is no necessary correlation of mere length with complexity of structure, it is clear on the other hand that something may be too brief to be very complex. Homer could not have written the *Iliad*, or Shakespeare *Hamlet*, in ten words or less. It seems reasonable, thus, to look for the simple forms of poetry in some area of discourse in which expression is severely restricted. Naturally one thinks at once of the more stringent verse-forms, the haiku particularly.

Here is a haiku by Issa, called "Spring Day":

> Departing, the spring day
> Lingers
> Where there is water.

Is this a poem? Certainly. A lyric poem? Surely. Is it the simplest kind of poem? It must be: it conveys only a single perception; if we try to divide that into parts, we have nothing. But if this is true, we have already established one boundary of lyric poetry; it begins with the very simplest kind. Not that I want to argue, mind you, that everything in the haiku pattern of five syllables plus seven plus five is a poem. I was amused to see a sign, gold-lettered on scarlet background, on the Hong Kong ferry:

> *Notice*
> Smoking and spitting
> Are strictly prohibited
> On these premises.

That has the verse-pattern, but I do not think it is a poem. Nor do I wish to contend that every haiku is a lyric. I merely think this one of Issa's is. We said it involved only a single perception; now, perception is not merely an exercise of sense, but a mental activity of a certain kind. Are there other elementary mental activities? Certainly; there must be absolutely elementary and indivisible activities of every sort— recollecting, recognizing, inferring, expecting, imagining, and the like, as well as of every emotional response. It would be wearisome to

illustrate them all; perhaps we need merely observe that the anony-
mous "O Westron Wind" involves a single wish for spring, so that the
lover can return to his beloved at home. And we may also observe that
each of them, if it enters into a *poem* as the wish enters into "O
Westron Wind," will produce a *lyric* poem.

It now occurs to me that these elements can be used *as* elements in a
more complex poem; for example, in a sequence of perceptions. Are
there such poems? I think at once of Theodore Roethke's fine poem,
"The Heron"; it is nothing other than a sequence of such perceptions.
Any such sequence, of course, must have a certain unity and continuity; but if it results in a poem, that poem is a lyric poem. Is this
possible for all the other elementary activities? Certainly. And again, if
a poem results, it is a lyric. Nor is it necessary that the activities be all
of the same kind; for example, a perception may lead to an emotion
and that to recollection and that to another emotion.

Let us observe something else. The "speaker," if I may use that
word, in Issa's poem is hardly characterized at all; he is simply someone capable of that perception and whatever it may imply. We know
something more about the speaker in "O Westron Wind:" he is a lover,
separated from his love by winter (we are not even sure that "he" is a
he.) Of his moral character we know nothing; we do not even know
whether the love is licit or illicit, or anything further. But, while
emotions and desires and choices and wishes are common to all mankind, *what* moves, *what* is desired, chosen, or wished may characterize
men indeed, as to their state of mind, disposition, or moral character.
It is obvious, then, that the character of the "speaker" in a lyric poem
may range from one absolutely universal to one very much particularized. Consider the difference, for example, between Issa's speaker and
Browning's in "Soliloquy of the Spanish Cloister."

We might note, also, that this sequence of ours can be of various
kinds; that it can, for instance, proceed in a straight line, or involve a
turning point, or several turning points; "Lycidas" and Keats's "Ode
to a Nightingale" involve turning points; but I shall pass over such
matters. What really concerns us is this: that events and activities of
the mind, if rendered into poems complete as such and no more, will
always result in lyric poems. I shall not define "poetry" for you; you
know the difference between Issa's haiku and the "haiku" on the Hong
Kong ferry. Now reflect that what goes on in the mind is purely
private; you can only know what goes on in the mind of another, even
your husband or wife, if it is somehow expressed. *Expression* is a word
we knock about a good deal; I shall strictly define it as—whatever
form it takes—the *external* manifestation of activities and events in the
mind that would otherwise remain private. *Internal.* So—granted we
have poetry—there is a poetry of *expression.* And it is lyric poetry. At

once we see, in the absurdity of the definition of lyric poetry as "the *poet's* innermost thoughts and feelings" a grain of truth: a lyric poetry of *private* thoughts and feelings, unknown unless expressed. *Whose* private thoughts and feelings? It does not matter; it matters very much what the thoughts and feelings are and how they are expressed. Unless, of course, by "whose" you mean, not Yeats or Keats, but the person in the poem. And notice that *External* events are here simply the circumstances of the internal or private events.

At this point I recall a poem somewhat unduly celebrated some thirty years ago: Marvell's "To His Coy Mistress." It is a superb poem, although I personally cannot—no doubt through poetic insensibility —read into it all of the profundities that better sensibilities have found in it. Whatever the case may be, there is no doubt about one thing: it is not simply an *expression*, as I defined the term, of internal conditions of a lover; it is an *act* (true, a verbal act, and these are no less real than physical acts, as some of you may have reason to know)—an act performed upon another person or persons. Let us not deceive ourselves here: Tennyson's *Ulysses looks* like an act but is not: it is merely *expression* masking as an act; Marvell's lover means business, and is operating upon his coy mistress precisely insofar as she is willing but coy, that is to say, temporizing; and like a sensible fellow, he addresses himself to the topic of Time. But, in any case, we must regard here, not an interior condition, but an external *act*. Is "To His Coy Mistress" a lyric poem? Why not? It has been so regarded by everyone. It follows that there is a lyric poem of the verbal act. There may be many verbal acts: of persuading, beseeching, commanding, informing, betraying, and so on. But we have an *act*. How did the coy mistress *react*? We have no idea, unless we suppose (illicitly) that she could not have resisted. Who is she? She is a mere circumstance of the act. Indeed, we ask nothing further of her; we are satisfied with the poem as it is.

We have seen that the elementary activities of mind in the private sphere might be extended in sequence. Basically, that is elementarily, Marvell's lover offers nothing but plea and reason; it is possible to imagine a *sequence* of such pleas, the lady in no way responding. This would give us a sequence of lyric poems. We can also suppose that the lover, here characterized as ardent and witty, can be generalized to the point where he is ardent simply, as in Marlowe's "Come live with me and be my love;" we can also suppose him to be particularized in character. It makes no difference; we are still within the areas of what we should call lyric poems. True, we might call them, as Browning did, "dramatic lyrics;" but all this means is that we have particularized character and circumstance. And here we may note something further: out of such elements alone, no matter how compounded, we should never be able to achieve the kind of construction we call *plot*. The same observation, of course, applies to the private experiences of which we have spoken.

Let us call this second major stage the *address*—the act—regardless of the verbal form it takes. So we have two major divisions, thus far: expression and address. Suppose we add a third: suppose the coy mistress *replies*. At once we have something different: not the expression of the private mental activity, not the act, (which may, by the way, be morally characteristic or not) in itself, but act and response or reaction. That is, *interaction*. At once we have a very different element; such elements, compounded, are capable of producing what we call a *plot*. As individual perception and passion and thought are swallowed up, so to speak, in act, individual act is here swallowed up in interaction; what results is a contexture of interaction. Yet there are lyric poems of interaction: for example, "The Nut-Brown Maid." So, it seems, we are approaching the limits of lyric.

We must, therefore, be very careful here. Such interplay or interaction (suppose we call it *colloquy*) can take various forms: utterances in turn, like lovers pledging mutual love; question and answer; demand and response; and things beside. All these may be found, of course, in plays as well as in lyrics. When do they overpass the bounds of lyric and become something else? Precisely when external circumstances and events cease to be mere *occasions* for individual action as purely individual action and become something prior; when the continuity of the external overrules the internal continuity of individual action and reaction; when, for example, the consequences of former actions or the working out of Nemesis or the changes of circumstance take priority over the individual. Under such conditions the individual action is intelligible and effective primarily in terms of what it subserves. But if external circumstances and events remain *secondary*, as ingredients in the individual act, the case is the reverse. If a poem results, it remains lyric. We can even use colloquies as elements, again, as elements in a sequence; and the elements can merely be juxtaposed or involve some type of progression such as addition (the one adding to the other) or repetition, or contrast, or dialectical progression, or opposition, or conflict. If the poet proceeds in this way, at the most he will produce something approaching a dramatic scene, as Browning does in "The Bishop Orders His Tomb at St. Praxed's Church" (though here the colloquy is represented through one speaker only); he will not produce a plot.

There is one further possibility. We may note that a framework of action—some sort of general action not serving as plot, but as successive *occasions* for lyric poems—is possible. To give instances: Meredith's "Modern Love," Wilfrid Scawen Blunt's "Esther," Eugene Lee-Hamilton's "Mima Bella," William Ellery Leonard's "Two Lives,"

Edna St. Vincent Millay's "Fatal Interview." There are of course other possibilities of organization—for example, as illustrating the various aspects of love. Whatever the organization, so long as it merely provides *occasions* for lyrics, the poem will remain lyrical.

Suppose we sum up. We have three basic lyrical phases: that of the private sphere, which involves the continuity of expression; that of the verbal act, which involves the continuity of address; and that of the colloquy, which involves the continuity of interchange or inter-action. All of these may entail the momentary (or elementary) or the sequential. They remain lyrical so long as their form is unaffected by any contexture in which they may be placed; for example, Shakespeare's lyrics in the plays are lyrics so long as their independence as wholes is not affected. In other words, lyric poetry presents individual action and reaction as wholes, unaffected by their context; the contexture of external events remains, not as conditions affecting them, but as occasions. Again, while they may contain within themselves a considerable narrative or dramatic portion, that portion is subordinate to the lyrical whole; thus the narrative of the wreck of the Deutschland, in the poem of that name, remains subservient to a lyrical whole, and Hopkins rightly remarked that his poem was not a narrative but an ode. Once we pass the bounds of that independence, however, once expression and address and colloquy become subservient to a further end as affecting their form as complete and whole in themselves, we have gone beyond the bounds of the lyric, and find ourselves in other and more complex forms.

Obviously private happenings in the mind, verbal acts, and colloquy or dialogue are not peculiar to the lyric forms; they may be found everywhere in the longer and more complex narrative and dramatic forms. But here they are parts, not wholes; they are subservient to some more comprehensive principle, such as *plot*; and, serving a function beyond themselves, they are seldom intelligible by themselves (a speech from a play is not intelligible by itself) or developed as they would be in lyrical treatment. The train of thought or passion and the verbal act are constantly subject to interruption or deflection from their course by external forces such as the speeches and actions of others; the colloquy is similarly subject. The difference, if I may use a somewhat homely comparison, is that between a balloon inflated to its proper shape, nothing affecting it but the internal forces of the gas, and a balloon subjected to the pressure of external forces which counteract the internal. Thus, as we move from simpler to more complex forms, the speech which might have been whole and complete in itself takes the form demanded by the scene; the scene takes the form demanded by the episode; the episode, the form demanded by the plot or some other comprehensive principle. As the principle becomes more and more comprehensive, the subservient parts are subject to further and further determination.

We may note a similar progression. In the lyric of mental experience or activity, that experience or activity is primary. In the lyric of the verbal act, it is no longer primary but merely a factor of the act. In the lyric of colloquy, the verbal act is no longer primary but a factor in the colloquy. And so on: each is sublated in the next.

We have found, I think, the boundaries of lyric territory, but we are far from knowing everything these boundaries contain. It should be clear even from this much consideration that there are different forms ruled by different principles, so that we can no longer speak, with any strictness at least, of *the* lyric in the sense of a single form. And we have not even touched upon such matters as the serious and the comic (for lyrics can be comic—"Soliloquy of the Spanish Cloister" is comic); matters which, since they are differentiations affecting form, will enter into the definitions of these forms. A further thing is clear—that it is futile to attempt a definition of lyric, if we mean by definition a statement of the nature or essence of somthing; for things of different natures cannot have one nature or definition. A corollary of this is that it is also futile to attempt to define poetry in general; for the same principle applies, and if lyric cannot be defined, neither can poetry.

THE POETIC PROCESS

The poetic process has been the subject of much discussion in our century. I do not think anyone would say that discussion has been in vain, but I also think that no one would consider it satisfactory. The difficulty is not that we have not found answers to our questions, but that we have found too many answers in too patent disagreement. The poetic process is a rational one; it is not. It is a conscious one; it is not. It is a voluntary one; it is not. It is a process analogous to other processes—of art, of communication, of scientific thought, even of biological, psychological, or political growth; it is not. The diversity of views may be partly explained by the fact that the poetic process is correlative with poetry and must be defined relatively to it, and that we do not always mean the same thing by the term *poetry*. We may indeed designate the same *objects*, but in designating them as poetry we usually point to quite different structural aspects of them. It is not astonishing that different structures should be produced by different processes. The mere fact that we talk about wholes and the relations of part to whole will not save us from ambiguity; a single poem may be viewed as any one of a number of different wholes, composed of quite different parts.

In general, discussions of the poetic process have tended to fall into one of three classes. The first of these, generalizing the process, analyzes the faculties or the activities supposedly involved and arranges them in their logical order, to produce distinct stages or periods of the process. The second describes the working habits of an individual poet in terms of characteristic external or internal circumstances or conditions. The third gives us, in the same terms, the history of the composition of a particular poem. To illustrate these in reverse order: W.D. Snodgrass's essay "The Finding of a Poem" tells us how he discovered the meaning—for him—of the elements entering into a particular poem; Paul Valéry's essays on his own poetry—"Poésie et

Reprinted from *Critical Inquiry*, vol. 2, no. 1 (Autumn 1975).

pensée abstraite," for example—generally describe his working habits and his experiences while at work; and the following passage gives a typical account of the poetic process as a series of logically ordered stages:

There is, first, a period of hard thinking, during which the mind explores the problems; then a period of relaxation, during which the rational processes of the mind are withdrawn from this particular problem; then the flash of insight which reveals the solution, organizes the symbols, or directs the thinking, during which the formula is tested, the work of art shaped and developed. . . . Graham Wallas calls the four stages Preparation, Incubation, Illumination, and Verification.[1]

I have no wish to seem ungrateful for such descriptions as we find in Mr. Snodgrass's and Valéry's accounts. I find them highly interesting, not merely when the poet himself provides them, but when they are the reconstructions of a competent scholar. As to the stage-or-period descriptions, I can only regard them as so many myths. They remind me of the more elementary manuals on how to write a term paper, and I doubt whether poets ever followed the former as I doubt whether students follow the latter. "Nature," says a great philosopher, "is not so neat."

What concerns me here, however, is not a matter of accuracy but of relevance. Whatever value these three kinds of accounts may have, they can have none as exhibiting the poetic process as such, because they are manifestly irrelevant to it. The stage-or-period account generalizes to such an extent that it ceases to have direct reference to poetry. We are a long way from poetry when we say of the process, as one writer does, that it is one "in which a whole-structure tends to obtain its optimal state," and that "similar processes occur everywhere in the biological and psychological field."[2] Such accounts are founded, not upon what is essential and peculiar to the poetic process, but upon resemblances which it may accidentally bear to other processes.

The second and third kinds, on the other hand, exceed in the direction of particularity, and are based upon what is peculiar either to the individual poet or the individual poem; hence they present the process as inextricably entangled with its accidents. All three kinds, therefore, may be said to base upon the accidental.

Moreover, the principle of order in all three is evidently not the one which obtains in the poetic process. The stage-account, as I have said, involves a logical or dialectical order, derived from a supposed

1. Wilbur L. Schramm, "Imaginative Writing," in *Literary Scholarship* (Chapel Hill, N. C., 1941), p. 183.

2. Rudolf Arnheim, "Psychological Notes on the Poetical Process," in *Poets at Work* (New York, 1948), p. 160.

priority of faculties or activities in abstraction from the thing produced. The second and third kinds entail a purely historical or
chronological order of the experiences and activities or a given poet. It
is impossible that they should be accounts of the poetic process as such;
for as T.S. Eliot remarks,

> It is not in the nature of things that there should be a point-for-point
> correspondence between the mental processes of any two poets. Not
> only do poems come into being in as many ways as there are poets; for
> the same poet . . . the process may vary from poem to poem. Every
> poem has its own embryological pattern.[3]

I will go further than Mr. Eliot, and say not only that no poem ever
was produced by the processes described, but also that none conceivably could be. All three select accidents of the poetic process and
arrange them in accidental order. If a poem results from any of them,
it must do so accidentally; in which case we might say that there is no
such thing as a poetic process. We cannot speak meaningfully of a
process of producing something by accident.

Caught as we seem to be between the hopelessly uniform One of the
stage-theory and the hopelessly multiple Many of the particular
descriptions, we may well ask whether there is such a thing as the
poetic process. If it is a process, it ought to have a definite beginning.
Where does it begin? If we are talking about the order in which a poet
happens to do or experience something, there is abundant evidence
that the process can begin anywhere—with a phrase, a rhythm, an
image, an idea—*anywhere.* If the poetic process has no definite beginning, does it have a definite ending, as processes are supposed to do?
One might be tempted to say that it does, that it always terminates in a
finished work. But when is a work finished? It is finished only when
the artist, for one reason or another, ceases to do anything more to it;
in short it is, as Valéry says, not so much finished as abandoned. The
"finished work" is thus simply the result of a process arbitrarily arrested.
The best warrant of completion is the satisfaction of the artist—a
satisfaction which, as any artist knows, may be purely temporary and
which may be justified or not, and which in any case does not prove
that the process might not have continued indefinitely. If there is no
definite ending, is there any definite order in which things must
happen in between? Here again, we have abundant evidence that
there is not.

This sounds like a very odd process indeed. But it is even odder than
it seems. It is a purely mental activity, as can be seen from the fact that

3. T. S. Eliot, Introduction to *Paul Valéry, the Art of Poetry* (New York, 1961), p.
xxi; originally published as vol. 7 of the *Collected Works of Paul Valéry,* Bollingen
Series, no. 45 (New York, 1958).

the poet may compose a poem entirely in his head before committing it to paper. As it is mental, it can have only one witness; and that witness is incompetent because he is not paying attention to the process but to the poem; in short, we have the paradox that in proportion as he is qualified, he is disqualified by his very qualification. I do not think you would find him an acceptable witness in court; for, besides the fact that he is looking another way when the thing happens, and is moreover engrossed in something else, he is in an unnaturally emotional state. Worse still, he does not fully know what he is doing or what is happening to him, for conscious as he may be of certain things, there are a great many others—some of these crucial beyond doubt—of which he must necessarily be unconscious. I do not use the term *unconscious* as the psychologists ordinarily do; I use it in reference to the skill which is essential to art, habit so perfectly instilled that it has become second nature, activity which is unconscious because it has become automatic.

As to whether the poet is rational during the process, that is a matter of how you define rational. My own experience is that, while the power of discursive reasoning—through, for example, a long chain of syllogisms—is greatly reduced, the intuitive powers are greatly extended, so that what might have been the conclusion of a long sorites is seen immediately, without the intervention of any middle term. What is more—and this is a point which might have interested David Hume —any rational activity during the process does not *feel* like reasoning; and ideas and images become more vivid than impressions of sense— another point that might have interested Hume. I do not think that he would have judged the poet to be in a normal condition; and of course we all know what Plato thought.

So here we are: we have viewed the poetic process from its most general description to its most particular without satisfaction, and we have disqualified the one witness who might have informed us. If there is no conception of the process beyond those we have been considering, we may abandon our investigation as hopeless.

Happily, an alternative can be found. If we assume that a poem—of whatever sort—is a certain kind of whole composed of parts, the process of producing it can be nothing other than the process of supplying the constitutive parts and ordering them into a whole. I mean "nothing other" in the very strictest sense. Whatever the poet may think or feel or do *as a human being,* he is operating as *poet* only insofar as he is constructing constitutive parts and assembling them into a whole; *in those operations only* does the poetic process consist. In this view, what he may think or feel is no more relevant than the thoughts and feelings of an architect as his building is being constructed—no more, even, than those of a hod carrier. Only his *effective activities*

count; as parts of the process, they should be seen, not in the chronological order in which the poet performs them, but in the order of their
relation to the whole. Whether as activities they are rational, voluntary,
conscious, or purposive is irrelevant; such terms are predicates of
human action generally, not of a specific process of making. Apply
them to cabinetmaking or automobile manufacture, and you will see
how little they can inform you of the specific natures of these processes.
They can do no more for the poetic process. Quite evidently, our
difficulty has been that we have tended to interpret the poetic process
in terms of the activities of the poet as man rather than as maker of a
specific product.

In this conception, where does the process begin? It begins whenever
a part is constructed to function as part of a determinate whole—not
with what is done first by the poet *as man,* but with what he does first
as poet. Where does it end? Upon completion of the whole. But the
process need not be completed in order to be a poetic process; it is that,
from the beginning and continuously thereafter so long as the parts
constructed continue to function with respect to the same whole. Its
order is, as I have said, not the chronological order in which the things
happened to be done, but the order of subordination of parts to a
whole.

Since the process is correlative with the whole product, it must
evidently vary as our conception of the whole varies. From this it
follows that there can be *no such thing as a single poetic process;* that
is, that rather than the one poetic process everyone seems to have been
looking for, there must be a number of processes, differing as their
products differ in kind. Tragedy, comedy, epic, and lyric, for instance,
are products different in kind, while entailing generally similar means
or materials; it is therefore clear that they cannot be produced by the
same process. Experience confirms this: a good lyric poet is not necessarily a good writer of tragedy, and the lyric poet who tries to compose
tragedy soon discovers that he must learn an additional art. As corol-
laries of the multiplicity of poetic processes, we may observe that there
can be no such thing as a single poetic faculty or a single poetic
character. Similarly, there are many arts, not a single art, or poetry.

If on the one hand these observations seem to complicate inquiry by
discovering multiplicity where we looked for unity, on the other hand
they simplify it, for we find processes specifically identical where these
relate to products specifically the same, and generally identical where
they relate to products generally the same.

Three chief advantages seem to me to be offered by this conception.
First, we shall be able to discuss the poetic processes themselves in a
clearly defined manner, as disengaged from the accidents of circumstance. We shall see them as solutions of the problems posed by the

conditions of form, and by comparing the materials and devices adopted with their relevant alternatives, we shall be able to compare what was done with what might have been done in terms of the resources of art, and so not merely to illuminate the method of the poet, but to judge his craftsmanship as well. We shall, in a word, be looking at the art of poetry as the poet himself looks at it, insofar as he is *looking as poet.*

Second, in so doing, we shall further be enabled, I think, to see how little commensurate modern criticism has been with art, and so be enabled not merely to supply certain deficiencies, but to remove the distortions they have brought about. The great area of the poetic art which has almost escaped our notice is that which the ancient rhetoricians called *euresis* or *inventio* and *taxis* or *dispositio.* I use these rhetorical analogues partly because we lack accurate terms today for such matters in poetry, and partly because we have never quite shaken off the rhetorical view of poetry, and so are likely to find them intelligible. What I have in mind is that we have become so engrossed with the verbal aspect of poetry that we have failed to see the immense area of nonverbal contrivance which is concealed behind the words, and which governs them and gives them their force. If we look clearly at the poetic processes, we shall see that it is impossible to produce poetry merely by stringing metaphors or ambiguities or paradoxes together, and that consequently theories which have proposed such hypotheses must be inadequate. We shall see, too, the impropriety of reducing poetic invention to brute subject matter, by the archetypal method or any other; and if we pursue this far enough, we may eventually escape from the rhetorical presuppositions which have constrained so much of our speculation.

Finally, we shall have eliminated nothing of interest. We need not forego, for instance, the discussion of the state of mind of the poet, or his working habits, or his experiences while working, or the chronological order of composition; we shall merely have supplied a criterion which permits us to see how these attendant circumstances are related, if at all, to a particular poem or to a particular kind of poetry. We shall see not less but more, and that more clearly and minutely. We shall lose nothing but something which was never desirable in the first place: the self-mystification which results when confusions are mistaken for problems.

TWO PLATONIC DIALOGUES:
A DIALOGUE ON
SYMBOLISM

I have just been wondering about something. You must have observed often enough that the bulk of criticism in any one age tends to center about certain favorite terms and concepts. Sometimes the favorites are taken from a quality, such as sublimity or correctness or liveliness; sometimes from a technical device which happens to be in fashion, such as irony or paradox; sometimes from some faculty supposedly essential to appreciation— taste, for instance—or to creation—for example, imagination. And you must have observed that, however they are derived, they exercise a considerable influence.

Indeed they do; they determine the ways in which critics of the period define poetry or any of the various kinds of literature; they enter into the formulation of principles and criteria, and in general establish precision in the whole discussion of literary matters.

And I suppose they must be terms and concepts of the most precise order, since, as you say, they give precision to everything else?

Well—

And, since they possess almost unquestioned sovereignty, the grounds of that sovereignty must be as clear and firm as possible?

These are just the points that always puzzle me. Theoretically, what you are suggesting ought to be true; but I, at least, have always had a great deal of trouble in finding out what these important terms meant, or why they should have been so important; and I have never found any very satisfactory answers. For example, I think it is much easier to say what Dryden meant by "tragedy" than to say what he meant by "justness" or "liveliness." I suppose some such circumstance must have led Professor Elton to make a glossary of critical terms in our age.

Doubtless our criticism is safe, then—thanks to Elton. It is comforting to think that one age, at least, has founded on rock.

Reprinted from *Critics and Criticism: Ancient and Modern*, ed. R. S. Crane (Chicago: University of Chicago Press, 1952).

You needn't be so sarcastic. Elton merely had a little card-file, with words like "ambiguity" and "symbol" written on the cards; and under each such title he set down a few remarks by Richards, Empson, Ransom, or some other distinguished critic. It was merely lexicography —perhaps not very good lexicography, either. It reminds me of Kant's notion of a lecture as a process by which ideas pass from the notebook of the professor to the notebook of the student, without passing through the head of either.

You think the glossary useless, then, because it involved no intellectual process?

Well—not utterly useless. But our age, like other ages, has its favorite central concepts, which I think are far from clear; and I can't see that Elton throws much light on them. We talk constantly these days about meaning, implication, suggestion, sign, image, symbol, metaphor, allegory, myth, and so forth; I am not sure that we know what we mean by those words; and when I look into Elton, I hear only the Tower of Babel. And, of course, given his sort of task, he can hardly be expected to deal with the cardinal questions.

The *cardinal* questions?

I was thinking of the term as Dante used it in its etymological sense. The questions on which these others turn, as a door on its hinge.

And these would be—?

The questions of the concepts back of the words. I doubt if you can have a good dictionary even of usages, if the concepts aren't clear. Put it this way: the cardinal question is not what this or that critic *means* by the term "symbol," but what a symbol *is*. Yes; I really think that, since poets are being so much praised or blamed for their use of symbols and are working so hard to invent and use them—since criticism has become so much a matter of symbolic exegesis—and since a lot of new theories of art declare art itself to be symbolic structure, we ought to know what a symbol is.

What a task you propose! You want to know, not the meaning of the word, but the nature of the thing meant by the word.

Precisely.

And how are you going to try to discover this?

Oh, I have no idea of attempting it by myself. But since we've opened the question, why not discuss it?

I hope you will not expect me to play Socrates.

No; why should we need Socrates? I have great faith in ordinary conversation. Perhaps you could just jog my mind with a few questions, and a few right answers might possibly fall out.

This seems to be a kind of piggy-bank theory of knowledge.

What if it is?

Very young children simply shake the bank any way at all, and get only a few coins after a great deal of effort. Older and more experienced ones learn to introduce a knife into the slot to guide the coins, and they very soon empty the bank.

Well?

I think we might do well to use a knife. Surely you know that in any inquiry the question must have a great influence upon the answer. If we were defining justice, and I asked you whether justice was a virtue or a vice, you would learn at least that justice is a virtue; whereas if I asked you whether it was pink or not-pink, you would learn that it is not-pink, which seems to me not nearly so useful. Socrates knew the sort of questions to ask; I don't. So, unless you are willing to play Socrates yourself—

I see; it appears we must have Socrates after all. Very well; invite him at once.

He is now, you must remember, only the shade of Socrates; he has suffered not only the oblivion of birth but the forgetfulness which follows death. I feel that he may come; the clock is striking midnight, a good hour for ghosts; and I will pour him a glass of this excellent muscatel, since a shade is supposed to drink the fragrance as we drink the wine.

A neat trick to get yourself an extra.

I, the shade of Socrates, have overheard you.

What, here so quickly?

I am present at all conversations where there is serious inquiry.

We were talking of modern critics.

I know nothing of them. But your predicament reminds me of a myth. May I tell it?—for it has never been recorded, and I think you are hardly likely to be acquainted with it.

By all means.

Well, then, I will tell you about the city of shadows. According to ancient legend, there was once a race of heroes, so remarkable for virtue and wisdom that they were godlike; and so the gods decided to admit them, mortal as they were, into heaven. Yet, because the heroes were mortal, they had shadows; and since heaven is a place of purest light, they were required to leave their shadows behind them on earth, so as not to sully that brightness. Thus the heroes passed into brilliance and joy; but their shadows languished behind them in darkness and misery, houseless and bodiless and, worse than either of these, inextricably entangled with one another—for, you must know, a shadow fears and detests absolute darkness even more than he does absolute light; in the latter he merely ceases to exist, while in the former he lies bound and wound and entangled with darkness and with other shadows and loses all identity and distinction. Thus it was with these shadows, until a god, I have forgotten which one, heard their lamentations and took pity on them. He built them a shadowy city of their own and, within it, a temple, wherein he set an altar; and upon this altar he placed a small piece of Reality, girdled with the fairest light, so that a shadow might have some knowledge of substance. In order to mark the way to this temple, he set faintly luminous signs in all the streets; and he gave them also such light as would confer identity upon them and permit them to see.

Very considerate.

So it was. However, the shadows were so taken with the signs that they neglected the Reality; they disputed endlessly as to which sign gave a clearer light or marked a better road; so that the god grew angry at last and turned the whole city into a maze and caused a great wind to cast down all the signs. Now the shadows were in utter confusion, quarreling as to which sign belonged where, until, at last, one who had been the shadow of the best of the heroes realized the vanity of such contentions and determined to seek out the Reality itself; for he thought that, once he had found it, he would possess the true treasure and, besides that, he would be able to restore order among the signs, for he would know which way they would have to point. His name, if I remember, was Lur; and I am told he obtained success. Now, it seems to me that this applies to your case.

That would seem to make us shadows.

So you are; and I, too, am a shade; and therefore we require, not true Philosophy, but its shadow—shall we say, skiatology? And yet this should be sufficiently nourishing to us; you have often seen that when a man eats, his shadow eats the shadow of his food, and leaves off eating when he does, so that presumably it, too, is full-fed? Let us, then, proceed to our shadow-banquet. You see I am holding something in my hand.

Yes, Socrates.

What is it?

I should say, a disk.

Look more closely at it.

It is made of metal.

Then you would say "metal disk" is an adequate name for it?

Yes.

And those disks you wear on your clothing—they are metal disks also?

No, Socrates, they are made of bone.

And then "bone disk" would be a good name for them?

No; they are called buttons, because of their use.

Then if this disk of mine has a use, it should be named according to its use, and not be simply called a disk.

Presumably.

And if I told you its use was to mark a place on a map, you would, say, call it a marker?

Yes.

And if I said it was to be used as money, you would call it a coin?

Yes.

If you will examine it now, closely, you will see that it is, in fact, a coin, although badly worn with age and use, I fear; and you will see that it is broken into two parts, which fit very closely together.

So it is.

We Greeks had a custom of breaking a coin thus when we made a contract; we called the broken halves *symbola*.

I have heard of that custom.

The broken coin, then, betokens a contract; and when we say that something is a "symbol," I suppose we mean that it betokens something.

Undoubtedly.

And if it were used in token of divorce or death or whatever, it would still be used as a symbol, and be called a "symbol"; but if used in token of nothing, it is simply a broken coin?

Quite so.

And what is meant by betokening something?

I should say it meant representing something.

Your photograph represents you?

Yes.

Does it symbolize you?

No; not necessarily.

You mean that not everything that represents is a symbol? For instance, if I were selling sand and showed you some grains, telling you that the rest would be of that order, these would represent, but not be symbols?

I should call them a sample.

What if you did not know what a book was, and I showed you this one as a representative? Is that a symbol or a sample?

I should call it an example.

And that plaster bust on your bookshelf, which I observe that someone has labeled "Socrates"?

That is a copy, Socrates, of a very famous bust of you.

It is a copy, then, of some original bust, but not a sample or example of it?

Yes.

And the original—is that a copy or a sample or example or symbol of me?

I should say rather that it was an imitation, in Aristotle's sense of the term.

I think I have heard of him and of his sense of the word "imitation." You mean by it, I presume, that the sculptor was not merely concerned with making a likeness of me but wanted also to make a good piece of sculpture, so that the bust, although it does not portray a handsome man, God knows, or portray an ugly man as handsome, is nevertheless a handsome work of art; whereas a copy gives only a replica and is handsome, middling fair, or ugly quite according to the original thing copied. I suppose that is what Aristotle also must have meant.

Yes, I should think so.

And I suppose you mean that "sample" should be used only when the things are homogeneous, like water or wine or honey or sand or cloth which is all of the same pattern and texture, so that a little represents the remainder, or the part, the whole; whereas an example is always one class of things or some individual as representative of a class into which it falls; and a copy, again, is a likeness of some individual thing.

Exactly.

But if representations differ thus, are they alike in any way?

They are alike in that they are all based upon some likeness.

So that a symbol, if it represents, must always bear some likeness to that which is symbolized.

Yes.

How marvelous, then, is the substance of air!

I do not follow you.

Spoken words are symbols, are they not?

Of course.

Then air in its motion must be able to make likenesses of everything which can be conceived.

You puzzle me.

And your photograph, after all, must be a symbol of you, and the best symbol, since it bears a very great likeness.

No; it is not a symbol at all, unless someone makes it so.

Then likeness and unlikeness are not necessarily connected with symbols?

Apparently not.

So a symbol may stand for anything, however unlike it?

So it would seem.

I suppose many poets must have used the sun as the symbol of darkness, or ice as the symbol of heat, and that you can quote some of these?

No, Socrates, I cannot; and I must admit that I cannot even conceive of the possibility.

We will accept that for the moment, although I am uncertain whether we are discussing the impossibility of the thing or the limitations of your powers of conception. Let us take another tack:

your photograph, though it represents you as a likeness, does not, you say, represent you, therefore, as a symbol; how might it represent you as a symbol?

I suppose by being taken for me.

I thought you implied earlier that knowledge, and not ignorance or madness, was necessary before something could be a symbol; for you said, I believe, that "bone disk" was not a good name for a button and that "button" was so called on account of knowledge of its use.

So I did.

Then if I took your photograph for you, would that not be ignorance?

Not if you did it deliberately, with the knowledge that it was not I.

But if I did such a thing deliberately, would not that be madness?

Not if you did not really take it for me.

So a symbol is something which is taken for something and yet not taken for it?

I am sorry, Socrates; perhaps I should have said "pretendedly taken for something."

So the user of symbols is a practitioner of one of the arts of pretense?

I think I see where that will land us, and I refuse to go that way. May I retract my statement that a symbol is something taken for something and start afresh?

By all means.

I will say, then, with Thomas Aquinas that a symbol is that thing which, to an intellective power, stands for something other than itself.

I do not understand.

It is used in place of something—a kind of substitution.

You mean that if you took down these curtains and put certain others in their place, the second would be symbols of the first?

No, not at all. A symbol is a convenient substitute for something impossible or difficult to use in itself, or to achieve, or something of the sort.

And, since it is used for it, has the same use?

Yes.

You have evidently found it impossible to obtain a doorstop; I presume that the book which holds the door open symbolizes the doorstop.

No, I should say it was used as a doorstop.

Yet the word "doorstop" symbolizes a doorstop?

Yes.

But surely the word itself could not be used as a doorstop.

Yes, but—a symbol is quite certainly used as some sort of substitute; words, for instance, are substitutes for thought.

I suppose that is why those who find thought impossible or inconvenient talk so much. But let us go back a little in the argument.

When we were talking of likeness and unlikeness, a certain thought occurred to me, and I should like to present it to you. I imagine I could use the book on your table as a symbol of knowledge.

Of course.

The book, however, remains exactly what it is?

Yes.

And so does knowledge remain what it is?

Yes.

Then both the symbol and the symbolized are such without any alteration of their natures?

Yes.

Then their natures could scarcely be the cause of one symbolizing the other—for, if their natures were the cause, it would be of the nature of the one to be a symbol and of the other to be the symbolized?

Yes.

Hence, if their natures are indifferent to this question, likeness and difference would also be indifferent; for the nature of a thing determines its similarity to, or difference from, another?

I have already told you, Socrates, that nothing is a symbol of itself.

Good; and you have also told me that anything can be a symbol of anything. Pehaps you will explain yourself.

I mean that the book is potentially a symbol; actually, it is not, unless something else makes it so.

To be something potentially and then to become it actually is to change?

Of course.

Will you explain how the book has changed? We have not touched it, and I see no difference between what it was and what it is. Yet, without changing, it seems now to be what it was not.

It has not changed in itself; it has changed in its relation to something else, wisdom.

My dear fellow! The relations between things must always be based upon characteristics of the things related?

Yes.

And while the characteristics remain the same, the relationship is the same, and when the characteristics differ, the relationship will differ also?

Yes.

Hence, surely, if the relationship has changed, the things have changed.

I'm afraid you have the better of me; I am puzzled.

I wonder if we are in any difficulty after all. I suppose I could use your paper knife, there, to cut book leaves.

Certainly.

In doing so, I should have to handle the knife itself and affect and

change it some way or other. Using it often enough, I should even wear
it out.

Certainly.

But I used the book as a symbol, without handling it. And it does not
show much wear as a result.

Of course not; that was a purely mental employment of the book.

I don't follow you.

You did not really use the book.

But if I did not really use the book, and a symbol must be used to be
a symbol, then the book could not possibly be a symbol?

I can't see how it could be a symbol.

And yet we made a symbol, without the physical use of anything?
Yes.

Clearly, then, a symbol exists independently of any physical use?
Yes.

And this would hold good in all instances, would it not, regardless of
what physical object was supposed to be involved?

Yes, Socrates.

Then I imagine that your Thomas Aquinas, as well as your contemporaries who talk of a symbol as a thing standing for some other thing,
could scarcely have meant that or known what they were saying if they
did mean it. For we have just seen that no thing can stand for any
other thing.

So it seems.

Well, then, if I did not really use the book, what did I use as a
symbol?

I know you will catch me out, but may I tentatively say the idea or
notion of the book?

Tentatively. And you may also tell me tentatively how one uses an
idea or notion.

We have already suggested, Socrates, that a relation is involved; I
shall say, therefore, a relationship of ideas or notions. Quite certainly
there is some sort of mental conjunction; the idea book is connected
with the idea of knowledge.

How do you mean, "connected"?

Identified.

My dear man; you told me that in order to recognize a symbol it was
necessary to distinguish it from the symbolized, or something to that
effect; how is this possible if the symbol and the symbolized are identified?

I will withdraw; I should have said there is a kind of attribution or
affirmation.

As when I say "The boy is brave" and conjoin the ideas of the boy
and bravery?

Yes, something like that.

Then the concept of the boy symbolizes the concept of bravery?

No, hang it! I shouldn't say that either. It must be some sort of fusing, some sort of unifying of the ideas, so that they become one and the same.

My friend, this is a strange task you impose on me and any other symbol-maker. I can grasp the idea of blackness and the idea of sphere, and thus compound the concept of a black sphere; but I do not tell myself that I have made the idea of blackness identical with the idea of sphericity or that I have made one idea out of two. If I really went on in that style, I should end up after all my thinking with only one idea. Rather it seems that I get, in my own way, three, and I prefer that. In any case, this has nothing to do with symbolism, for these ideas do not symbolize each other.

Very well; I will hazard again. A concept is a symbol when it has been so frequently associated with another in experience that it brings the latter at once to mind.

By heaven! You speak as if you never took off your shoes before going to bed or before taking a bath; or as if you did so only infrequently.

I don't follow you.

You do remove your shoes on such occasions, I hope, and I hope also that these occasions are not too infrequent?

Of course.

But does the removing of shoes symbolize bathing or going to bed?

Not necessarily.

On the other hand, we could make their removal symbolize these things even without the habitual association you speak of?

Yes.

Then, clearly, inquiry into association will not help us much here.

I am afraid you are right. I suppose you will go on now to prove that it is impossible there should be symbols in the mind, just as you proved there were none outside the mind; so that we shall have no such thing as a symbol after all.

I have a similar dread myself; I should be very much disheartened, were it not that our conversation has suddenly reminded me of something.

What?

We sound like men who are looking at bricks and other building materials; men who have a vague idea of what a house is but are utterly ignorant of any such thing as an architect or an art of architecture, and who are consequently much puzzled as to how the materials could ever be assembled into a house.

I do not see how that helps any.

What would you advise such men to do? Would you not suggest that they learn about the architect and his powers?

I suppose so.

It seems to me that the architect, in this case, would be the soul.

Oh, Lord, Socrates! This is the twentieth century; the soul is now out of fashion.

I observe that it is indeed, in more ways than one. Why should that deter us?

Many now would refuse to admit its existence.

I suppose our most formidable opponents would claim it to be impossible?

Yes, certainly.

Well, then, let us cheerfully confront our strongest enemies at once and deal with them, and perhaps the others will not trouble us. I suppose that by calling the soul "impossible" they mean that there must be some cause why it could not be?

Yes.

This cause would have to be eternal—for if it ceased to exist for one moment, it would be false to say the soul is impossible?

Yes.

I should be most interested in their evidence for the eternal existence of this cause. However, let that be; let me ask you instead: for something to be actual, its potentiality must be existent first?

Of course.

For any act or operation to be performed, there must be something capable of performing that act or operation?

Yes.

That something itself must, however, exist actually and not merely potentially? For instance, if a man becomes a father, the power of reproduction must have been in him; but that power must have been an actuality and not existed merely in potential form—as in the man, say, when he was himself still a fetus.

Quite so.

And this, far from being impossible, is necessary.

Yes.

And by "necessary" we mean "impossible that it should not exist"?

Yes.

But, obviously, we are actually capable of mental acts, and the power to do these must therefore exist and have actual existence, and that necessarily?

Yes.

This, then, whatever it is, I will call the "soul"; I shall treat it discreetly and modestly, attributing to this mystery only such powers as it itself evinces in action. Are our enemies still on the field?

I believe they have withdrawn.

Good! Now, we obviously can compare ideas?

Certainly.

We can separate and conjoin them, distinguish and liken them?

To be sure.

Affirm, deny? Order the less general under the more general?

Yes.

Distinguish the true, the false, the probable, improbable, possible, necessary, impossible? And otherwise evaluate?

Yes.

Believe, disbelieve; and suppose that which we do not believe?

Yes.

Then the soul must have these powers?

Necessarily.

And be able to form pictures of some particular thing, and to turn these into ideas which are more general; and again to convert these ideas back into pictures? For instance, to form a picture of a certain tree, and out of it to get the idea of a tree; and again, having the idea of a tree, to envision a tree?

Yes.

And, surely, with all this activity, the soul must be busy?

Very.

I think I see in my mind's eye this busy soul of ours, seated amid her many treasures, counting and evaluating and ordering them. Such as she can deal with quickly and easily, she handles directly; but treasures are brought in to her constantly, in enormous measure; and in her haste and business she must often assign to one thing the value of another.

Doubtless.

Certainly, too, with all this business, she is sometimes fatigued and confused, and reckons the false as true, and the true as false, and is then in error.

Yes.

But sometimes she supposes something to have the value of another quite deliberately, although she knows it does not; for she is in haste to get on with her reckoning and hopes to set all her accounts in order one day.

Indeed.

There is no doubt that whatever evaluation she sets upon such things will have to stand in her accounts until she is ready to give a better reckoning.

No doubt at all.

Doubtless, too, these ideas may be said to have values in themselves; but, until the true reckoning, these values are superseded by the assigned values. Shall we give a name to these?

Why not?

What shall we call them?

Socrates, I know that, if I do not call them "symbols" immediately, you will presently force me to; so I yield at once. Let us call them "symbols."

I think we should rather call them the "symbolized."

Very well: the symbolized.

The concept or idea which is a symbol will have its own value, but the soul will deal with it as having the value assigned to it. This value is not of truth or falsity, or goodness or badness, but of meaning. The concept of physical sight, for instance, may have the value of intellectual vision; it will then mean intellectual vision. Otherwise it remains simply the concept of physical sight.

I see.

But will the world not think we are mad? Are not words, whether spoken or written, considered symbols by everybody—whereas we have shown that only a mental idea or concept can be a symbol?

I suppose the world will be furious.

Let us, then, to lessen its rage, call words "secondary symbols." For they are only a sort of signal to entertain a concept; and, without such a relation of concepts as we have described, they could never be symbols in any sense.

Please explain.

A spoken word is merely a sound, is it not, and capable on utterance only of raising the impression or idea of itself as sound in the mind of the hearer. That is, unless the idea of that sound is given the value of a certain other concept by the soul.

I see.

It would appear, then, that symbolism has to do not with things but with a mode of conception; a supposition, contrary to known fact, that one concept has the value of some other concept; does it not seem so?

Yes, it does.

I should now like to distinguish symbols from other things which are often confused with them.

Proceed.

They are different, for instance, from signs. Fever, for example, is a sign of illness, because it is an effect of which illness may be a cause; since it is a sign, we may infer from its presence that illness exists. But fever is not a symbol of illness. For if the concept of fever is given the value of the concept of illness, the inference from fever to illness would be absurd, seeing that, in granting the fever to be illness, we have already assumed the point to be inferred.

The question would be begged, undoubtedly.

A sign, therefore, must be said to have implication rather than meaning; we must reserve meaning for symbols.

True.

Meaning depends always upon knowledge of the symbols, singly and in conjunction, and never upon implication or inference, unless certain of the symbols are unclear or lacking, as in unfinished sentences or as in innuendoes, which are a kind of incompletely stated argument; or unless some apparent impossibility of meaning arises, as in irony.

I do not quite follow that.

Why, you would surely know, let us say, such individual words as "Socrates," "Plato," "is," "well," "ill," "and," "but," "not," and so on?

I think I can be credited with that much.

Some of these are significs, having meaning in themselves, and others have no meaning in themselves but show how the significs are to be related to one another—would you not agree?

Yes.

And if I said, "Socrates" or any other of these words, there would be no necessity of inference, unless you did not know what the word meant?

Yes.

Then if I said "Socrates is ill," there would be no question of inference; the meaning of the parts would immediately give the meaning of the whole, since all parts of the meaning are expressed?

Yes.

But, should I say "Socrates is ill, but Plato . . . ," something is missing? And you would have to infer the missing part, would you not?

I see.

And similarly, in innuendo, one expresses the part which implies what one really means but does not express what one really means; and in irony, one says the opposite of what one means, counting on the fact that the hearer will recognize the impossibility of what is being said and infer the contrary, which one really intends.—Heaven forgive us!

What is the matter?

Here we have been sitting and chatting like two old women about things that are not symbols, as if our business were finished and we could be at leisure, when we have hardly begun.

What do you mean?

It seems to me that we have discussed symbols only in their poorest and barest variety, when they barely deserve that name, and we have said nothing of the truer and better variety.

You leave me in the dark.

Suppose you saw me pounding a nail with a stone—I should in a sense be hammering, should I not?

Yes.

And yet a stone is hardly a hammer and would deserve its name only from its use in this instance, and barely at that.

Yes.

I should be ridiculous if I said that I owned a hammer or knew how to use one, if that were all I had and knew how to use.

True.

I should be—should I not?—like a man riding a pig and vaunting it for a charger?

Very much.

By heaven! Now that I have ridden my pig and seen it for such, I will never rest until I have mounted a noble charger. Will you help me into the saddle?

Gladly; but how?

We were right, were we not, in insisting that nothing can be called a symbol in the true sense unless it can be used as a symbol; just as nothing can be called a hammer if it is utterly incapable of being used as a hammer—however much it might resemble a hammer?

I think so.

So that a painting of a man is not really a man, and the painted eye not really an eye, no matter how good the likeness to man or eye. These are mere appearances or falsities because they will not fulfill the functions of the things they mimic?

I agree.

We have, then, it appears, four classes of things. Shall I tell you what they are? The first is the class of things that have neither the use nor the appearance of certain others and hence are never confused with them. The second is the class of resemblances and appearances, which, however, are utterly useless with respect to the function of the things they resemble. Here, in our case, belong all sophistry and word-jugglings and meaningless distinctions and such speeches as the speaker himself does not understand. Thirdly, the class of things which may be used for a given purpose, but only crudely; for their nature does not suit that purpose; they are used only out of necessity or convenience, for lack of a better; they are hammers and knives and what-not only because something else wills them to be. It was amid these that we sat down so contentedly, thinking they were symbols, like barbarians happy with their stone trash and never dreaming of the marvelous tools of civilization.

Enough metaphors. Go on.

Well, then, there is a fourth class—that of the things which have both a use and a nature suited to the use. The real hammer, I suppose, has a form and material exactly suited to its special use, and to the circumstances of its use? And so our true symbol must also have a form and matter especially suited to its function?

Yes.

Since symbols are ideas, I suppose their materials must be the ideas which are parts of them.

I don't follow.

You have the idea of a circle?

Yes.

Surely the parts of this idea are center-point and curved line and radius and so on?

I don't see that; surely I can envision a circle without them.

You could prove, I suppose, that this circle you envision is really a circle? Or do you mean that you use the term loosely?

I see what you mean, and I withdraw. You mean that the idea of a circle cannot be formed without reference to some such parts as you mention; I, of course, was speaking only of an image or fantasm.

I suppose the form of an idea will be the synthesis of the parts of this idea; as the idea of a circle is the synthesis of the parts of the idea circle. Your fantasm, too, had a form; the curved line which made it had to be conceived as complete in all its parts, or you would not have envisioned a full circle.

Yes.

Similarly, the idea of a black sphere would be impossible without concepts of blackness and sphericity? For these are its immediate parts?

Yes.

And this indifferently whether the black sphere is the symbol or the symbolized?

I cannot see how there could be any difference.

Well, now; suppose I were trying to symbolize the concept of a sphere; would the concept of a circle or of a triangle be a better symbol?

I should say, the circle.

The sphere could exist without the triangle, but not without the circle? For the sphere is a circle fully revolved on a diameter, and any plane passing through it must always produce a circle; but a triangle could never generate a sphere, or form any part of it as sphere; and spheres could be if triangles had never existed.

I see.

The circle is, then, a cause of the existence of the sphere, whereas the triangle is not?

Yes.

And the keystone, because it is the cause of the existence of the arch, would be a better symbol of it than any other stone.

Doubtless.

The materials of the concept of the symbol, then, must always be drawn from some part of the concept of the symbolized, without which that latter could not be? That is, from a cause?

That seems reasonable enough.

The symbol gives a kind of understanding of the symbolized; this is scarcely possible without conveying a cause?

I think that makes it clearer.

There must be five ways, then, in which the symbolized is connected with the symbol, must there not? Resemblances of form or shape or nature would, I think, be one of these; such was the case with our circle and sphere.

Yes.

Again, the parts would stand for the whole, or the materials for the synthesis. For instance, the keystone or the arch might stand for the house, I think, or the victim for the murder.

No doubt.

And any instrumental causes as well; thus sword and shield might symbolize the art of war; and any agency might symbolize whatever was done by it. This is why workman's tools are so often chosen as symbols of their craft or trade.

Certainly.

And, surely, of things that have a use, purpose, function, or result, each may be symbolized by its proper work or use? The shipbuilder will, I think, be willing to have his art represented by a ship, and the engineer to have his represented by bridge or bastion.

True.

Lastly, we shall have a whole class of accidental concomitants of the aforementioned classes, arising out of confusion with the true causes just mentioned or out of historical happenings or customs or legends or analogies, and so forth. For example, members of a given religious cult will be most likely to take as symbols things connected with the most crucial articles of their faith, or a nation will accept something connected with some important event or period in its history.

Yes.

That which is distinctive and more immediately connected with the symbolized will always be the better symbol, will it not? I think, for example, that bricks are a better symbol of the building art than, say, clay; for clay is also used by the potter and the sculptor and the brickmaker; and something more immediately connected with the building art will be better still.

Certainly.

This is because whatever is immediate will always bring the symbolized more powerfully and vividly to mind than would the remote.

Beyond question.

Yet, it seems to me, we are no closer to our symbol, our true symbol, than an account of general attributes would be to a definition or than a description would be to an image.

Please explain.

I presume that an account of general attributes and a definition are alike in that they present to the mind some concept or idea, which is never of any particular thing but always of some universal?

Quite so.

And in this they differ from description and image, which are of the particular and present to the mind not a concept or idea but a fantasm or picture?

Yes.

The fantasm is to the idea as the particular to the universal, is it not?

Yes.

And an account of general attributes and a definition have nothing to do with the accidents connected with the particular thing, but with its essence; whereas for description and image it is the accidents which are more important than the essence, for they convey more of the particular? You would insist, for instance, if I described a particular man, that I should not simply call him man or unfeathered biped or rational animal, but that I should include his height, shape, size, facial appearance, colors, and other particulars, all of which are, however, no part of the concept "man" but are accidental to the individual?

I would.

A concept is surely distinct from a fantasm? Although the mind cannot think without fantasms which attend thought, so that you cannot think circle without envisioning a circle, there is still a difference between the idea, which is not a picture, and the fantasm, which is?

True.

I am glad you have not gone astray on that point, which confused so great a philosopher even as David Hume. Our general account and our definition must differ, then, from description and image.

Yes.

But surely an account of attributes is not the same as a definition? The account contains attributes which are true and sometimes essential, without resulting in a clear idea of the nature of the thing; until the proper attributes are selected from among these and gathered in proper arrangement into the unity of a definition, no clear idea of the nature of the thing results; but it results immediately from the definition. I speak, of course, only of true accounts and definitions.

Yes.

So the account provides, as it were, materials only for the definition.

Yes.

The same is true, I think, of the relation between description and image. For the description gives a mass of characteristics of the thing, characteristics which the thing might possess under any and all circumstances; from these the mind might frame a number of pictures, but only because it happened to frame them, just as the mind, if it chose, might assemble the characteristics of an account into a number of definitions or notions of the nature of something.

True.

Whereas a definition impels the mind to a single notion which is the notion of the nature of the thing, and an image impels the mind to a single fantasm.

Yes.

Similarly, I suppose, we must distinguish the materials of the symbol from the true symbol—which surely possesses the power to set before the mind the concept intended, and no other?

Surely.

What, then, shall we say about the form of our symbols? For our argument has gone to show that we must not talk merely about their matter if we are to have true symbols.

I am afraid I cannot help you, Socrates.

I presume that, possessing the concept of the symbol, however compounded of certain materials, we should have only that concept and no more? For instance, while a circle could symbolize a sphere, having the concept of a circle is to have that concept and not that of a sphere?

Right.

Unless, to be sure, that concept contains some indication that it is more than that concept.

How could it do that?

I have observed that even your cartoonists, when they represent a sphere by a circle, always add to the circle something to indicate that it is more than a circle; they give it shading or a high light or something of the sort, which a mere circle would not have.

You are right.

And, by this indication of something which is incompatible with circle, they show that something more than circle is intended?

Yes.

Without such indication, I presume, the mind would be content to take circle as circle; but meeting a contradiction, it is restless and will not be satisfied until it has resolved that contradiction?

Even so.

The contradiction between circular form and spherical high light will, however, be resolved when the mind discovers that a sphere is intended?

True.

Then we must advise our symbolists to be sure to have some such indication in their symbols, to give them power to force the mind toward that which is intended, or their symbols will not be recognized as symbols.

Certainly we must.

But the indication will have to be a true index of the thing symbolized; otherwise our circle will be taken erroneously for a wheel or something other than the sphere intended.

Yes.

But, given the proper selection of the proper materials and such an index, the mind will pass instantly to the symbolized, being impelled by the symbol.

Beyond doubt.

Since we do not only think but also often feel toward that which we think and since the thing symbolized will have a certain nature which may be good or bad, and hence lovable or hateful, presumably our index and all other parts of our symbol will have to be so framed that the appropriate emotions will be evoked. For example, if a man conceives Death as benign and merciful, it would be absurd to symbolize it by some concept which was hideous and evil, like that of a rotting skeleton.

Certainly.

Anyone who wishes to invent true and powerful symbols will have, therefore, to study that concept which he wishes to symbolize and determine its most striking and important attributes, that is, those which determine the conception and our emotions toward it; next, he will have to find or invent something which incorporates these attributes; and with these he will have to combine the index. Suppose, for example, that a symbol-maker conceived of a certain way of life, which concept he wished to symbolize; and suppose, on casting about in his mind, he thought it best typified by the kind of life led in a certan city—say, Byzantium. Now, it seems to me that if his thought runs on "life such as at Byzantium," he has only an example; if on "life like that at Byzantium," only an analogue, so that, on putting it into words, a metaphor will result; but if he so frames his conception of Byzantium that it is not a mere mirror, as examples and analogues are, but, as it were, a window, a transparency through which we see the thing he truly intends; then and then alone has he made a symbol.

You seem to think that symbols are not, after all, metaphors.

And should I? Whatever name we give to our symbol will now apply immediately to the symbolized, and thus differ from metaphor; for a metaphor is only the name of a certain thing transferred to its similar in respect to a certain similarity, although their concepts remain distinct; whereas the name of the true symbol will stand not metaphorically but directly for the symbolized; because the concept of the symbol has been identified with that of the symbolized.

I think you are right.

And shall we let this stand, then, for our account of symbols?

I think we may well do that.

Yet is seems to me that we have said nothing of symbolic poetry.

How is that? Isn't it simply poetry which utilizes such symbols as you have described?

My friend, in the first sense in which we talked of symbols, any user of language is a symbolist; the poet, since he uses language, can hardly avoid symbols of that sort.

That is true; but what of those who use the last kind of symbols you mentioned?

Could not such symbols be used in any form of composition?

I suppose they might.

Then it seems to me that we have said nothing about symbolic poetry because we have never discussed poetry; and therefore we must push farther, if you are willing.

I am willing.

We should be talking again of materials only, and of only part of these, if we discussed symbols; we must consider what the poet distinctively does as a poet, if there is one kind of poet only, or what the several kinds do if there are several, since one account for very different kinds might be so general that, in fitting all, it fitted none.

I agree.

The poet, it seems to me, builds wholes; in this he is unlike the binder of faggots or the money-tellers, who care only about totals.

I wish you would explain that.

If you bought a shoe from me, you would be very much surprised, I think, if I handed you merely a number of pieces, even if they were all correctly shaped and if all the necessary parts were there; you would demand to have them assembled, and not stitched together anyhow, but assembled correctly; for a shoe is a whole and not a total; whereas a sum of money or a bundle of faggots is merely a total and requires no particular arrangement.

I see.

A poet, then, constructs wholes. For he does not throw the parts together anyhow, but assembles them, and that properly according to his art, and is much annoyed if anyone spoils the order, say, by transposing lines or stanzas.

Yes.

And that which has a certain characteristic, as a whole, is surely more possessed of that characteristic than that which possesses it only in part? For instance, that which is beautiful as a whole is more beautiful than that which is beautiful only in part, and that which as a whole is good is better than that which is good only in a part?

Surely.

Then the poet whose poem is symbolic as a whole will be more truly a symbolic poet than one whose work is symbolic only in part?

Yes.

Then it seems to me that we must examine these wholes, and that according to their differences. For if we say that all art is symbolic, we say nothing of the poet save that he is an artist; if we say that all poetry is symbolic, we say merely that he is a poet.

Certainly.

Well, then, consider: does it not seem to you that there are two very broadly different kinds of poets, according to the different wholes which they make?

I am sure it will seem so if you discuss them.

On the one hand, there are those who set some kind of human activity before us, whether with many episodes and characters, as your novelists do, or with only a single character at a moment of passion or decision, as lyric poets so often do. In setting such activity before us, they are concerned primarily with the beauty of the poem, which, being beautiful, must give us pleasure.

I fancy, Socrates, that you will not find many critics at present who think pleasure important enough to be the end of poetry.

Then I should ask them with what swine they have lain, to have so low a conception of pleasure?

I merely present their objection; I do not share their opinion.

I wonder if they would think the lot of the just man less pleasurable or more painful than the lot of the unjust; or if they think there is no difference between the pleasures of noble and ignoble men. For they talk as if they suffered from profound moral ignorance. But to resume: I was speaking of high art, not of a swine's swill; and I was saying that certain poets sought to effect beauty by their imitation. I did not say that they sought to give us pleasure; the beauty is not for the sake of the pleasure but, rather, *results* in pleasure: two very different things. Let us call them "imitators" or "mimetic poets."

Very well.

On the other hand, there are those who seek to persuade us of some doctrine, that is, either merely to instruct us or to get us to feel a certain emotional disposition toward it. Now that I think of it, I suppose there is a third group in between these; the group of the entertainers, who are concerned merely with giving pleasure and offer only so much beauty or instruction as will be conducive to pleasure. Here belong your comedians, who will do anything to raise a laugh, and the sentimentalists, who will do anything to start a pleasant tear, and your popular moralists, who deal in what everyone knows because those who utter what we have always approved flatter us and give us pleasure. I can scarcely, however, consider them real poets; so perhaps, after all, we have two classes of poets—the mimetic and the didactic.

Very well; but I doubt also whether critics will accept this distinction, for they are likely to claim that all poetry is didactic, or something of the sort.

They would admit, I hope, some difference between Homer and Dante?

I doubt whether they would admit anything.

Then we must show them. If you were seeking to imitate an action, the action itself would give unity to the imitation?

I think so.

But if you were to inculcate some doctrine by way of representing some action—as in moral allegory, for example—completeness would depend not upon the action but upon the doctrine? Your poem would be complete only when the doctrine was completely expressed and when you had done everything you could to advance it?

Yes.

And the parts of the mimetic action would depend upon the action itself and whatever was necessary or probable within that, but the parts of the doctrinal action would be selected with a view to the doctrine and its statement?

True.

Homer and Dante you would regard, I presume, as both successful poets.

Very.

Is there any doctrine which as a whole binds the poem of Dante together?

I think there is.

Will you state it?

There are several levels of significance, and doctrines corresponding to each of these, all binding the work together as a whole; the allegorical subject, which is "man as by good or ill deserts, occasioned through free choice, he becomes liable to rewarding or punishing justice," is intended to enforce certain moral doctrines, practically, with the end of "removing those living in this life from the state of misery and leading them to a state of felicity."

And you would say that the parts and the whole are regulated by the moral doctrine and selected and shown in reference to it?

I would, since Dante himself says so.

Would you tell me what doctrine similarly underlies Homer?

That, I think, would be very difficult to say, whether you talked of the *Iliad* or the *Odyssey*.

And what would you say if I tried to persuade you of something and never made clear what it was of which I sought to persuade you?

I should say that you had not been very successful.

But Homer is successful, I think you said.

He is successful in a quite different way.

Then there must be those two different kinds of poets and poetry?

It would appear so.

It would be dreadful to confuse these two poets, would it not? For if we regard both as didactic, Dante appears excellent and Homer very poor, inasmuch as we cannot even tell what he is urging upon us; or if we regard both as mimetic, the reverse would be the case; for surely Dante is not much of a plotmaker; his incidents do not follow on each other as incidents, but as incidents representing a doctrine.

True.

To read them without regard to this distinction would be also, I think, to plunge ourselves into totally incorrect interpretation; we should puzzle ourselves indefinitely trying to find the doctrine behind Homer or trying to justify the practice of Dante without regard to the doctrine.

I agree in part; but I do not understand how, unless we are forced to the doctrine, that is, persuaded of it, we can get much out of Dante as you describe him; whereas I myself remain unpersuaded of it, and yet—quite illicitly, it would appear by your argument—get pleasure out of him, just as out of Homer.

My friend, I observe that you have Cicero and Demosthenes and many other orators on your shelves. I hope you read them with pleasure.

I do. Invariably.

They inevitably persuade you?

No. I see what you mean; I am pleased by the art of the orator, even though I am not persuaded.

Precisely; and, besides, we have not said that the one kind does not please and the other does not instruct, or anything so foolish; we have said that the one is concerned with beauty of form and the other with inculcation of doctrine.

I think I see it better.

To return to our distinction: we should find a similar distinction, I think between the comic poet and the satirist, even if the latter is what we call "comic" and even if he deals with the general rather than, as do the writers of invectives and lampoons, with the particular. For the comic poet merely presents the ridiculous, whereas the comic satirist seeks to convince us that something *is* ridiculous.

Yes.

Then the mimetic and the didactic poets build different wholes?
Yes.
And these different wholes may involve different parts?
Yes.
The mimetic poem will have to include as its parts the action, I presume, and that along with character and thought; for it will imitate not merely a string of unqualified events, at which we might laugh or weep as we chose, but morally determinate actions, which would govern our feelings. For I suppose even death and murder might be considered serious or amusing, depending on the light in which they are regarded.
Yes; people are nowadays very much amused by things like *Kind Hearts and Coronets* and *Arsenic and Old Lace*, both of which involve a string of murders; and they are also greatly amused by the cartoons of Charles Adams, dealing with subjects which, in their usual conception, would be horrible and morbid.
The mimetic poet will also present what he is imitating in a certain manner—for instance, either dramatically or narratively; and he may either present the action in its proper order or convert it, and there are many other things relating to manner of representation, I should imagine. All this will be a second part. Lastly, there is the part of the medium, or words.
Yes.
And symbols are possible in all these parts, I think; for example, the characters and their actions and, in short, the plot as a whole may be symbolic.
As in Kafka's *The Castle* or Joyce's *Ulysses*.
Or there may be symbolism of narrative or dramatic manner.
Yes; a play called *Our Town* would exemplify that, for, while the plot is not symbolic, the dramatic representation is.
Or, finally, there is symbolism of diction; for a poet might symbolize brute nature by a tiger or a hawk, and call it by their names; and this would be like metaphor, and yet different from it, as we have argued.
Yes.
But poems are wholes, and a whole must always have some principal part?
Yes.
And surely it is the principal part which gives its nature to the whole, and not some subordinate part? And here the principal part would be the action, since it is the thing imitated? For without it I fear we should have no imitation at all.
Surely.

Our true symbolic poet of the mimetic kind must then make his action symbolic, if he wishes to impart the symbolic character to the whole.

Yes; and with a few exceptions like William Blake, poets have done this only recently. But Rimbaud and Joyce and Yeats and Kafka are certainly of that order, and so is Eliot.

And what of our didactic poet? The parts of the whole which he makes seem to me to be very different.

How?

He must make or intimate clearly some statement, which is his doctrine or thesis in the emotional or intellectual light in which he wishes us to accept it; and he must offer some sort of proof, whether logical or the kind of thing that in a certain frame of mind we should accept as logical, even if he merely presents himself as a good man and indicates that all good men must think or feel as he does in the matter. And there are many ways of proof; for example, he may offer us a story which implies his thesis, either by induction, as in the exemplum, or by deduction, as in the allegory, or by analogy, as in the parable and the fable. All this, thesis and proof alike, belongs to what we may call the "argument."

Why not?

On the other hand, he must use words. So there is a second part, clearly subordinate, I think, to the first part; for the words would be selected with a view to the argument and not, I should hope, the arguments selected with a view to the words—I cannot imagine the latter procedure as convincing anyone.

Nor can I.

The argument, therefore, is clearly the principal part; and our didactic poet will be a symbolist if that is made symbolically.

I suppose Ezra Pound's *Cantos* is of that sort, and perhaps certain things of Robinson Jeffers.

Now, I think, we have fashioned our mimetic and our didactic poets, noble fellows both, and we are able to say when either will or will not be a symbolist. Are you satisfied with our account?

I think I have still a few difficulties, Socrates; not so much with what you have said as with what arises beyond all this. I am still uncertain about whether allegorists and myth-makers are symbolists; and I am not clear, therefore, whether Dante and Spenser are symbolists or not.

By "allegorist" you mean, I presume, someone who uses personification and makes such abstract things as the virtues and vices into people?

Yes.

And does the rendition and elaboration of his poem depend upon the virtue or vice, primarily, or upon the convention that he is representing them as persons and must therefore assign them appropriate costumes, appearances, and so on?

Upon the latter, I should say.

Whereas the rendition of the symbol is rather determined by the thing symbolized, is it not?

I see; they are in a manner the reverse of each other.

Moreover, symbolism is possible apart from analogy—is it not?— whereas allegory never would be.

I agree.

And allegory is finite, since, once one has carried the traits from the personification to the quality personified, the process is complete; whereas, once one has reached the concept symbolized, one is left with the contemplation of it; and besides, it in turn may be made the symbol of something further?

Yes, I see; there is something transparent, as you said, about symbols and something opaque about allegory. But what of the myth-makers?

My friend, we saw that the poet, whether mimetic or didactic, required knowledge of some sort, both of his craft and of that which he represented?

Yes.

Apart from knowledge, he could never achieve plausibility of action or character or argument?

He could not.

So long as he presents this knowledge in terms of its manifestations in particular causes, we may call him "poet" and nothing more; a very honorable thing. But what if he seeks to convey this knowledge itself, wholly divorced from all particulars and accidents? He must needs do this by some myth or fable, and we may call him a "myth-maker" whether he uses a symbol or parable or allegory; and that is to call him both "poet" and "philosopher." Surely, your Yeats did this in his work "A Vision"; and Eliot, also, in his myth of Wheel and still point.

I see.

And now I must be going, since it is nearly dawn and since the wine in the goblet has yielded nearly all its fragrance; but your question has reminded me that I left the myth of the shadow-city unfinished. May I finish, since only a word or two remains?

By all means.

Well, then: Lur, our shadow, found the place of the temple by his journey; but he discovered also that the god in his anger had locked the gates so that no one could enter. Yet a mirror had been hung in the vast hall, so that, although he could not see the Reality, yet he could see its reflection. And he saw that there were many other approaches to the temple by ways not his and that these too offered a view, although a different view from his, and like it only in that they too were of reflections only. And, being a shadow, he was content; for the shadow must be content with the shadow of knowledge and rise as if full-fed from the shadow of food. Are you not also content?

I am content.

A DIALOGUE ON
THE FUNCTION OF ART
IN SOCIETY

$\mathbf{M}$y twentieth century friends summoned me quite late—indeed, long after midnight—by their usual method of setting out a glass of wine for me, in the belief that the souls of the dead are attracted by the aroma. When I appeared, a vigorous discussion was going on between the Humanist and the Mathematician, as to whether humanistic or mathematical studies were superior, a dispute in which I found myself immediately involved, for the Mathematician turned to me at once and said, smiling:

I'm glad you have come, Socrates; perhaps you can put some sense into this fellow's head, for I can't; he keeps babbling that humanistic studies are superior because they are concerned with art, which he thinks superior to everything else; whereas I very sensibly maintain that the sciences are obviously most useful to society and that, since mathematics is the queen of the sciences, it is clearly superior to every other branch of study. Do you suppose you can help me convince him?

I don't know, I said; perhaps he has very powerful arguments.

So I have, Socrates, said the Humanist; powerful and simple ones. There are three classes of goods which have nothing to do with each other: the admirable, the necessary, and the useful. I maintain that the very fact which my opponent has so insistently repeated, that art has no use, shows that it is admirable and supreme, for the useful is always servile. I assert that art is the flower and ornament of society, and one of the final goods pursued by man. That is all, really; as you see, the argument consists of self-evident truths.

Doubtless they will be self-evident when I understand them, I said; in the mean-time, will you tell me what benefit art, as a final good, confers? For it is my impression that all goods confer benefits.

Everyone knows that, he replied; art tends to make everyone more content with himself and with others.

Reprinted from *Chicago Review*, vol. 16, no. 4 (1964). Originally in Spanish, in *La Torre*, vol. 1, no. 1 (1953).

Given art, the just man will then be more content with his justice, and the wise man with his wisdom?

Precisely.

And the unjust man will be more content with his injustice, and the fool with his folly? And the wise will be content with the folly of the fool, and the just with the injustice of the unjust?

I dislike to admit that, Socrates, but I suppose I must.

You dislike to admit it because this would not be of benefit to the just and the unjust and the wise and the unwise?

If you put it that way, yes.

Then we must have better grounds for finding art admirable; for if its benefit is that it makes everyone content with himself and with others, this is not much of a benefit.

Very well, he said, let me try again. What I meant was that art is a virtue in itself, and is to be esteemed as such; just as we admit the excellence of a single virtue, and its benefit both to the individual who has it and to his society, whether he is a good man or a bad one.

Would you agree or would you not that the distinguishing mark of virtue is that it cannot be carried to excess, and that, therefore, anything which can be carried to excess cannot be a virtue?

I would agree.

Then what would you say of a society in which every individual was constantly engaged in either the production or the appreciation of art? Surely all would starve, wouldn't they? And certainly every useful trade and profession would disappear.

I suppose so.

Then art cannot possibly be a virtue?

I fear not.

But if art is not virtue, I presume that the production of art cannot be a virtuous activity, and the product of art is not a product of virtue, and the enjoyment of art also cannot be a virtuous occupation.

But, Socrates, surely art may be combined with virtue.

I fear I do not understand. The wise man, in action, will be wholly occupied with his wisdom, I should imagine.

Doubtless he would.

And similarly the just man, in action, will be wholly occupied with his justice, and the brave with his bravery, and the temperate with his temperance?

Yes.

Then I fail to see how these men can combine virtue with art, unless one can simultaneously be wholly occupied with one thing and partly with another.

Socrates, the just or wise or any man must sometimes relax, and not engage in action.

My friend, if you say that, I shall give you a choice; either you must hold that the virtuous man in relaxing also relaxes in his virtue, and if that is the case, art is clearly vicious, for it is the opposite of virtue; or you must hold that he merely rests from action, in which case art is useful only when virtue is useless, and a distraction when virtue is active.

Very well, Socrates, art is not admirable if you prefer, for I know your arguments are tending that way; but at least let me not be pushed into saying that art is useless.

It is useful, then?

Certainly.

Well, then—to whom and for what?

In everything, and to everyone.

To the carpenter or the bridge builder or the cobbler or any other artisan in his craft of useful production?

In that respect, no.

Well—to the farmer or herdsman or anyone else of the sort? Or is it not the case that art, if it is useful, is so when these and all masters of trades are inactive and useless?

Never mind that, Socrates; my real meaning is that the ideas of beauty and of utility are very closely associated, although beauty transcends utility. For example, a really useful ax or any other tool is beautiful in its way because it is perfectly determined to its function, and a well-painted ax goes beyond that form dictated by utility to be more beautiful still.

And it is precisely in achieving this greater beauty that art is useful?

Precisely.

But surely it is useless and not useful to go beyond utility? No, no, I said, this is fantastic; you are simply playing cat and mouse with me; for on your argument it turns out that the crafts we supposed useful produce things which are perfectly fitted to their function, and hence beautiful, and hence useless; whereas the fine arts are useful because they produce things which are perfectly fitted to perform a function which they do not have; and the more functional a thing is, the more beautiful it is, whereas the beautiful itself is not functional, and heaven only knows what other miraculous paradoxes.

Very well; I will take the position that beauty is functional simply, if you will.

It is not what I will—never mind. you would grant that a toad or a weed has a form perfectly adapted to its function, would you not? And a mud-scow is shaped to do precisely what it is supposed to do?

Why do you ask?

I was not aware that any of these would be called beautiful, although they seem to be perfectly fitted to their functions. Conversely, the lily and the diamond are thought to be beautiful, yet the idea of the mode of life of one, or of any possible function of the other, never enters our heads.

That is right.

Well, then, it would appear that beauty is, in its very essence, useless, and art, if it is concerned with beauty, is aimed at something of no use.

Very well, Socrates; you have gained another point. But there is one thing that you will never convince me of: that art is not a necessity. I feel in my heart that it is certainly that to me; and I hold that on no other proof but that the feeling comes from the heart, which is certainly superior in any case to reason and all the ingenious proofs and disproofs which come from reason.

Hold on, I said; if your proof depends on the warrant that the heart is superior to reason, it depends upon reason, for the proposition that the heart is superior could only have come from the reason. But let us finish. There are two kinds of necessity, are there not? For water is necessary to all men, but liquor only to the drunkard?

Yes.

Well, are the arts necessary to all men, or only to a few? If you say "everyone" again, I shall again ask you, to whom specifically?

You have won again, Socrates; but I protest that these are phantom arguments.

You must excuse me, I said; I am only the phantom of Socrates, as you know; and it is not surprising that a phantom should use phantom arguments.

Don't mind him, Socrates, said the Mathematician; you have taken him down nicely. Now, if you will only show the superiority of mathematics to all other studies, I'll be grateful to you. I suppose you would agree that mathematics is the only real and certain knowledge man has; and that its usefulness is obvious everywhere, for all the sciences which have to do with the nature of things formulate their knowledge in mathematical terms and formulas, and engineering has used mathematics to produce untold miracles and to multiply incalculably the power of man. Further, mathematics furnishes a standard by which the methods and principles of all other sciences—even logic —may be judged. But you would agree, wouldn't you, that we mathematicians have pretty well solved the Sphinx's riddle of the universe?

I don't know, I said. Let us see. I suppose that mathematics is concerned with number or quantum, and that this is distinct from the nature of things—otherwise the sciences of mathematics and physics, say, would hardly be distinct?

Yes, surely.

And when the mathematician measures a table, does he do so in respect to its being a table, or in respect to its being something measurable, such as a surface or length or something of the sort?

The latter.

And if he does know what a table is, that knowledge is not required for his measurements; moreover, mathematics will not provide knowledge of what a table is, except in respect of quantity? Similarly, in the matter of some attribute of the table—say, whiteness—he may measure the whiteness but cannot as mathematician know what it is?

True.

Then, generally, mathematics neither requires a knowledge of the nature of things, nor provides it.

Certainly, Socrates; mathematics is an abstract science. What of it?

You remarked, I think, that other sciences which do deal with the natures of things—physics and chemistry, for example—formulate their knowledge in terms of mathematics?

So I did.

Then if mathematics involves no concepts save those of quanta or number, and the other sciences formulate their knowledge of natures in terms of quanta, neither will be able to discuss the true natures of things?

Perhaps not. Would you like to state the true nature of water, if H_2O is not that?

It is not my business to state the true nature of water or of anything else at the moment; my point is that H_2O obviously does not state it, for that is the statement of a quantum; and we have agreed that quantum is not the nature of anything except quantum.

So we have.

Now, I suppose, the goodness or badness of something is always in reference to its function; for instance, the goodness or badness of a horse is in reference to its function as a horse, and similarly, that of a man, in reference to his function as man?

Certainly.

This function, surely, is determined by the nature of a thing—for instance, the function of horse is determined by the nature of horse?

Undoubtedly.

Then, I suppose, mathematics will be quite unable, by itself, to judge the goodness or badness of anything; since it has nothing to do with natures other than number. But then, it will be unable to judge even itself, surely? For mathematics is knowledge, and yet knowledge is not a number or quantum.

True.

Therefore it is incapable of judging its own methods, or those of any other science, and can neither discuss truth nor falsity, validity nor fallacy, since surely these also are not numbers or quanta?

Well—I suppose.

Do not suppose—agree or argue. It cannot then be, can it, the queen of the sciences, if not qualified precisely in respect to these qualifications you specified as its claims to be queen?

I fear it cannot.

You have claimed great usefulness for it and for the other sciences; I suppose that whatever is of great use may also be greatly abused, unless it has within itself some principles which direct it solely to the good.

Yes.

But mathematics and these other sciences have no concept of the good, and therefore are unable to have any such directing principle?

True enough, but what are you driving at?

My friend, I will tell you quickly, for a child could see it. If mathematics is as you describe it, and the other sciences are as well, they are very powerful and therefore very dangerous both to society and to themselves. They are dangerous because, offering great power which is not necessarily ordered to the good, they will tempt the ambitious to seize them and abuse them, to the detriment of society; moreover, if they multiply the power of man, they permit a tyrant to enslave the rest of mankind in hopeless perpetuity. But they are also dangerous to themselves; for if tyrants seize them and use them, their ends and methods will be perverted until they can no longer be called sciences; and hence these sciences contain the seeds of their own destruction. The true scientist will undoubtedly suffer doubly, for he will suffer both as scientist and as man. Tell me frankly whether you are not beginning to see evidence of this in your own century.

I fear indeed that I am.

Beware, then; if you have solved the riddle of the Sphinx, fear the misfortunes of Oedipus which follow.

At this point the Humanist said bitterly: Socrates, you have just reduced all culture to ashes; why don't you go ahead and destroy society, government, and man himself, together with all other good things as well?

Heaven forbid, I said, that I should ever destroy anything good. But surely you do not mean that society and government are necessarily good.

Merciful heaven! he exclaimed. Will you leave nothing untouched? Show us how society and government could possibly be bad.

I would rather consider what society and government are, and what they are when they are good, and what may be done to improve or preserve them. Suppose, since you are so convinced they are always good, you tell me what they are.

A society is men gathered together for benefit. That is why, as I say, it is always necessarily good.

Benefit to themselves, or to others?

To themselves, of course.

Then a group of bandits would be a society?

No, I will change that, and say benefit both to themselves and to others.

It is to a criminal's benefit, and to the benefit of others that he be restrained from action, is it not?

Of course.

Then I suppose a prisonful of criminals would be a society?

Of course not.

Accept it as an instance or alter your definition; for it fits your definition.

Would you like me to say that society is not a grouping and that it is to no one's benefit?

No, for that would be absurd. Tell me rather what sort of group it is, and for what benefit gathered. For example, I imagine that a number of strangers sheltering in a cave during a storm would not be a society, nor would the spectators at a puppet-show, nor a thousand things, all of which involve grouping for benefit.

Then I will say, it is any group gathered to supply the basic necessities of life for each other. Hence, necessarily good.

Then is a family a society?

No, the family is a natural group, society is an artificial one. And government is therefore instituted to protect it. Hence also necessarily good.

From what you say, I remarked, society appears to grow out of the necessities of the individual, and government to arise out of the necessity to maintain society.

That is correct.

Both, then, are aimed at some good; moreover, government is for the sake of the society, and society for the sake of the individual; these are the goods at which they aim, if I follow you.

Of course.

But surely the goods of the individual must be more than the basic necessities of life, such as subsistence and safety.

Why should they be?

My friend, you will soon be, like some social fools of your day, admiring societies and governments like those of the ant and the bee, and building their own accordingly. Who would be a member of such, unless coerced by want and fear?

Well. . . .

Let us remember that we are building for men, not for insects; and let us say to all such, go to the ant, thou sluggard, but do not be so sluggish as to steal his form of government. No, let us say that good society and government have the end, not merely of permitting man to live, but to live as well as possible; and the good of the individual necessarily involves virtue, as well as all other possible excellences of person and fortune.

Very well.

Then, according to what we have said, the good society must be one in which the good social member is also a good man; and the good government is one in which the good man is also the good citizen. Thus social and political theory must be founded on ethics, rather than ethics being founded on them. For if the state is allowed to define what happiness and virtue are, the most corrupt state can claim that all its citizens are happy and good.

Beyond doubt.

Then how shall we ensure that our society and government produce the good man?

Good laws, Socrates, for one, and religion, and moral and political philosophy.

An excellent answer, excellent, and yet I wonder whether it is really sufficient.

What on earth do you mean, Socrates?

It is difficult to state. Let me put it this way. Anything which is held together is bound either from within or from without or from both, is it not? For instance a barrel or a bundle of faggots is held together from without, and a chair by its internal jointings, while a really stout chest is held together both internally by its mortises and externally by its bands. And I suppose that this double binding is always stronger than either internal or external force alone. Now, are not laws a sort of external binding—for they are a pressure from without upon the individual, to make him do what he does not necessarily want to do? And religion similarly, unless the individual happens to be truly pious? Moreover, laws are general, and there may be much slipperiness as to which particular action fits under which law, especially when laws conflict. This difficulty religion escapes when priest or minister gives particular counsel; but religion requires the faith of the individual before it can affect him; now faith cannot be commanded or constrained; hence, those who most need such guidance are those who most often will not submit to it because they do not believe in it. Again, both law and religion, wonderful and beneficial as they are, teach by punishment and reward, salvation and damnation, so that the individual is likely to do the good act and abstain from the wrong, not because one is right and the other wrong, but from hope or fear of something else. And these emotions of hope and fear are too inconstant to found everything on; he who hopes may soon despair, and he who fears may presently grow confident.

Well—there is still moral and political philosophy.

But these deal with concepts, do they not, and proceed by reason?

What if they do? Your point is, I think, that the individual himself must desire the right things; surely correct concepts and good reasoning will instill such desire.

I wonder if they will. You have a concept of love and another of hate. Do these move you either to love or to hate? Can one be reasoned into or out of love? I fear that reason and concepts can hardly instill desire and aversion, though they may sometimes modify them, or discover what means may lead to one's desire. Beyond that they can scarcely affect human conduct; for, apart from the fact that the good or the bad are desirable or the reverse, why should they move us to action, as *ideas*, any more than the ideas of square or triangle?

Well, then, what does instill desire and increase it?

We may observe, may we not, a certain interconnection between desire and emotion? For instance, if we desire something, a whole train of emotions such as hope, fear, joy, grief, and so on are produced in us, according to whether we do or do not achieve it? Conversely, emotion instigates desire; for instance, anger produces the desire to retaliate, and love the desire to benefit, and pity the desire to assist. Again, emotions are produced by opinions attended by images, either of the sense or of the imagination, are they not? For example, the sight or imagination of an animal about to attack one will produce fear, if it is attended by the opinion that it is dangerous and about to attack; but without the opinion of imminent danger, it will not. And the image of someone suffering, attended by the opinion that the misfortune is undeserved, will produce pity; but without these, pity can never be excited.

Very well, but I still see no solution.

Come, let us consider: we said that both society and government, when good, were for the benefit of every individual, did we not? That benefit, moreover, was the greatest conceivable, since it included virtue and all the constituents of happiness. Why, then, should anyone fail to achieve that benefit? For surely anyone would prefer the whole of benefit in preference to any part of it, unless he were mad, or so disordered by passion as to be nearly so, or otherwise disabled?

Continue.

I suppose the man who acts well has the ability to see the consequences of good or bad actions, and to distinguish good from bad, and to hold firmly to the course of the good; and that it is precisely in respect to these three things that the man who does not act well must be disabled?

Surely.

The third of these is due to weakness of will, which is the absence of a habit of choice; the first two, if we were right about desire and emotion, are due to weakness of imagination, and to failure to reason out consequences. Hence an immediate gratification seems more attractive than a remote one; the bad is preferred to the good simply because neither is conceived with sufficient vividness and completeness. And a man who acts badly thinks that he is acting in his own interest, which he supposes counter to the interests of others because he believes them also to be ruled by self-interest; whereas the fact is that his true interest necessarily involves the interest of others, for that is why society and government were framed; thus he is not acting in his own interest, after all.

Beyond doubt.

To make this man good, we must first free him from his supposed self-interest, must we not?

Beyond doubt.

Well, then, by heaven, we have to ask ourselves whether there is any faculty which, setting vivid images of good and bad before his senses or his imagination, does so in complete abstraction from his self-interest, and forces him to distinguish good from bad, and choose the good. Do you know of any that will serve?

No.

What a pity! Merely observe; this faculty, were there such, would be of inestimable value, since it would have the power of moving man from within, whereas all others that move him do so from without; thus we should have our double binding, which is most necessary since, as you said, society and government are not natural but artificial gatherings.

Come, come, Socrates, don't be coquettish; we know that you know. What is this mysterious faculty?

My friend, I wish I knew. The only candidate I can think of has already been tried and sentenced and executed.

I don't follow you.

Let me explain. People seeing a play, if it is a good one, are very much moved, aren't they?

Yes.

If moved emotionally, they are feeling some form of pleasure or pain at what the characters do or undergo? And surely they would not feel pleasure or pain unless what happened were in accord or not with their desires; therefore they must actually desire the characters to do or endure good or evil?

Certainly.

Yet surely it is not to the self-interest of anyone in the audience to have good or evil befall the characters? For what have these to do with them?

Surely not.

And is this reaction of the audience a random one, as each person happens to favor one character and dislike another, or do all favor some and dislike others?

The latter, certainly.

How curious! Your audience will undoubtedly contain good and bad, like and unlike; yet whatever their differences, here all will operate in the same way, on the same principle! All will feel the same emotion of pity or fear or grief or mirth at exactly the same moment— as indeed their behavior shows—provided they are attending and following what goes on. And tell me, who is it they favor or dislike, the good or the bad—or is their favor or dislike based on other grounds?

It is based on these grounds; they inevitably favor the good and dislike the bad.

Then surely they must be able somehow, here, to distinguish these? And to discern good and evil fortune and action?

Yes.

And they laugh at comedy, where all is unimportant, and do not take the characters and their fortunes seriously, whereas the reverse is true in tragedy? And therefore they can distinguish important from unimportant?

Certainly.

And they wish good for the good, and bad for the bad, and so must make some choice of action and fortune?

They do.

And tell me—the dramatist must be able to depict the good man as good, and the bad as bad, and misfortune as misfortune, and so on, in order to effect this response in the audience?

Of course.

And can he also depict a villain as a good man, and a good man as a villain?

No, Socrates, that he can't; nor can he confuse misfortune with good fortune, or anything of the sort; his audience will detect that instantly and be annoyed.

Remarkable! Then this art is in its essence true and just; although the dramatist seeks primarily to write a good play, he must necessarily follow virtue in order to do so. And in order to construct a good plot, he must consider the consequences of character and action; all of which he presents in true colors, and as vividly realized as possible. This, I suppose, is the reason why the audience can here distinguish and choose so well; for the reason must lie in the art and in the artist, otherwise the audience, which itself is heterogeneous, could not react so uniformly.

Surely.

Notice how delicate the morality of the audience is: in tragedy they prefer, to the supposedly "happy" ending, the material disaster of the hero, if only he will ultimately perform some noble act of repentance or restitution, even if it means his death; in comedy, they wish the clownish hero every kind of happiness save that which is too noble for him.

Right.

Well, then, distinguishing repeatedly between good and bad, repeatedly choosing between right and wrong, repeatedly calculating the consequences of actions, will they not form some habit out of all this repetition, and will not such a habit be good?

Undoubtedly.

But are the forms of drama unique in possessing this extraordinary power, or do epic and comic-epic and other forms of poetry and fiction possess it also?

I see no reason why they should not.

Nor do I. And perhaps painting and sculpture and pantomimic dancing share in it, too—for none of these can depict the good as bad or the bad as good, any more than they can depict the weak as strong or the ugly as beautiful. Similarly, we are moved immediately by music, and instantly recognize it as noble or jocose; for music plays on the soul itself, and the soul can scarcely be deceived in its own motions. So let this be our statement of the role of art in society and government: the artist, in pursuing the Beautiful, must necessarily advance the Good.

Well said.

Shall we say briefly what our humanist must be like? For it is his role to interpret and teach what the artist creates. It is clear that he must conceive of his knowledge as a science, and a noble one; not patterning its methods upon other sciences, but utilizing the most exact methods appropriate to its subject. He must then, certainly, be skilled in dialectic, so that he can inquire, attack, and defend; otherwise he will lose sight of the true greatness of his subject, and only praise it falsely—just as you, my friend, lost sight of it and so praised it.

You are right.

He must also be trained in philosophy, particularly in the matter of the principles, methods, and organization of the sciences; hence he must know metaphysics; besides which he should be trained in moral and political philosophy, and especially in psychology, since art comes from the soul and works upon the soul. He must also know the whole body of the arts, and their history; he must, however, know the theory of forms before the history, since the history will be of changing forms. Also he must know languages and their principles, and color-theory, and whatever else pertains to the various media of art. And we will demand also that he be well acquainted with the art of his own day, for although he will not have the last word on that, he will have the first. Do you think, if he knows all these things, he will be in danger of being disesteemed?

On the contrary.

Let him earn his honor then, and perform his function. But consider: will he not improve his science, and will that not improve art, and art in turn improve man and society? And will not the notion of what is good change with each stage of improvement—for what the child thinks good differs from what the youth thinks so, and what the youth thinks, from the mature man?

I should think so.

Well, then—may not man at last transcend himself? For you know the law of nature that the lower species by striving becomes a higher.

I don't follow you.

I have only a moment; it is near the time when shades must depart, and the fragrance is nearly gone from the wine in my goblet. I will therefore tell you of this mystery as quickly as I can, by telling you Plato's dream of the Tower. He dreamed it on his death-bed; it was the first thing he told me of after his death.

He dreamed that he was on a gigantic Loom; chaos and storm were above and around, but he thought he saw, in a dim and wildly shaken light, great cascades of water, fire, earth, and air roaring to feed the Loom, like giant threads. He knew he was a figure in a mighty tapestry; all about him he saw every kind of repulsive beast and plant being woven; but the fair forms of plant and animal, and the fairer form of man, were not there. The tapestry moved upon the Loom, and when any piece of it was finished, the myriad figures in it separated and fell away, and the pattern of their arangement was lost. Then he too was finished, and fell backwards into darkness; but at the last moment he saw himself to be, not a man, but a great fish; also he caught a glimpse of a huge Figure in the shadows, working the Loom, and he thought that this too had the form of a fish; but a giant snake that fell with him cried that the Workman in the dark was a snake, and a mighty lizard that it was a lizard; and Plato supposed, therefore, confused and dim as his thought was, that each thing had seen the Workman as its own likeness. He fell with the other creatures into what he took to be a swarming fen, where all wallowed, mating and devouring in their attempt to re-unite themselves and so restore the original pattern; but refusing that writhing mass, he swam until he came to a bank and endeavored to climb it, impossible as that seemed, and as he strove, legs were furnished him; on emerging, he saw by lightning-flashes that he stood within a great Tower, with a stair winding slowly up its inner sides. This stair he began to climb, and as he did, the Minotaur passed him, going downward, garlanded and drunk with blood and wine;

Pasiphaë followed close behind; he saw also Myrrha slipping slowly down the stair, gazing wildly at her hand, the fingers of which were beginning to put forth leaves. The first landing, he saw was guarded by Furies; but on his passing them they turned to Sirens, and wooed him to return, showing him the stair below in a paradisiacal light, as the fairest of gardens. Yet he saw that he had now regained his human form, like the creatures around him; therefore he went upward, through a strange throng of what he took to be madmen, for some clutched fiery crowns and scepters, others flaming swords, and still others blazing coins, while all cried bitterly for water to assuage the pains of their burns. Plato, I say, ascended, not so much out of desire as out of such pain as the iron, if it were sentient, might feel when drawn by the magnet; however, he was by no means assisted by anything; on the contrary, the anguish of the ascent took all his strength. Ever he climbed into the darkness, and as he did, the darkness retreated; and when he had passed the Furies who guarded the second landing, he found himself in the company of figures majestic and tall as those who stalk the tragic stage; but he, too, now was tall, as tall as any. Happy Oedipus was there, blessing his blindness; and priestly Tiresias, and Homer; all had precious jewels set in their eyesockets, through which they saw, they said, better than with eyes. Hand in hand Plato climbed with them; at the tower's top, they all stared in wonder at each other, for they had all grown exactly alike; but, glorious as they were, were not men nor anything they had ever seen. And then they stared at the spacious heaven and saw to their amazement a gigantic Form, like what they had become, but indescribably more splendid; and they were drawn up to it through the clear air, as stars to a greater star. And Plato heard his own voice singing, together with the voices of all the others: "We praise Thee, we praise Thee; not in Thy Image didst Thou make us, but Thou hast caused us to make ourselves in Thy Image."

AN OUTLINE OF
POETIC THEORY

W hen, in any field of learning, discussions of the subject are based upon different principles, employ different methods, and reach different conclusions, such differences tend to be interpreted, by expert and layman alike, as real disagreement. The differences are not of themselves dangerous to the subject; the tendency to interpret them as contradictions is. The dogmatist, however sound in his own method, usually regards them as signs of the chaos that must await any who depart from his position. The syncretist regards them as signs that all positions are at least partly false, and collects "truths," which frequently lose, in his synthesis, not only their supporting arguments but their original significance as well. The skeptic, finally, interprets such differences as implying the impossibility of philosophical knowledge in the field. All these views are potentially harmful to learning in so far as, in suppressing discussion, they suppress some (and in the case of skepticism, all) of the problems and because, consequently, they retard or even arrest progress within the subject. Skepticism, indeed, is most dangerous of all, for it does not arrest progress merely in certain respects but arrests it wholly; and, once given head, it does not pause until it has also canceled whatever has been achieved in the past.

Criticism in our time is a sort of Tower of Babel. Moreover, it is not merely a linguistic but also a methodological Babel; yet, in the very pursuit of this analogy, it is well to remember that at Babel men did not begin to talk nonsense; they merely began to talk what *seemed* like nonsense to their fellows. A statement is not false merely because it is unintelligible; though it will have to be made intelligible before we can say whether it is true. The extreme diversity of contemporary criticism is no more alarming than—and, indeed, it is connected

Reprinted from *Critiques and Essays in Criticism, 1920–1948*, ed. Robert Wooster Stallman (New York: Ronald Press Co., 1949).

with—the similar diversity of contemporary philosophy; and the chief import of both is of the need for some critique which shall examine radically how such diversity arises, by considering what aspects of a given subject are amenable to treatment, what problems they pose, and how these may be diversely formulated. For the diverse may be contradictory or not; theories of criticism which are not contradictory or incompatible may be translated into one another or brought to supplement one another, and a just decision may be given between those which are really contradictory, provided that we can isolate the differences of formulation from the differences of truths and falsities. True interpretation is impossible when one system is examined in terms of another, as is true refutation when the refutative arguments are systematically different from those against which they are directed. To propose such a critique is, in effect, to state the possibility of a fourth philosophic attitude: that of pluralism. Dogmatism holds the truth of a single position and the falsity, in some degree at least, of all others; syncretism holds the partial falsity of all; skepticism the total falsity of all. All these take into their consideration doctrines alone; pluralism, taking both doctrine and method into account, holds the possibility of a plurality of formulations of truth and of philosophic procedures—in short, of a plurality of valid philosophies.

Such pluralism is possible both in philosophy and in criticism because criticism is a department of philosophy. A given comprehensive philosophy invariably develops a certain view of art; the critical theories of Plato, Aristotle, Hume, and Kant, for instance, are not any random views but are generated and determined by their respective philosophies. And while a given criticism or theory of art may not originate in a comprehensive philosophy and may resist reference to one already existent, it is not therefore really independent of a more comprehensive system, for the discussion of art must entail assumptions which involve more than art; it is merely part of a whole as yet undeveloped. In short, since criticism or the theory of art is part of philosophy, it has the same bases as philosophy and is determinate or variable according to the same principles.

It is impossible within the scope of this essay to discuss all the factors in the foundations of philosophies and criticisms; but perhaps a rough and partial statement may serve for illustration. I propose that the number of possible critical positions is relative to the number of possible philosophic positions and that the latter is determined by two principal considerations: (1) the number of aspects of a subject which can be brought into discussion, as constituting its *subject matter;* (2) the kinds of basic dialectic which may be exerted upon that subject matter. I draw this distinction between the subject and the subject matter: the subject is what is talked about; the subject matter is that subject in so far as it is represented or implied in the discussion. Philosophers do not discuss *subjects themselves;* they can discuss only so much as the terms or materials of the discussion permit; and that is the subject matter. We cannot discuss what we cannot, first of all, mention, or what we cannot bring to mind. In other words, any discussion of a "subject" is relative to its formulation. But, further, any discursive reasoning must employ some method of reasoning or inference; and, since there are various possible systems of inference, we may say that a given discussion is a function of its subject matter and of the dialectic, i.e., system of inference, exerted upon that subject matter.

Whatever art in itself may be, as a *subject*, it is clear that criticism has employed certain aspects of it as subject matters. Thus one aspect of an art is its product; another, the instrumentality, active or passive, which produced the product; another, the product as relative to or determined by that instrumentality, and hence as a sign of the nature of that instrumentality, whether this last be viewed as actual or potential. Another is the relation of an art to a certain subject or means, as a consequence, and hence as a sign, of these; still another aspect is its production of a certain effect, either of activity or of passivity, upon those who are its spectators or auditors; and, lastly, there is the art viewed as instrumental to that effect. We may sum up all this by saying that criticism has viewed art variously as a product; as an activity or passivity of the artist; as certain faculties or as a certain character of the artist; as a certain activity or passivity of the audience; as certain faculties or as a certain character of the audience; as an instrument; or as a sign, either of certain charcteristics of the artist or his audience or of something else involved in art, e.g., its means, subject, etc.

The significances which the term "poem" assumes in critical discussions may illustrate this. In its most obvious meaning it refers to the product of the poetic art; but critics have often used it to refer to what they considered more important aspects of poetic art or have differentiated it by reference to such aspects. Thus those who think that it is characterized by its instrumentality mean by "instrumentality" either the poet or the poetic powers; those who define poetry in terms of the poet see the poet as active craftsman or as the passive instrument of his inspiration or as a mixture of the two; while those who define poetry in terms of poetic powers see the poet as possessed of faculties or qualities either of a certain kind or of a certain degree. With these differences, both consequently view the poem as a kind of behavior of the poet; and for both, the literal poem—the product—becomes a sign of that behavior, which is, in turn, a sign of the poetic character or faculties. Others find that the poem properly exists in the audience; the audience is the true poet, for, without it, the poem could never come to life; and the audience, like the poet, can be viewed as actualizing certain active

or passive potentialities or merely as possessing such potentialities—
hence the theories of "audience-participation" (the active view) or "art
as experience" (the passive view), etc. Finally, "poem" may mean the
end to which the product is instrumental, e.g., the psychological cure
or ethical or political attitude or behavior.

These seem like "conflicting views"; hence they have been treated so
in the history of criticism. If "conflicting" merely means "different,"
there is no quarrel, for these views are different enough. But if it means
"contradictory" or "inconsistent," nothing could be more absurd. For,
in the first place, all these doctrines have different references, and it is
impossible to have contradiction except in the same reference; and,
secondly, where contradiction exists, one view must be false if the
other is true, whereas all these views are perfectly true in their proper
senses, for all are founded upon perfectly obvious aspects of art, poetic
or otherwise. Nor, if they are not contradictory, are they inconsistent,
in the sense that they proceed from, or result in, contradiction; for,
asserting the existence of certain aspects of art as they do, they are all
true in some sense, and it is impossible for true propositions to be
inconsistent. Indeed, nothing prevents certain philosophers, like Plato
and Aristotle, from investigating all these aspects of art.

Whatever aspect of art a critic may fix upon, he usually seeks to
explain its nature by reference to certain causes or reasons; thus those
who are concerned with the product of art, for instance, have thought
to explain the nature of the product by reference to its matter or
medium, to the subject represented or depicted, to the depictive method
of the artist or some other productive cause, or to the end or effect of
the product; and some have employed merely one of these causes or
reasons, while others have used several or all. Aristotle, for instance,
employs differentiations of object, means, manner, and effect to define
tragedy, whereas a critic like Richard Hurd finds the nature of poetry
adequately defined by its subject matter.

I have remarked that the kind of dialectic exerted upon the subject
matter is the other determinant of a given mode of criticism. The
variety of dialectics is an exceedingly complex question, but we may
occupy ourselves here only with a single characteristic of dialectics—
their concern with likeness or difference, or both. The integral or
likeness-dialectic reaches solutions by combination of like with like; the
differential or difference-dialectic, by the separation of dissimilars.
Thus a criticism integral in its dialectic resolves its questions by referring poetry, for example, to some analogue of poetry, finding characteristics of poetry which are shared by the analogue; whereas a criticism
differential in its dialectic resolves its questions by separating poetry
from its analogues, finding characteristics which are peculiar to poetry.

Thus—to confine our illustrations to the various criticisms which deal with the product of art—we find criticisms differing as they center on either the subject matter of art or its medium or its productive cause or its end or several of these, and as they proceed integrally or differentially. Subject-matter criticism of the integral kind resolves the subject matter of the arts into something not peculiar to the arts, on the basis of likeness; and the principles of art, when so found, are always the principles of things other than art as well. Thus Plotinus finds the beautiful in art to consist in the imitation of the beautiful; but inquiry into that characteristic, for him, shows it to be common also to natural objects and to actions, and so upward to the Beauty which is almost indifferentiable from the Good; and the ultimate solution of artistic as well as of all other problems lies, for him, in the contemplation of God. Differential criticism of this order, on the other hand, separates the kinds of subject matter and argues on the basis of such separation, either to distinguish the arts from other faculties or activities or to distinguish them *inter se*.

In pure subject-matter criticisms, once the subject matter has been found, it determines all other questions, e.g., of artistic capacity or character or of the techniques, forms, processes, criteria, and ends of art. For example, if the subject matter in the raw, so to speak, is all-sufficient, the characteristics of the artist tend to appear as sharpness of observation and readiness of comprehension; if the subject matter requires order and selection, correlative capacities for order and selection are constituents of the artistic character; and so on. A similar determination operates throughout all other problems: criteria, for instance, are produced from some correspondence or opposition, absolute or qualified, between the subject and the medium, or the artist, or the effect. Thus many of the theories of artistic realism have as their criterion the absolute correspondence of the effects of art with those of reality itself; art is thus copyistic, and the work is a "slice of life," all formal criteria (such as order) being supplanted by attributes of the reality. Where the subject matter of art is opposed to the reality, however—whether it requires an order and selection not found in reality or differs from reality even more radically—such correspondence is qualified, or even negated, as in modern nonrepresentationalist theories.

Comparably, criticisms centering on the medium can be integral or differential, and solve their problems through reference to the medium. The integral criticism of this order is exemplified in the innumerable attempts to find general criteria for all literature, whether poetic, historical, philosophic, or personal, on the ground that all literature employs words; and the differential criticism is exemplified in the theories of men like I. A. Richards and Cleanth Brooks, who seek to differentiate poetry from prose by differentiation of the kind of diction employed in each, in order to discriminate appropriate criteria for each. The character of the artist varies as the character of the medium is stated; where the medium is viewed as indifferent to form, the capacities of the artist are at the maximum, and, conversely, where the medium is viewed as tending toward form, the artist frequently appears as a kind of midwife to nature, assisting the bronze or the marble to a form which it implicitly contains. Criteria, again, can be found by consideration of the degree to which a given work actualizes or fulfils the potentialities of the medium.

When the productive cause is central, the integral criticism establishes analogies between the artist or the artistic process and some more general cause, e.g., nature or natural process, or God and the divine creative process (Coleridge). Extreme criticisms of this order reduce the art-product almost to a by-product of the artistic character; Fracastoro and Carlyle, for example, refuse to limit the name of poet to those who actually write poems, since poetry is merely incidental to the possession of poetical character. Differential criticism of this kind, again, confines the conception of the artist to the unique maker of a certain product. When discussion centers on the natural elements of the artist, the artistic character lies outside the possibility of any deliberate achievement, as in Hazlitt; conversely, when the artistic character is defined in terms of acquired traits or disciplines (as in Reynolds), discussion of genius and inspiration is at a minimum, and the artistic character itself appears as amenable to art and, indeed, often as the *chef d'oeuvre* of the artist.

When criticism turns on the ends of art, integral and differential dialectics are again possible; the ends of art can be analogized to other purposes of men or to some natural or divine teleology or, conversely, can be differentiated from all else. And, here, as above, the nature of the problems and of their solutions is determined by the choice of the ground-term.

All such criticism may be called "partial," for each attempts to resolve all problems by consideration only of a part. All fix upon a single *cause*, in Aristotle's sense of the word, and account for everything in terms of it, as if one were to account for a chair merely in terms of its wood or merely in terms of its maker. None permits a full account, for the respects in which art is compared with, or contrasted to, other things are always only a part of its actual characteristics. This partiality remains, even if several of these causal factors are combined, unless, indeed, all are involved.

As opposed to such partial criticisms, there are comprehensive criticisms such as those of Plato and Aristotle, the former being primarily integral, the latter primarily differential, although each includes both likeness and difference. These systems permit not only the discussion of all aspects of art but a full causal account; for, whereas Aristotle makes the maximum differentiation of causes, Platonic dialectic employs only a single cause, but one subsuming all. The difference—not in truth or in cogency of argument but in *adequacy*—between comprehensive and partial systems can be readily seen by comparing, say, Aristotle with the "Aristotelian" Scaliger: Aristotle can discuss any aspect of poetry, but Scaliger, basing all merely upon the medium and viewing that only in its most general light—the universal power of language being to express fact or opinion—thereby confines himself to the treatment of poetry only as the instrument of instruction.[1]

Recognition of the methodological differences between systems of criticism, and of their consequent respective powers and limitations, quickly establishes the fact that twenty-five centuries of inquiry have not been spent in vain. On the contrary, the partial systems of criticism correct and supplement one another, the comprehensive intertranslate, to form a vast body of poetic knowledge; and contemporary theorists, instead of constantly seeking new bases for criticism, would do better to examine the bases of such criticisms as we have and so avail themselves of that knowledge. Many a modern theory of criticism would have died a-borning, had its author done a little more reading as he thought, or thinking as he read. Critical knowledge, like all knowledge, must be constantly extended; but no one is very likely to extend it who is not fully aware of what has already been accomplished or of what consequences follow from such accomplishments.

If a plurality of valid and true kinds of criticism is possible, choice must still be exercised, for it is impossible to employ all methods simultaneously, and the selection of method is by no means a matter of indifference. Choice is determined by the questions one wishes to ask and the form of answer one requires and by the relative adequacy of given systems. The discovery of properties peculiar to a given kind of poetry demands a differential method, as that of properties which poetry holds in common with other things requires an integral method. If one wishes to know the nature of a given kind of poetry, as a certain *synolon* or composite, a whole and its parts specified with the maximum differentiation possible without the destruction of the universals upon which science depends, an Aristotelian criticism is requisite; if one proposes to view poetry in terms of principles of maximum community, a Platonic criticism is demanded. Every philosophy is addressed only to certain questions and can answer them only in certain forms.

II

In the method of Aristotle, which underlies the following sketch, poetics is a science concerned with the differentiation and analysis of

1. See Bernard Weinberg, "Scaliger versus Aristotle on Poetics," *Modern Philology* 39 (1942): 337–60.

poetic forms or species in terms of all the causes which converge to produce their respective emotional effects. Scientific knowledge falls into three classes: theoretical, practical, and productive. The end of the first class, comprising metaphysics, mathematics, and the natural sciences, is knowledge; that of the second, comprising ethics and politics, is action; that of the third, comprising the fine and the useful arts, is some product over and above the actions which produce. Only the theoretical sciences are exact; the productive sciences, or arts, are less exact than the practical, since they involve a greater number of principles, and principles derived from many other sciences.

The poetics of a given species takes as its starting point the definition of the product, i.e., a statement of the nature of the whole composite produced by an art, and thence proceeds by hypothetical reasoning to treat of the questions specific to that whole and its parts. Such analysis does not exhaust all aspects of the art; but any which it excludes are referred to other sciences. Thus the consideration of art as a skill falls under ethics; that of art as a political and social instrument, under politics; and that of art as a mode of being, under metaphysics, in accordance with the general Aristotelian practice of assigning questions to their appropriate sciences. A given special poetics, therefore, does not treat centrally of the faculties requisite for production, or of the effects to be produced by art, but of the special product, viewed as a differentiable synthesis of differentiable parts, and, as such, having the capacity or power (*dynamis*) of producing certain peculiar effects.

Before we can consider the various special arts of poetry, however, we must discuss the significance of certain concepts of a more general nature. Unity, beauty, and imitation, for instance, relate to things other than poetry but are not therefore less important to poetic discussion. The term "imitation" is used coextensively with "artificial"; it differentiates art from nature. Natural things have an internal principle of motion and rest, whereas artificial things—a chair or a table—have, qua products of art, no such principle; they change through propensities not of their form but of their matter. Natural and artificial things alike are composites of form and matter; but art imposes a form upon a matter which is not naturally disposed to assume, of itself, such a form. The acorn of itself grows into the oak; the stone does not of itself become a statue or tend to become a statue rather than a column. Art may be said to imitate nature either in the sense that the form of the product derives from natural form (e.g., the human form in the painting resembles the natural human form) or in the sense that the artistic process resembles the natural (e.g., artificial fever in the art of medicine does what fever does naturally). The useful and the fine arts are both imitative; but the latter have as their end the imitation itself, as a form possessed of beauty. Since every imitation has some form imposed somehow upon some matter for some end, specification of all these factors results in a definition of a given species of art; e.g., by specifying *what* is imitated in tragedy (object of imitation), *in what* (means of imitation), *how* (manner of imitation), and to what effect we construct the definition of tragedy. Such definitions are the principles from which reasoning proceeds in the arts; if a certain product or whole is to be produced, it will have a certain number of parts of a certain nature ordered in a certain way, etc.[2]

A poem has unity in the sense in which anything which has continuity is unified; but, more than that, it is one in that it has a single form and is an ordered and complete whole. A piece of wire is one because it is continuous, and if you break the continuity you have two pieces; but some things are totals rather than wholes—a cord of wood, for instance, because the parts need merely be present, and not in any particular arrangement—and others are wholes proper, because they are not only complete and have all their parts but also have them in the proper arrangement, i.e., the least important ordered to its superior part, and so on until the principal part is reached. Parts of a shoe stitched together anyhow are one in the sense of continuity, but not one in the sense of assemblage into a certain single form, the shoe; a poem is similarly an ordered and complete whole.

Moreover, it is not only a whole, but one of a certain nature; it is an imitation in a certain means; hence, since a given means can imitate only certain objects (color and line cannot imitate the course of thought, or musical tones a face), poetry must imitate action, character, or thought; for a given means can be used to imitate only something having the same characteristics as it or something of whose characteristics its own characteristics are signs, and speech (the medium of poetry) is either action or the sign of action, character, and passion. (For example, painting can represent color directly, but the third dimension only by signs, such as perspective diminution, faintness, etc., of objects.) Media are not such things as certain pigments or stones but such as line, color, mass, musical tones, rhythms, and words. The object imitated, therefore, must be some form which these can take or which they can imply by signs. Hence inference plays a large role in all the arts.

Inference and perception serve to institute opinions and mental images concerning the object, and opinions and mental images produce emotion. We see or infer the object to be such and such, and, according to our opinion of what it is, we react emotionally in a certain specific way. If we have the opinion, we react, whether the thing, in fact, is so or not; and if we do not have it, we do not react, whether the

2. It should be borne in mind that the present discussion applies strictly only to what I have elsewhere called "mimetic," as distinguished from "didactic," poetry. See below p. 251.

thing is so or not. The opinion that a disaster is imminent produces fear; and the opinion that the victim suffers undeservedly produces pity; and so on.

Emotions are mental pains (e.g., pity), pleasures (e.g., joy), or impulses (e.g., anger) instigated by opinion. The basis of our emotions toward art may be explained as follows: We feel some emotion, some form of pleasure or pain, because our desires are frustrated or satisfied; we feel the desires because we are friendly or hostile to, or favor or do not favor, the characters set before us and because we approve or disapprove of events; and we are friendly or hostile to the characters because of their ethical traits; in brief, we side with the good against the bad or, in the absence of significant differentiations of moral character, upon grounds still moral, as with the oppressed against the oppressor, with the weak against the strong, etc., our judgment now being primarily of the action rather than of the agents.

Since the object of imitation as we conceive it determines the emotions which we feel and since moral differentiation lies at the basis of our conception of the object, the possible objects of imitation in poetry, drama, and fiction may be schematized in terms of extremes, as follows: The serious, i.e., what we take seriously, comprises characters conspicuously better or worse than we are or at any rate such as are like ourselves and such as we can strongly sympathize with, in states of marked pleasure or pain or in fortunes markedly good or bad. The comic, i.e., the ridiculous, comprises characters as involved in embarrassment or discomfiture to whom we are neither friendly nor hostile, of an inferiority not painful to us. We love or hate or sympathize profoundly with the serious characters; we favor or do not favor or condescend to the comic. Serious and comic both divide into two parallel classes: the former into the tragic kind, in which the character is better than we, and the punitive, in which the character is worse; the latter into what may be called "lout-comic," in which the character, though good natured or good, is mad, eccentric, imprudent, or stupid, and the "rogue-comic," in which the character is clever but morally deficient. These kinds are illustrated in drama by *Hamlet, The Duchess of Malfi, She Stoops to Conquer,* and *The Alchemist;* the protagonists in these are, respectively, a man better than we, wicked men (the brothers of the Duchess), a good man with a ridiculous foible, and rogues. Between these extremes of the serious and the comic lie what I have called the "sympathetic" or the antipathetic; i.e., forms in which the morality of the characters does not function in the production of emotional effect so much as does our judgment of the events as, for example, just or unjust; the man is indifferent, but the suffering is greater than even a criminal should undergo, etc. The emotions produced by the contrary objects are themselves contrary; for instance, the pity and fear of tragedy are opposed by the moral vindictiveness and the confidence of retribution in the punitive kinds. Again, the emotions are contrary as the events are contrary; that is, the spectacle of a good man going from good fortune to misfortune or from a pleasant to a painful state effects emotions contrary to those evoked by the spectacle of a good man going from misfortune to fortune or from pain to pleasure. Again, comic "catastrophe" is mere embarrassment or discomfiture, and effects emotions contrary to those produced by catastrophe in the serious forms.

In short, the emotions we feel in poetry are, generally speaking, states of pleasure and pain induced by mental images of the actions, fortunes, and conditions of characters to whom we are well or ill disposed, in a greater or lesser degree, because of our opinions of their moral character or, such failing, because of our natural sympathy or antipathy; or, in other words, our emotions are determined by the object of imitation and vary with it. Emotion in art results, thus, not because we believe the thing "real" but because we vividly contemplate it, i.e., are induced by the work of art to make mental images of it. Compare such expressions as "He was horrified at the mere thought of it," "The very notion filled him with ecstasy," etc.

Pleasure, in general, is a settling of the soul into its natural condition; pleasure in poetry results primarily from the imitation of the object and secondarily from such embellishments as rhythm, ornamental language, and generally any such development of the parts as is naturally pleasing. Where the object of imitation is itself pleasant and vividly depicted, pleasure is direct; when the object is unpleasant, pleasure results from the catharsis or purgation of the painful emotions aroused in us, as in tragedy. Pleasure is commensurate, in other words, with the beauty of the poetic form; and distinctive forms, as they have peculiar beauties, evoke peculiar pleasures.[3]

By "beauty" I mean the excellence of perceptible form in a composite continuum which is a whole; and by "excellence of perceptible form" I mean the possession of perceptible magnitude in accordance with a mean determined by the whole as a whole of such-and-such quality, composed of such-and-such parts. Assuming that parts of the number and quality required for the whole have been provided and ordered hierarchically to the principal part, the whole will be beautiful if that prime part is beautiful; and that part, as a continuity, must have magnitude and be composed of parts (e.g., plot, the prime part of tragedy, has magnitude and has parts); since it has magnitude, it admits of the more and the less, and hence of excess and deficiency, and consequently of a definite and proper mean between them, which constitutes its beauty. Specifically, in terms of the form itself, this mean is a

---

3. For a further discussion of the relation between pleasure and poetry see p. 251.

proportion between whole and part and, consequently, is relative to the different wholes and parts; in reference to perception, it is a mean between such minuteness of the parts and such extension of the whole as would interfere with the perception of the parts, as of their proper qualities, and as in interrelation with each other and the whole. Thus in tragedy the mean of plot-magnitude lies between the length required for the necessary or probable connection of the incidents and the limit imposed by the tragic change of fortunes. The constituents of beauty are, therefore, definiteness, order, and symmetry; the last being such commensurability of the parts as renders a thing self-determined, a measure to itself, as it were; for example, plot is symmetrical when complication and denouement are commensurate. As a thing departs from its proper magnitude, it either is spoiled (i.e., retains its nature but loses its beauty) or is destroyed (i.e., loses even its nature). Compare a drawing of a beautiful head: alter its definitive magnitude to a degree, and the beauty is lost; alter it further, and it is no longer recognizable as a head.

III

These questions are not peculiarly poetic ones but rather matters belonging to metaphysics, psychology, and ethics. The problems we now approach, however, are poetic and may be divided into two kinds—general questions, common to all the poetic arts, and special questions, peculiar to a given poetic art. Biology offers a parallel; for some attributes are common to all forms of life, others are peculiar. Similarly with poetics; some questions come about merely because the imitation is of action, like Aristotle's discussion of plot prior to chapter 13, others because of something specific, like his discussion of the tragic plot, imitating a certain kind of action. I shall here deal with both kinds, though illustratively only, and take up first the question of the definition of forms.

In their scientific order, all the arts, as I have said, begin with definitions of their specific products as wholes, which they utilize as the principle or starting point of their reasoning. These definitions, far from being arbitrary resolutions, must be collected from a conspectus of the historical growth of the species to which they relate; a kind of art, to be known and defined, must first actually exist. Not every aspect of the growth of artistic species, however, is relevant to their artistic character; hence their historical development must be examined in terms of their character as imitations. No single line of differentiation suffices for the separation of species. Most broadly, the arts are distinguished in terms of their media, for, since nothing can be made actual which is not potentially in the medium, the potentialities of the medium, as matter, determine all else; yet the means, even when

fully differentiated, singly and in combination, is insufficient for specific distinction, for arts which have the same means may imitate
opposite objects, as do comedy and tragedy. In turn, objects may be
differentiated, but even such further differentiation is not definitive,
for imitations may still differ in manner, although the possibilities of
manner are now broadly determined. With the distinction of modes or
manners of imitation, the account of the parts of imitation qua imitation is complete, and the historical survey of the rise of the arts—the
synthesis of these differentiated parts into distinct wholes—is now
possible. Such history begins as the causes emerge. The poetic arts, like
the other fine arts, originate in instinct, some matter being given a
form not natural to it, by an external efficiency, for the sake of the
pleasure produced. Yet, though imitation is natural to man, instinct is
insufficient to account for the further development of art; for art
ramifies rather than remains constant, as the universal cause of instinct
would suggest; and its ramifications are determined by the character of
the artist: the noble minded imitate the noble, the low-minded the
low. Even so, the tale is not complete: for art develops further until a
form is achieved and valued for its own sake. Art passes, thus, through
three stages—the instinctive, the ethical or practical, and the artistic—
the first two of which are determined by the nature and character of
the artist, and the last by the form. The achievement of form is
signalized by a revolution in the ordering and constitution of the parts:
once the specifically pleasurable effect has luckily been produced, the
part which is primarily effective becomes principal, develops its proper
extension and qualities, and all other parts readjust to it, in their
proper artistic order. A distinctive synthesis—a species of art—has now
formed, and its poetics may begin, for the formulation of the distinctive means, object, manner, and effect of the synthesis gives all four of
the causes which are collectively, but not singly, peculiar to it, and a
definition results.

  Aristotle has frequently been defended on the ground that all poetic
species reduce to those which he has enumerated, and more frequently
attacked on the ground that they do not. Both defense and attack are
mistaken, the former because it makes poetics predictive, the latter
because it assumes that, since Aristotle did not define certain species,
his theory could not afford a basis for their definition. In fact, as the
above account has shown, the poetics of a given species must always
develop after the species has come into actual being, the definition
being formed by induction; but, on the other hand, the poetic arts in
their development do not leave their bases; they do not cease to have
means, objects, and manners, or even the differentiations of these
mentioned by Aristotle; they merely differentiate these further and
produce new syntheses. The distinction between narrative and dramatic manner, for instance, has not been rendered obsolete, although it

affords no significant distinction, in itself, between Homer and Henry James; yet, to distinguish them, we must begin with the different possibilities of telling, as opposed to impersonating, and discriminate the various complexities of narrative device.

Once object, means, manner, and effect have been specified to the emerging species, the definition of the artistic whole which so results permits an analysis into parts; and when the principal part has been identified and the order of importance of the remaining parts established, the proper construction of the principal part must be ascertained. That part is itself a whole composed of parts, and these parts—its beginning, middle, and end—must be determined, and the character of their conjunction—necessity and probability—must be shown. But the whole is not only a whole, but a whole of some magnitude; and, since it is, moreover, to be a beautiful whole, it must be a whole of some definite magnitude. As I have remarked, this definite magnitude lies in a mean between excess of the part and excess of the whole, the former producing such vast extension that the whole cannot be comprehended, the latter such minuteness that the parts cannot be apprehended. This formula, however, is general and must be specified to the species of art involved. Relatively to perception, it must always be determined in the temporal arts by the limits of memory, since in these arts the parts are not coexistent but successive and, consequently, must be remembered if the whole is to be comprehended; but even this is relative to the species, differences of the parts and wholes of which impose different burdens upon the memory. (A given lyric might be too long to be remembered, while a given tragedy might not.) The wholeness, completeness, and unity of the principal part once established, the part can be divided into its species; hence, for example, Aristotle divides plots into simple and complex, which are different wholes, since the complex plot consists of differentiable parts (peripety and discovery) according to the efficient cause of the change of fortunes with which tragedy is concerned.

"Aristotelian" criticism has frequently centered merely upon this much, to produce mere *Formalismus*; but Aristotle himself goes farther. The principal part is only materially a whole, complete, one, etc.: formally, it has an effect or power of a certain specific order; tragic action, for instance, is not merely action, nor even serious action, but action differentiated by a certain act—the tragic deed committed in a certain way by the tragic hero—and Aristotle, investigating the possibilities of character and action, determines which of these result in the tragic effect—the "working or power" of tragedy—is the form. Comparably, the poetics of any species must be addressed to the differentiation of its principal part, since it is this that primarily determines the emotional effect.

Once the principal part has been treated, the subordinate parts can be dealt with in the order of their importance and according to their causes, the final cause of each being to serve its superior part, the formal cause being the beauty of the part itself. The whole analysis, thus, not merely indicates the possibilities of poetic construction but discriminates among them as better or worse, to exhibit the construction of a synthesis beautiful as a whole, composed of parts of the maximum beauty consistent with that whole, and productive of its proper emotional effects to a maximum degree.

The method—one of multiple differentiation and systematic resolution of maximal composites into their least parts—may obviously be extended to poetic species which have emerged since Aristotle. Aristotle distinguishes broadly and between extremes; later theorists in his method must follow the basic lines and go farther. For example, his poetics, as we have it, deals only with such poetry as has plot, i.e., such as imitates a *system* of actions. These are maximal forms; there are, that is, no "larger" poetic forms or any which have more parts than these; smaller forms, such as the species of lyric, can be treated by carrying such systems back to their elements.

Four kinds of action or behavior can thus be distinguished, without regard to seriousness or comicality, etc.: (1) a single character acting in a single closed situation. By "closed situation" I mean here one in which the character's activity, however it may have been initiated or however it may be terminated, is *uncomplicated* by any other agency. Most of what we call lyric poetry belongs here: any poem in which the character commits some verbal act (threatening, persuading, beseeching) upon someone existing only as the object of his action (Marvell's "To His Coy Mistress"), or deliberates or muses (Keats's "Ode to a Nightingale"), or is moved by passion (Landor's "Mother, I Cannot Mind My Wheel"). (2) Two or more characters in a single closed situation. "Closed situation" here means "uncomplicated by any other agency than the characters originally present and remaining so throughout." This parallels the notion of "scene" in French classical drama; here belong all the *real* colloquies of persons acting upon and reacting to one another (e.g., Browning's "The Bishop Orders His Tomb"), although not the metaphorical colloquies, such as dialogues between Body and Soul, etc. (3) A collection of such "scenes" as I have just mentioned about some central incident, to constitute an "episode" (Arnold's *Sohrab and Rustum*). (4) A system of such episodes, constituting the grand plot of tragedy, comedy, and epic which is treated by Aristotle.

These are whole and complete "actions"; hence the first differs from a speech in a play, the second from a dramatic scene, the third from a fragment of a tragedy; nevertheless, it is clear that, *in a sense*, the combination of speeches produces a scene, that of scenes an episode, that of episodes a plot. These classifications must not be confused with species; they are not poetic species but lines of differentiation of the object of imitation which must be taken into account in defining species. Similar analysis of means and manner would extend Aristotle's system to include all poetic forms.

So much for Aristotle's general method and his apparatus for the definition of forms; I shall presently return to such questions again, in order to sketch a special poetics, but for the moment I wish to deal with three more problems of general poetics: those of unexpectedness, suspense, and representation, although we can do little more here than touch on general points.

All emotions are greater if produced from their contraries—for example, fear in one who has been confident—and the unexpected effects just this. Like suspense, it is common to all temporal arts, the parts as well as the wholes, for whatever involves temporal succession may involve anticipation, and wherever we have anticipation we may have the unexpected. Expectation is the active entertainment of the opinion that something is necessary or probable at a given time, place, in certain relations, etc. The audience must infer, and infer incorrectly; they have the premises, so to speak, for otherwise what happens would be improbable; but they cannot connect them to infer correctly, for otherwise what happens would be expected. Since they do not infer the probable, and do infer the improbable, two things must be noted: the causes of wrong inference and the causes of failure to infer rightly. Since the premises must be considered together for inference and since the audience will reason only from premises which they actively entertain and take to be true, failure to infer will be due to (1) forming no opinion or forming a contradictory one, so that one or both of the premises will not be used; (2) failure to collect the premises, although both are entertained; (3) failure to infer correctly, although both are entertained and collected. All these can be developed to show what the poet may possibly do: for instance, opinion can be prevented by the use of remote signs (i.e., such as involve many references), or many and apparently contradictory signs, ambiguity of words or acts; acceptance as true can be prevented by the use of unusual consequents, by contrariety to general belief, by dependence upon the words of an apparently untrustworthy character, or by contradiction of an apparently trustworthy one; and so on.

All these things lead to nonexpectation; but the truly unexpected comes about when the thing is not only not expected but contrary to expectation. This will happen if the poet provides premises which seem to prove the contrary. It is best when failure to infer the right thing and the faulty inference are brought about by the same premises. This is effected by the use of qualification. For example, if A happens, B usually follows, except in circumstance C, but if that circumstance happens, the opposite of B results; now if C is bound to happen, but people do not know that, they will expect B after A, whereas the opposite results. Surprise will vary in degree with expectation of the contrary; consequently, the audience will be most surprised when they are most convinced that B will happen. The less important, apparently, the reversing circumstance, the more surprise. Again, since the all-but-completed process makes its end most probable, expectation will be highest here; hence reversal just before the end will be most surprising. This underlies many "hair's-breadth escapes." Most surprising of all is the double unexpected, which occurs when from A comes the unexpected result B, which leads to the previously expected result C, which is now unexpected as the result of B. This is exemplified in Sophocles's *Oedipus*, where the inquiry into blood-guilt leads to the question of parentage, which seems at some remove; but the question of parentage resolves unexpectedly the question of blood-guilt.

Suspense is anxiety caused by extended anticipation—hence (1) by the uncertainty of what we wish to know and (2) by delay of what we wish to have happen, although we know it already. (Gossips are in the first state before they have been told the scandal, in the second until they impart it.) The first results whenever we want to know either the event or the circumstances of the event, whether in past, present, or future time; hence the poet must avoid the necessary, the impossible, or the completely probable, or that which is unimportant either way, for we are never in suspense about these; instead, he must choose the equally probable or else that which is probable with a chance of its not happening, and something which is of a markedly pleasant, painful, good, evil, or marvelous nature. Suspense of the second order is produced by unexpected frustration, by having the thing seem just about to happen, and then probably averting it. The anticipated thing must have importance exceeding the suspense; otherwise irritation and indifference result.

Representation—what parts of the action are told or shown, and how, and what is left to inference—is a question of manner of imitation. Obviously, poets sometimes exhibit more than the action (e.g., tragic poets exhibit events which are not part of the plot), sometimes less, leaving the rest to inference; sometimes follow the plot-order, sometimes convert it (e.g., using flashbacks); exhibit some things on a large and others on a small scale; and there are many other possibilities as well. It is impossible here to do more than suggest; in general, representation is determined by necessity and probability, emotional effect, and ornament, i.e., these are the main reasons for representing something. The poet must represent things which by their omission or their being left to inference would make the action improbable; hence, if an event is generally improbable but probable in a given circumstance, it must be represented in that circumstance (e.g., Antony's speech in *Julius Caesar*). Again, he must omit whatever would contradict the specific emotional effect (hence disgusting scenes, such as the cooking of Thyestes' children, are omitted, since disgust counteracts pity) or include what would augment the effect (hence scenes of lamentation and suffering in tragedy, since these make us poignantly aware of the anguish of the hero). Masques, pageants, progresses, etc., are ornaments. Representation, whether narrative or dramatic, always makes things more vivid, and the latter is more vivid than the former; and it affords the audience knowledge, whether directly or through inference by signs. In any poetic work the audience must at certain times know some things and not know others; generally the denouement discloses all, except in works which have wonder as their prime effect. Unless the audience knows somewhat, emotion is impossible, for emotion depends upon opinion; and unless it is ignorant of certain things, unexpectedness and some kinds of suspense are impossible. Hence in any work something is withheld until the end: either how the action began or continued or how it ends; the audience is ignorant of one or several of the following circumstances: agent, instrument, act, object, manner, purpose, result, time, place, concomitants. What must be concealed is the primary question; the next is the order in which things must be disclosed; and theory can make available to the poet a calculus of the frame of mind of the audience, of the nature of emotions, etc., to determine the order of representation which will produce the maximum emotional effect.

All these questions can be developed to afford a vast body of working suggestions for the poet and of criteria for the critic; I shall be happy if I have suggested, even faintly, the character of the problems and the method of their treatment.

IV

We have seen that in any special poetics—whether that of tragedy or epic or some kind of lyric or novel—reasoning proceeds from the distinctive whole which is the product of art to determine what parts must be assembled if such a whole, beautiful of its kind, is to result, and that such terms as "whole," "part," "beauty," etc., must be specified to the given art, because, for example, the beauty of a tragedy is not the same as the beauty of a lyric, any more than the distinctive beauty of a horse is the same as that of a man. Indeed, lyrics and tragedies even have some different parts; for instance, a lyric does not have plot, but plot is, in fact, the principal part of tragedy.

We may illustrate the nature of a special poetics a little further by outlining briefly that of the species to which Yeats's "Sailing to Byzantium" belongs.[4] It is a species which imitates a serious action of the first order mentioned above, i.e., one involving a single character in a closed situation, and the character is not simply in passion, nor is he acting upon another character, but has performed an act actualizing and instancing his moral character, that is, has made a moral choice. It is dramatic in manner—the character speaks in his own person; and the medium is words embellished by rhythm and rhyme. Its effect is something that, in the absence of a comprehensive analysis of the emotions, we can only call a kind of noble joy or exaltation.

There are four parts of this poetic composite: choice, character, thought, and diction. For choice is the activity, and thought and character are the causes of the activity, and diction is the means. The choice, or deliberative activity of choosing, is the principal part, for reasons analogous to those which make plot the principal part of tragedy. Next in importance comes character; next thought; and last, diction.[5]

4. For a detailed "grammatical" analysis see pp. 5ff.

5. Nowadays when the nature of poetry has become so uncertain that everyone is trying to define it, definitions usually begin: "Poetry is words which, or language which, or discourse which," and so forth. As a matter of fact, it is nothing of the kind. Just as we should not define a chair as wood which has such and such characteristics—for a chair is not a kind of wood but a kind of furniture—so we ought not to define poetry as a kind of language. The chair is not wood but wooden; poetry is not words but verbal. In one sense, of course, the words are of the utmost importance; if they are not the right words or if we do not grasp them, we do not grasp the poem. In another sense, they are the least important element in the poem, for they do not determine the character of anything else in the poem; on the contrary, they are determined by everything else. They are the only things we see or hear; yet they are governed by imperceptible things which are inferred from them. And when we are moved by poetry, we are not moved by the words, except in so far as sound and rhythm move us; we are moved by the things that the words stand for.

A gifted British poet, G. S. Fraser, has objected to these remarks on diction ("Some Notes on Poetic Diction," *Penguin New Writing*, no. 37 [1949], pp. 116 ff.): "I think, on the contrary, that criticism should pay a very close attention to diction. I agree with Mr. Allen Tate: 'For, in the long run, whatever the poet's philosophy may be, however wide may be the extension of his meaning . . . by his language shall you know him.' And I do not find that Mr. Olson's sturdy-looking piece of reasoning stands up very well to my regretful probing. In what sense is it true that we are simply 'moved by the things that the words stand for,' and not by the words themselves? Certainly not in any sense in which other words would do as well: in which the fullest paraphrase, or the most intelligent exposition, would be a substitute for the original poem. And certainly not in any sense in which the situation that the poem refers to, if we were capable of imagining that *without* words—if, for instance, we could draw a picture of it—would be a substitute for the original poem, either. Not, that is, in any sense, in which 'the things the words stand for' means merely the kind of physical object, abstract concept, or emotional state at which the words point. The pointing is the least of it."

The "activity" of the character is thought or deliberation producing choice determined by rational principles; it is thus, as I once remarked, a kind of argument or arguing. But there is a difference between logical proof and such poetic argument as we have here; in logical proof the conclusion is determined by the premises; here it is, of course, mediated by the character of the man arguing, just as argument in a novel or a play is not supposed to be consistent with the premises but with the character. The limits of the activity are the limits of the deliberation; the parts of the activity are the phases of that deliberation, and they are conjoined by necessity and probability.

This species of poem, then, if it is to be beautiful, must have a certain definite magnitude as determined by the specific whole and its parts; and the proper magnitude will be the fullest extension possible, not exceeding the limits mentioned above, and accomplished by phases connected necessarily or probably. This is, it will be noted, different from the magnitude proper to comedy or tragedy, and even different from the magnitude proper to a speech exhibiting choice in any of these; for example, tragedy does not aim at making its constituent speeches or actions as full and perfectly rounded as possible absolutely, but only qualifiedly, in so far as that is compatible with the plot. Hence in properly made drama there are few if any "complete" speeches, let alone speeches developed to what would be their best proportions

---

I willingly concede what I have never debated: that diction is very important to poetry; that, as Tate suggests, distinction of language is an important index of poetic power (although I cannot agree that it is the sole index or even the prime index); that criticism ought to pay the utmost attention to diction; that, as T. S. Eliot has said, the poet is likely to be extraordinarily interested in, and skilful with, language; that we are not "moved by the things that the words stand for" in any sense that would allow us to dispense with the particular words by which the "things" are constituted for us; and all similar propositions. The point is not whether diction is important, but whether it is more or less important than certain other elements *in* the poem. In one respect, I repeat, it is the most important; the reader, if he does not grasp the words, cannot grasp anything further, and the poet, if he cannot find the appropriate words and arrange them properly, has not written a poem. In another respect, however, the words are the least important, in that they are governed and determined by every other element in the poem. There is agreement on all hands that words "function" in poetry; there should be no difficulty therefore, no matter how we conceive of the structure of poetry, in seeing that words must be subordinate to their functions, for they are selected and arranged with a view to these. Mr. Fraser himself has no difficulty with this fact, although he is disturbed by my statement of the fact; for he goes on to discuss (pp. 123 ff.) "a wide-scale current use of poetic diction in a really vicious sense to disguise a failure of choice, a confusion of character, or a lack of clear thought"; and he also remarks (p. 126) that "one cannot ask people to express themselves as confusingly as possible, in the hope that their confusions will prove to have a clear underlying structure; for, as Mr. Schwartz truly says, 'if this were the only kind of poetry ... most poetry would not be worth reading.' "

independently of the whole; this is true even in declamatory drama, where the speeches are of more importance than in the better kinds.

The activity, however, is not merely to be complete and whole, with its parts probably interrelated; it must effect certain serious emotions in us by exhibiting the happiness or misery of certain characters whom we take seriously. Hence the character must be better than we, but not so completely noble as to be beyond all suffering; for such people are godlike and can awaken only our admiration, for they are in a sense removed from such misfortunes as can excite dolorous emotions. Moreover, the choice imitated cannot be any choice, even of a moral order, but one which makes all the difference between happiness and misery; and, since it is choice, it must be accomplished with full knowledge and in accordance with rational principle, or as the man of rational prudence would determine it. Again, it must be choice not contingent upon the actions or natures of others, but as determined by the agent. And there must be no mistake (*hamartia*) here, as in tragedy; for, since this is a single incident, *hamartia* is not requisite to make future consequences probable.

We could proceed indefinitely here, as on all of these points; my intention, I repeat, is the merest illustration.

V

Thus far we have proceeded on the supposition that the imitative poetic arts have as their ends certain pleasures, produced through their play upon our emotions. Certainly, these are ends of art and such as any consideration of art must embrace; but to suppose that art has no further effect and that it may have no further ends relative to these is vastly to underestimate the powers of art. It exercises, for example, a compelling influence upon human action—individual, social, or political—for among the causes of the misdirection of human action are the failure to conceive vividly and the failure to conceive apart from self-interest; and these are failures which art above all other things is potent to avert, since it vivifies, and since in art we must view man on his merits and not in relation to our private interests. It is not that art teaches by precept, as older generations thought, nor that it moves to action; but clearly it inculcates moral attitudes; it determines our feelings toward characters of a certain kind for no other reason than that they are such characters. The ethical function of art, therefore, is never in opposition to the purely artistic end; on the contrary, it is best achieved when the artistic end has been best accomplished, for it is only a further consequence of the powers of art. The same thing is true of any political or social ends of art, provided that the state be a good state or the society a moral society. To reflect on these things is to realize the importance and value of art, which, excellent in itself, becomes ever more excellent as we view it in ever more general relations.

Yet these relations can scarcely be recognized unless we first recognize the distinctive powers of each form of poetic art; these relations are possible, indeed, because art has, first of all, certain powers. And it is to these powers, in all their variety and force, that the poetic method of Artistotle is directed. Indeed, the most distinctive characteristic of Aristotle as critic seems to be that he founds his poetic science upon the emotional effects peculiar to the various species of art and reasons thence to the works which must be constructed to achieve them.

5

METACRITICISM

ART AND SCIENCE

The sciences are, of course, knowledge; the theory of the arts—aesthetics, criticism, call it what you will—claims to be knowledge also. Since the claim is made, or more often, assumed, some sort of comparison is invited. Few who trouble to make the comparison would doubt that the sciences are in a far superior condition. In the sciences, theory and practice have gone hand in hand, with miraculous results. Scientific discussion is so clear and so uniform that failure to understand it can only be due to lack of intelligence or training. Agreement on method is such that, in any subject, method is spoken of in the singular rather than in the plural, and such that researchers in very distantly related fields may still engage in the most complex cooperation. When dissension arises among scientists, it is about matters frankly admitted to be hypothetical or speculative. In science it is common for many researchers to arrive independently at the same conclusion. Even the predictions of science, while not always accurate, are held always to be worthy of serious consideration, grounded as they are upon what is universally recognized as relevant and probable.

In science the known and the unknown, the certain and the conjectural, are sharply distinct. Agreement upon what constitutes scientific knowledge, both in general and in particular, sets out a clear course of study and makes easy the evaluation of projects and researchers. The qualifications of a scientist in a given field are so plain, and so plainly manifest, that there can be no question as to who is qualified, and little question as to the degree of his eminence in his field.

Artistic or critical theory is practically in a contrary condition. Theory and labor have hardly gone hand in hand. Most artists would feel that theory has been too abstruse or too tenuous to be of much help to them. The mistaken judgments of critics are often attributed to their

theories; their correct ones seldom are. Theories are at such variance
that the artist or critic who trusted all would end in hopeless confusion.
The terminology of artistic theory is neither clear nor uniform; it has
not only generated much purely verbal dispute, but has also led to the
questioning of propositions that, in a happier state of the subject,
would have been recognized as unquestionably true. No point of
doctrine, however chief and principal, is as yet beyond dispute; there is
no agreement on method, perhaps none even on the possibility of
method. No clear course of study can be laid out; such integrations of
endeavor as are common in science are impossible here; and it is
impossible also to obtain agreement upon the qualifications of the
critic, the signs which manifest these qualifications, the value of a
given critical project, or the degree of eminence—except in very
general terms—of a given critic.

Science seems to be a matter of the things studied rather than of the
man studying; constant addition and progress are possible, and at
death the scientist, even the ordinary one, leaves his knowledge behind
him, solid as coral, for others to build upon; his unsolved problems can
be safely left to his heirs for solution. Artistic theory seems to be so
much a matter of the man studying rather than of the things studied
that each particular theory, if it does not die with its author, seems to
have a history only of perversion and corruption. How even an
eminent critic would have extended or completed his theory, what
might have been his answers to questions or objections, remain matter
for conjecture only. We find much change, but little progress. In short,
whereas the theories of the sciences display all the marks of knowledge,
those of the arts seem nothing more than witnesses of changing opinion
and taste.

It is thus necessary for me, speaking twenty-odd centuries after Plato
and Aristotle, to pose once more the question of whether the arts are
subjects of knowledge: whether, that is, we may have more than
historical information about artists, techniques, theories, and products
or art. I say "once more," for the question is very old. Plato, you may
remember, raised it in the *Ion* and elsewhere, and decided, incidentally, in the negative. Aristotle, on the other hand, thought that the arts
were subjects of scientific inquiry, and found a place for them in his system as the productive or poetic sciences: his *Poetics* remains, like the
Acropolis, a ruin which testifies to what had been built. Many other
philosophers also included theories of art in their philosophies—Bacon,
Hume, Kant, Hegel, Comte, Croce, Collingwood, Santayana, to
mention a few—and French nineteenth-century critics like Taine and
Brunetière thought that art might be brought to a scientific study.
Indeed, a precursor of mine at the University of Chicago—the late
Professor R. G. Moulton—sought to establish the scientific study of
literature on inductive principles.

It might seem that a question so ancient, so far from settled after so many men of genius sought to answer it, ought either to be dismissed as insoluble or answered in the negative. A chimera of human thought, perhaps, like the quadrature of the circle? Perhaps, but after many centuries it was demonstrated that the circle could not be squared; we have, at least, no such demonstration that there may be no scientific knowledge of art. In fact, it would be very odd if such knowledge turned out to be impossible. Why should we be able to examine and explain the things of nature—the most vast, the most minute, the most ancient, the most recent—and not the things of art, which we can always perceive as wholes, and which have a history shorter than the history of man? The things of nature are innumerable; they are vastly more complex, composed of many more parts in many more relations, these parts composed of yet others; they are possessed of many more properties and functions; they are composed of matter which is mysterious to us and which must also be investigated; their forms and qualities, when we grasp them, are greatly different from the forms and qualities with which sensation presents us (remember Sir Arthur Eddington and his two tables—one his worktable as he was familiar with it, the other the same table as the science of physics saw it); moreover, to finish my list, the things of nature are produced by causes extremely obscure and abstract, for purposes equally so. In comparison, the things of art are very few; the smallest frog pond produces more in days than all our artists have produced in all the centuries. The things of art are produced from materials familiar to us; indeed, it is our familiarity with their properties that induces us to use them. The things of art all have forms perceptible to sense. Man is himself the maker of them, the devices and techniques of their production are all his own discoveries, the purpose behind them is his own, the forms themselves are his own perceptions and conceptions.

How is it, then, that in a field apparently so open to inquiry, so little—if anything—is known? Take poetry, for instance; nobody seems to know what it is. Our century has spawned innumerable new definitions of poetry; and you may be sure that when everybody offers a definition of something—especially when each definition is different— there is general ignorance as to what it is. (There is also the interesting fact that unless you know in some sense what a thing is, you are very far from scientific knowledge of it.) In music, there is no theory which can explain, plainly and demonstrably, what the effects of the *Eroica* Symphony are, or why it should be in one key rather than another, or why the movements must be in a certain order, or why the Funeral March from the A Flat Sonata, suitably transposed and scored, might not have been used instead of the one we have, or how all the parts make up a whole. The theory of painting or of sculpture is in no better shape. In all the arts we know what we see or hear, we know what we like or dislike, what we call good or bad, major or minor; but we are—under questioning, at least—at a loss to classify the works by kind, or to defend the criteria by which we judge them. It is a curious thing that in the so-called mechanical arts or crafts (car making, rocket manufacture, whatever) the importance of knowledge has always been clear, and it has always been clear what was knowledge and what was not; in the fine arts it is different. It is a curious thing that if you make a chair, a great many people can tell you whether it was well made or not, whereas if you propose the same chair to critics as a beautiful object, the dogs of war are at once let loose.

How is this? There are several reasons for this. First, whereas in the sciences men have tended to remain within a given method and develop it as far as possible, in critical theory—particularly in modern times—men have tended to multiply approaches, and when they have attempted to develop a given approach, uncertainties as to method have thrown them off. You have an instance of this in the innumerable attempts of critics, in the Renaissance and later, to follow in the path of Aristotle—attempts which led to misunderstandings and confusions so extraordinary that even among the best theorists today most have an utterly distorted notion of what Aristotle held. Suppose the *Poetics* of Aristotle had been influential in antiquity, as it was not, and known throughout the Middle Ages, as it was not, and suppose that it had been extended and developed by men perfectly aware of the workings of his method, as it was not; we should now have a substantial body of knowledge of the poetic arts. Of a single order only, of course; but we should have had something like the vertical progress in science when men build upon the work of those who went before them; whereas artistic theory instead multiplied approaches, as I have said, so that its progress has been horizontal rather than vertical.

p. 333

Second, the arts, as bodies of knowledge, are in a peculiar situation. Perhaps I can put it this way: if you adopt Aristotle's division of sciences into the theoretical (metaphysics, mathematics, natural science) the practical (ethics and politics), and the productive sciences or arts, then the practical sciences are dependent upon the theoretical, while the productive sciences are dependent upon both the theoretical and the practical sciences. For example, in the poetics of tragedy, you have to deal with concepts such as those of whole, part, unity, completeness, magnitude, beauty, order, seriousness, simplicitly, complexity. But these are by no means concepts specific to tragedy; the poetics of tragedy merely specifies them to tragedy; as concepts they are derived from some other science. It is not within the province of the poetics of tragedy to state what unity or completeness or wholeness is; these are questions of metaphysics; the poetics of tragedy can (and must) state what these are in tragedy, that is, when a tragedy is one or whole or complete. The poetics of tragedy derives, in this fashion, from several precedent sciences. Now this dependency of poetics on other sciences, while it varies in kind and degree in the various systems, is something unavoidable; perhaps it is at its minimum in systems such as those of Schelling and Coleridge, in which the human act of creation is similar to the divine act of Creation, but even then poetics is dependent upon theology at the very least. Because of this dependency, poetics must always be founded on more principles, and on principles more remote from first principles, and hence less certain, than the sciences upon which it is dependent; consequently it must also be less exact than they. Moreover, poetics must be affected by the condition of the sciences on which it depends; where these fail in demonstration, or leave gaps, or develop in directions not relevant to poetics, the foundations of poetics can hardly be scientific.

The necessary dependency of which I speak has had other consequences. Aware of the inexactness of their subject matter, theorists of art have often sought to model their methods on more exact or more prestigious sciences, or confused the treatments of art which these afford with treatments of art proper, or adopted the same criteria for knowledge in art as those in more exact sciences. Whenever this happens, the theory of art suffers a check, for the theorists labor, not in their own field, but unwittingly in the fields of their admiration, usually with insufficient training and knowledge, and thus usually to no great effect. For example, when literary study—not too long ago— modelled upon history, students of literature became literary historians, usually rather bad ones; when there were startling developments in psychology and psychoanalysis, critics became psychologists and psychoanalysts; and so on. In a word, artistic theory is supposed to become exact when it apes something more exact; it becomes scientific, supposedly, by aping other sciences. Underlying such suppositions are two other suppositions: first, that the theories of the past contradict, indeed virtually cancel, one another, or that if they do not, they are at any rate obsolete and have no value for works of later date; second, that there is some single set of doctrines which constitutes the totality of truth, that there is one single method capable of producing these, and that all other methods and doctrines are to be valued, to the degree in which they approach this ideal.

Do the various theories of art in fact contradict one another? They do so indeed, if one restricts his views to words only, the critical vocabulary, without examining the meanings and functions of the words in their particular contexts. Thirty years ago Professor Richard McKeon published an essay in which he traced the diversity of meanings of the term *imitation* (Greek, *mimesis*, Latin, *imitatio*) in antiquity, and showed how the meanings varied from philosopher to philosopher, from critic to critic. The term has indeed been used diversely since antiquity; and so, too, has every other important critical term. Things are infinite, words are finite, as Aristotle remarked in the *De Sophisticis Elenchis;* consequently words must be ambiguous, for one word must stand for many things. In philosophic discourse a word has, first of all, one of its conventional or dictionary meanings, always general; this is modified or specified further by the context in which it appears; and this, in turn, is modified or specified by its function within that context. For example, if you are reading Aristotle's *Poetics* and do not know what the word *mimesis* means, you look it up and find that it means imitation. You are highly pleased, and proceed; but you do not yet know the meaning of the term, for you do not yet know what aspects of imitation are under consideration. When you know these, you still do not know the meaning of the term; indeed, you will not know it until you know the general system of ideas in which the term is placed and its place in that system; for example, you will hardly understand it unless you know of Aristotle's categories and the many implications of these, of his theory of causes, of his distinctions between nature and art, and so on, and unless you realize that imitation is the key term to his poetics, the one on which everything depends. Hamilton Fyfe remarked that the term mimesis in Aristotle requires a treatise for explanation. Precisely; that is why you cannot find its meaning in a lexicon.

It is a verifiable fact—I wish I could say an easily verifiable fact, but it is not, for it requires a great deal of work to verify it—that while philosophers use relatively similar terminology, because of the nature of language, they use terms quite differently, because of the nature of their thought; and this of course applies to those who theorize about art. To have precisely the same meaning, terms must have the same general meaning as specified further by the same aspect under consideration—for example, if I say "furniture" you understand me only generally until you see what I predicate of it, or what classes I divide it into; and the terms must have the same position in the same system. Consider this, and you will see that the possibility that philosophers are using their terms with the same meaning is relatively small.

And so we come to the question of contradiction. If I say "X is Y" and you say "X is not Y," and if by X I mean *paper* and by Y *cheap*, whereas by X you mean *cows* and by Y *graceful*, you have scarcely contradicted me. Contradiction can occur only when precisely the same predicate has been affirmed and denied of the same subject—that is, both subjects must have the same meaning, and so must both predicates. This is just what we saw as very unlikely a moment ago. Once we realize this, the apparent contradictions—and, for that matter, the apparent agreements—disappear. They are replaced by a vast variety of quite different statements, verbally similar, but verbally only, meaning and implying quite different things. And the discourses which these statements constitute do not represent one continuous discussion, by any means. If, in Robert Maynard Hutchins's phrase, they make up the "Great Conversation," that Conversation is what St. Augustine thought all conversation is—a series of crossed monologues; discourses dealing with different subject-matters, using different principles by different methods to produce different conclusions.

But—to come to the second supposition—surely among these there is, or else there is still to be discovered, a set of statements conveying the whole truth, and one single method which is the right method. First of all, the very possibility of language depends on the fact that sounds or their written symbols may be given meaning. Once they have been given meaning, they become words. The giving of meaning is always determinate—that is, the word means *this* and does not not mean *that*. From this it follows that all language is selective; it selects from the innumerable things and their attributes that which it stands for, that which it means. For example, if I say "chair," I signify a set of objects from whose attributes I select only those which make them chairs. These objects are many things besides chairs, and they have a host of attributes which have nothing to do with their being chairs, and they are this or that kind of chair, of this or that material, and they have a host of individual attributes—they are each in a certain place, each is someone's property, and so on; but when I say "chair" I ignore all this and select certain attributes only. And if the word could stand not only for these, but for all the other attributes of chairs as well, it could no longer signify them as chairs. I find this to be true of any word I can think of; no word will stand for the totality of things in the totality of their attributes; even such words as "all," "totality," "everything" will not, for they signify things collectively but not individually, or for things distributively but not collectively, whenever they are used in any single sense. Signification is therefore necessarily finite, whereas the universe consists of infinitely numerous things with infinitely numerous attributes. We can have no word for what has not been in some way differentiated; to differentiate is to select.

Language is also restrictive—that is, once a term has been given a particular meaning, we can speak of no more than the term permits, so long as that particular meaning obtains. This is to say that our use of terms restricts us to the discussion of the things or characteristics selected by those terms. Let a circle be whatever it is in reality, it is for the geometer only what he has defined it as being. The universe itself, whatever it may be in fact, becomes for my discussion only what I say it is, and contracts itself to the limits of my discourse.

Consider what this means. Any philosopher, though he profess to talk about the universe, must in fact confine himself to the universe of his discourse. Any philosophic problem must be relative to its formulation; and since any solution to a problem is relative to the problem, the solution must also be relative to that formulation. But that formulation, as we have seen, must be finite. It follows that there can be no single philosophic system embracing all truth; and by the same token, no method which is the only right method.

There must, therefore, be a plurality of valid systems and methods. How many? This seems a staggering question until we reflect that the arts, considered as bodies of knowledge, are a part of philosophy and hence are subject to whatever variations may be found in philosophy generally. That is, there are as many possible systems of theory of art as there are of philosophy generally. Induction supports this view, for every philosopher who comprehends a philosophy of art in his system develops his own distinctive philosophy of art. Compare Plato, Aristotle, Hume, Kant, and Hegel, for example, and you will see at once what I mean. But then, if there are as many possible systems of artistic theory as there are of philosophy generally, how many kinds of philosophic systems are there? This seems an even more staggering question; but I believe that we can answer it as well, at least in very broad outline. We can answer it if we can discover on what philosophic variation depends.

It is a function of only two things: first, the fundamental dialectic of the system; second, the subject-matter on which the dialectic is exerted. Any philosophy which contains discursive reasoning—that is, which involves inference—has a fundamental dialectic. By dialectic I mean the system which permits inference, and by inference I mean the derivation of propositions from other propositions or concepts from concepts by any consequential principle whatsoever. Thus division into classes is inference based upon the principle of division; combination of classes into one is inference based upon the principle of combination; similarly, any resolution of propositions into component propositions or any synthesis of propositions into a compound proposition, or any syllogism in any sense of the term "syllogism," is inference.

All inference involves three conditions. I can best illustrate these by considering an inference verbally expressed. In such inference, first, the terms used must be significant and retain their significance unchanged; second, it must be possible to combine them into significant structures for assertion and denial; third, there must be some principle of validation. Take for example the syllogism *All men are mortal, Socrates is a man, therefore Socrates is mortal.* The inference would be impossible if the terms were not significant and did not retain that significance unchanged; if the terms were combined in a way that admitted neither assertion nor denial; and if there were no principle by which the assertion of the premises entailed the assertion also of the conclusion. This last I have just called the principle of validation; it is the principle (which, incidentally, may vary from system to system) by which the assertion or denial of one thing necessitates the assertion or denial of another. Thus, if you told me that you liked the three statements of my syllogism very much and thought that they were true, but refused to believe that the third followed from the first two, you would be challenging my principle of validation.

Now the principle of validation in any system is a function of the first condition I mentioned, that is, of the significance of terms. We can see this easily enough from the following. Suppose I responded to your objection by pointing out that my argument was in the mode called Barbara; if you now challenged the validity of the mode, I should point out that the syllogism had a universal major premise and an affirmative minor, and so followed the rules of the first figure; if you challenged these, I should appeal to the general rule of all syllogism, the so-called *dictum de omni et nullo*; if you challenged this, I should have to fall back upon the principle of contradiction and the consequences of using terms in a given significance; if you were still recalcitrant here, I should have reached my limit, I could argue no further. Clearly, then, the principle of validation depends upon the employment of terms.

I have said that the principle of validation may vary; in the same fashion the concept of truth may vary from system to system. For Plato a term may be true; for Aristotle, truth is predicable only of propositions; for Anselm there are several kinds of truth, for example, truth of discourse, truth of opinion, truth of essence, truth of action; for Aquinas, truth is the adequation of thought and thing; for Hume, a correspondence of idea with impression.

What I have been trying to put before you is that validity of argument and truth are not absolutes, but variables which alter with different systems. There is not one truth and there is not one logic; this last point you can verify by noting that every philosopher who treats the subject constructs his own logic—compare Aristotle, Hobbes, and Hume, for instance. There are dialectics based wholly upon likeness, others based wholly on difference, some on both; some on qualified, others on unqualified likeness and difference. There is indeed a bewildering variety, and you may well be bewildered. But is it so very strange, after all?--you have the same thing, to a lesser degree, in the sciences; in geometry, for instance. Are the internal angles of a triangle equal to one hundred and eighty degrees? For Euclid, yes; for Lobachevsky, no, they are less; for Riemann, no, they are more. Is there a contradiction here? By no means; all are correct; the differences are due to different conceptions of space.

And in the same fashion—to leave dialectic and proceed to the

second point, the subject matter on which the dialectic is exerted—
there are many possible conceptions of art. Let me for simplicity's sake
mention only some of those that occur frequently or importantly in the
history of discussion. Art may be conceived either as an object, thing or
product; or as an activity of the artist, or a passivity of the artist, or as
certain faculties or a certain character of the artist; or as a certain
activity or passivity of the audience, or certain faculties or a certain
character of the audience; or as an instrument to some end; or as a
sign, either of the character or activity or passivity of the artist or the
audience or of the nature of something else involved in art. These, I
must warn you, are only very general heads; each of them may be
specified much further, and, of course, they generate different species
of artistic theory.

We may illustrate them by considering the different senses in which
the term "poem" appears in discussions of poetry. The most common
sense is that of the product of art, a certain form imposed upon words,
whatever the theorist takes that to be. But, other critics argue, the
product is only one aspect, perhaps an unimportant aspect, of the
poetic art; the issue of real importance is the human instrumentality
which produces; and some argue that this is the actualization of certain
powers, others that it is the possession of the powers themselves; and
this is a matter of whether you conceive of the artist as an active
craftsman or as a medium of inspiration. For both, the true poem is the
poetic behavior of the poet; the poem is thus merely a sign or witness
that the man is a poet. Others, again, argue that the poem only exists
in the audience; and the audience can either be seen as a collaborator
in the poem—"audience-participation," which is the view of the audience as active, or "art as experience," in which the audience is passive.
Finally, the poem may be considered as an instrument to some end; for
example, of mental therapy or moral or political reform.

These look like "conflicting views"; hence they have invariably been
treated as such in the history of criticism. If the term "conflicting"
means merely "different," we need not quarrel; surely these views are
different. But if it means "contradictory," nothing could be more
absurd. For it is clear that all these statements have different subjects,
and, as we saw, it is impossible to have contradiction except with
reference to the same subject; again, where contradiction really exists,
one view must be false if the other is true, whereas all of these views are
perfectly true; all of them are founded upon perfectly obvious and
undeniable aspects of art. I am not arguing that no critic ever contradicts another, for that would be equivalent to proclaiming human
infallibility; but I shall say that the men of the past were no more fools
than we are, and that where such contradiction in fact exists, one or
the other is in error; and his error is not the consequence of his view,
but strictly *his* error.

Indeed, nothing prevents any given philosopher from investigating all of these aspects: Plato and Aristotle, for instance, did just that. The apparent conflict of views is really only a difference in the imposition of names; a difference of what we saw earlier as the poverty of language as opposed to the richness of ideas. As I have suggested, however, such differences do not stop here, for specific differences turn up within these general heads. For example, although two men are speaking of the poetic activity, that activity also has many aspects, and consequently there may be "conflict" upon the questions of whether the poetic activity "is" this aspect or not. This in turn leads to other "conflicts"; for instance, since the poetic activity involves some reasoning, anyone who fixes upon its rational aspect is bound to find the poetic character to consist in the possession of certain rational faculties, whereas, since the poetic activity also comprises nonrational elements such as passion and imagination, one who fixes upon these is bound to find the poetic character to consist of non-rational faculties.

Even if two theorists have fixed upon the same aspect, they may still differ in what may be called their causal analysis. I find this difficult of statement; but let me use Aristotle's scheme of four causes—formal, material, efficient, and final—as illustration here, since it offers certain advantages. Suppose, then, two theorists have fixed upon the poetic activity, they may still differ in that one fixes upon the material cause, the other the formal cause of that activity. In a sense this is merely further differentiation of the aspect, of course; but the distinction cross-cuts the other line of differentiation. And since the meaning of the term *art* shifts from product to productive faculty and so on through the other senses I have mentioned, the concepts of the form, matter, end, and productive cause—the causal concepts—shift accordingly. If art is viewed as a product, that is, a work of art, its matter or medium is tone and rhythm, color and line, words and rhythm, and so on; its form is taken from some form of the things, whatever they may be, that we call the subjects of art; in short, all causes are determined by the aspect of art as product. If art is viewed as some passivity induced in the audience—the artistic experience in the passive sense— the matter or medium becomes situate in the audience, as certain propensities to conception or passion, and its form is the actualization of these in the experience. The product or work of art now appears as the stimulus or productive cause of that experience. If art is viewed as an activity of the audience, the form of art now appears as an activity of the audience, and the work now appears as powers realized in the audience (material cause) or as a stimulus (efficient cause). A similar shift follows whatever other aspects of art may be selected in a given critical dialectic. These are not conflicts any more than the supposed conflicts mentioned earlier; there are simply consequences of the diverse orientations of diverse systems of theory.

After all this argument, it should be quite evident that if the sciences

have produced an enormous number of consequences from relatively
few approaches—this is what I called vertical progress—artistic theory
has progressed horizontally, producing an enormous number of approaches with relatively few consequences—as, perhaps, has philosophy. Quite possibly both should change directions, as in fact they have
done before; for the relation of the sciences to humanistic studies in the
seventeenth century, for instance, is not unlike that of the humanistic
studies to the sciences in the twentieth century.

It should be evident, too, that the artistic theories of the past are by
no means to be dismissed as obsolete, irrelevant, or contradictory. Very
unfortunately, critics and theorists of this century, more than of any
other, have tended to slight the past, to have only the most superficial
acquaintance with it, to pick over half-heartedly a minute part of it in
search of an occasional jewel, or to neglect it wholly. This is done of
course from ignorance, but the ignorance proceeds from folly. If the
past contained nothing but errors, we could learn from its errors; if it
contained nothing but unsolved problems, we could learn what the
problems were. (You will remember that Darwin said it was harder to
see what the problems were than to solve them; and by the way he was
echoing Aristotle who said that the right putting of the problem was
half the answer.) A foolish contempt of the past has led theorists to
start *de novo*, as if nothing had been done before, and since many of
them were literary men without philosophic or scientific training, they
produced a mass of inept definitions, preposterous proofs, and ridiculous hypotheses. This contempt sprang partly from the desire to keep
up with the sciences, partly from the conviction that the older theories
could have little relevance to the newer kinds of art.

Yet the past is the foundation of the future, and indeed, as I have
been trying to suggest, a great part of that foundation has been very
soundly laid; we have only to examine it carefully and probe it thoroughly, to see how soundly. It contains all of the major and basic
approaches; in fact, you may find many a modern theorist working on
a problem— a supposedly new problem—which was solved long ago,
by someone whose works he should have read, or read carefully. No
doubt it is possible to surpass Roman rhetorical theory, for example,
but there is a greater likelihood of doing this if you have some acquaintance with it.

If there is to be scientific knowledge of art, then, what is necessary
first of all is to understand the past, to read its theoretical literature in
its own terms, not in ours; and this involves such analysis of method,
only much more precise and thorough, as I mentioned earlier. To do so
is, among other things, to avoid much foolish contention. For example,
Aristotle's statement that plot is more important than character has
been the target of constant attack by persons who ignored his proofs of
this point (indeed, I have never seen these proofs given any attention)

and who never troubled to observe that he used these terms in senses quite different from the modern ones. Yet, if it is necessary to understand the past, it is also necessary not to be misled by it, for mistakes have been made—and unfortunately, the mistakes have probably been much more influential than what was sound.

Once the true has been separated from the false, it is, of course, necessary to build upon it. Let me take the *Poetics* of Aristotle once more as an example. This contains principles upon which it is possible to build a theory commensurate with every development in mimetic literature—fiction, drama, and poetry—since Aristotle's day; perhaps a theory of all the arts could be built from it; but few theorists have attempted to do so. It suggests a host of problems. What would his theory of comedy have been? How would he have dealt with subsequent developments in tragedy and epic? What would have been his treatment of forms which have emerged since his time? Some may maintain that Aristotle himself is the only one who could answer such questions; they may well be right; but to take that view is to presume that Aristotle had, not a method, but a mere knack for doing something nobody else could—for a scientific method can be used by others; it is also to turn what might have been a valuable scientific program into an archaeological object. But I am not merely suggesting an extension of Aristotle; I am suggesting the development of every valid approach.

If there is to be what I have called vertical progress in the science of art, there are certain internal and external conditions that will have to be fulfilled; I mean that things will have to be done both within and without the disciplines concerned with art. Internally, certain disciplines will have to be developed and improved. The greatest weaknesses of theorists and critics in the present day is an inability to discover a problem and formulate it precisely, to examine it on all sides, and to solve it on sound evidence. This is due to lack of philosophic training, particularly training in logic; and it is as serious a deficiency in a humanist as would be a lack of training in a scientist. Particularly, when men have been properly trained, such disciplines as hermeneutics must be developed. Hermeneutics is the discipline of interpreting and proving the interpretation of literary works as literary works; and development of it will enable us to separate sound from unsound interpretations. For example, there is a clutter of absurd interpretations of Hamlet, which most scholars recognize as absurd but are unable to refute; indeed, in most areas of literary study it is impossible to establish a small point about a poem or novel without first clearing away all the rubbish that has accumulated about it. A sense of evidence is of course required in areas other than interpretation; if scholars are to have it, there must be very serious revisions in all graduate curricula.

Externally, the sciences must come to the assistance of the arts. You will remember that I spoke of the dependency of poetic sciences on other branches of learning; very unfortunately, some of these have developed in directions utterly useless to art, while failing to supply things that are necessary. I have psychology particularly in mind. I do not at all mean, let me say, that I want more Freud on Da Vinci and Dostoevsky, more Ernest Jones on Hamlet, more Jung on archetypes; I do not want any more Dr. Edmund Bergler on the artistic temperament as a neurosis brought about by weaning. But all of the arts operate on man, affect man, and it is crucial to have, for instance, a theory of the emotions which complexly sets out the various families of emotion in all their degrees with all their causes. Modern psychology seems to have reduced them to as few as possible—so that I myself have had to go back to the earlier systems which discriminated among them. Barbey D'Aurévilly is said to have had a palette with every kind of pigment beside him as he wrote; he had keyed these to symbolize the various emotions and shades of emotion, and he would make a small dot of color before he wrote each line, to remind himself of the emotional effect he was trying to get. I admire that man; and psychologists would do well, in my view to take a hint from him.

Suppose the arts are brought into a scientific condition—what then? I do not care to make any great promises or to put forth any great prospectuses; our age is already littered with broken promises and unfulfilled prospectuses. I certainly do not think that everyone will become an artist or a critic as a consequence. I am not at all certain that art itself will improve—some great artists seem to have done very well on very poor theories—but criticism might improve; a consummation devoutly to be wished. No, I think the utmost I can claim is that we shall have more knowledge, and since the things of art are made by man, and about man, and for man, we shall know something more about man. And I think that is important. I once wrote a poem in which I revised the legend of Oedipus and the Sphinx. When the Sphinx posed her famous riddle, the Oedipus of my poem answered "Man." But instead of giving up at that point, my Sphinx responded that man was the answer to all questions, but that the answer was meaningless unless Oedipus knew what man was. Alas, he did not know; and so the Sphinx continued to ravage the world, and has done so ever since, and will continue to do so until her second and more difficult riddle has been solved.

ON VALUE JUDGMENTS
IN THE ARTS

T he history of criticism, like the history of philosophy, contains certain persistent problems—problems which emerge again and again, in one dialectical context or another, transformed by fresh formulation and resolved in terms of that formulation, only to resurface upon objection to the solution and perhaps to the formulation as well. "Here is the problem, solved at last." Is it? It presently appears that the question was incorrectly asked, incorrectly prosecuted, and incorrectly answered. The problem itself, thus, seems some vague and elusive entity remaining beyond all discussion, sometimes approached but never touched, mocking the efforts of the best minds to capture and subdue it. The problems of value judgment in the arts are among these persistent problems.

The layman is usually surprised to find that the questions which have apparently baffled philosophers are the very ones which he supposes the simplest to ask and easiest to answer. What could be simpler and easier than to say *what* a work of art is, *whether* it is good or bad, and *why* it is so? This is a painting; it is bad; it is bad because the subject is ugly. This is a poem; it is good; it is good because it expresses fine sentiments effectively. Surely these are basic matters; if they are not clear, what can be? That, so far as he is concerned, is the end of the matter; anything further is mere supersubtlety, and perhaps sophistry as well.

While such matters are indeed basic, in all the arts and sciences the appearance is often very far from the reality, and what seems obvious is not necessarily so. Certainly we make value judgments constantly in life, could not conduct our lives without making them; even animals seem to make them; and probably there could be no greater dispraise of a man than to say he has no sense of values and cannot tell good from bad, for that implies that he is disqualified utterly for anything more than vegetable life. Yet the apparently simple resolves on analysis into the actually complex. What is so simple as eating or walking? The

Reprinted from *Critical Inquiry*, vol. 1, no. 1 (September 1974).

physiologist does not find such matters simple. The analysis of value judgments proves on examination so complicated as to have generated the most conflicting views. I will not review them here except to say that in present discussion the criteria of judgment remain a matter of controversy; that the essence of forms of art—for example, the "nature" of tragedy or comedy—is still a subject of dispute; that it has been alleged that a statement of value is not really a proposition at all, neither true nor false, as incapable either of verification or falsification, that such a statement is nothing more than an affective expression, wholly personal, and as such having nothing to do with general or universal values. In short, it is difficult if not impossible to find a single point, however trivial or however crucial, which is generally— let alone universally—accepted as certain and established beyond doubt.

Confronted with such a bedlam of conflicting claims, one might well recoil in disgust, concluding that the problems are impossible of solution and that all discussion of them is vain. It is possible, however, to draw another and better inference: to wit, that there is no such thing as an absolute and all-comprehending philosophy or an absolute and all-comprehending critical theory; that the solution of any problem is always relative to its formulation and that no problem can be completely formulated; that any solution is a function, not merely of a subject matter but of the particular dialectic employed upon it; and that consequently what seems like dissent may merely be methodological difference or a concern with different aspects of the subject.[1] It is hardly strange that those who start at different points and move by different means in different directions should end up in different places. In any case, this affords no real ground for skepticism. The prevalence of supposed error may convince many that there is no truth, but in reality error *proves* truth: that is, if there is in fact error, there must in fact be truth, for these are correlatives one of which cannot exist without the other.

It seems absurd, in an essay on values, to raise the question of whether values actually exist. As I have already intimated, the conduct even of animal life is dependent upon the recognition of them. It seems absurd as well to ask whether there are values in art: if there were none, no artist would pursue his art, works would never be evaluated, and people in general would never be attracted or repelled by them. Values exist and we make judgments about them, correct or incorrect. It is more profitable, rather, to ask what we mean by a value and in what sense it exists; what a value judgment is, and what is involved in

1. See my discussion of dialectic and critical method in "The Dialectical Foundations of Critical Pluralism," which follows this essay.

it, what kinds there are, and what the conditions of sound judgment may be.

While we speak of something as having value and so make "value" an attribute of the thing, the value is not a discernible property of the thing itself; it is a certain relation between the thing—indeed in terms of real or supposed properties of the thing—and something further. It exists as a relationship exists, and the term "value" is a relative term. To make this clearer: an object has a certain size and has this in itself; it is, however, "great" or "small" only in reference to something further, although indeed in virtue of its size. Or a chemical substance has a certain chemical property; but it is "poisonous" or "medicinal" or "nutritious"—these are evaluative terms—only in reference to something else. As there are variations in the relation, the "value" itself changes: for example, what is "nutritious" to one organism may be "poisonous" to another, or what is "medicinal" in certain quantities or under certain circumstances may be "poisonous" in others, and so on. A "value" is thus a relative attribute of something in virtue of certain discernible properties as these relate to something else. It "really" exists, as a relation "really" exists, for example, parenthood. We may, however, form a true or false conception of that relation and so make true or false value judgments. For example, the history of medicine is full of instances of things at one time thought curative and at another deleterious. And there may be value judgments of a value: for example, something is nutritious, but more or less nutritious than something else, or the nutritious is better than the palatable.

When we discuss the value of a work of art we are confronted immediately with two difficulties: the terms we use, and the peculiar character of art. No one, to my knowledge, has ever doubted that an artist produces a *form* of some kind, and that in any discussion of art *as art* that form must somehow be considered; but the terms we use generally have no reference to form. We miss the form in various ways. (1) We use terms that are nonartistic—that is, terms that refer to something external to the work, as when we speak of the subject of a painting, of *what was depicted* rather than the *depiction* of it, though we know full well that what we respond to is not what was depicted but the depiction of it. "This is a play about Oedipus"—what does that tell us of the diverse forms produced by Sophocles, Seneca, Dryden, Voltaire, Gide, Cocteau? (2) Or again, we use terms which are analogical, for example, the "rhythm" of a painting; the difficulty with these is that they are ambiguous and also that, while they may relate to the work, they can designate it only insofar as there is similarity between it and the analogue. (3) Again, we use terms which seem to designate a single form when in fact they refer to forms of the utmost heterogeneity, as when we speak of "the novel"; this usually arises out of the indiscriminate application of the term over some considerable span of history, so that the "historical slippage" of meaning is gradual and goes unnoticed. As the term broadens in meaning to include more and more heterogeneous forms, the essence of each is lost, and the term comes to apply only to accidental analogies between the forms. In the end very little can then be said, involving only the abstract and general accidents of likeness. Henry James's *The Art of Fiction,* Percy Lubbock's *The Craft of Fiction,* and E. M. Forster's *Aspects of the Novel* illustrate this condition perfectly. The complaint that it is impossible to discuss tragedy because the term has been diversely employed and its proffered justification (usually nowadays with citations from Wittgenstein) stem from this condition. The complaint and the justification are both trivial, and the solution of the difficulty is simple. All that is necessary is to distinguish the different senses of the term by distinguishing the different *things* to which it is applied. Language is ambiguous, and we use it ambiguously; this in no way implies that the ambiguities cannot be cleared up. (4) Finally, we may use terms which indeed have reference to the form of the work but place the part for the whole; that is, terms which are elements in its definition but do not constitute the complete definition. Thus we designate something, not through the form proper but through the device or method used, as in "drama," "sculpture," "etching," "collage," or through the means or medium, as in "charcoal sketch," "watercolor," "oil painting." The point is not that the object is not, say, a drama or a watercolor; of course it is. The point is rather that these terms do not as such refer to the form and refer to it completely. If in fact they stipulated form, all charcoal sketches would be alike in form, and all oil paintings, and all dramas. One consequence of speaking in such a fashion is that we are likely to confuse the method with the form and talk of, say, "the nature of drama" as though all drama were of the same "nature," whereas the dramatic method is used in a wide variety of forms; or to confuse the medium or means with the form and to assume that the work can have no properties beyond those of its medium, as though artists did not exist and all art were simply nature.

Perhaps more might be said on this topic, but we must leave it to consider what I earlier called "the peculiar character of art." In the first place, while we speak of "seeing" a painting or sculpture, of "hearing" a piece of music, we do not in fact do so. It is true that deprived of the sense entailed we should be shut off from the art entirely; but the sense is merely the starting point. The form is shaped within the artist's mind; the sensory materials are merely what is necessary to manifest that form and, through the operation of various faculties, convey it to the mind of spectator, auditor, or reader. We need not go into the analysis of these faculties, we need merely show that more than the senses is involved. And this is easy. In all of the temporal arts, for example, the parts of the whole exist at different times, and unless the earlier were retained in memory—for they have ceased to be—the whole could never be grasped. Without the functioning of memory, music for instance would be for us simply a series of isolated notes, unrelated to each other; melody would be impossible; we should never be able to recognize a recurrent theme; in short, music itself would cease to exist for us. All the representative or imitative arts would be impossible; we could never recognize what was being imitated, since recognition depends upon the operation of some faculty which can compare a present impression with a memory and find a likeness. Indeed, we should never even be able to recognize any work of art *as a work of art* on the basis of sense alone; it would simply be for us, as it is for cattle or fowl, one more object in a world of objects. We do not see the painting, we see the colored paint; we do not hear the music, we hear sounds; we come to perception of the painting or the music through the operation of other faculties than sense. In every act of production the artist takes sensible materials and structures them into suprasensible relations which eventually constitute the *form of the work;* in every act of appreciation we grasp some (or possibly all) of these relations eventually to constitute our *perception* of the form of the work. The form and the perception are clearly two different things; it is conceivable even that the perception may be more valuable than the perceived; but it is accurate only insofar as it is similar to or identical with the perceived.

Moreover, a work of art is a particular, and a special kind of particular. It cannot be known through a universal. I can know that any particular member of the frog genus *Dendrobates* is brilliantly colored and extremely venomous and that its venom attacks the neuromuscular apparatus of an organism, because I know this is true of the genus, and I can know this without ever having encountered a *Dendrobates;* but I cannot know any particulars about *Hamlet* because I know about tragedy. Euripides' *Tyro* is a lost work; it was a tragedy; what do you know of it? Further, the work of art is a particular that cannot be known through the account of someone else. I can know a great deal about the Paine Mountains or the Kalahari desert through the accounts of others; but no account can give me the form of the Diabelli Variations or Michelangelo's *Moses.* I may learn accidental bits and pieces from accounts; the form I must experience directly, through the workings of my own mind upon the data of my own sensations.

A work of art is not merely a particular; it is a *unique* particular. It has its qualities to be, not an individual representative of its class, but what it is uniquely. It does not, like a natural thing, animal or plant,

[handwritten margin notes: "Effete, faulty logic." and "Chorus actors three trim. iambic un- essential un- happiness of human life"]

have such and such qualities because it belongs to such and such a class or species: it belongs to a class (a *constructed* class) because it has such and such qualities. Its materials are not programmed, so to speak, as the natural materials of seed and semen are, to develop into predetermined forms, geranium rather than daisy or kit fox rather than cougar. Its materials are indifferent to form, and without human intervention would remain inert; marble or bronze may take this form or that, Venus or Mars, dove or lion, or no form at all. In nature an internal cause, a cause inherent in the material, is most important; in art an external cause—the artist—is most important. In nature it is the universal which is most authoritative; once we have grasped the universal we know a natural law according to which anything that falls under the universal will be such and such with such and such qualities and functions. In art it is the particular which is most authoritative; there are no rules or laws of art; the work is, as we say, a law unto itself. Any generalization which we may make about it is a generalization and nothing more, and has its validity only because the particulars validate it. Any class into which we put it is not a species in the proper sense, existing in the way a natural kind exists (say, *Dendrobates*), but a constructed class, the resultant simply of our grouping together a number of similars. The fact that the arts have their origin in human nature, that the evolution of arts resembles natural evolution, that innumerable analogies may be found between art and nature must by no means deceive us into thinking that art *is* nature.

A further point: a work of art is a composite whole of more or less complexity. The greater the complexity, the greater the number of structures it is likely to contain; there is the difficulty, then, that one of these may be mistaken for the final structure, that is, the *form*, of the work. To take a parallel from nature, the human body is a skeletal structure, a venous structure, a neural structure, and so on; it is difficult to identify among all these the structure that is primary. Or consider a poem; it may contain many structures—linguistic, rhetorical, logical, structures of ideas, structures of metaphor or image, etc.— and critics fix upon one or another of these claiming it to be *the* structure, with the result that there is a good deal of confusion and dissension.

To sum up: a work of art is a structuring of sensory materials into some form perceptible to sense, and this perceptible form is itself the basis or material for the construction of what I shall call a mental or conceptual form (this term includes emotion and imagination as well as intellect). It is particular; it is unique; its form must be perceived, that is, known directly. It is complex and may contain multiple structures. This, then, is what is to be perceived. Let us consider the consequences of these characteristics for the perceiver. Since sensory materials are involved, there must first of all be an accurate perception of these as well as the sensible form which they compound. To illustrate: looking up at a bough in the jungle, I see a patch of brown, a patch of orange, and blue; these are the sensory elements. They are conjoined and in their conjunction compose a shape; this is the sensible form. (Whether I go on to interpret that shape as a bird or, more specifically, a toucan is another matter.)

Again, these sensory data must be correctly interpreted, as for example that the figure in the painting is that of a man; and this interpretation, since it is in respect to a particular, is an opinion and may be right or wrong. As an opinion and one with reference to a particular which is unique, it is incapable of demonstration. This is not, however, to say that it is incapable of *proof;* it is provable by reference to the primary sensory data, or, in the case of compositions that entail notation, to that notation which gives rise to them—for example, in literature the text, in music the score. Proof here is such proof as we use in evidence of the fact: for example, you doubt my assertion that the object in my hand is a pipe; I exhibit it and prove that I am right. It is possible, especially in the arts that involve notation, that there will be ambiguity of notation, or (as in music especially) incompleteness of notation, or some other possibility of multiple interpretation; in such cases there must be a comparison of the probabilities of the interpretations, as well as the probability of deliberate ambiguity, as in a pun.[2] Ambiguity is of course possible in other arts; people are still puzzled about what is represented by Picasso's sculpture in Chicago's Civic Center Plaza, for instance. Moreover, the arts also involve symbolism and allegory and esoteric reference; customs officers have seized many an Indian or Oriental picture of a human copulating with an animal on the assumption that it was pornographic, whereas in certain cultures such things have a religious significance.

In brief, then, starting with the data, the perceiver will through various mental processes build up in his mind a concept of the form of the work with such substructures as it may contain. These processes will of course include imagination and emotion; they will also, however, involve opinion, and each opinion will be based upon preceding opinions and should be provable from them. Each constitutes a hypothesis, and all enter into the compound hypothesis as to the form, which derives its probability from its constituents as a compound proposition derives its truth or probability from the truth or probability of its constituent propositions.

2. See my discussion of some problems of interpretation in *"Hamlet* and the Hermeneutics of Drama," pp. 75–91.

Ideally the concept of form will be identical with the form; in
actuality it will vary from it and be better or worse—provably—as it
approaches or deviates from it. The variations will spring from variations in perceivers of powers of perception, inference, imagination,
etc., as well as variations in knowledge, experience, etc. When one
considers the extraordinary range of such human variations as well as
the complexity of the processes, it is not astonishing that there is so
much disagreement and dissension about a particular work; it is astonishing that there is not more.

II

I have dealt with the peculiar character of art at such length because
I consider that value and the standards by which we evaluate are
contingent upon *what* we are evaluating. There is, of course, an
alternative to this view—the Platonic alternative—in which all things
are referred ultimately to some Ideal which is at once Being and Value
and Standard, and are judged in terms of their approximation to it. I
have no quarrel with this alternative; it simply does not pose or answer
the questions I have in mind. It is one thing to regard all values in
terms of their likenesses, as ultimately One, another to regard them as
different, and at present I am concerned with their differences. One
may talk either of the Good or of various goods, and usually we talk in
terms of the latter. A girl is good, a plane is good, food is good; but if
we define what we mean in each case we come out with something
different. A girl is good if she is chaste, a plane if it is safe, fast, and
commodious, food if it is palatable and nutritious; a plane is not good
because it is palatable and nutritious, nor a girl because she is safe, fast,
and commodious. Thus, if we differentiate values, values are contingent upon what we are evaluating.

We must distinguish, too, between a statement of a value and a
judgment of value. Let us consider the former first. If, as I said, a
value involves correlation, and if a value is predicated of something, it
is clear that the predicate of a value statement must always be a
relative term. Now—for our purposes at least—there are two kinds of
such relatives: those in which the correlative is specific, obvious, or
understood (whatever you would like to call it), and those in which it is
not. If I say "She is a mother," the predicate is a relative term, but
unless "mother" is a metaphor the correlative is obvious; she is a
mother *of offspring*. The statement constitutes a proposition, that is,
an assertion or denial which can be considered in terms of its truth or
falsity. If, on the other hand, I say "This work is his greatest," the
correlative, unless I have previously specified it, is indefinite. It is
impossible to consider the truth or falsity of this because we do not
have a complete proposition, though the statement may be complete as

a sentence. Great in what aspect? Great in regard to what standard? We cannot tell. A statement of this sort cannot be judged as true or false or even as fully intelligible unless the correlative is specified. We do not know what the predicate *means.*

Indeed, we cannot even tell what the predicate is *of.* Is it a predicate of the thing supposedly judged, or of the "judge" himself? All of us at some time or other have heard a lover say "She's a *beautiful* girl!" and on meeting the beloved been appalled to discover the wide discrepancy between claim and fact. In such instances the statement involves an attribute, not of the girl but of her lover, or at most some connection between uncertain and indistinct attributes of the girl as cause and an effect on her lover. As such it is no doubt true, but it is unverifiable as far as we are concerned, and we do not consider it as a proposition but as an emotional expression. And if we respond, out of politeness, "Yes —she's beautiful," that is not a proposition either but agreement for the sake of courtesy.

A complete proposition will result, then, only when there is a specified correlative. Now, propositions of value are thought to be true or false, probable or improbable, upon some foundation or ground; evidently, then, it is not merely the predicate which is relative but the proposition as a whole—unless it is prima facie impossible or absurd, as when it is self-contradictory—is a correlative of something which warrants it, and the warranting correlative is found either in the judge or the thing judged, or both. Thus we commonly distinguish between value-propositions in five principal ways: (1) as subjective or objective; (2) as proceeding from emotion or reason; (3) as proceeding from the expert or the inexpert, or some other qualification or disqualification of the judge; (4) as held by an individual or by people generally; and (5) as the consequence of the application of some standard.

The subjective is supposed to arise immediately out of emotion or feeling or some other affection, without reference to any criterion, just as our response when the dentist's drill strikes a nerve does not involve reference to any criterion. The objective is generally supposed to be immediate also, as arising immediately from the properties of the work without reference to the subject who does the evaluating. The subjective is thought to be basically exclamatory in nature and hence nonpropositional. This is obviously false, since every exclamation can either be converted into a proposition—for example, "Ouch!" is equivalent to "This is painful"—or includes a proposition—for example, "How beautiful!" includes the proposition "This is beautiful." The subjective is supposedly inferior in validity to the objective, as involving the "personal element"; yet in fact there is no reason why the former should not be equal or superior in validity to the latter. The truth or falsity of an opinion or proposition is not dependent upon who holds it but upon

that concerning which it is an opinion. Moreover, to distrust the
subjective completely, precisely because it is subjective, is to call in
question sensation and observation and hence to undermine the foundations of all art and science—indeed, to make these impossible. But in
actuality, unless we use the term "objective" metaphorically, the objective is really impossible; whatever the inherent value of a work, the
value *placed* on it in an evaluation is obviously a function of something
external to it, that is, the person evaluating. Subjective and objective
are thus the same thing; that is, both are "subjective"; their only
difference lies in that whereas the subjective acknowledges the predicates to be attributes of the person evaluating, the objective supposes
them to be attributes of what is being evaluated. But this supposition is
itself a subjective manifestation.

Similarly, the judgment which proceeds from emotion is generally
thought inferior to one proceeding from reason. Granted that emotion
often affects judgment, the originating faculty has no bearing on the
truth or falsity of opinion. Emotion may generate true opinion as
readily as reason may generate false. In the same way, expert
judgment may be wrong and inexpert right; the many wrong and the
individual right; judgment from standard or criterion may consult the
wrong standard or apply it incorrectly.

All of these suppositions have a measure of truth in them; in fact,
each represents a probability, for example, it is probable that emotion
will distort judgment or that expert opinion is better than inexpert.
The difficulty is that they are all at one remove from what is to be
directly evaluated, that is, they deal with probabilities about the judge
rather than probabilities about the judged; moreover, they require our
acceptance of the first probability in order to establish the second,
which is in an entirely different genus, for a work is not in the same
genus as the man judging. Again, some of them contradict each other;
for example, the probability that the opinion of the expert (who are
individuals and few) is superior to that of the inexpert (who are many)
contradicts the probability that the opinion of the many is better than
that of the few. The probability of our judgment, thus, would seem to
have nothing to do with its intrinsic probability but to be dependent
upon which warranting probability we choose to invoke, and to vary
with it.

It would appear, then, that we are caught in a situation in which we
can only appeal to "the best judges" on the one hand or "the best
works" on the other. But this is a vicious circle. Who are the best judges
of music? Those who judge the best composers as best. Who are the
best composers? Those whom the best judges judge to be best. This
certainly represents the actual state of affairs, but it does not help us to
identify the best judges or the best works. Unless the circle can be
broken, we can simply go round and round, like goldfish in a bowl.

III

If we are to break that circle, we must recognize first of all that since a value proposition involves some correlative proposition which is its warrant of probability, and since it derives its probability from that warrant, a value proposition becomes a *judgment* of value only when it is *the conclusion of some argument involving values.* Thus, except for the fifth—the case of a standard—in all the cases we have been examining—subjective versus objective, emotive versus rational, etc. —the correlative proposition constituted a premise (a major premise) from which the judgment followed as conclusion. The syllogisms can readily be stated,[3] but upon their statement it will at once appear that they do not constitute proof but are all forms of a material fallacy which in the old logical terminology was called the *argumentum ad verecundiam*—the argument in terms of reverence or respect. With the exception of the fifth, they are all appeals to authority of one kind or another, the difference being in what is taken as authoritative. Authority, famously, has a nose of wax which can be bent in either direction; in any case, no arguments of this sort will establish the point in question.

At this juncture we may review our discussion to see what light it sheds on the conditions of value judgment. A work of art entails sensible materials which must be accurately perceived as such, and the only proof of the existence of the traits of these is that they can be perceived by others. There should therefore be (1) a perceptible characteristic or trait. Moreover, this trait should (2) be "essential" to the work, that is, as entering into some verifiable structural relation and not merely accidental. (3) The sensible elements enter into some sensible form which must be accurately perceived and (4) correctly interpreted.[4] (5) The suprasensible substructures must be grasped in their totality and in their various interrelations, the greater always subsuming the lesser, until they constitute the final subsumptive whole which is the form of the work.

All of this has to do, of course, with the structuring of a complex concept which shall be commensurate with, and provably true or probable with respect to, the form of the work. Since what is involved is a unique particular, this concept when predicated of the work will constitute, as we saw, a complex opinion or hypothesis. It is obviously impossible to escape the "personal element" or to go beyond opinion;

3. The syllogisms would be framed thus: "Whatever is considered best by objective (rational, expert, popular) judgment is in fact best; this is considered best by objective (rational, etc.) judgment, therefore, etc."

4. I do not at all mean that all art is imitative or representative but merely that, say, a swirl is grasped as a swirl.

but this does not mean that we cannot achieve as much certainty as possible or that "one opinion is as good as another."

The work has its own inherent value or values apart from any evaluation of it, and its value attaches to it *particularly;* it is not valuable as a piece of gold is valuable because gold is valuable but because of what it uniquely *is.* For example, a tragedy is not valuable merely because it is a tragedy. Now, when we evaluate, we form a conception of that value which again is an opinion—an opinion contingent upon our opinion of the form—and when this is expressed in words it is what we have called a value statement. To be a complete proposition—not merely to be considered as true or false but even to be considered as intelligible—the predicate of this statement must have a specific correlative; and the probability of the proposition is dependent upon some warranting proposition, or, in other words, the judgment of value is the conclusion of some argument involving values.

Of the five principal kinds of warrant which we examined, only the reference to a standard holds a possibility of being relevant to value; not any and every standard, however, but some standard specifically. Here we must make a distinction. Standards of measurement require no defense—they are matters of convenience or custom or whatever, warranted by acceptance. Astronomical distances are measured in light-years for convenience; areas of land may be measured in terms of acres or hectares or manzanas according to the customary units of measure in a given country. Standards that have to do with good or bad, benefit or harm, pleasure or pain, on the other hand, may require some justification or defense, and it is obvious that the standards consulted in judgments of art are of this sort. Since they relate to a value which is contingent upon the form, clearly they must (6) represent an actual value and (7) be appropriate to that form, and since they have reference to a trait they must (8) be appropriate to that trait. Finally, since the value judgment is the conclusion of a syllogism, that syllogism must be (9) a valid syllogism and, since the proof is to be verified by others, (10) clearly and unequivocally expressed in words.

We have, then, ten conditions of sound value judgment; and value judgments are provable or liable to objection with reference to these. As I have indicated, the first five relate to the concept of the work, the last five to the establishment of the judgment as such. For convenience and clarity they may be summarized as follows:

1. There must be a perceptible characteristic or trait
2. It must be essential to the work and not accidental
3. The sensible form must be accurately perceived
4. It must be correctly interpreted
5. The suprasensible substructures must be grasped in their totality

and in the totality of their relations as constituting the final
subsumptive whole which is the form of the work

6. The standard or criterion must represent an actual value
7. It must be appropriate to the form
8. It must be appropriate to the characteristic or trait
9. The value syllogism must be a valid syllogism
10. It must be clearly and unequivocally expressed (hence, it may
    contain no metaphors)

Perhaps all of these are sufficiently clear except for 2, 6, 7, and 8. In
saying that the trait must be "essential," I have no intention of
stipulating what the essence of a given form is. That is a question of the
theory of forms, and I am not now constructing a theory of forms; I am
discussing the conditions of value judgment in theories generally. Any
theory eventually involves discussion of kinds of forms, and what is
"essential", is here simply whatever is related to a kind *as a kind.*
However a given art and its kinds may be differentiated or defined,
there will be aspects of the work which will not relate to it; these
inartistic aspects I call "accidental." These will *ex hypothesi* be
irrelevant also to value judgment. For example, the fact that a work is
made of inferior or worthless materials—"junk" objects—has no
bearing on its value as a work of art.

In saying that the standard or criterion must represent an actual
value, I mean that it represents an actual good. This no doubt needs
explanation. An ethical act is not good because it is in accord with an
ethical rule; on the contrary, an ethical rule is valid because it is in
accord with ethical action which is good. If virtue did not exist in
particular acts, philosophies of ethics would be impossible; if particular kind or brave acts did not exist, we should have neither concepts
of nor words for kindness or bravery. The authority and the quality
exist in the particular, not in the universal. Moreover, the more specific
is always more authoritative than the more general, as closer to the
supremely authoritative particular. It is the same with art, as I have
already intimated; the particular has a good or goods which constitute
its value; out of the experience of many like particulars we form a
conception of a general projected excellence which becomes a criterion
or standard, and we judge the particulars comparatively as they
approximate to it. That criterion may have other criteria subordinate
to it or may itself be subordinate to other criteria; for example, in
literature criteria of style are generally regarded as subordinate to
criteria relating to other aspects of a work which are considered more
important than style, and criteria which relate to the work as a whole
are regarded as superior to criteria which relate to the parts.

The good represented by the criterion is either self-evident or generally accepted or must be argued dialectically; the same possibilities
exist with respect to its relation to other criteria as superior or subordinate to them. There may be "true" criteria or "false" criteria; a
criterion is "true" if it represents an actual good; otherwise it is "false."
Even supposing it to be a true criterion, however, it may be inappropriate either to the form or to the trait. We cannot appropriately judge
a comedy, for example, by all of the criteria which pertain to a
tragedy; similarly, if a character in a drama is merely sketched, we
cannot judge it to be insufficiently developed without reference to its
function in the drama. Again, criteria appropriate to one part of a
work are not necessarily appropriate to another; for example, those
appropriate to diction are not necessarily so to plot or character. The
criteria applying to one art, also, are not necessarily applicable to
another; it would be ridiculous to demand of music everything that we
should demand of a sculpture.

We may grasp the importance of the ten conditions of judgment by
considering what happens when they are violated. To take a particularly horrible example, a man uttered the following judgment: "Tschai-
kowsky is the greatest composer because he is the most nationalistic." This is an absurd judgment (we must remember that the fact
that judgments can be absurd is a proof that they can also be sound)
which violates all of the conditions with the possible exception of the
formal validity of the value syllogism. What does "nationalism" mean
(10)? To what perceptible trait is it related (1)? How is it essential
to the works (2)? How is it related to musical form or interpretation
(3,4,5)? To make this brief, does "nationalistic" represent a value, and
how is it appropriate to music (6,7,8)?

To take another example which is deliberately ridiculous; in Kafka's
story "Die Sängerin der Mäuser" the mice annually arrange a concert
by a beautiful blonde singer on the coldest day in winter and pack
themselves tightly into the concert hall; they enjoy the concert im-
mensely because the day on which it is held is the only winter day on
which they are warm. Obviously this violates all of the conditions
except 6 and 10; for while comfort is an undoubted value and while
their judgment is expressed unequivocally, nothing in it relates to
music or the quality of the performance.

Bad judgments abound in the newspapers and journals, even in the
writings of serious critics. "The sheer fun of *Hamlet* sets it above other
Shakespearean works"(1). "The Preludes of Chopin can be sung by a
child," said George Sand in praise of them, and was echoed by James
Huneker (2). Edwin Muir judges Henry James unfavorably because he
"excludes three-quarters of life where another would make some effort
to subdue it" (6,7,8). "It is this shimmeriness which is the chief contri-

bution of D. H. Lawrence to novelistic technique," writes the author of a book on the novel (1, 10). The examples might be multiplied, but perhaps this is sufficient illustration.

IV

Thus far we have been considering value judgments as though they were all of one kind. There are, however, various kinds, differing in both matter and form, and we have now to examine these and see whether their differences require any modification of the foregoing statements. We may note first of all the difference between simple and compound value judgments. A simple value judgment is indivisible into other value judgments; a compound one is so divisible. If I say "This word [in a poem] is apt" or "This image is vivid," the judgment is simple; if I say "His diction is apt" or "His imagery is vivid," I am making a summary judgment which combines judgments of all the instances of his use of diction or construction of imagery; the proposition is a conjunction which asserts the truth of all of its constituents and hence is true only if all its constituents are true. Since a value judgment, in the sense in which we have been using the term—as, that is, a judgment with a supporting reason—is the conclusion of a syllogism, clearly the premises must be sufficient to necessitate the conclusion, and different conclusions will require different premises, so that in this case the syllogism will be different. "All words that are appropriate to [the thing intended, the character, the emotion, or whatever is involved] are apt; this word is appropriate to, etc.; hence it is apt" is quite different from "All words etc.; his diction in every instance is, etc.; hence his diction is apt." Full proof would require consideration of every instance, whether we say "always," "generally," or "seldom"; practically, however, the matter is not usually carried that far.

Such compound propositions have compound subjects; it is possible also to have single subjects with compound predicates as well as compound subjects with compound predicates (I am speaking, of course, of *logical*, as opposed to *grammatical*, subjects and predicates). All require analysis into their constituents and, in full proof, establishment of each of them.

When a value judgment is both simple and proximate (by "proximate" I mean following immediately from the descriptive proposition which gives the perceptible trait), we are likely to be unaware that we are syllogizing; nevertheless, if a reason is given, the syllogism has been made. If I say "The word 'ask'st' in Arnold's sonnet "To a Friend" is bad because it is difficult to pronounce," I have made a syllogism: all words that are difficult to pronounce are bad, this word is difficult to pronounce, ergo, it is bad. If I say that the whole line of verse is bad—"Who prop, thou ask'st, in these bad days, my mind?"—there will be a proximate compound value judgment, the minor premise of the syllogism involving such predicates as "halting and labored rhythmically," "difficult to pronounce," etc.

Besides simple and compound value judgments as such, there are comparative value judgments. That these are compound is evident upon analysis: if I say that *A* is better than *B*, I assume that *A* and *B* have a certain trait or traits in respect to which they are comparable and, in certain cases, some common standard to which they may be appropriately referred; and such assumption is clearly a compound proposition, in fact, a conjunction. Moreover, it is evident that comparative judgments are *posterior* to value judgments as such; they are based upon *preceding* judgments of the values of *A* and *B*. Clearly, then, these stipulations must be added to the ten conditions already discovered when we deal with comparatives.

We may take as a typical syllogism of comparative judgment Aristotle's proof that tragedy is a higher form of art than epic:

> Whatever form of art better achieves the poetic effect
> is the higher form
> Tragedy better achieves the poetic effect
>
> Therefore tragedy is the higher form.
>
> [*Poetics* 26.1462b.11–14]

There are obviously many different possibilities of comparison. The apparent potentialities of a given form may be compared with what is achieved in it ("Given the limitations of the haiku, it is extraordinary what Buson ... "). Device may be compared with device, part with part, part with whole, degree with degree, quality with quality, value with value (i.e., criterion with criterion), work with work, form with form, and so on. The principles underlying all are now perhaps clear: all judgments go back ultimately to proximate value judgments based upon descriptive propositions, the predicate of which signifies a perceptible trait; simple judgments entail the ten conditions discussed; compound ones are to be resolved into their constituents and the required premises determined for each; the comparative judgments entail the further conditions that the things compared have a common trait which is the basis of comparison and that the values of each be determined by prior value syllogisms.

Full syllogistic exposition would be extremely tiresome; the proofs therefore should be abridged. If the value judgment is unchallenged, abridgment is possible by avoiding the obvious, concentrating on the crucial, using enthymeme rather than syllogism, or, better still, condensing the syllogism to a single sentence. The stock syllogism on Socrates and his mortality, for example, can be reduced to "Socrates, being man, is mortal." Even a lengthy sorites permits of such reduction by giving the major and minor terms and the successive middles. For example, "He is avaricious; hence suffers unbounded desire; hence is perpetually dissatisfied; hence miserable; hence not to be taken as a model by those who wish to be happy." Further condensation can be achieved by the use of summary propositions if the instances summarized are obvious. If the judgment is challenged, the objections determine the parts to be argued.

V

We have seen that a value is a relative attribute of something in virtue of certain discernible properties as these relate to something else and that the arts utilize sensible forms to produce suprasensible or conceptual forms. All evaluations, therefore, must depend immediately or remotely upon a descriptive proposition which has as its subject the sensible form or some part of it and some perceptible trait as its predicate.

The question arises, as both critics and philosophers have been aware, how the descriptive can give rise to the evaluative. The question is not so difficult as it seems. Consider our word "ask'st." It contains a combination of consonants difficult to pronounce and harsh to hear; it is unpleasant; the unpleasant is a form of the bad. We move quite easily from the property to the value. So much for the word itself; but it is part of a line of verse. Does its function in the line (which would be a form of good) require its difficulty and harshness? If it did, the evaluation of the greater part, the line, would overcall the evaluation of the lesser, the word; we should then excuse the ugliness of the word as requisite to serve some higher function than that of euphony. But it does not; the line itself is made up of other ugly combinations of sound, is halting and laborious in its rhythm, is in no way expressive, through emphasis, of the meaning, or through signs, of the condition of the supposed speaker; and the words in the question are far from their natural order. The line itself is bad, and the word is worse for not serving more than a grammatical function in it. Is the composition of the line required by its part in the poem? If so, etc.; if not, etc. But if the word were itself euphonious and served some higher function in the line, and if the line were euphonious and expressive and served some higher function in the part of the poem which includes it, we should have a compounding of goods, though they would be goods of a different kind (e.g., euphony is a different good from expressiveness).

We may see from this that something may be good in itself and good with reference to something further, as well as that there are different *kinds, degrees, quantities,* and *orders* of goods. We shall have, then, a multiplicity of criteria as representing the good in itself and the good with reference to something else, as well as those representing kinds, degrees, quantities, and orders of good; but the criteria will always be goods; and the bad will be judged against a criterion which represents a good, for the bad is judged in terms of the good and not conversely. Moreover, pleasure is here obviously a good, but it would be insufficient to stop at that point; there are different kinds of pleasure (the pleasure taken in euphonious sounds is different from that taken in expressiveness), different degrees of pleasure (some sounds are more pleasant than others which are pleasant), different quantities of pleasure (*this* work offers a greater variety of pleasures than *that*), and different orders of pleasure (the distinctively human pleasures are of a higher order than those which man has in common with other animals, and even among physical pleasures some are thought higher than others).

Here again, however, certain problems arise. First, if we speak of the pleasure produced by art we have evidently gone from the work to something external to it, that is, the perceiver. Is the work, then, something incomplete in itself requiring the complement of the perceiver, as R. G. Collingwood argued? The answer is that the work is complete in itself and has its given value or good, the *potentiality* to produce certain pleasurable emotions, concepts, etc., which is however the *actuality* of its form. The pleasure produced is certainly extrinsic to it; the capacity to produce it is as certainly intrinsic. The difficulty comes about through a failure to distinguish the actual from the potential. Consider, as a simple instance of what I mean, a riddle. A question involving an apparent self-contradiction is puzzling; I may make a riddle, then, by making a question which involves an apparent self-contradiction, and the riddle will be complete in itself and an *actuality* when I have made it. It will have the *potentiality* to puzzle someone, who will have solved the riddle when he apprehends the true form of the implied assertion, namely, what it really says as opposed to its *apparent* self-contradiction: "When is a door not a door? When it's a jar."

Again, it is evident from the argument that we can derive criteria from an analysis of the goods. But are criteria prior or posterior to judgment? For if criteria are not prior to judgment, how do we know the goods as goods? And if they are not posterior to judgment, how can we derive them from the goods? This would seem once more to involve us in a circle. Indeed there is circularity here, but not that of a vicious circle; there is circularity in the sense in which all science is circular, going from particulars to principles and returning from principles to particulars. The value of works of art is obviously realized prior to our judgment; they exist and they are good; but we can no more apprehend their value than we can apprehend their form without directly experiencing them. We come to the knowledge of values and criteria in art as we do in ethics, by experience; we cannot be taught them as we are taught theorems in mathematics. Out of repeated experiences we come to form the concept of a standard, as out of repeated experiences of the particular we frame the notion of the universal. We can be taught that Shakespeare is *great;* we must teach ourselves the *greatness* of Shakespeare. In short, in our coming to know it, the good of the work is prior; in our proof of its value, in reasoned judgment, it is the conclusion of an inference and is posterior.

A further difficulty, often raised as an unanswerable and final objection to the possibility of sound judgment, is the matter of variations. I have said something on that point already, but it may be well to add a word or two. If all artistic judgment involves a certain characteristic of a work which is referred in a certain way to a certain standard, it is evident that if the same characteristic were referred in the same way to the same standard, and this by everybody, all value judgments would be identical; there would be no variation in judgment. By the same token, it is clear that if judgments differ, they must differ in respect to at least one of these. We have, therefore, the heads of possible agreement or disagreement. Now, if "disagreeing" judgments are based upon different characteristics, I deny that there is disagreement; we cannot be in disagreement while talking about totally different subjects. "This horse is white" in no way disagrees with "That horse is black." Similarly, there can be no disagreement if the standards differ or are differently referred to. There is simply difference.

Apart from incomplete or inaccurate perception of the fact, which does not permit of logical formulation, the chief cause of variation lies in the standard or criterion. Critics tend to go astray here in six principal ways. First, there is the criterion which is false absolutely because it does not represent a value. T.S. Eliot's "impersonality" is an example; personality and impersonality have nothing to do with the value of art. Second, there is the criterion which is so vague that it is really inapplicable by anyone other than the critic who uses it; Arnold's "high seriousness" is of this sort. Third, there is the criterion taken as absolute when it applies only with qualification; Eliot's "intensity" exemplifies this, for it is absurd to demand intensity of all poetry, or, for that matter, to demand "high seriousness" of it. Fourth, there is the criterion applied too narrowly; quarrels about unity, for instance, frequently turn on the failure to realize that there may be many kinds of unifying principles and consequently many kinds of unity. Fifth, inappropriate criteria are invoked, as when those of one art are applied indiscriminately to another. Finally, the rank or order of values is mistaken, as when a lower value like "concision" or "purity of language" is set above higher values, or when craftsmanship is valued above all else.

It is evident, thus, that we also evaluate values and systems of value themselves, and if we are to do so by reason, we must reason dialectically. No good can be higher than a good which includes it, or a good to which it is instrumental, or be absolutely good if, taken in combination with something bad, it makes the result worse, as courage in the evil man only makes him more dangerous; we must take major premises such as these to argue the orderings of goods.

There are, then, values and kinds and degrees and quantities and orders of values, and we come to know the *Summum Bonum* in each art as we do the *Summum Bonum* in life. We come to know more about art as we come to know more about life, and we begin to realize its true importance only when we realize that, important as art is, it would not be so important if other things were not *more* important. And our conception of art and its values must be qualified always by the reflection that we shall never know all about them, but that neither this fact nor the inexactness of the subject gives us license for imprecision. We shall never know all about art or the values of art until all art is at an end; meanwhile, artists will continue to instruct us.

THE DIALECTICAL FOUNDATIONS OF
CRITICAL PLURALISM

T here is something ironic in the fact that, in the seventeenth century, the scientist was frequently the object of ridicule, while the critic of the arts—particularly the critic of letters—was held in high respect. That particular wheel of fortune has certainly come full circle. Few, I think, would now contest the assertion that the sciences are at present in a condition far superior to that of the arts, or, at any rate, of that portion of the arts which entitles them to consideration as departments of knowledge; and indeed, the reasons for this assertion may seem only too obvious, too numerous, and too absolute. In the sciences, theory and practice have gone fairly hand in hand, and labor has patently been fruitful in the highest degree; and as a consequence, the fantasies of the Arabian Nights, or the even wilder dreams of a Verne, have been rendered commonplace. Scientific discussion is so clear and so uniform that failure to comprehend it is attributed to a lack of intelligence or of training in the hearer, rather than to a fault in the discussion itself. Such is the agreement on method that one tends to speak of scientific method in the singular rather than in the plural; and it is such, too, that the most complex cooperation is possible between researchers in fields of study utterly remote from one another. If dissension arises between scientists, it is either in the extension of science to matters which are not viewed as scientific, or in the consideration of questions which are frankly admitted to be hypothetical or speculative. It is common in science for many researchers to arrive independently at the same conclusion; and even the predictions of science, while not always accurate in themselves, are nevertheless held always to be worthy of serious consideration, and always to be grounded upon assumptions universally recognized as relevant and probable.

In science, the known is sharply distinguished from the unknown and each from the conjectural; and the agreement, both general and particular, upon what constitutes scientific knowledge prescribes a

Reprinted from *Texas Quarterly*, vol. 9, no. 1 (spring 1966).

clear course of study, and makes easy the assessment both of enterprises and of researchers. For example, the qualifications which constitute a man as a scientist in a given field are thought to be themselves so perfectly plain, and so manifest in their tokens, that there is generally little, if any, disagreement, not only as to who are the first and second ranking practitioners of a given science, but perhaps even as to who are the twenty-first and twenty-second. Finally, we may say to terminate a list that might be prolonged indefinitely, science seems so much to be a matter of the things studied rather than the man studying, that constant progress and incrementation is possible; at death the eminent scientist leaves behind him like coral the residue of his knowledge; even his unsolved problems can safely be left to his heirs for solution.

The state of the arts, considered as departments of knowledge, might be accurately as well as tersely indicated by remarking that it seems in all these respects to be the very contrary of the condition of science; but doubtless it may be useful to trace these differences more clearly. In the criticism of the arts, it would appear, labor has been almost fruitless; theory has been too abstruse and too general to be of much assistance either in the production or the judgment of artistic objects; and dissension over theory is such that, were artist or critic to lend an ear to all claims, he would quickly find himself in the situation of the father and son in the old German fable, and end by carrying the ass. The terminology of artistic criticism, far from promoting understanding by its clarity and uniformity, has by its ambiguity and irregularity often supplanted the problems of art as a subject for dissension, and has often provided a fruitful ground for cavils upon propositions the truth of which, in a happier state of the subject, would have been recognized as unquestionable. There is perhaps no point of doctrine, however chief and principal, which has not been repeatedly and vigorously denied; and there is not only no agreement upon method, but none even upon the possibility or impossibility of method. Since there is no agreement upon the constitution of critical knowledge, no clear course of study can be laid out and such integrations of endeavor as we have observed to be common enough in science are impossible; equally impossible would be any attempt to state the qualifications of the critic, or the signs which manifest these, in a manner satisfactory to any considerable number even of the expert. The attempt to evaluate a given critic or a given critical project is consequently sure to provoke sharp controversy; and the theory of art seems to be so much a matter of the man studying rather than of the things studied, that each particular theory may almost be said to die with its author; how a given critic would have extended or completed his theory, what would be his views on this or that work left untreated, and what his answers to certain objectors or innovators, remain questions for conjecture only. Critical progress seems impossible; instead there is only change; and the phrase *quot homines tot sententiae* seems to have been invented for the arts. In short, whereas the theories of the sciences seem to bear all the marks which betoken the existence of knowledge, the theories of the arts seem to bear only those of *opinion* and *taste;* and it is a somber sign that in the curricula of most modern universities, criticism, in the sense of the theory of art, is not recognized as a subject of graduate education, that is, is not recognized as a true department of knowledge capable of instruction, demonstration, and extension. Contemplating the condition of the sciences, we are reminded of a vast and valuable estate, accurately surveyed, certainly established in possession, admirably tilled, perfectly administered; contemplating that of the arts, we find all in disrepair, little work going forward, the title in constant litigation, and the sheriff advancing to seize the whole.

One would suppose that the superiority of the condition of the sciences, if thus evident, could scarcely have escaped the notice of the humanists themselves; and in fact their dissatisfaction and alarm even antedate the rise of empirical science. The notable progress of these sciences, however, quickly produced a tendency to compare the relative conditions of art and science, and that tendency seems to have resulted, so far as humanists were concerned, in two sharply different attitudes. The first of these supposes that the arts differ totally in their subjects from the sciences, treating values not less real or important, or, as is frequently claimed, even more grandiose, despite their intractability to precise formulation. The arts, according to this position, involve infinite variation, either because each work of art is unique, or because manifestations of taste are so, or because in some way extreme particularity or extreme generality necessitates imprecision. On this ground the condition of artistic studies can be defended; for, it is asserted, while such studies are imprecise, and are grounded upon taste or immediate perception rather than upon strict proof, their objects are wholly inaccessible to science; and advocates of this position tend consequently to view with contempt any endeavor to render the arts "scientific," interpreting such effort as an indication that the subject matter of the arts has been inadequately or falsely conceived. The second attitude is that the inexactness of artistic study is lamentable, and its consequence has generally been an attempt to limit artistic study to such matters as might be dealt with precisely—to what might be generally susceptible of observation or proof; and on these grounds it has been frequently suggested that humanistic study restrict itself to such subjects as philosophy, bibliography, or the history of the arts, modelling its methods after those of the empirical sciences, or after those of "scientific" history. Of these two attitudes one may say that it is unlikely that both are wholly false, for they have been maintained over a long period by men of exceptional sensitivity, intelligence, and learning; but *per contra* it is clearly impossible that both should be wholly true.The former, based on consideration of the subject matter, draws conclusions about method; the latter, founded upon suppositions about method, draws conclusions about the subject matter; and there is the curious possibility that each of these positions may be in error precisely through what each claims to know best and to consider most important, for if there is error in both, it must arise in the former from erroneous conception of the subject matter, and in the latter, from erroneous conception of method. At any rate, the disadvantages of each may be clearly seen, for the former, while it pretends to deal with issues of some scope and grandeur, leads to such inexactness as frequently to make discussion impossible, or hardly worth the trouble if it is possible; and the latter, while it pretends to great precision, tends to exercise its impressive apparatus upon trivialities, or, at any rate, to avoid all those issues which are commonly considered to be of principal importance in the arts; and both tend only to confirm that inferiority of the arts which each had originally sought to correct.

The truth of the first view consists perhaps in its contention that the subject matter must be dealt with adequately, that the subject matter must determine method, and that method can be no more exact than the subject matter will permit; the truth of the second, perhaps, in its insistence that the arts are not absolutely inexact, and that a certain rigor of method, at any rate, is consequently possible. But both seem to have fallen into error through the same assumption, namely, that method in the arts is the exact counterpart of method in the sciences; for it is only upon that assumption that their conclusions follow. If the subject matter of the arts is inexact in gross as both views assume, both conclude rather more than their premises will permit; proponents of the first view should have concluded, not that method is impossible, but rather that method appropriate to an exact subject matter is impossible; while proponents of the second view should have concluded, not that much of the subject matter should be excised from consideration, but that much of the subject matter is inaccessible to the method of the exact sciences. With the addition of this observation, both are in effect brought to agreement, for both deny the applicability of the methods of the exact sciences to the subject matter of art as a whole, and both are consistent with the possibility of some method other than that of the exact sciences.

That professors of the arts should have had difficulty with problems arising from consideration of the subject matter and method of the arts is not surprising, for these are problems not of a special art or group of arts, but of some more general field of inquiry. They are more general than art precisely because they involve the establishment of the principles of art, for no art, science, or faculty can demonstrate its own principles without circularity. As determining or as related to artistic principles, these problems, extra-artistic though they be, are of the highest importance to the arts, and that importance has been manifest through their constant recurrence in discussion whenever the principles of art have been called into question, or whenever the techniques of art have required a foundation. As a matter of fact, artistic theory has been chiefly of two kinds: the technical, and the metaphysical or dialectical. Serious contemporary criticism, for instance, when it is not merely particular commentary or interpretation of the "text-creeping" variety, is almost exclusively metaphysical, for it seeks to deal with such problems as the mode of existence of a work of art, the place of art among the sciences, and the establishment of appropriate principles and method in art. The constant attempts to find some philosophic basis for theory and practice suggest that critics and artists alike feel the necessity of some conjunction of art with philosophy.

One is likely to recall that this conjunction has not always been absent; for both Plato and Aristotle conceived of the arts, and indeed the sciences also, as parts of philosophy, and treated them as such. For Plato the arts and the sciences were based upon hypotheses which could be verified by dialectic, and it is as functioning in this role that he speaks of dialectic as the "coping-stone" of the sciences. For Aristotle, who also thought that no art or science could demonstrate its own principles, problems such as those relating to the organization of the sciences were metaphysical in character, and it was metaphysics which dealt with all questions too general and too primary for any of the special sciences. For the former, all knowledge was one because all things contained a principle of similarity; for the latter, the sciences were compendent despite their diversity, for they sprang from the same discipline.

How long the sciences were allowed to remain in such interconnection is a question, really, of how long the Platonic and the Aristotelian philosophies survived their authors; and, while both men seem not to have lacked disciples, even their immediate successors in the Academy and in the Lyceum appear to have attacked crucial doctrines and to have made important changes in the systems of the masters. The long history of Platonism and Aristotelianism which is so frequently and so diversely recounted by philosophers is, after all, a history of their doctrines rather than of their systems; and it is a history of the shifting meanings, and the consequent adoption or rejection, of those doctrines as they appear in systems different from, and sometimes even opposed to, the systems of Plato and Aristotle. The history of philosophy has often been asserted to be the history of Plato or of Aristotle or of both; if that is true, the masters possessed, in addition to their other talents, the capacities of Proteus for assuming a multiplicity of strange forms.

Gradually, at least, their successors appear to have separated philosophy from science, some devoting themselves to special sciences, others to such moral, metaphysical, and logical studies as are at present thought to comprise philosophic, as opposed to scientific, subjects. While later philosophers beyond number have attempted to repair the schism thus introduced, the notable absence of fully developed theories of art founded upon fully developed philosophic bases suggests that the restoration has hardly been complete. Bacon, Hobbes, and Hume—to mention only a few examples—all relocate the arts and the sciences in the philosophic corpus; but none of these does more than sketch the bases from which a theory of art might be developed. The innumerable artistic theories of a more specific character, on the other hand, appear to rest upon foundations which are at best only hypothetical. It is fairly safe to say, therefore, either that Plato and Aristotle afford the last instances of an adequate correlation of philosophy, science, and art, or that, if any later correlation exists, humanists have remained unaffected by it.

Why should such correlation of the fields of knowledge be so important as to affect the whole career of the arts? A really accurate answer would be a very lengthy one; but perhaps all of its details would stem from one central fact. The arts, more than any other branch of knowledge, derive their principles from other branches of knowledge. The practical sciences, such as ethics and politics, depend upon the theoretical (for instance, ethics is obviously dependent upon psychology); but the arts depend upon both the theoretical and the practical sciences. This may be seen readily enough by examining a few of the important questions of the arts. The question of the nature of a work of art involves a theory of definition which is metaphysical or logical in character. The question of the process of reasoning in the arts is of a similar order. The human activities represented by the arts offer problems of subject matter which involve both ethics and physics. The effects of art on its audience offer problems which involve ethics and psychology.

The arts, consequently, must be less exact than the theoretical sciences, and less exact even than the practical sciences; for they are contingent upon these. But if the arts involve the other sciences, they are also distinct from them; poetics, for instance, is not ethics or psychology because it involves ethics or psychology; and the failure to differentiate properly the arts from the sciences which they involve has had an obvious enough effect upon their development. When poetics, for example, is regarded as a department of grammar or of rhetoric, as happened so frequently in the course of the history of criticism, only such aspects of poetry can be treated as are relevant to the theory of grammar or of rhetoric. Such reductions of one body of knowledge to another are brought about, of course, by the absence or inoperancy of philosophic disciplines which determine the interrelations of the sciences. The very possibility of a science depends upon the possibility of distinguishing a certain subject matter; and this in turn depends upon the possibility of some discipline equipped to make such distinctions.

The question may very well arise why the sciences should have progressed while the arts did not, if the separation from philosophy is the cause of the failure of the arts to progress; for, as we have remarked earlier, the sciences also were thus separated. Perhaps we have already answered this in part. The case of the sciences is really quite different. Their objects permit observation, experimentation, and calculation in ways in which the objects of art do not; as a consequence they allow the accumulation of facts to a degree which assists greatly in the framing, correction, and rejection of hypotheses. I am speaking of course purely of the empirical sciences; the mathematical sciences, because of their populational bases, have been relatively independent of empirical fact, and have progressed chiefly by the drawing of consequences. All of these sciences, moreover, deal with clearly defined aspects of their subjects, at least as compared with artistic studies. The latter, on the other hand, neither have their proper provinces clearly marked out, nor deal with groups and classifications so distinct as the natural kinds; nor do they permit such clear and absolute reasoning, nor such clear apprehension of the fact. Moreover, whereas the sciences have rather quickly fastened upon methods and employed them until they became or seemed to become obsolete, artistic studies have frequently been occupied simultaneously with questions of knowledge and questions of method.

On the conviction, then, that some examination of the philosophic foundations of criticism is requisite for the proper development of the theory of the arts, I propose to take up some of the relations which exist between philosophy and criticism.

II

The arts, considered as bodies of knowledge, are a part of philosophy. Consequently they are subject to whatever variations of method may be found in philosophy generally. In other words, there are as many varieties of philosophy of art as there are of philosophy generally. Such variety in philosophies of art has been advanced as the chief argument for skepticism in art (the latest manifestation of which is the so-called Critical Relativism), just as such variety in philosophy has been advanced as an argument for general philosophic skepticism. The

[right margin, handwritten:] p. 296
cf. ————
McCormick

assumption of the skeptics in both instances is the same. It is that this variety is equivalent to contradiction, every philosophic *sic* being canceled by a philosophic *non*. Since this assumption in effect implies the impossibility of any constructive philosophy, it is worth examining at some length. We may examine it best, I think, by first looking into the causes of philosophic variety, and by secondly observing whether any contradiction in fact is present.

We may begin by noting that all systems of philosophy have entertained or assumed some theory of discourse, either positive or negative, and that this theory has invariably affected the formulations of the philosophy. By "positive or negative" theories of discourse I mean that, according to the philosophy, language or some other system of signs is capable or incapable, absolutely or in certain respects, of serving as the vehicle of philosophic thought. Thus a philosophy completely positive in its theory of discourse would hold that all things are effable or sayable (I believe there has never been such a philosophy), while a philosophy completely negative in its theory of discourse would hold that all things are ineffable or unsayable. The Cynic who preferred the motion of a finger to speech affords some idea of the latter, although he is hardly a perfect example, for he evidently thought only that language was an inadequate vehicle. The extremes are perhaps hypothetical rather than actual; most philosophies, at least, would lie in a middle ground; but that middle ground offers the greatest possibilities of variation, so as to admit almost a polar opposition. For there is not only an extraordinary difference in the degree of efficiency or inefficiency attributed to language or other signs, but language and its proper function are quite variously conceived as well.

Nevertheless, there are certain properties of language which perhaps would be granted by all. In the first place, language is necessarily abstractive or selective. That is, it is impossible for language to signify the totality of existence; if it did, it would be nonsignificant. If I say "chair," I signify this object by a term which is selective. It does not stand for all the attributes of this object, as for example that it is my property, that it was made in Philadelphia, and so on; it stands only for those attributes signified by the term "chair." And if "chair" stood not only for these, but for all other things or attributes as well, we should, if that were the only name for the object, have no term for chair. The term would in a sense stand for everything and for nothing. I find this to be true of any term I can think of: no term will stand for the totality of things in the totality of their attributes in the totality of their modes of conception, and so forth; even such terms as "all," "totality," "everything" will not, for they stand for things collectively but not separately, or for things distributively but not collectively. I may indeed broaden or generalize the meaning of a term, or narrow or specify it; but it will stand, still, for such-and-such, and not for something else. In other words, language is impossible unless we can say of its constituents that they function in this way and not in that. The basis of language is thus determination; its elements must function determinately, whatever we take the function of language to be. I can have no term for what has not been in some way differentiated. The development of language bears this out; as new things appear, or as we become aware of things, we devise new names for them, but not until we have differentiated them from other things. Similarly, philosophers are always inventing new terms, since they are making new distinctions; whereas the universe consists of infinite things with infinite attributes capable of being conceived in infinite modes of conception; signification is therefore necessarily finite.

The second characteristic of language which must engage us may be called its *restrictiveness*. Once we have fixed the selectiveness of a term—given it a particular meaning—we can speak of no more than that term permits, so long as that particular meaning obtains. In other words, by the use of any terms we are committed to the discussion of the characteristics or things selected by those terms. Terms may, of course, be generalized or specified in their meanings, or given entirely different meanings; but as the selectiveness of each term is determined, discussion is restricted by the selection until there is a change of meaning. Let a circle be ever so many things in reality, it is for the geometrician only what he has defined it as being. However complex and variable literary style may be, the critic who defines it as the choice and arrangement of words can deal only with such characteristics of style as these terms select. The universe itself, whatever it may be in fact, becomes for my discussion only what I *say* it is, and contracts itself to the limits of my discourse. I can talk about only what I can distinguish and mention.

Let us consider what this means for philosophic discussion. It means, first of all, that any philosophic problem is relative to its formulation. Secondly, since any solution to a philosophic problem is relative to the problem, any solution is relative also to that formulation of the problem. Any philosopher, consequently, though he profess to talk about the universe, in fact must confine himself to what we may call the *universe of his discourse*. This in itself may seem sufficient to account for most of the variety of doctrine among philosophers, for it suggests the possibility that they are talking about different things; but indeed this is only part of the matter.

Any philosophy which contains discursive reasoning, as opposed to intuitive or contemplative reasoning—any philosophy, that is, which involves inference—has a fundamental dialectic or dialectics. By dialectic I mean the system of inference which in a given philosophy permits inference: the logic of the philosophic system as a whole, so to speak. And by inference I mean not merely what is ordinarily called inference, as for example, the syllogism, (the enthymeme, the hypothetical syllogisms, and so on) but inference in the broadest sense: the derivation of one proposition from another. Thus division into classes is inference based upon the principle of division; combination of classes into one is inference based upon the principle of combination; and similarly, any resolution of propositions into propositional components, or any synthesis of propositions into a compound proposition is inference.

Philosophies vary according to the dialectics on which they are based. Hence, if we can determine in what respects dialectics may vary, we shall be enabled to account for variation in philosophy. Now, inference is possible only under certain conditions. (1) Significant expressions must be used. This may seem open to immediate objection: What about the nonsense-syllogisms, so commonly employed in elementary logic texts?—"All kenets are kreteks, no kreteks are keleps, therefore, etcetera!" The answer is that these are not nonsense-syllogisms; kenets, kreteks, and keleps are not nonsense words. Very clearly they stand for terms of the specific kind requisite for a given kind of logic; and they stand for terms distinct from each other; they are no more nonsense than would be the abstract symbols A, B, C, precisely because they are just such abstract symbols. Unless they can be supposed to have such minimal meaning, inference is impossible; hence, as I have just said, significant expressions must be used. (The same thing holds if we suppose inference to be conceptual, nonverbal inference; for the selectiveness and restrictiveness of which we spoke apply also to concepts.) (2) It must be possible to make propositions, in some sense true or false. This is perfectly clear from our definition of inference, for we said that inference involves propositions. (3) There must be some principle of validation—some principle, that is, which is the warrant of valid reasoning. To illustrate this, we may say that it is what is brought into question whenever in a given argument both the premises and the conclusion are granted to be true, but the necessity of the conclusion as following from the premises, is denied. Thus if I offer a syllogism and you grant the truth of both premises and conclusion, but deny that syllogism is valid argumentative procedure, you are calling in question the principle of validation of my argument. It may be noted that there are in some systems of proof only general principles of validation, whereas in others there are both general and special ones. Thus the *dictum de omni et nullo* is general with respect to syllogistic reasoning; the rules of figure (for example, that in the first figure of the assertoric syllogism the major premise must always be universal, the minor always affirmative) are special, and the rule that *Barbara,* the first mood of the first figure, is valid is more special still.

To sum this up: Every dialectic is characterized by (1) its *semantic orientation,* the linguistic or signal devices, including concepts if these are conceived as in signal relation, as in attachment to their meanings; (2) its *propositional structures,* and correlatively with this, its *truth value;* (3) its *principle or principles of validation.* There are, therefore, respects in which dialectics agree or differ, and according to which they vary; and we must now inquire into what relations may prevail between these elements of dialectic.

That the principle of validation derives from the semantic orientation of the philosophic system can be seen from two observations. In the first place, I might first of all respond to your objection—to go back to the case mentioned above—by pointing out that I had argued in the mode *Barbara;* if you challenge the mode, I answer by showing that the syllogism follows the rules of the first figure; if you challenge these, I appeal to the *dictum de omni et nullo;* presently, being pushed farther, I must fall back upon the Principle of Contradiction and the consequences of the employment of terms in a given significance or semantic attachment. In other words, the method of argument rests ultimately upon the semantic orientation of a given system. But we may argue this point from the opposite direction as well. Let us suppose two hypothetical universes. Let us suppose first a universe consisting of three things, A, B, and C, all absolutely identical with each other. It will now be plain that, as any characteristic possessed by any one of these things will be shared by any other, I may reason from what is known about any one to what is unknown about any other; and the method of argument will be analogical, i.e., operate by total analogy. Should my analogical reasoning be called into question, I should respond by indicating the total likeness of the things in the universe. On the other hand, suppose now a universe of three things absolutely dissimilar; analogical reasoning now becomes invalid. In the first case, then, nothing but analogical reasoning is valid; in the second, analogical reasoning could never be valid. Since in fact the universe is composed of likenesses and differences, these "universes" are hypothetical, as I said; but the possibility of a philosopher's *formulation* of the universe, that is, *his universe of discourse,* as comprising total likeness or total difference is perfectly clear; and this semantic orientation will obviously determine the validity within his system of this or that kind of reasoning. That is, since the formulation is always selective, as we saw, nothing prevents the selection merely of likenesses or merely of differences; in which cases the methods of reasoning would be determined exactly as if the real universe, over and above

[handwritten marginal note: A = B = C ? The letters themselves are not identical!]

discussion, had only such characteristics, just as in the hypothetical cases mentioned.

The principle of validation, therefore, derives from the semantic orientation of the system; so, too, does the propositional structure with its attendant values of truth and falsity. The importance of this point can scarcely be overestimated: I am saying that the nature of the statements we can make, and the significance of truth and falsity, are variable from system to system, and depend upon semantic orientation. This can be seen from the following considerations. Suppose we have a terminology consisting only of three terms, "justice," "green," "not-green." It will then be true to say, "Justice is not-green." But suppose we extend the terminology to include a distinction between "colored" and "not-colored," and place "green" and "not-green" under colored. It will not be true, now, that justice is not-green; for that would imply that it was colored. The true proposition now is "Justice is not-colored." Thus a proposition true in one context has become false in another, and we conclude that the truth and falsity of a proposition can vary with, for they are dependent upon, the semantic orientation of the system. But this is supposing, of course, a single sense of truth and falsity; whereas even in this sense, terms vary. For instance, in one system, truth is correspondence of thought to thing; thought to word in another; word to thing in still another.

Finally, the structure of propositions must vary with the semantic orientation. How it varies specifically we shall shortly see; but to speak generally at this moment, that it does vary can be seen from the fact that some logicians define the structure of the proposition as class-inclusion or -exclusion, others as subject-predicate relation, and so forth; and that it must vary with the semantic orientation is evident from the fact that such terms as *class, subject, predicate,* or any others in which propositions are defined or explained, must always have reference to the universe of discourse.

Everything, therefore, appears to hang upon the semantic orientation of the dialectical system; and variations in propositional structures and in principles of validation are clearly due, as we have just seen, to that same origin. Evidently, then, if we can grasp the various possibilities of such orientation, we shall have a key to the various possible basic dialectics, and through these a key to our whole problem.

Now, as I have already suggested, dialectics may deal merely with likenesses, or merely with differences (the dialectics mentioned in connection with the two hypothetical universes were simple instances of these) or with both. This much is, I trust, clear; we need only to show how this is a matter of the functioning of terms, that is, of semantic orientation. But this is simple enough. Terms are selective, as we saw; and they may either specify or generalize. General terms stand for classes or groups of things in respect of some likeness. When the likeness is likeness in the sense of literally the same attribute or set of attributes, the term is univocal. For example, "animal" is a univocal term as applied to a horse and a man; when we state what we mean by "animal" as applied to a horse, it is precisely what we mean by it as applied to man. If a term is applied to two things, but not in respect of any likeness, the term is equivocal; an example would be "colt" as applied to a horse and a gun. Finally, if a term is applied to things not literally alike in such a fashion as to make the term univocal, nor yet so unconnected as to make the term equivocal, it is an analogical term. Strictly, analogical terms are those which stand for things different in definition, but similar in their relation to other things. They always imply a proportion; hence their name. An example is the term *justice* as employed in Plato's *Republic*, both to signify a moral virtue of the individual and an attribute of the State: the moral virtue *justice* is to the individual as the attribute *justice* is to the State. Or, again, *harmony* as applied to musical tones and to the soul; for here also, A:B::C:D.

We have just found now, as a matter of fact, two respects in which dialectics differ. The first is their concern with likeness or difference. The second will be evident if we reflect that analogical terms may always transcend any literal distinction made by univocal terms; that is, an analogical term can always group together things that univocal terms would separate. The reason for this, of course, is that two things which are not literally alike may still be in proportional relation. Now, it is evident that as we follow lines of likeness we ascend to more and more general terms; and these terms may always be predicated on the terms below, whether analogical or equivocal. For instance, ox and man are animal, animal and plant are living organism, living organism and inanimate matter are substance. But if we are predicating univocally, we reach an upward limit of predication: what univocal term, for instance, is predicable of substance and something else? Not being or existence; for substance exists differently from, say, quality or quantity. On the other hand, if we are predicating analogically, we may proceed upward until we have brought everything under one class; that is, the limit is not reached until we have identified, or subsumed under one term, everything that was within our concern. These are obviously, then, two different kinds of predication; they amount to this, that in saying "A is B," the former uses the copula "is" qualifiedly, making a distinction between "is" as "is essentially" and as "is accidentally"; whereas the latter uses the copula absolutely, making no such distinction. Aristotle and Plato illustrate these differences; the former is constantly criticizing the latter's combinations and divisions of classes.

The semantic orientation of dialectics, then, will vary according to whether likeness or difference or both are involved, and according to whether there is absolute or qualified predication. But there is also a third respect of variation. It has already been suggested that every philosophy must have some theory of discourse, negative or positive. Now, discourse as employed by philosophy has two principal functions: (1) significative and (2) evocative. Conceived in its significative function, language signifies or stands for things, of which it is in some respect an adequate sign. Conceived in its evocative function, however, language does not, strictly speaking, stand for things; it produces or evokes concepts of things; and its adequacy is determined, not according to whether it is precise in signification, but according to whether it evokes an adequate idea or concept. These are quite opposite positions, as may be observed: according to the first, adequate concepts are produced because language adequately signifies things; according to the latter because adequate concepts are produced.

It will be noted that these remarks turn on three terms in certain interrelation or lack of interrelation with each other: *things, thoughts,* and *words.* All dialectic turns on the interrelation of this triad, or on the absence of interrelations of this triad; and the theories of discourse which we have just been discussing are in fact only certain special positive or negative interrelations. Thus the significative theory assumes a correspondence of a certain order between words and things, such that a certain correspondence follows between concepts and things. The evocative theory, on the other hand, assumes the opposite. Again, if no correspondence of any kind or degree can be assumed between words and concepts, or words and things, discourse is absolutely impossible; words neither can stand for anything nor can bring the mind to think of anything.

Other things are notable about the triad. One term can be made primary, and inference can proceed from one to another, or can not, according to the correspondences or incorrespondences established. Philosophy has frequently begun, that is, with a scrutiny of things, to determine thoughts, and words; or with thoughts, to determine things and words; or with words, to determine things and thoughts. The shift normally occurs through doubt or denial of some warrant. Thus, if sensation which is the warrant of the existence or of the natures of changing existences, or if intellection, which is the warrant of the unchanging, be questioned, philosophy shifts to a primarily epistemic concern, and problems that were problems of metaphysics or physics either vanish or are translated into problems of perception and conception. And cognition can be made demonstrative or indemonstrative of

[margin annotations: denotative & connotative?; ?; actions?; ?; action]

existences, depending upon whether or not some correspondence can be established between thoughts and things. Augustine and Descartes, for example, are able to develop from a *doubt of knowledge* a philosophy of things, for they are able to find a correspondence between thought which is ultimately insusceptible of doubt, and unknown existence. Hume, on the contrary, disallows such correspondence on the ground that "nothing is ever present to the mind except its own perceptions," and consequently can develop a philosophy of what is perceived and conceived *qua* perceived and conceived only (impressions and ideas); things outside such cognitions, that is, the extra-mental, remain impossible of demonstration, and are held to exist only through "animal faith." Since thought is reflexive (I may think about thought) knowledge is still possible about thought, even if thought and existence are incorrespondent.

To sum up: Dialectics vary according to their semantic orientation, their propositional structure and truth-values, and their principles of validation. The two last were seen to depend upon and to vary with the first. In reference to semantic orientation, dialectics vary according to the following respects: (1) their foundation upon likeness, difference, or both; (2) their employment of the copula absolutely or qualifiedly; (3) their concern with things, thoughts, and words; (4) in the event of their concern with both likeness and difference, the primacy of one or the other (thus Plato is primarily concerned with the former, Aristotle with the latter); (5) in the event of their concern with two or all of the triad, the primacy of one or another relative to a given enquiry or demonstration; (6) in the same event, the number and nature of the terms selected from the triad; (7) the nature of the correspondences or incorrespondences established between members of the triad. This last matter is extremely complex and delicate, and cannot be handled here.

Henceforth we shall call dialectics total or partial; a total dialectic may be defined as one which involves both likeness and difference, and which involves all members of the triad in correspondence, so that inference may involve all three. All other dialectics will be considered partial. In addition, we shall henceforth call likeness-dialectics integral, and difference-dialectics differential, dialectics. Partial integral dialectics will tend to identify whatever lies within the scope of their concern. Language may be prior or posterior to thought, as explained above; accordingly, truth for these systems consists either in the proper signification of things, or the proper evocation of concepts. Terms will be analogical, and the principle of validation will invariably be analogy or, if likeness is complete, identity.

To illustrate these points, we may examine certain specific cases. Let us suppose, first of all, that a philosophic system is oriented, or addressed, wholly to changing things, and employs only differential and never integrating terms—terms, that is, only of difference and never of likeness. This would occur if one insisted that all things are unique (maximum differentiation); that though A is a ball and B is a ball, each is unique. This is not mere sophistry; there is a sense in which these statements are true. The whiteness of A is not the same as that of B if we mean the individual whiteness; and the material of A is not the same as that of B, though both are made of rubber; nor is sphericity in one the same as sphericity in the other—each has, like a moon, its distinctive mountains and valleys. Consequently, in the view of philosophers who talk this way, to call A and B by any term implying similarity, whether ball, sphere, white object, or anything else, is to commit serious error.

Such philosophies, therefore, employ differential terms to discriminate A from B; and since constant change alone is admitted to their purview, object A must also be discriminated from itself, for A at one time is different from A at another. Nor is even this a sophistry; for not only is the individual whiteness of A different from that of B, but the whiteness of A at one moment is different from the whiteness of A at another; for each is a mere moment in a flux. Two broadly different kinds of dialectic develop from this position; they may be regarded as extreme and as modified forms, respectively. The extreme form is based upon the attempt to signify individual subjects and to attribute to these individual predicates. For example, "This pencil is this yellow". If the position is pushed to a real extreme, signification becomes impossible, since words are finite, while things, attributes, and moments are infinite; in a more moderate view, absolute precision is indeed impossible, but a relative degree of accuracy may be achieved by specification; the moment, though informulable, may be suggested, as by the type of proposition just cited. The second kind of dialectic employs more general terms,—not, however, universals; for the terms are *ex hypothesi* ambiguous. Since for both of these systems language is ambiguous, the dialectic frequently takes the form of an analytical discipline intended to improve the accuracy of language, or to avoid the psychological confusions which language may induce; this is the general function of the Korzybskian and other semantics with which we have been deluged of late.

For these systems such principles as the Law of Identity, the Law of Contradiction, and the Law of Excluded Middle, so generally accepted as axiomatic by most systems of philosophy, are false, for all of them can be taken as denying the flux which is under surveillance. A is not the same as A, for there is change; I cannot even signify A, strictly, for while I note it, it is one thing, while I name it, another. A is both B and not B; far from being impossible and false, this is perhaps the truest of propositions, in the view of these philosophies; for it is the very formula of change. The A which is B becomes not B. Nor is this sophistry; for in the absence of any distinction between potentiality and actuality, i.e., between A which is actually B and potentially not B, A is certainly both B and not B. The problem which occupied certain logicians of the nineteenth century may be recalled here. It would seem, they argue, that a bar of iron heated at one extremity and chilled at the other would be both hot and cold; consequently the law of contradiction seems to be in doubt, for the bar is both hot and not hot, cold and not cold; if we distinguish the ends of the bar, however, the difficulty disappears, for the end which is hot is not that which is cold, and so the principle has been rescued. But, it must be noted, the truth of the Law of Contradiction in this instance, and in all instances, depends upon whether we draw a certain distinction; if, for example, we do not draw it here, the bar may truly be said to be both hot and not hot. In a word, such principles of logic as these are not universal principles, but phenomena of certain dialectics, brought about by the semantic orientation of the systems. Fundamental though they be made for some dialectics, they may be utterly false or irrelevant to others. In this instance, the distinction has shifted the discussion from the bar to its two ends; what, however, if we wish to speak of the bar? Again, it was a frequent notion that a subject with contradictory attributes was absolutely inconceivable; but in that case, we may ask, how did this bar happen to be conceived?

In the extremest view of these dialectics, the object cannot be signified, for discourse, as finite, cannot be infinitely specified; cannot be perceived, for it has changed from what we perceived even as we perceived it; cannot be contemplated, for the same reason; and cannot be acted upon, for what we would act upon is gone before we can act. Thus Heracleitus remarked that we cannot step into the same river twice; indeed, we cannot step into it even once. Applied to things, these dialectics produce such flux-philosophies as that of Heracleitus; applied to thoughts, such skepticisms as the philosophies of Pyrrho and Sextus Empiricus; applied to words or signs, such "semanticisms" as that of Korzybski.

All of these dialectics are valid, relative to the differentiated individuals which comprise their universe of discourse; and they should be considered, not as the barest sophistries, but as efforts to deal with the most fugitive aspects of things. Extended beyond their proper limits and asserted to have universal and absolute application, as has so often happened, they reveal startling weaknesses; their just, although partial, observations become sheer absurdities, their principles antinomies.

According to these systems only motion or change is real, while rest is illusory; that position was the consequence, as we have seen, of an address to individual things and their individual attributes as these appear in infinitesimal time, or, in other words, the consequence of the treatment of absolute dissimilars or of dissimilars approaching the absolute. Precisely the opposite state of affairs is produced if dialectic is shifted from such concern to a concern with absolute similars, by a denial of individual differences. If difference is impossible, change is impossible, for change moves between different poles. The dialectic now turns on the reduction of the many to the one; motion is only an appearance, individual forms being only fleeting appearances of the One which is beyond change. The Law of Identity is now absolute, as are the other laws mentioned earlier; thus Parmenides, who held this position laid down as principles that Being is Being (identity), that it is Being and not No-Being (contradiction) and that anything must be one or the other (excluded middle).

Different as the extremes of integral and differential dialectics are, they amount to the same thing in certain respects. Both end up with an unique subject of which only unique predicates may be asserted, though in the first case these subjects are many, and in the second but one; and since neither permits of universal terms, both make impossible the construction of demonstrative science. Thus for Heracleitus there is no science of the changing sensibles, although perhaps one may attain divine reason, or knowledge of the universal law; and for Parmenides, the One alone is existent and knowable, though but little can be said of it; all science, save metaphysics, is thus impossible.

Parmenides and Heracleitus deal with things; as dialectic shifts to thoughts or words, its basic characteristics remain the same. In other words, as the subject matter is shifted, the formal character of dialectic is not necessarily altered. The reason for this is clear enough: in describing the foundation and development of these dialectics we were not talking of peculiarities of things, but of likeness and difference, which may be found in concepts and signs as well.

The extent to which theories of discourse influence the dialectic in which they occur may be seen by a brief comparison of Plato and Aristotle. We have previously spoken of the distinction between language as significative and as evocative. A species of the latter—language as mnemonic—achieves its adequacy not through signification but through recollection of an adequate concept. This immediately affects the terminology and propositional structure of the system: propositions are asserted to be true, not by virtue of the existence of things and attributes signified by them, nor by any fixation of meaning, but by virtue of their efficacy in recalling to the mind a truth once known and now forgotten, that is, by virtue of their capacity to stimulate memory. Thus in the dialogues of Plato the interlocutor is part of the argument proper; the guarantee of truth is his recollection of the truth, once the dialectician has properly prepared him for it; and the warrant of the argument is similarly found in him, for the Platonic dialectic does not turn on written or spoken words, but upon words in the soul; and argument or proof is no mere formal collocation of terms and propositions, but, as it were, the soul's journey toward truth. Thus it is no accident that Plato wrote his arguments in dialogue form, his doctrines in epistle and treatise form. Aristotle, on the other hand, constructed a logic based upon the significative and not the evocative or recollective powers of language, and one consequently in no way dependent upon hearers for the truth of its propositions and the cogency of its arguments. Two premises imply a conclusion in the Aristotelian logic through their form and matter, regardless of whether a hearer assent or dissent; for truth is not grounded upon assent but upon the existence of the things signified in accord with their signification; and comparably, validity of argument rests only upon a certain collocation of terms. Only in the Aristotelian dialectic (reasoning from opinion) is the assent of the hearer important to the argument; demonstration, however, is determined by the nature of things; and it is also no accident that Aristotle developed his sciences in treatise-form, while he utilized the dialogue for popular exposition, in which opinion might play a leading role. Again, upon this difference rests the possibility of a formal logic for Aristotle; Plato, on the other hand, develops not a formal logic, but a dialectic; while the procedure of the dialectician can be described, as in the *Phaedrus*, the "know-how" of the matter lies in him and resists formulation; thus Plato resists the reduction of arguments to topics, and would doubtless have raised objections on a similar basis to the whole dialectic of Aristotle. The radical difference seems to lie in their diverse conceptions of knowledge: Aristotle thought that it began with sense, Plato that it antedated birth; and these different correlations of thought with thing result in different conceptions of language.

The dialectic of Aristotle is primarily differential, while that of Plato is primarily integral; but that both are concerned with likeness and difference is perfectly clear; for the foundations of Plato's method are combination and division, the former being integral, the latter differential, and similarly Aristotle can group things together, as well as differentiate them. But Aristotle makes the substance-accident distinction whereas Plato does not; and as a consequence of this distinction, Aristotle divides likenesses and differences into substantial and accidental, with the profoundest results to his system. For it, along with the other differences just mentioned, appears to produce all the other differences in their systems. At the root of all this lies a difference in what we have called semantic orientation. Plato opposes a real and changeless intellectual world to an apparent and changing sensible world, whereas Aristotle makes no such opposition. As a consequence, Plato opposes sensation to knowledge, whereas Aristotle finds the genesis of knowledge in sensation. Given his distinctive concern and its formulation in significative rather than evocative language, Aristotle naturally must hold the principle which is the underlying condition of significative language specified to literal terms; the four causes (literal distinctions of causation), the ten categories (the upward limits of literal predication), the distinction of the sciences (the sciences as distinguished in terms of the four causes), thereafter follow in train. Given his distinctive concern and its formulation in evocative (mnemonic) rather than significative language, Plato may disregard all the formal specifications indispensable to a system of fixed and univocal terms, using language to stimulate the mind toward truths beyond language; and dialectic is heuristic only, and only a recollective heuristic, for the truths have been known and forgotten. Since all things have a principle of similarity, an integral dialectic is possible; and since they also have principles of difference, a differential dialectic is possible as well (hence combination and division as discussed in the *Phaedrus*). Reasoning is proportional, that is, analogical, following the divisions of the divided line; for conjecture is to belief as understanding is to reason, and in parallel, shadows are to things as hypotheses are to ideas. Hence any question may move from science to science. For example, the question of the nature of the sophist eventually ends in metaphysics, traversing the boundaries of the sciences. Method is unitary, that is, the same for all inquiry, since the likenesses and differences are not restricted as they are in Aristotle by genera of things.

Dialectical adequacy is a question of whether the various possible elements of dialectic, as we have defined them, have been selected and organized in such fashion as to permit the maximum statement and solution of philosophical problems. By "solution" I mean, of course, positive solution; it is always easy to state problems so that they cannot be solved or to reach the solution that the problem cannot be solved. On this view of dialectical adequacy, it is obvious that the total dialectics alone are adequate, although both total and partial are valid, in the sense that they permit true propositions and cogent reasoning. Plato and Aristotle, thus, are instances of total dialectics, while Hume and Hobbes are examples of the partial kind. Hume is partial in the sense that he does not employ the whole triad, for his system permits the demonstrative treatment of no problems beyond those of perceptions. Hobbes, on the other hand, is partial in respect to likeness and difference; for he reduces all attributes to body, motion, and figure, which is equivalent to shutting out all considerations which are not analogues of the attributes of the physical body in local motion. In short, he begins with a likeness which is insufficiently general, and although his method thereafter is differential, the controlling analogue restricts his view of almost everything. (Modern psychologists who treat all problems of human learning in terms of the behavior of a rat in a maze make an exactly similar reduction.)

Speaking most generally, we may distinguish four kinds of philosophy: the dogmatic, the syncretic, the skeptical, and the pluralist. By dogmatic I mean what the skeptics did when they employed the term; that is, any affirmative philosophy, such as that of Plato or Aristotle. The other three are really philosophies about philosophy; the syncretic holds that any given dogmatic philosophy is false as a whole but perhaps true in part, so that a philosophic synthesis can be made; the skeptical, that any given dogmatic philosophy is false both as a whole and in part; and the pluralist, that many valid, and several adequate philosophies are possible. Dogmatism results from the application of any one dialectical method to immediate philosophic subject matter; the other three forms result, most generally, from the application of a dialectic to various philosophical treatments of certain subject matter. The two middle forms consider the doctrines alone of the dogmatists; the last considers doctrines in terms of the methods which generated them, that is, in the context of method. Thus Cicero may be taken as an example of the syncretic philosopher, and Sextus Empiricus as an example of the skeptic. The present essay perhaps sufficiently illustrates philosophical pluralism.

Skepticism, always the chief enemy of philosophical enterprise, is always based upon a partial dialectic. It comes about either from an address to the uniqueness of things, concepts, or signs, so that universals become impossible; or from other partiality in respect to likeness and difference; or from inadequate correlation of the triad, as in the case of Hume; or from a mere *sic et non* balancing of doctrines, without taking into account the method which makes them mean what they mean. The skeptic indeed is always a dogmatic in disguise; for he is always insisting upon one and only one formulation of truth, and is disturbed by the fact that there seems to be more than one. Failing to see the proper causes of such variety, he concludes that all philosophy is false.

We may conclude this rough sketch with two observations. First any partial dialectic may supplement (1) a similar dialectic oriented to a different subject matter; (2) its obverse dialectic oriented to the same subject (for example, an integral dialectic supplements a differential, or vice versa); (3) thing-dialectics may be supplemented by conceptual or verbal dialectics, conceptual by thing- and verbal-dialectics, and so on. Secondly, any adequate total dialectic may be translated into any other adequate total dialectic. The difference between supplementation and translation is, I hope, clear; it is a question of whether one may add on, and thus provide something not afforded by the original system, or whether one can restate simply, say, an Aristotelian doctrine in terms of Plato.

Partial dialectics of a differential order approach the individual in some sense—either the individual thing or object, or at some moment of its existence. Hence they are invariably concerned with changing things. Insofar as they are really differential, they must involve differential terms; propositions are possible if both subject and predicate can be qualified to the requisite determinacy, that is, adequately differentiated, but are impossible if the individuals cannot be conceived, perceived, or signified. Language may be made prior to thought, in the sense that things can be signified which cannot be conceived, for example, some moment of existence too fleeting, or some magnitude too great or too small, for conception. Or, conversely, thought may be made prior to language, in the sense that things can be conceived which are ineffable. According to the propositional structure possible in a given system, argument will either be impossible, or, given systematic difference, proceed by negation or contrariety; or finally, by mere differentiation. For example, if A is the negative of B, then attributes of A must be negatives of attributes of B; if it is the contrary, its attributes must be contraries. Here systematic difference is present. If however there is no certain differential relation between A and B, argument is impossible, except for mere differentiation. That is, one might still argue that since A is different from B, their attributes are different. This however is indefinite and indeterminate, for one cannot infer what attributes B has, but only that they differ from those of A.

We may now proceed to investigate the application of these remarks to the criticism of the arts.

III

According to the preceding account of dialectics, they are six in number; two partial in respect of their concern with likeness or difference exclusively; two partial in respect of their concern with or correlation of some part only of the triad of things, thoughts, and words; and two total, as concerned not only with both likeness and difference, but also with all members of the triad in some positive connection which permits cross-inference. These are, I repeat, the basic kinds in terms of extremes; but there are obviously various species of these. On our supposition that there is a correspondence between the number of possible kinds of criticism, there would seem, then, to be six basic kinds of criticism—viewed solely, of course, in terms of their dialectical form. If we add in the diverse subjects to which these may be addressed, that is, view criticism materially as well as formally, there are naturally more. We must consequently attempt to discern the kinds of matter which may be involved.

The kinds of matter to which the dialectics of criticism may be addressed divide most generally according to the various senses of the term *art*. Since, as we have suggested, a term is always connected with some aspect of something, we may grasp the various senses of the term *art* by considering what aspects we may differentiate. It will be sufficient doubtless to mention only the principal aspects—those that tend to recur frequently, or occur importantly, in the history of criticism. Art, then, may be said to embrace the notion of some kind of object or thing produced, that is, a product; produced through some kind of human instrumentality, either active or passive; resulting in some way from the nature of the instrumentality, and as such, a sign of the nature of that instrumentality and of its potentialities or faculties; related to a certain subject and a certain medium, and consequently a sign of these also; related to some kind of purpose, and producing some kind of effect, either of activity or passivity, upon auditor or spectator; and as so viewed, instrumental to that effect.

To state this a little differently—art may be viewed either as an object, thing, or product; or as an activity of the artist, or as a passivity of the artist, or as certain faculties or a certain character of the artist; or as a certain activity or passivity of the audience, or as certain faculties or a certain character of the audience; or as an instrument of some kind; or as a sign, either of the character or activity or passivity of the artist or of the audience, or of the nature of something else involved in art. Speaking generally, art appears thus as product, activity, passivity, instrument, faculty, and sign, although these terms must be qualified as I have just qualified them.

These remarks may be illustrated by considering the different senses in which the term *poem* appears in discussions of poetry. The primary sense is that of the product of the art, a certain form imposed upon words, whatever the critic takes that to be. But, other critics argue, the product is only one aspect, and perhaps a relatively unimportant aspect, of the poetic art; the issue of real importance is the human instrumentality which produces; and some argue that this is an actualization of potentialities, others that it is the potentialities themselves. The former see the poet as either active or passive or both; he appears either as a craftsman actively making something, or as the mere instrument of his inspiration, or as a combination of the two. For these, the true poem is the poetic behavior of the poet. The latter class sees the poet simply as possessing certain faculties or qualities, or as possessing them in a certain degree, and tends to identify the poem with the mere possession of these. Since the product is for both classes a consequence of its agency, it appears as a sign of the nature of that agency. Other critics, again, argue that the poem properly exists in the audience: the audience is the true poet, for without it the poem could never come to life; and the audience, like the poet, can be viewed as actualizing certain passive or active potentialities, or merely as possessing such potentialities—thus the theories of "audience-participation" (the activity view) or of "art as experience" (the passivity view). Finally, the poem may be considered as a kind of instrument, relative to some end; for example, of mental therapy or social reform.

These look like "conflicting views"; hence they have invariably been treated as such in the history of criticism. If the term "conflicting" means merely "different," we need have no quarrel with the term; certainly these views are different. But if it means "contradictory," nothing could be more absurd. For, in the first place, all of these doctrines have different subjects; and it is impossible to have contradiction except with reference to the same subject; and second, where contradiction exists, one view must be false if the other is true, whereas all of these views are perfectly true in their proper senses; for all of them are founded upon perfectly obvious aspects of art. Nor, if they are not contradictory, are they inconsistent, in the sense that they logically proceed from or result in contradiction, for we have just argued that they are all true in some sense, and it is impossible for true propositions to be inconsistent. They may indeed be irrelevant to each other; but that is hardly the point at issue. Again, I am not arguing that no critic ever contradicts another, for that would be equivalent to proclaiming human infallibility; but I shall say that, where such contradiction in fact exists, one of the men is in error; and that his error is not the consequence of any one of these views, but strictly *his* error.

In fact, nothing prevents any given philosopher from investigating all of these aspects: Plato and Aristotle, for instance, did just that. The apparent conflict of views is really only a difference in the imposition of names; that is, it is a difference of what we have called semantic orientation. Nor do these differences stop here, for they turn up within these aspects; for example, although two men are speaking of the poetic activity, that activity also has many aspects, and consequently there may be "conflict" upon these questions of whether the poetic activity "is" this aspect or that. This in turn leads to other "conflicts"; for instance, since the poetic activity involves some reasoning, anyone who fixes upon its rational aspect is bound to find the poetic character to consist in the possession of certain rational faculties; whereas, since the poetic activity also comprises elements which are nonrational (for example, individual temperament, let us say), one who fixes upon the nonrational aspect of the activity is prone to find the poetic character one possessed of certain nonrational faculties.

Even if two critics have fixed upon the same aspect in a certain differentiation, at whatever point of differentiation, they may still differ in what may be called their *causal* analysis. I find this difficult to state; but let me use Aristotle's scheme of four causes—formal, material, efficient, and final—as illustrative here, since it offers certain advantages. Suppose, then, two critics have fixed upon the same aspect—say, poetic activity, or some specific aspect of that activity— they may still differ in that one fixes upon the material cause of that activity, the other upon its formal cause, or in that one fixes upon all the causes, another upon certain ones only. In a sense this is merely further differentiation of the aspect, of course; but the distinction, it is clear, cross-cuts the other line of differentiation, for it may occur at any point.

Since, as we have seen, the meaning of the term *art* shifts from its aspect as product or object to its aspect as productive agency, and so on throughout the list given above, the concepts of the form, matter, end, and producer—the causal concepts, in a word—shift accordingly. If art is viewed as a product, that is, a work of art, its matter or medium is tone and rhythm, color and line, words and rhythm, and things of a like order; its form is taken from some form of the things, whatever they may be, that we tend to call the subjects of art; in short, the causes are determined by the aspect as product. If art is viewed as some passivity induced in the audience—the artistic experience in the passive sense—the matter or medium of art becomes situated in the audience; it is certain propensities to thought or passion in the audience, and its form is the actualization of these in the experience of a series of emotions or concepts. And the product itself may now appear, under the guise of the stimulus of these emotions and thoughts, as the productive cause. If art is viewed as some activity in the audience, the product may appear either as the stimulus of or the signal for such activity (productive cause) or as the potentialities which in some sense are actualized in or by the audience (material cause); and the form of art may now appear as the activity of the audience. A similar shift follows whatever other aspects or determinations of aspects of art may be selected in a given critical dialectic. These are not conflicts any more than the supposed conflicts mentioned earlier; they are simply consequences of the semantic orientations of diverse systems of criticism. Indeed, the "causal" analysis I have just employed is no absolute thing, but is itself a consequence of dialectical method, and critics and philosophers may distinguish more causes or fewer, or distinguish them differently, or even, as Hobbes did, roll them all into one, and collapse that with effect.

The kinds of critical systems, then, will vary according to these matters which are elements of the formulation of critical problems, and according to the type of dialectic exerted upon the problem as thus formulated. Since, as I remarked earlier, we can philosophize only about what we can signify or evoke conceptually, it is clear that our solutions can only be such as are relative to the problem as formulated and such as our methods will permit. The most complex problems, in actuality, may be given a simple or rather a simple-minded formulation; and so formulated, will result in a simple-minded solution or perhaps none at all.

The actual number of kinds of criticism, differentiated as we have suggested, is indefinite, but we may enumerate certain modes which are important in the history of criticism. The following ten kinds may be offered as principal: for any one of the aspects of art mentioned above five kinds of integral critical dialectics, four concerned with any one and the fifth with all four of the causes just mentioned; and five kinds of differential critical dialectics, four again concerned with any one of the causes, and the fifth with all. Plato exemplifies the total integral critical dialectic; all causal factors can ultimately be assimilated to subject-matter, and the products of the arts can consequently be viewed, like the things of nature, as imitations of the Ideas. Aristotle exemplifies the total differential critical dialectic; by adequate differentiation, these factors can be specified so that they are collectively commensurate with the various species of art. Definitions of the species thus result (compare the four-cause definition of tragedy in the *Poetics*) and these definitions serve as principles of reasoning from which the whole art, for example of tragedy, can be developed. Hurd and Spence are concerned with subject matter, the former differentially, the latter integrally; Longinus and Newman, with the productive cause; Lessing and I. A. Richards with the medium; Hume and Allison, with the effect.

But the mere names of critics who exemplify these kinds of criticism mean little; doubtless it will be more illuminating to discuss the criticisms themselves. I shall consider only the kinds which deal with the product of art. Criticism which is based upon the subject matter of the product of art is, as I have suggested, of two kinds, integral and differential. Both, in a sense, have the same line of argument, for both are enabled to solve all the problems which fall within their purview by reference to the subject matter. In a sense, however, they follow opposite lines; for the integral kind proceeds by resolving the subject matter of the arts into something which is not peculiar to the arts, on the basis of likenesses which can be found. The principles of art in such systems are never to be found within the arts themselves, peculiarly; rather the arts appear as an instance, perhaps even an inferior instance, of the manifestation of these principles. The differential criticism, on the other hand, separates the kinds of subject matter and argues on the basis of such separation, either to distinguish the arts from other faculties or activities, or to differentiate them *inter se.* What the former establishes is likeness; the latter, difference. Thus Plotinus finds the beautiful in art to consist in the imitation of the beautiful; but inquiry into that characteristic shows it to be common also to natural objects and actions, and so upward to the Beauty which is almost indifferentiable from the Good. The ultimate solution of artistic as of all problems thus lies for Plotinus in the contemplation of God. This is the extreme of this particular kind of integral dialectic; it reduces all variety to the One; and Plotinus is perfectly clear about its analogical character; "in such a total," he says, "analogy will make every part a sign." Hobbes, on the other hand, proceeds by differentiating "the three regions of mankind, Court, City and Country" to differentiate "three sorts of Poesy, Heroique, Scommatique, and Pastorall." But the subject matter of poetry is differentiated also from the subject matter of other discourse: "the subject of a poem is the manners of men, not natural causes; manners presented, not dictated; and manners feigned, as the name of Poesy imports, not found in men." Poetry is thus distinct in its subject matter from natural or moral philosophy or from history.

Once the subject of the arts has been described in these systems, it determines the solutions of all artistic problems. Thus the qualities which define the artist, the possibilities of artistic form and effect, the criteria of art, and so on, yield of ready solution. If the subject matter in the raw, so to speak, is all-sufficient, the only requisite characteristic of the artist is sharpness of observation or readiness of comprehension; if it is thought to require order and selection, faculties which permit this (for example, the imagination) are added; if the subject of art becomes purely imaginary, in the sense of being quite independent of the real, observation drops out; and so on. A similar determination operates throughout all other problems. It is evident that the terms *nature* and *art* fluctuate according to the system; for once the artistic faculties have been defined, for example, all the rest is nature. Thus there exist systems of literary criticism in which the power of expression in words is natural, since, given that the poet is impregnated with his subject, the words will follow as a matter of course, that is, naturally; and conversely, there are systems in which the power of expression is acquired by art, since the mere conception of the subject is thought insufficient to produce a work of literary art.

In such systems the criteria of art derive from some correspondence absolute or qualified, between the subject and the medium, the subject and the author, or the subject and the effect—in a word, between the subject and any one or more of the remaining terms. For example, a good many of the theories of artistic realism have as their solitary criterion the absolute correspondence of the effect produced by the

work of art with the effect produced by reality itself, the subject matter
in such systems being nothing other than reality itself; art is copyistic,
and the work is a "slice of life." Where the subject matter of art is
opposed to reality, however—whether it requires a selection and order
that reality does not have, or whether it differs from it still more
radically—correspondence must be qualified and indeed this may be
pushed to an extreme where any correspondence is undesirable (compare modern nonrepresentationalist theories). Again, a hierarchy of
subject matters is often established; where the subject is all-important,
the artistic species are also ordered hierarchically, according to the
hierarchy of subjects. Otherwise, any simple relation is denied.

The derivation of artistic criteria in a subject matter criticism from
an absolute correspondence between subject and effect is well illustrated by the position of one of the interlocutors in Dryden's *Essay of
Dramatic Poesie*. Crites establishes the three unities of time, place, and
action by a simple reference to the subject imitated by poetry; since a
day is the natural unit of time, a natural physical locale the natural
unit of place, and a single real action the natural unit of action, a play
must confine itself to the action of a single day, in a single locale, and
so forth, or it will strike its audience as improbable. In a word, poetic
probability is here absolutely determined by natural probability; the
argument is from what is unitary or probable in nature to what must
be unitary or probable in art. Eugenius, who responds to this argument, argues in precisely the opposite fashion, determining the subject
matter of poetry from the effect; it is not what is probable or necessary
in nature which determines poetic probability, but what will impress
the audience as probable or necessary. Hence the unities are relative to
the opinion of the audience; the unity of place, for instance, is not
maintained merely when the locale is actually one and the same, but
also when any change of place is so slight as to leave unaffected the
impression of the audience that the place is one. A comparable opposition exists between the positions of the other two interlocutors, Lisi-
deius and Neander.

In criticisms in which the medium of art is the chief referent, the
capacities of the medium, treated either integrally or differentially,
afford the grounds for all argument; thus analogies discovered between
the media of the several arts, or between artificial and natural matter,
can be brought to identify the subject matter of art, or to define the
capacities of the artist, or to determine the effects or ends of art; or,
conversely, the establishment of differences between media can be
made to yield differentiations in these other matters. A common instance of the first is the tendency to inquire into the general criteria of
literature, whether poetic, historical, philosophic, or personal, on the
ground that all literature employs words; and a common instance of

the second is the tendency, particularly frequent in contemporary criticism, and exemplified by men like I. A. Richards and Cleanth Brooks, to seek to differentiate poetry from prose, or poetry from science, by differentiation of the kind of diction employed. Thus Richards differentiates poetry by the ambiguity of its diction, and Brooks by its paradoxical quality of diction. The fashion in which examination of the medium permits the identification of the proper subject matter of an art is well illustrated by Lessing's *Laocoon;* Lessing counters the thesis of Spence in the *Polymetis,* analogizing the subject matters of painting and of poetry, by reference to the sharply differing possibilities of their respective media, which necessitate different subject matters for each. The criteria in all such critical dialectics derive from an analysis of the capacities of the medium, either assumed as the same matter hierarchically ordered, or as a hierarchy of different matter; thus arts, or species of art, or particular works of art, can be ranked according to the extent to which they realize the potentialities of their medium or media; and the artist frequently appears merely as a kind of midwife to nature, assisting the bronze or the marble toward a form which the material implicitly contains, or which it is even claimed, often enough, to necessitate.

Where the discussion turns on the artificer or the productive cause, it has a tendency to turn into an analytic either of the artistic process or of those characteristics of the productive agency which are thought to influence the production. This occurs whether the agency be conceived as a mental faculty, an individual artist, a school of artists, a society, or some agency more general still. In its extremer forms this dialectic reduces the art product to the status almost of a by-product of the character or the characteristic action which produced it; often, indeed, the product is dismissed as incidental. Thus Fracastoro and Carlyle both refuse to limit the name of poet to those who actually write poems; the essential element is the possession of the poetical character, and the actual writing of poems is only one, and by no means the most important one, necessarily, of many ways in which the poetic character is manifested. Frequently, also, the term *poem* is extended to include any manifestation whatever of that character. In certain forms of this dialectic the artistic character lies outside the possibilities of any deliberate achievement, and the discussion then turns on genius, as in Hazlitt, or on inspiration, as in Valéry, or even on a kind of opportunity, as in Proust; that is, the artistic capacity is assumed, respectively here as constant and actual (genius), or potentially constant and only intermittently actual (inspiration), or as something incidental to the character of the artist. Conversely, the artistic character is sometimes regarded as itself amenable to art; the discussion then is chiefly of the disciplines by which the artistic character is to be achieved, as in Longinus, who analyses what the artist of the Sublime must *be*, or in Reynolds, who analyses what the painter must *do*. Frequently, the character of the artist, in this view, appears as his *chef d'oeuvre;* compare Browning's remark about Shakespeare, to the effect that his works were merely exercises by which he perfected his soul. If the analogy of the artistic process or act is to moral action, the character of the artist appears as his moral character; if to political action, as his character qua citizen or ruler; if to natural activities or processes, the analysis is in terms of natural forces (cf. Nietsche, Freud). Sainte-Beuve, for example, takes all aspects of the individual character into account to explain the work as a whole of any given figure. In such dialectics—Sainte Beuve's, for example—criteria such as unity are drawn from some unity of the producing agency, whether it be personal individuality, the unity of some impulse or purpose, or whatever. Unless some particular import can be found in the distinctions between genera or species of artistic works, such distinctions tend to be denied or ignored, or, in some instances, re-drawn in terms of characteristics more significantly related to the character of the productive agency. Thus Schiller reclassifies poetry into naive and sentimental, for example. The product exists simply as a residue significant of a certain kind of activity which, in turn, is significant of a certain kind of productive agency; in a word, art is reduced to behavior. (This position is contemporarily well illustrated in the critic of Kenneth Burke, who holds poetry to be symbolic action, and hence to be properly analyzable in terms of the poet. His dialectic, however, is differential, whereas that of Sainte-Beuve was integral. The latter could ask "What is a classic?" ignoring the distinctions between philosophy, poetry, science, history, memoirs, and even, as in the case of Madame Récamier, mere behavior; Mr. Burke, on the other hand, differentiates the various employments of discourse and even the technical devices involved in a given work.)

When criticism is founded upon the ends of art, integral and differential dialectics are again possible; the ends of art can be analogized to other purposes of man, or to some natural or divine teleology, or so differentiated as to be peculiar to art or certain species of art, or even to the individual in some sense. Broadly speaking, there are two kinds of values which thus emerge, the *per se* and the *per aliud;* the former some intrinsic value, such as the pleasure afforded by art, the latter some extrinsic value, which attaches to art as an instrumentality. They may be fused or opposed; Plato, for example, fuses them, and Tolstoy opposes them, denying the role of Beauty in art, and insisting upon a criterion of usefulness. As in the above-mentioned dialectics, the nature of both the problems and their solutions is determined by the choice of the ground-term.

These eight kinds of criticism—one integral and one differential for each of the four heads—are all partial dialectics, as I have suggested earlier; hence, although they have invariably been treated as conflicting, they are supplementary rather than contradictory. Their opposite characters result, not from the truth of some and the falsity of others, but from the fact that each formulates the problems of art differently; more precisely, each attempts to resolve all the problems of art by consideration only of a part. Each therefore involves a distortion which any other seeks to correct; but the correction in turn involves a similar distortion. This may be illustrated by a reference to the dispute, already mentioned, between Crites and Eugenius in Dryden's Essay. It is true, as Crites assumes, that natural probability determines poetic probability; but it does not do so absolutely, for in that case the opinion of the audience would always have to be in conformity with nature (compare Aristotle's point on the preferability of the probable impossible to the improbable possible); and it is true, as Eugenius assumes, that the opinion of the audience determines poetic probability, but again it does not do so absolutely; for then nature would always have to conform to the opinion of the audience. Nevertheless, neither position is really false, for each is true relative to its particular formulation in each case. The opposition is indeed no more mysterious, and no more contradictory, than would be, say, the oppositions which might be found in the accounts given of the same subject by a physicist and a mathematician; for both single out different aspects of the subject for their discussions.

All in fact fix only upon a single cause, in the Aristotelian sense of the word, and seek to answer all questions about art in terms of that cause. We may take as parallels the following. Suppose there were four kinds of answers to the questions raised about some object, say, a chair; and let us suppose these answers as differentiated into four causes, material, formal, efficient, and final. Anyone who now speaks in terms of a single cause only must attempt to answer all questions in terms of that cause. The man who fixes upon the material cause, for instance, must explain the form which the wood assumes (that is, chairness) as a tendency or property of the wood itself; the productive agency also lies within the wood, the chairmaker being nothing more than, as it were, a favorable circumstance for its manifestation; and so on. (Compare the early Greek physicists, who talked of nature exclusively in terms of its matter.) In quite comparable fashion, these critical dialectics tend frequently to talk of the subject matter, not only as subject matter, but as medium, productive agency, and end; or of medium as subject matter, agency, and end; and so on. In any of these cases, however, discussion is possible only of so much of these other causes as can be reduced to the cause in terms of which the analysis is being made.

Certain consequences result from each of these reductions respectively. When the problems of art are stated wholly in terms of the subject matter of art, art is in effect reduced to the things which it imitates or represents; it is either identified with its subject directly, or it becomes a kind of discourse about its subject—each art employing its own variety of symbols—and can be judged in terms of its truth and falsity, either to the individual or the universal, and commended or blamed as it possesses the qualities of its subject, or possesses them in a better or worse degree. That is, the form of the work of art is discussed by the critic, but only insofar as it bears comparison with the form of the subject; terms like part and whole, for instance, are defined by reference to the parts or the whole of the subject. When the problems of art are stated wholly in terms of the medium, the form of the work can indeed be discussed, but only *qua* an incident to the medium; and all the problems tend to turn on the work as possessing or not possessing, as increasing or lessening, the properties of the medium. When the statement is exclusively in terms of the productive agency, art appears, as we said earlier, either as traits or activities of that agency, and the form of the work is stated in terms of the potentialities of the agency. Finally, when the statement is in terms of ends, effects, or functions, art appears either as an instrument or as a kind of object or organism possessed of certain properties.

If these considerations are reexamined, it appears that in the first case, the work of art appears as the medium of its subject matter; in the second, as the subject matter of its medium; in the third, as the effect or aim of its productive agency; in the last, as the productive agency of its effect or aim. None of these permits the statement of the nature of a work of art in a full integral or a full differential fashion, for the respects in which the work is compared or contrasted are always only a part of its actual properties. The first position states, sometimes with great accuracy, the imitative relationship of the work to its subject, but fails generally to account for the potentialities of the medium, the methods by which the work is produced, or the effects which it has. The second, similarly, can point out well enough what potentialities of the medium have been realized, but not what the realizations them- selves are, nor how or why they have been brought about. The third can show how the work proceeds from the producer, but not what it is, nor why or how it has been made; the last can state the effect, but, like the other modes, burkes all but its own proper questions. In other words, if we suppose that a work of art is a product, made in some way of some matter not natural to it, having a form in some way similar to the form of its subject matter, and producing some kind of effect or result, then the first position fails to envisage the product as distinct from the things which it imitates or stimulates; the second fails to separate it as a composite from the matter of which it is composed, and hence fails to state it as a form; the third fails to distinguish it properly qua product from the productive agency; the fourth fails to distinguish it from anything else having the same effect. All tend, consequently, in one way or another to break down the distinction between art and nature—they "naturalize" art in some way, that is, analogize art to nature. If they proceed integrally the analogy is transcended by other analogies (for example, art and nature having been collapsed, both together are collapsed with something else), and if they proceed differentially, the analogy determines the differentiation (compare our earlier remarks on Hobbes, relative to his controlling analogy.)

From the point of view of Plato, these positions would be unsatisfactory because not enough is differentiated originally to make the final analogy all-embracing; from the point of view of Aristotle, not enough is differentiated originally to set up proper lines of differentiation, for example, the failure to distinguish the artificial product, which is like a natural thing, and which is produced by human activity, from the thing which it resembles or from the activity which produced it, collapses the theoretical, practical, and productive sciences. Each of these four sources of integral or differential dialectic states the nature of the work exclusively in terms of the subject, medium, producer, or end. Plato recognizes all of these to transcend them in a continuously integral dialectic; the Platonic Dialectic fuses all art and science ultimately, but by no merely partial account of either. Aristotle takes these and differentiates them until they are collectively peculiar to a species of art, when they form a definition of that species.

If this essay has succeeded in its intention, it should be evident that there are many valid kinds of criticism, concerned with different aspects of art and utilizing different methods in their investigations; it should be clear, too, why they are valid and why they differ, and how each system must have its own peculiar limitations and powers. If this excursion into meta-logic and meta-method has wholly succeeded, it has established the foundations of critical pluralism. I shall hope that at the very least it has shown that form and similar cardinal terms of criticism suffer shifts in meaning as they are employed in the contexts of one method or another; and that consequently, in proposing questions which involve them, we are proposing not one question but many, and that to answer these wholly we shall have to find as many answers as we have questions.

INDEX